SHARKS OF THE AIR

SHARKS OF THE AIR

Willy Messerschmitt and How He Built the World's First Operational Jet Fighter

JAMES NEAL HARVEY

CASEMATE

Philadelphia & Oxford

First published in the United States of America and Great Britain in 2011.
Reprinted as a paperback in 2020 by
CASEMATE PUBLISHERS
1950 Lawrence Road, Havertown, PA 19083, USA
and
The Old Music Hall, 106–108 Cowley Road, Oxford OX4 1JE, UK

Copyright 2011 © James Neal Harvey

Paperback edition: ISBN 978-1-61200-892-9
Digital edition: ISBN 978-1-61200-023-7

A CIP record for this book is available from the British Library.

Printed and bound in the United States of America.

For a complete list of Casemate titles please contact:

CASEMATE PUBLISHERS (US)
Telephone (610) 853-9131
Fax (610) 853-9146
Email: casemate@casematepublishers.com
www.casematepublishers.com

CASEMATE PUBLISHERS (UK)
Telephone (01865) 241249
Email: casemate-uk@casematepublishers.co.uk
www.casematepublishers.co.uk

CONTENTS

For Ursula, with all my love.

PROLOGUE

On 26 July 1944, an RAF Mosquito of 544 Squadron flew over Munich at an altitude of 28,000 feet. The aircraft carried no bombs, and had no armament; its mission was photographic reconnaissance. Flight Lieutenant A.E. Wall was at the controls. His navigator was Pilot Officer A.S. Lobban.

Munich was heavily defended by 88mm anti-aircraft guns and by Luftwaffe fighters based just to the east of the city at Flughaven Riem. Wall and Lobban weren't worried, however. Flak put up by the German gunners was rarely effective at this height, and the Mosquito could outrun any of the Bf-109s and Fw-190s that might try to intercept it.

Nevertheless, the RAF airmen were keenly alert, as they had been since taking off from their base at Benson, Oxfordshire, early that morning. As combat veterans they realized their aircraft could be the victim of a lucky hit by an 88, or could be attacked by fighters at any moment. So as Wall handled the flying and Lobban lay in the nose and operated the camera, each man also kept a sharp eye out for impending danger.

It was a good day for their mission. The weather was bright and sunny, the air unusually clear for the midpoint of the brief Bavarian summer. A scattering of clouds drifted lazily across the sky, but the white puffs of cumulus were no hindrance to visibility.

As he looked down from the left side of the cockpit, Wall could distinguish only a few landmarks. He saw the *bahnhof* and the railroad tracks extending from it, and he also thought he could make out the twin spires of Munich's famous old church, the *Frauenkirche*, but he wasn't positive. Many of the other buildings were in ruins as a result of

1

bombing raids carried out by the RAF at night, and by the USAAF in daylight. A feature that was easier to identify was the Isar, the river that ran through the center of the city.

One thing he could not pick out was the BMW factory, though he knew it was on the northern outskirts. The Bayerische Motoren Werke was a major engine manufacturer, and that was one of the reasons RAF Intelligence had sent the Mosquito to take aerial photographs.

As an auto-racing enthusiast, Wall was familiar with BMW's history. The company had been founded in 1916 to build aircraft engines under license from Daimler-Benz, which was why its famous blue-and-white emblem depicted whirling propeller blades. Both Mercedes and BMW engines had been used to power many German airplanes, including the Fokker D-VII, the outstanding fighter of the First World War.

Following the armistice, Germany had been forbidden by the Versailles Treaty to build aircraft. Therefore, in the 1920s BMW began manufacturing autos and motorcycles, and later built race cars that competed at England' s Brooklands track. Today the plant was a vital contributor to the German war effort, once again turning out a wide range of engines, principally for airplanes and tanks.

But what was the factory' s present condition? Had it been badly damaged, or even destroyed? Or would the photos indicate it was still in operation? If it were, Allied bombers would be sent to hit it again.

As Wall flew back and forth over the battered industrial area of the city, Lobban triggered the shutter, shooting frame after frame of black-and-white film. The Mosquito was ideal for this kind of work, very stable in the air. In fact it was remarkable in many respects, and like every pilot who flew it, Wall held the type in high regard. Yet its design was so unorthodox that when first conceived, the airplane had come close to not being produced at all.

Built by De Havilland, the Mosquito was 41 feet long, with a wingspan of 54 feet. It was powered by two liquid-cooled twelve-cylinder Rolls-Royce Merlin engines that together provided 3,000 horsepower. Its range with two drop tanks was 1,905 miles, more than enough for it to fly from its base in England to the target and back.

But those aspects of the design were not what made it unique among contemporary military aircraft. What set the Mosquito apart was that it was built almost entirely of wood.

Such a radical idea had come about thanks to foresight on the part of De Havilland's engineers when they began planning a new medium bomber. Anticipating the war by several years, they reasoned that the metals required for conventional construction would one day be in short supply. Then why not build the new airplane of molded plywood, and some parts even of balsa wood?

Predictably, officials of the British Air Ministry considered that a foolish idea. They said the days of wooden airplanes in combat were long past, and directed De Havilland to put the project aside and concentrate on building its Flamingo troop carriers and Tiger Moth trainers.

But when the Battle of Britain raged in the skies over England, the De Havilland factory at Hatfield worked feverishly to produce a prototype of the Mosquito. It was test-flown by Geoffrey De Havilland Jr. on 25 November 1940, and proved to be an excellent performer.

The Mosquito was then rushed into production, and eventually it became the most versatile aircraft in the war. It played many different roles: as a bomber carrying 4,000 pounds of high explosives, as a day fighter, as a radar-equipped night fighter, as a mine layer, as a pathfinder, as a supporter of ground troops, as an air ambulance, as a military transport. But it also served as a platform for reconnaissance photography, as it did above Munich on this mild summer day.

After a few minutes of circling, Flight Lieutenant Wall decided he and Lobban had achieved the mission's objective. He was tired of sucking oxygen through his smelly rubber mask, and his electrically heated flying suit was uncomfortably warm. He told his navigator it was time to pack it in.

Plenty of flak was coming up by then. The sky was marked by ugly black bursts, though none of them came close to their aircraft. Lobban got back into his seat and said Wall should turn to a heading of 285 degrees.

At that point the Mosquito was still over the northern part of the city. As Wall banked to turn on course, the strong rays of the sun caused him to squint. He knew he'd have to contend with the glare all the way back to base.

Suddenly Lobban called out, "Hey, what's this? Bandit at six o' clock! And closing fast!"

Wall was surprised. How could an enemy fighter have reached their altitude so quickly, without being seen?

There was no time to think about it—he had to pull away from the attacker in a hurry. Getting caught by a fighter that no doubt mounted cannons while he was flying a wooden airplane armed with nothing but a camera was not a welcome prospect. He shoved the throttles and prop controls forward, and reset the fuel mixture to full rich. The powerful engines immediately responded, and the Mosquito sprinted ahead.

The aircraft's rated maximum speed was 420 mph, but when pushed, it could do better than that. In the thin air Wall felt sure no Messerschmitt or Focke-Wulf could overtake it. All he had to do was keep the throttles wide open and fly straight and level, and the enemy would be left far behind.

He was wrong.

"Still closing on us," Lobban shouted.

Wall couldn't quite believe it. But a glance in the rear-view mirror told him it was true; though the Mosquito's airspeed was now 430 mph, their pursuer was rapidly reducing the distance between them.

There was one way Wall could fly even faster. He put the airplane into a shallow dive, and the needle of the airspeed indicator quickly moved to 440 mph. Then to 450, 460, 470. Already well past its do-not-exceed speed, the Mosquito began vibrating roughly. Keep going at this rate, Wall thought, and you'll tear the wings off. He drew the stick back and brought the Mosquito level.

Now the enemy not only stayed with his aircraft, but came closer still. And began firing its guns. Tracers streaked past the Mosquito, inches above the cockpit canopy.

"Break!" Lobban yelled.

Wall backed off the throttles, and swung left. The attacker flashed by, and as it did, he got his first good look at it.

So did Lobban. "Bloody thing's got no props!"

Indeed it didn't. The enemy aircraft was a low-winged monoplane with two large engine pods, and a configuration different from any Wall had ever seen before. It looked like a shark. A shark with wings.

The strange airplane was turning toward them. It didn't seem to be all that maneuverable, perhaps because of its enormous speed. At least it appeared to require a great amount of space to come about.

Wall knew his fighter tactics. If he could turn more tightly than the other airplane, he might be able to keep it from getting a clean shot at them. He added power and reversed course, heading directly toward it.

The two aircraft began closing at a combined speed of nearly 1,000 mph. To Wall it was as if he was flying toward a bullet, in a projectile of his own. The enemy airplane fired again, but it was not lined up quite well enough to hit them. At the last possible moment, Wall flicked the ailerons and sent the Mosquito past the attacker. Then he continued to turn hard, G-forces pushing him deeper into his seat.

As he'd hoped, it took longer for the other airplane to swing around. Again he headed directly toward it. And again he flew by before fire from its guns could strike the Mosquito. But on the next pass his opponent made a smart move, beginning his turn only a fraction of a second after Wall began his. Then he dove, and climbed toward the British aircraft from underneath, firing his cannons as he came.

Wall heard a loud bang. The Mosquito lurched and shuddered, and he struggled to maintain control, but at least the aircraft was still flying. The only response he could think of was to try another dive of his own. He pushed the stick forward, and as he did, he caught sight of a tower of cumulus below and off to his left.

Stick over, left rudder. The Mosquito flashed downward, and an instant later was enveloped in cloud. It was like flying in a bowl of milk, with the view through the windscreen solid white. But to the men in the cockpit, nothing could have looked better.

Wall then began circling, so as to remain inside the protective vapor. There was considerable turbulence, though that was nothing compared with the possibility of explosive cannon shells punching more holes in the airplane.

"See if you can check the damage," Wall ordered.

Lobban left his seat and opened the inner hatch. As he did, a strong rush of wind entered the airplane. After a few moments he closed the hatch and returned. "The outer hatch is gone," he reported. "Blown clean off."

"Anything else?"

"Not that I could see. Although there could be."

Wall went on circling for another minute or two. Finally he said, "Watch it now, we're coming out."

When their aircraft emerged from the last swirling wisps of cloud, the two men swiveled their heads rapidly and saw nothing but a few more flak bursts here and there. The mysterious attacker had disappeared. By now they were drained emotionally as well as physically, and were damp with sweat. But they were careful not to let their guard down, and continued to scan the vast blue sky.

Another problem arose: the aircraft's vibrations were growing worse. Wall reduced speed, and that helped a little. But would the Mosquito hold together until they made it back to England? He asked the navigator whether another base was closer.

Lobban looked at his charts. "There's Fermo, in Italy. It's near the Adriatic Coast."

"Heading?"

"One-six-five."

Wall gently turned to the prescribed course. As they flew on they encountered no further problems from either flak or enemy fighters. But on crossing over the snow-capped Austrian Alps the Mosquito went on shaking, as if it too had been unnerved by the unexpected attack.

Neither man had much to say then. Lobban watched for features in the landscape, while Wall concentrated on nursing the aircraft through the high mountain air. The Merlins' cylinder head temperatures were dangerously high, which was not a surprise, considering how the engines had been revved. Wall reduced power further.

Again he wondered about the strange enemy airplane. With no propellers, he concluded that it had to have been a jet. There were rumors that the Germans had succeeded in developing such machines. A few months earlier, American pilots in a flight of Mustangs claimed to have seen three of them while flying over the North Sea. When the Mustang pilots tried to engage, the twin-engine monoplanes simply zoomed away and disappeared.

But by whatever means today's attacker was powered, it had clearly displayed fantastic speed. In fact, its performance represented not just a step forward, but a giant leap. That in itself was amazing. Usually when a new type appeared, it might be as much as 20 or 30 mph faster than its rivals—the Mosquito itself had been such a machine. Yet this enemy airplane was at least *100 mph faster!*

What advantage might that suddenly give the Germans? Would they be able to produce the jets in large quantities? If they did, would the new airplanes' speed enable them to outfight anything else?

By this time in the war, the Allied air forces were much stronger than the Luftwaffe. Enemy fighters were often outnumbered twenty-to-one and more, and it was obvious that many of the German pilots were inexperienced replacements. In fact, for the huge fleets of British and American bombers that pounded the cities in Germany around the clock, flak presented as much a hazard as did the Luftwaffe. Would the new aircraft tip the balance in the Germans' favor?

Not likely. For all the hard fighting that continued on every front, the Nazis' defeat was inevitable. Then why didn't they surrender now, and save millions of lives on both sides?

Only a few days earlier, the Allies had learned of a plot in which a group of high-ranking German officers had tried to assassinate Hitler. Probably they'd thought that with Hitler finally removed it would be possible to end the war. So at least some among the ranks were willing to face the facts.

Or were they? Certainly the enemy continued to produce new kinds of exotic weapons. The V-1 buzz bombs were causing death and destruction as they rained down on London, and according to British Intelligence, Germany had still more deadly devices in the works.

Seen in that light, the incredibly fast aircraft that had attacked the Mosquito that day was another in a long series of scientific break-throughs, leading to questions that were extremely puzzling. What kind of people were the Germans? Why did they embrace war, and go on fighting when all hope of victory was lost? Whatever the reasons, Wall despised them for killing many of his comrades, and for the pain and horror they'd caused England.

As he went on struggling to hold the Mosquito on an even keel, he caught sight of sunlight glinting on water, some miles ahead. Lobban saw it too, and pointed exultantly. "Look there," he called out. "The Adriatic!"

They'd make it to Fermo after all. Wall throttled back and began losing altitude. Soon they'd be on the ground, and he'd write a report on today's mission. And have himself a much-needed drink.

But the questions continued to swirl about in his mind. What drove the Germans? What was it that enabled them, against all odds, to produce technology that often kept them ahead of everyone else?

And who was the aeronautical genius behind the fighter that attacked them today?

PART I

TAKING FLIGHT

1.

In the summer of 1909 Ferdinand Messerschmitt, a prosperous Frankfurt businessman, took his wife Anna Maria and their five children by train to Lake Constance for a vacation. The huge lake was in the foothills of the Alps, bordered by Germany, Austria and Switzerland. The Messerschmitts stayed in a charming old inn near Meersburg and enjoyed the natural beauty of their surroundings, hiking on the forest trails and swimming in the lake's icy waters.

One of the other towns on the north shore was Friedrichshafen, site of the world's foremost builder of rigid airships, a company owned by Count von Zeppelin. His LZ-1 had made its maiden flight in 1900 and was the first dirigible to fly successfully. Fascinated by the idea of air travel, Messerschmitt wanted to see Count von Zeppelin's flying machines for himself, so he hired a carriage to transport the family to Friedrichshafen.

Of Messerschmitt's offspring, the one most enthusiastic about the trip was the younger of his two sons. The boy's name was Wilhelm Emil, but throughout his life he would be called Willy. He'd been born in Frankfurt on 26 June 1898.

An excellent student, Willy had a particular aptitude for mathematics. Like his father, he was interested in all types of machines, and avidly read newspaper articles describing vehicles such as Gottlieb Daimler's automobiles, and Hildebrand & Wolfmüller's motorcycles. But most of all, he was enthralled by stories of aircraft. That same summer the Frenchman Louis Blériot had crossed the English Channel in his monoplane, completing the voyage in a mere 40 minutes. Willy thought that an amazing feat.

When the Messerschmitts arrived at *Luftschiffbau Zeppelin,* an airship was tethered outside the great barn-like hangar, being prepared by workers for a cross-country flight. Designated the LZ6, the dirigible was 128 meters long and 12 meters in diameter, and carried beneath it an open gondola for the three-man crew and five passengers. The aluminum frame was covered with cloth, and lift was provided by 17 cells containing 11,298 cubic meters of hydrogen gas. Two 15hp Daimler internal combustion engines, each turning two propellers, supplied power.

To Willy, the ship seemed almost too large to leave the ground. As he and the others watched, the mooring lines were cast off, and the dirigible began to rise into the air. It was a thrilling sight, one he would never forget.

Engines thrumming, its passengers waving and people on the ground waving back, the enormous airship slowly climbed to an altitude of 300 meters. It flew out over the lake, and then turned and headed north. Willy's rapt gaze followed the craft until at last it disappeared over the horizon.

From then on, the boy continued to read everything he could find on the subject of flight, marveling at the exploits of daredevil airmen in Europe and America. Later his father took him to the International Aviation Exhibition in Frankfurt, where they watched gliding displays.

The gliders were primitive affairs. Constructed of wood, cloth and wire, they had a high wing and a tail, and a fuselage that was simply an open framework. The pilot sat out front, hands and feet on the controls. But as crude as they were, the craft seized the boy's imagination.

Ferdinand Messerschmitt then returned to Bamberg, the Bavarian city where he'd been born. Following the death of his father, he was expected to take over the family business, a hotel and restaurant called the Weinhaus Messerschmitt. In addition to accommodating guests, the place also sold imported wines. An elegant, three-story white building, it was on Langestrasse, facing the Schonleinsplatz.

When Willy was twelve, his father introduced him to Friedrich Harth, an architect whose hobby was building and flying gliders. Harth was surrounded by a group of young aviation enthusiasts who donated their time and energy to assisting him. Willy eagerly joined the group.

Although younger than the others, the boy was more industrious than any of them. Harth saw that he had a unique talent and encouraged him, which helped guide Willy in his decision to spend his life designing and building aircraft. Over the next few years he helped construct a number of prize-winning gliders, and soon outstripped Harth in his ability as a designer.

When World War I broke out, Willy's heroes were the pilots in the Imperial German Air Service. The thought of valiant airmen sending their enemies crashing to earth in flames was tremendously exciting for him. How wonderful it must be for the victors!

Then on 28 April 1916, his father died. Willy was devastated. Ferdinand Messerschmitt had generously given him unfailing support in his quest to become an aircraft designer. But Ferdinand's death also caused a crisis in the Messerschmitt family. The Weinhaus had thrived under his direction, but was now without a leader. Willy could not fill the role; he had no experience in the business, and certainly no interest in it. Fortunately his older brother, Ferdinand Jr., agreed to take it over.

By that time Willy had grown to manhood. Tall and muscular, he had a long straight nose and a slightly protuberant jaw, and his black hair was brushed straight back from his high forehead. His eyes were deep-set and dark, with an intensity that revealed a fiercely competitive nature.

Early in 1917, he was inducted into the army. He hoped to be assigned to duties involving aviation, but instead he underwent training in a mortar battery. Before his unit was sent to the front, however, he was transferred to the Air Service. He was stationed at Schleissheim, an airfield near Munich that was known as the cradle of Bavarian aviation. He was a member of a ground crew, and though he would have no opportunity to fly, at least he could work on airplanes.

As the war ground on, the tide increasingly turned against Germany. In the battles of Ypres and Verdun and the Somme she'd lost thousands of men, and at Passchendaele and Cambrai she lost thousands more. In the spring offensive of 1918 alone, she suffered 168,000 casualties. When Messerschmitt went home on leave he found there was hardly a family in Bamberg that had not lost a father or a son. He also saw many wounded veterans hobbling about the streets, some missing arms or legs. Several of Willy's own boyhood acquaintances had been killed.

The United States then entered the conflict. In June the Americans won the battles of Belleau Wood and Chateau-Thierry, and in the fall they joined the French and British in the Meuse-Argonne offensive that led to the German surrender.

When the Armistice was declared on 11 November 1918, Messerschmitt bitterly resented his nation's defeat. His anger deepened when he learned the terms of the Treaty of Versailles, which Germany was forced to sign in 1919.

The treaty required Germany to give up 13 percent of her national territory and all of her overseas colonies, plus 16 percent of her coalfields and half her iron and steel industries. She was not allowed to build aircraft, submarines, or artillery, and was required to pay 132 billion Reischmarks in reparations. The already weak economy collapsed. People bartered to obtain food, and many died of disease and starvation.

Despite the hardships, the Weinhaus Messerschmitt survived.The family drew from its large stocks of wines, trading them to meet their needs, and in time the business began to recover. As for Willy, he was more eager than ever to pursue his dreams. He continued to build gliders, several of which set endurance records. He was determined that no matter how many obstacles stood in his way, he would become a successful aircraft designer.

2.

To reach his goals, Willy knew he'd need a first-rate education. This led him to enroll in the Technische Hochschule of Munich, an excellent engineering university. His family paid his tuition, and he lived frugally in Schwabing, a neighborhood favored by students and artists.

At the time, the political situation in Germany was chaotic. Kaiser Wilhelm had abdicated, and Friedrich Ebert, leader of the German Social Democrat Party, was elected Chancellor. The government became the Weimar Republic. But in Munich, the head of the German Communist Party, Eugen Levine, proclaimed that the Bavarian Republic would have its own laws.

Levine drew his ideas from the Russian Marxists, making private ownership of a business prohibited. Peoples' homes would be expropriated and given over to the poor, and paper money would be abolished. To enforce his decrees, he established a military unit called the Red Guards.

Fearing that this development would lead to Germany falling under Communist rule, Chancellor Ebert sent troops into Bavaria, where government officials were arrested and executed. Members of the Red Guards were killed or imprisoned, and Eugen Levine was shot by a firing squad. But German politics remained in turmoil. Assassinations were rife, and a number of private armies, so-called Freikorps led by former military commanders, hunted and killed radicals.

At this time a new group emerged. This was the National Socialist German Workers Party, the Nazis. Their leader was a strangely intense young man named Adolf Hitler, a native of Austria who'd been a corporal in the German Army. During the war Hitler had won the Iron Cross for valor and was temporarily blinded by poison gas. After the Armistice he entered politics, which he approached like a religion.

Physically, the Nazi leader was unimpressive. His shoulders were narrow and his hips wide, and he was slightly less than average in height. Beneath his prominent nose was a black toothbrush mustache that made him look almost comical. Yet despite this, he was a mesmerizing speaker.

In his hours-long speeches he would literally shout to the audience that Germany had lost the war because the Communists and Jews in the homeland had stabbed the armed forces in the back! The outrageously punitive Versailles Treaty must be disavowed! Germany must once again take her rightful place among the leading nations of the world! To back him up he formed a private army called the Sturm Abteilung, or SA, a gang of thugs also known as the Brownshirts. They wore swastika armbands and crushed anyone who spoke out against their leader.

Though Willy Messerschmitt shared the Nazis' views toward the hated Versailles Treaty, he did not join the party. He was preoccupied with his studies, which included a heavy load of courses in physics, mathematics and mechanical engineering. Then too, Munich offered many pleasant distractions for students. In the beer halls a stein of good Bavarian brew cost only a few pfennigs, and there were plenty of compliant girls. Willy much enjoyed the Bohemian lifestyle.

Yet his interest in designing and building gliders was as keen as ever. He resumed his association with Harth, and the two collaborated on several new sailplanes. Most of the ideas for them came from Willy.

On 21 September 1921 conditions at the gliding center in the Rhön Mountains were ideal. With Harth at the controls, Willy's latest sailplane lifted off and eventually reached an altitude of 150 meters. It was in the air an astonishing 21 minutes and 37 seconds, a new world record for endurance.

A few months later, Harth was flying another of Willy's designs when a sudden wind shift caused the glider to crash. Harth suffered major injuries, and never flew again.

Willy was still a student at the university. To supply funds for his projects, he set up a gliding school on the Wasserkuppe, and charged tuition. As a replacement for Harth, he chose Wolf Hirth, an outstanding pilot.

Willy then built a new sailplane. Like all others, it was steered by wing warping, but to reduce drag, Willy eliminated the pylon atop the wing that held the wires used for warping. Instead, two struts ran from the keel of the glider up to the wing. The new method improved performance considerably. Messerschmitt also rejected the two-spar wing design favored by other builders, and constructed his glider's wing with a single spar. It was ingeniously contrived to withstand stress, via a unique bracing arrangement that Messerschmitt patented.

In 1922, Germany underwent another crisis. Under the terms of the Versailles Treaty, France and England demanded payment of the 132 billion Reichsmarks they claimed Germany owed.

To meet the enormous obligation Germany printed more money, and the result was runaway inflation. In January 1923 the exchange rate was four marks to the U.S. dollar, but by the end of the year a dollar cost 4,000,000,000 marks. Hunger riots took place, and because money was worthless, the debt remained unpaid. France used Germany's failure to pay as an excuse to seize the Ruhr Valley, where Germany's coal, iron and steel industries were located. The French army occupied the region.

As a result of inflation, Willy had no funds to build his next glider, so he made do with used parts. To reduce drag as much as possible, he put the warping controls inside the wing, and instead of an open framework of steel tubing, he enclosed the fuselage with plywood panels. Drag was greatly lessened, but the aircraft was hard to handle and was demolished in a crash. Sudden warping of the wing had shifted the center of pressure in the airfoil, which resulted in structural failure.

To correct the faults, Willy designed a new type of airfoil with a fixed center of pressure, which eliminated the problem. Designated the

Gottingen 535, the airfoil is used in the construction of gliders to this day.

For the Rhön Competition of 1923, Willy designed a sailplane that featured his new airfoil. He entered two examples in the trial. His pilot would be Hans Hackmack.

With the wind out of the west at 20 meters per second, the sailplane took off and attained the remarkable altitude of 303 meters, or just under 1,000 feet. No other aircraft in the competition was able to soar anywhere near that high. Willy then convinced the faculty of the Technische Hochschule to accept his sailplane as the thesis for his degree in mechanical engineering, and at the age of 25, he graduated as a *Diplom Ingenieur*.

On 13 August Gustav Stresemann became Chancellor of Germany. Stresemann sold some of his nation's remaining assets in order to pay the reparations, and Germans responded by being enraged that the Weimar government did not stand up to their former enemies.

But Adolf Hitler saw the situation as his main chance. The Nazi party was now a powerful group of 55,000 well-organized followers, and with the help of the former fighter pilot Hermann Göring, Hitler attempted a coup. When officials attended a rally in a beer hall in Munich on 8 November, Göring had SA storm troopers surround the place.

Hitler rushed into the hall and fired a pistol, shouting, "The national revolution has begun!" His Nazis would march to Berlin, he proclaimed, and overthrow the government, making General Erich Ludendorff head of the army. The crowd roared its approval and sang, "Deutschland Uber Alles."

But "the beer hall putsch" failed. In a melee the following day, the police killed 16 Nazis and lost three of their own. Hitler fled into hiding. Later he was arrested and tried, fully expecting to be shot, but instead, a sympathetic judge sentenced him to five years in prison.

At that point an exciting opportunity arose for Messerschmitt. Germans were forbidden to build airplanes, but not gliders. So why not equip light aircraft with small engines, and call them powered gliders? Willy decided to start his own company, to manufacture this new type of aircraft.

As he made his plans, another determined individual was busy making his. In cell number 11 in Landsberg Castle, Adolf Hitler went on spouting his ideas to anyone who would listen. His followers urged him to write a book about his beliefs and political theories, but Hitler was no writer. While raving about Germany's enemies, he was often barely coherent, so he dictated his thoughts to a student at Munich University who fashioned them into a book.

The writer was Rudolf Hess. Dark haired with bushy black eyebrows, Hess was also a former fighter pilot. The original title of the book was "Four Years of Struggle Against Lies, Stupidity and Cowardice," but eventually an editor would change it to "Mein Kampf," which meant, "My Struggle."

As this was transpiring, Messerschmitt struggled with his own projects. When at last inflation was brought under control and Germany began her economic recovery, his brother was able to lend the funds necessary for Willy to launch his venture.

3.

The new company was called *Flugzeugbau Messerschmitt Bamberg*. Willy did his designing in his room on the second floor of the Weinhaus, and rented space in the nearby Murrmann Brewery for construction.

The Rhön Competition of 1924 was the first to allow powered gliders to take part. Messerschmitt intended to enter one or two machines in the meet, reasoning that if they performed well, it would give his fledgling firm a huge boost.

The new aircraft, designated the S15, had a single-spar wing, with a span of 14 meters. The fuselage was again enclosed in plywood panels, but there were significant differences. The leading edge of the wing was faced in smoothly curved plywood to help it slip through the air. And instead of a belly skid, a pair of large disc wheels were joined to an axle under the fuselage. Also, the fuselage was longer, because the weight of an engine required the center of gravity to be farther aft.

The most important difference would be the engine itself. Willy would have to use one of small size, resulting in less power. However, that didn't trouble him. The aircraft would weigh slightly less than 400 pounds without the pilot—and to be on the safe side, he'd be sure to hire a slender airman to fly it.

The engine he chose was built by Douglas Co. in England. It was a three and one-half horsepower 500cc motorcycle plant with twin, horizontally opposed cylinders. A two-stroke, it ran on a mixture of oil and gasoline. That saved weight, because there was no need for valves and an oil reservoir.

By late spring, the airplane was ready for a flight test. Willy and his crew of five workers hauled it from the brewery to the airfield, a broad meadow near the town. For a pilot, Willy had hired Heinz Seywald, a short, slim man who had learned to fly in the German Air Service during the war, and later had gained experience in flying gliders.

Word had circulated that Messerschmitt was about to try out his new flying machine, and a crowd gathered to watch. They chattered excitedly, as if attending a football match.

Seywald climbed into the cockpit, and Willy grasped the propeller. He'd have to spin it to his right, because British engines ran opposite from the German. He gave the prop a downward tug and the Douglas caught, belching a cloud of oily blue smoke and buzzing loudly.

Seywald advanced the throttle, and after a roll of 200 meters the S15 took off. The aircraft made several flights that day, and on the longest one it stayed in the air for 43 minutes. Seywald thrilled the crowd by banking and diving and then circling over the town of Bamberg at an altitude of 600 meters.

Knowing the value of publicity, Willy had made sure that there would be a reporter on hand from *Flugsport*, the leading magazine for flying enthusiasts. The writer's glowing article drew the attention of a flight school in Würzburg. The school already owned three Messerschmitt gliders, and they quickly placed an order for an S15.

Now Willy began building the examples that would compete at Rhön. They were similar to the S15, and Messerschmitt was confident they would win more than their share of prizes. The first was a single-seater, designated the S16a. Willy named it Rudi, after his younger brother Rudolf. Once again the engine was a Douglas twin, but this one provided 14 hp. The other airplane was the S16b, a two-seater. Willy called that one Betti, the nickname of his younger sister Elizabeth.

There were several important changes in the two new aircraft. One was the use of ailerons instead of wing warping. In another, each airplane's wing could be folded back, to facilitate towing. The cockpit was enclosed, so the pilot had no forward visibility, but had to look out the side windows.

When test-flown, both these aircraft performed well and delivered excellent fuel economy. At a speed of 115 kph, and with a pilot and passenger aboard, the Betti flew 3.2 kilometers per liter of fuel consumed. Confident he had a pair of winners, Messerschmitt and his crew eagerly transported the S16s to Rhön. Seywald had again been chosen to fly them.

This was the most important event yet held at Rhön. Every designer and pilot with an interest in light aircraft was there, as were many journalists and a great crowd of spectators. It was not until late in the day that Seywald was cleared to take off. He put the graceful Rudi through its paces, diving and zooming, and the aircraft performed beautifully.

But with the airplane at an altitude of 200 meters, the propeller suddenly tore loose from its block and spun away. Seywald closed the throttle and switched off the magneto. He made a spiraling approach and put the nose down, but it was too late. The S16a slammed to the earth.

Messerschmitt and his crew ran to the airplane. Seywald was bruised and dazed, and the Rudi was a wreck. Willy said he'd find another pilot to fly the Betti, but Seywald wouldn't hear of it. He insisted on continuing with the S16b, and eventually convinced Messerschmitt to let him fly it. The demonstration would be the last of the day.

In the gathering dusk Seywald took off, and the S16b acquitted itself admirably. The determined pilot put it through many of the same maneuvers, and added a few others, including Dutch rolls and power stalls. Everything worked perfectly, except for the chain that turned the propeller. A link snapped, and the flailing chain wrapped itself around the engine's drive shaft. The engine abruptly quit, and once again Seywald found himself flying a powered aircraft with no power.

This time he was in luck. The wind was light and steady, and he had no trouble landing the hobbled aircraft. Though the Betti was only slightly damaged, Messerschmitt considered it another debacle. He'd entered the first two powered airplanes he'd ever designed, and both had failed. He and his crew began packing up the S16b and the wreckage of her sister ship. It was a grim task.

As they went about their task, a man approached Willy and introduced himself. His name was Theo Croneiss, a name that rang a bell. Messerschmitt was aware that Croneiss had been a fighter pilot in the war, and that he'd racked up a record of five kills.

Theo Croneiss was a big man, cheerful and outgoing. He surprised Messerschmitt by congratulating him on having built two very good light airplanes. The engine problems, he said, were not the fault of the designer.

After an otherwise distressing day, that observation was good to hear—but what Croneiss said next was even better. He told Willy he was about to start a flying school, and on the basis of what he'd seen of the young designer's work, he wanted to equip the school with aircraft built by the Messerschmitt Company.

Willy was elated. He realized at once that this could be a turning point in his career.

4.

As he began designing the new airplane, Willy decided to change the designation from "S," which stood for *Segelflugzeug,* or sailplane, to "M" for Messerschmitt. Thus the design that Willy created for Croneiss was named the M17.

As a major improvement, he built a sheet steel bulkhead to which an engine could be attached with four bolts. He also made sure that, unlike the S16s, the M17 had a strong firewall behind the bulkhead to protect the airplane's occupants.

When the first of the M17s were delivered in the spring of 1925, Croneiss was delighted. The new airplanes were easy to fly, had very good performance, and were cheap to operate and maintain. He put them to work as trainers for his students, and also looked around for air meets in which they might compete.

The most interesting possibility was the *Oberfrankenflug.* It was the best-known aerial competition in Germany, taking place in May. Croneiss entered one of his M17's, and flew the airplane himself. The M17 won first prize for altitude, as well as first prize for speed. It was obvious that the new aircraft was the best in its class.

The M17 proved it again in September, during the International Flight Competition in Munich. That meet attracted not only German designers, but other designers from all over Europe. The M17 won first prize in every event.

Not only did the success bring him more orders for airplanes, but added to Messerschmitt's fame, which in turn encouraged more students to enroll in the flight school. Adventurous young men who wanted to fly wanted most to learn from Theo Croneiss in an M17.

The following September, an M17 startled the world. Equipped with a 29 hp Bristol twin and fitted with extra fuel tanks in place of a passenger, it flew from Bamberg over the Alps to Rome, a distance of 1620 kilometers. Total time in the air was 14 hours and 20 minutes.

In the meantime, officials in France and Britain were arguing that Germany was in violation of the Versailles Treaty by again building airplanes. The German government countered by pointing out that the nation's aircraft firms were constructing only planes intended for peaceful use. Because the Versailles Treaty referred specifically to military aircraft, which Germany was not building, the restrictions were then lifted.

Nevertheless, there were stirrings among veterans of the German Air Service. A few had found jobs as pilots, or like Theo Croneiss, had started flying schools. Most of them, however, had been reduced to scratching out a living. They believed that under the proper leadership, Germany would one day resurrect her former military might and exact revenge on her enemies. As a consequence, many became zealous followers of Adolf Hitler.

Prominent among them was Rudolf Hess. Hitler placed complete trust in the former fighter pilot, who was given a high position in the party.

Also given a high position was Hermann Göring. Hitler said of him, "I like Göring. I made him head of my *Sturm Abteilung*. He is the only one who ran the S.A. properly. I gave him a disheveled rabble. In a very short time he organized a division of 11,000 men."

Theo Croneiss had joined the Nazi party early on. He introduced Messerschmitt to Göring and Hess, who admired the youthful aircraft designer for his outstanding talent. Yet Willy still had not become a member of the party, preferring instead to concentrate on his business. Croneiss again contributed to its growth by founding the *Nordbayrische Verkehrsflug*, or North Bavarian Airline, and choosing Messerschmitt to build his equipment.

Croneiss's company would be a feeder airline, enabling its passengers to connect from small airports to large ones, where they would embark on flights of greater distance. The airplanes Messerschmitt was to supply would accommodate only three passengers and their baggage plus the pilot.

At this point Willy decided to convert his firm to a privately held stock company. Its name was now *Messerschmitt Flugzeugbau GmbH*

Bamberg. Although he still owed his brother a considerable sum from his original loan, Willy owned all the shares.

His next aircraft was designated the M18. Like the M17, it was a high-wing monoplane. In designing it, Messerschmitt decided to cover the fuselage with stressed aluminum rather than plywood, as a safety factor—plywood tended to splinter in a crash. In July 1926, the first of the M18's entered service. They performed well, with no maintenance problems; thanks to the four-bolt attachment, mechanics could replace an M18's engine with a fresh one in less than an hour.

The following year Willy built the five-passenger M18b. The airplane was remarkable for its economy of operation, which airlines measured then as they do today, by cost per passenger kilometer flown. The cost of operating the M18 was roughly one-fourth that of airplanes built by other manufacturers. No wonder Willy sold M18s not only to German companies but also to airlines in other European countries, notably Spain and Italy.

In 1927 another challenge arose. This was the *Sachsenflug,* a competition offering a prize of 60,000 Reichsmarks for a light airplane with the best empty weight to payload ratio. Messerschmitt's entry would not only be a new airplane, but it would also be based on what was for him a new concept. For the first time, he would build a low-wing monoplane. The result was the M19. The aircraft was an open cockpit single-seater, and was the first aircraft in the world to lift more than its own weight. The airplane weighed a mere 308 pounds, yet its payload was 440 pounds. Willy's achievement was one that many experts had thought impossible.

Croneiss flew the M19 in the Sachsenflug trials, and so superior was the airplane to all other entries that the competition was virtually over before it began. The M19 triumphed, and Willy was awarded the prize of 60,000 marks.

He invested the entire sum in his company.

5.

By the late 1920s Adolf Hitler was again making his presence known in German politics. He'd been released from prison on 20 December 1924, and for a few years had been living in comfort at Berchtesgaden in the Bavarian Alps. He traveled to rallies in an open Mercedes bought for him by the Nazi party, and never failed to excite audiences with his rant-ing. Nazi membership grew to 108,000, with many sympathizers among non-members.

Hitler's personal life changed as well. Women had always thought him odd, and shied away. But now that he'd become a prominent polit-ical figure, they flocked around him. Some of the women who knew him intimately whispered that he was sadomasochistic, and at times impo-tent. He was also rumored to have contracted syphilis from a whore, which might explain his hatred of prostitutes.

None of this had a negative impact on Hitler's public image. In part this was due to the work of his propaganda chief Josef Goebbels, an evil genius when it came to manipulating the media. Goebbels worked hard to present Hitler as more a statesman than a rabble-rouser, though his speeches were as fiery as ever.

At this time Germany's Ministry of Aviation wanted to promote growth in the industry, so both the Weimar Republic and the Bavarian government invested in a number of aircraft manufacturing companies, which was actually a way subsidizing them. The stated reason was that expanded air travel would be good for the nation's economy. But there was also a less obvious rationale. Some officials were members of the Nazi party, and believed that air power could become a vital factor in Germany's military resurgence.

One of the companies asking for financial help was the *Bayerische Flugzeugwerke AG* in Augsburg. BFW had been formed in 1916 to build Albatros fighters for the German Air Service, and now the direc-tors wanted the firm to become an important builder of aircraft once again. They petitioned the Bavarian government to invest in the com-pany, and the request was granted. Willy Messerschmitt then asked for a similar subsidy, but the government saw no reason to support more than one aircraft manufacturer in Bavaria. Messerschmitt was told he should merge his company with BFW.

Willy was taken aback. He'd never considered working for any firm but his own. The directors of BFW, on the other hand, were all for uni-fication. Not only would the company be getting an infusion of capital, but it would also gain an aircraft designer who was considered one of the best in Germany.

After lengthy discussions, Willy finally agreed to the merger. He would become both chief designer of BFW and a member of the board of directors. He would be paid a handsome salary and would also receive license fees on the sale of any aircraft he had designed before the merger. Moreover, he would be in a management position with a larger, well-financed company, which would enable him to compete with the nation's leading aircraft manufacturers.

He signed the deal on 8 September 1927. He was only 29 years old, and had graduated from the Technische Hochschule just four years earlier. Now as the chief designer of BFW he was virtually given a free hand.

Immediately he began overhauling the company's development program. He brought in his own assistants, and hired a number of talented engineers. And then he won his first big order—it came from Deutsche Lufthansa, Germany's national airline.

The head of Lufthansa was Erhard Milch, who directed BFW to build a new transport that would carry ten passengers on long-range flights. The contract called for the delivery of two aircraft, with more to follow. This was an auspicious beginning for the next stage of Willy's career. Or so he thought.

Like Messerschmitt, Milch was surprisingly young to hold so important a position. And also like Willy, he was supremely confident of his own abilities. But except for those qualities, the two men were polar opposites. For one thing, Milch was a Prussian. Born in Wilhelmshaven on 30 March 1892, he was educated at the Anklam Military Academy, graduating first in his class. During the war he served in the German Air Service, and though not a pilot, he attained the rank of captain and commanded the 204th Reconnaissance unit.

Following the Armistice, Milch formed a small airline, which after a succession of mergers became *Deutsche Lufthansa*. His administrative skills were such that in 1926, at the age of 35, he was made the managing director.

Milch was a superb executive. Short and stocky, with blue eyes and thinning sandy hair, he could be charming when the situation called for it. But he was also ruthless. In his business dealings he had a reputation for bearing grudges.

In their first meetings, Milch and Messerschmitt got along well. Milch was pleased that Germany's outstanding designer would build the new transport, and he was eager to see the proposal.

Messerschmitt used the M18 as the basis for his design. To provide more power, he installed a 500 hp BMW radial engine. By February 1928 the aircraft was ready for a test flight. With Milch and other representatives of Lufthansa on hand, the M20 took off smoothly and performed a series of maneuvers.

Everything went perfectly, until the pilot put the M20 into a dive. As its speed increased, fabric on the upper surface of the wing began to tear away. The pilot panicked. He jumped out of the aircraft and pulled his parachute's ripcord, and as he dangled in the harness, the M20 dove straight down and crashed. Seeing this, Milch concluded that the machine had suffered from structural weaknesses. There was no discussion. He simply left the field and cancelled the order for the two aircraft.

Messerschmitt was deeply disappointed. He insisted on an investigation, and examination of the wreckage revealed that the problem with the fabric was minor. The airplane could have landed safely.

To prove that his design was sound, Messerschmitt went ahead and built the second M20. Identical to the first except for stronger wing fabric, it was tested on 3 August 1928. The aircraft performed flawlessly in every maneuver, including a number of steep dives.

The M20 was then certified as ready for airline service, and Milch reinstated the order. Messerschmitt was relieved that he'd been vindicated, and the following spring another M20 was delivered. So cost-efficient were the new transports, and so popular with passengers, that the airline ordered four more.

Now for the first time, Willy had money to spend on himself. He bought a comfortable house in a quiet residential neighborhood of Augsburg, and a new 2-liter Mercedes sedan. He had many female admirers, though little time for them; as usual, he preferred burying himself in his work.

But there was one young woman he found highly attractive, even though he considered her out of reach. She was the Baroness Lilly von Michel-Raulino Stromeyer. A dark-haired beauty who was seven years older than Messerschmitt, the Baroness had been born into one of Bamberg's richest families. The Michel-Raulinos lived in a mansion filled with antiques and fine art; at a time when few people owned automobiles, members of the family could be seen riding in a chauffeured Horch limousine.

In 1919 Lilly had married Otto Stromeyer, who also came from a wealthy family. Otto wore wire-rimmed spectacles and rarely smiled, but he was a shrewd financier, and his dealings added greatly to the Stromeyer coffers.

The Baroness had money in her own right. Following the marriage she and Otto formed the Stromeyer-Raulino Financial Group, which was successful in a number of ventures. Over time, they had three sons.

When Messerschmitt began to make a name for himself as an aircraft designer, Lilly took an interest in him and his exploits. She believed aviation had a bright future, and made it a point to get to know Willy and discuss his ideas with him. Though most men of that era were put off by intelligent women who were knowledgeable about business and politics, Willy was captivated by the Baroness. She had a remarkably quick mind, and was better informed on matters of finance than he was; she was also quite beautiful.

At this point BFW was suddenly faced with a severe crisis. As was often the case, politics was at the root of it, and unless the emergency could somehow be favorably resolved, the company would soon be bankrupt.

6.

The problem stemmed from partisan dissension in the German government. In the Weimar Republic, as well as in Bavaria, there were loud outcries by peace advocates that money was being wasted on aviation subsidies. It was a nefarious attempt, they said, to rearm Germany. The Reichstag reacted by cutting off revenue to the aviation firms.

The viability of a company like BFW depended greatly on cash flow. With their subsidy cut, they would be unable to buy construction materials and pay the work force, making it impossible to fill the orders on the books. The banks were no help; they regarded aviation as much too risky, especially at a time when money was tight.

Desperate for a way out, Willy asked the Baroness for help. She agreed to take steps on his behalf, and suggested to her husband that the Stromeyer-Raulino Financial Group come to the rescue. Although Otto was initially reluctant, the Group finally bought 87.5% of the company's shares, and the remaining 12.5% went to Messerschmitt.

For Willy, there were many advantages. Most important, the company was saved from bankruptcy, but an additional advantage was that BFW would now have the input of financial expertise. And Willy would have even greater freedom as chief designer than he'd had under the current board of directors. With sufficient capital, BFW thrived. The company delivered several more M20 transports to Lufthansa, much to the satisfaction of Erhard Milch, who was pleased with their performance and cost-efficiency.

As always, Messerschmitt constantly improved his products. He followed the M20 with the M20b, a more powerful version of the transport. So well was the M20b received that Milch ordered ten more, which BFW was able to deliver over a span of three years.

The company's profits were soon rewarding the Stromeyer-Raulino Group for its investment. Otto Stromeyer kept a sharp eye on the books, and as long as BFW was making money, he was satisfied. He was rarely seen at the Augsburg plant. The Baroness, on the other hand, visited often. She found aviation an engrossing business, and never tired of discussing with Willy his plans for future growth. It was clear to her that he was both a visionary and an inventive genius.

In order not to distract him from the many issues that needed his attention during the day, they began having dinner together in Augsburg's *gemütlich* restaurants. He discovered that in addition to her astute business judgment, she had a tender feminine side as well. This attraction eventually led to meetings at Messerschmitt's home.

Lilly was fascinated by the young designer. He was bold and adventurous, willing to take almost any chance to reach his goals. These qualities made him quite different from her husband, whose stuffiness bored her. What happened next was inevitable.

Over a period of several months, Lilly frequently spent nights with Messerschmitt. They had fallen deeply in love, and she was convinced she'd found the man she wanted to be with for the rest of her life. Needless to say, he felt the same way about her.

With characteristic decisiveness, the Baroness divorced Stromeyer and moved in with Willy. She brought her youngest son, Eberhard, while the two older boys stayed with their father. She hired a cook and a maid, and saw to it that the Messerschmitt home was furnished tastefully. Bavarian citizens were largely Catholic, and though such conduct was considered scandalous, Messerschmitt and Lilly ignored the cackling busybodies.

Willy was very happy with the new turn his life had taken. He was not only in love, but had someone he could trust completely for sound business advice. Additionally, he and young Eberhard were getting along well.

BFW kept busy filling the orders from Lufthansa. But unfortunately, on a cold day in the winter of 1928, the pilot of an M20b flew into a heavy squall. The aircraft crashed, and all aboard were killed. Although bad weather was the obvious cause, Erhard Milch suspected that design faults might have contributed to the mishap. He therefore insisted that a similar Lufthansa M20b be put through a rigorous flight test.

Conducting the test would be Hans Hackmack, the same pilot who in 1923 had set an altitude record while flying a Messerschmitt glider. Hackmack was now Lufthansa's chief test pilot, as well as a close friend of Milch. In the test, Hackmack conducted power-on and power-off stalls, dives and sharp turns. All maneuvers were performed without incident, but then, for some unexplained reason, the M20b went into a vertical power dive. Hackmack failed to pull out, and died in the crash.

When the news reached Milch, he became furious. Refusing to consider the possibility of pilot error, he blamed Messerschmitt. The designer-built airplanes, Milch claimed, were unsafe. According to him, Messerschmitt had been personally responsible for the deaths of the Lufthansa passengers and crew in the first crash, and now his careless-ness had led to the death of his friend Hackmack as well.

Milch immediately cancelled the balance of the orders for M20s and demanded that the firm return the money it had so far been paid. He swore that Lufthansa would never buy another airplane that had been designed by Willy Messerschmitt.

The cancellations were a crippling blow. BFW could not meet Milch's demand for reimbursement, and his attacks discouraged other customers from buying BFW aircraft. Willy filed a lawsuit against Lufthansa, and a legal battle ensued.

During this time, the Baroness used her own funds to help support the company; friends also lent what money they could. Yet the losses continued to mount. Unable to pay its creditors, BFW was again faced with bankruptcy.

It was then that Messerschmitt designed a new aircraft, the M23. A low-wing sport monoplane with two open cockpits in tandem, it was light and fast, and became an immediate hit. It sold well, winning a number of competitions.

Nevertheless, this didn't keep BFW from sinking deeper into debt.

At the end of the year the firm declared bankruptcy, and soon it would have to close altogether. Even with the help of the Baroness, Messerschmitt was unable to find a solution.

Then came a ray of light. The court found there was no proof that structural weaknesses had caused the M20b accidents, and ruled that Lufthansa must reinstate its orders. BFW was ordered to build the remaining transports and deliver them to the airline.

Milch's hostility toward Messerschmitt then became white-hot. He would never forgive the designer for the death of his friend, and from then on he'd do everything in his power to make trouble for him. In turn, Messerschmitt felt Milch was rancorous and vengeful. The two men would remain enemies for the rest of their lives.

Despite the animosity, work on the transports resumed. As BFW began to deliver them to Lufthansa, payments from the airline brought in desperately needed funds. However, much time would pass before the company could emerge from bankruptcy.

In 1928, the German Ministry of Aviation quietly approached Messerschmitt and asked him to design and build a trainer and a bomber. Willy agreed, but to his chagrin he was told both aircraft must be biplanes, a configuration he considered outmoded.

Resignedly, he built prototypes. The M21 trainer and the M22 bomber were the only biplanes he designed in his entire career. He was not pleased with them, and neither was the Air Ministry. BFW received no orders for the airplanes.

But Messerschmitt was not discouraged. He began building sport airplanes with glass-enclosed cockpits and such drag-reducing features as faired landing gear struts. He also added large flaps and wing slats to enable his aircraft to land at slow speeds. The use of slats was an ingenious idea that originated with George Handley Page, a British aeronautical engineer who built heavy bombers in World War I. Messerschmitt visited Page in England and was given a demonstration of the devices.

The slats were long strips attached to the leading edges of the wings. They were spring-mounted, and when the aircraft was aloft the slats were held in place by air pressure. As the aircraft slowed to land, the pressure lessened and the slats extended a few inches. This gave the wings added lift, and made it possible for the aircraft to settle without stalling.

Among Messerschmitt's friends were many veterans of the German Air Service who were also members of the Nazi party. They were certain that Hitler's rise was unstoppable, and urged Willy to join the party. Although Messerschmitt believed in most of the party's principles, he was not anti-Semitic. He agreed with those who considered Adolf Hitler a messianic leader, but questioned whether or not Hitler could actually take power. Willy decided to be prudent and wait; he would see for himself.

As he hesitated, fate dealt the nation another unexpected blow. In October 1929, the U.S. stock market crashed, causing a financial catastrophe in Germany as well as in America.

7.

The reason the crash had such a disastrous effect on the German economy was because so many of the nation's industries depended on investments from the United States. But suddenly that source of capital disappeared, and as a result, Germany was hit harder than any other European country. By the end of 1930, unemployment was at 4,000,000 and rising.

Adolf Hitler had predicted the calamity more than a year earlier, and now people saw that as proof of his acuity. What Germany needed, Hitler insisted, was the kind of strong government that only he could provide. When speaking to union members, Hitler assured them that he was a true socialist and that he would institute programs beneficial to them. But at the same time he told industrialists that he only pretended to be a socialist. Reassured, a number of rich industrialists, including Alfred Krupp and Fritz Thyssen, contributed money to his cause.

The truth was that Hitler wanted to establish his own brand of socialism in Germany, modeled on that of Italy's dictator Benito Mussolini, whom he admired. The government under Il Duce consisted of one central power with absolute authority over all aspects of society, both civilian and military. This was in fact fascism, and Hitler regarded it as the perfect system for Germany—but of course, with himself at its head.

The Nazi party was now increasing its strength. Hermann Göring had been elected a deputy in the Reichstag, and so had Josef Goebbels, with other party members gaining seats as well. Göring's successor as head of Hitler's private army, the SA, was longtime party member Ernst Röhm. Under the openly homosexual Röhm, the SA grew to 400,000 men. Röhm's Brownshirts were notorious for frequently attacking and murdering Hitler's enemies.

During this turbulent period, Milch made sure Lufthansa issued no further orders to BFW. Because of the broader economic downturn, the airline was suffering from severe financial troubles of its own. Messerschmitt, his funds limited, concentrated on building new lightplanes. Despite his M29 winning every competition it entered, he was unable to get contracts to build larger aircraft.

Economic conditions in Germany became even more disastrous. Hitler challenged President Paul von Hindenburg in a national election and was defeated, resulting in his party being banned. Hindenburg appointed Franz von Papen Chancellor.

Von Papen lifted the ban on the Brownshirts, which would prove to be a mistake—Röhm's storm troopers promptly killed 86 members of the Communist party. In July 1932 von Papen called an election in hopes of gathering support for his government, but he would soon find this was yet another mistake. The Nazis won 230 seats and became the largest party in the Reichstag.

The group of industrialists that had financially supported Hitler's cause then petitioned President Hindenburg to install Hitler as Chancellor. Physically weak and increasingly senile, Hindenburg assented. Adolf Hitler became Chancellor of Germany in January 1933. He was 43 years old.

The following month Göring met with industrialists and demanded additional large sums of money. This resulted in the industrialists donating 3,000,000 Reichsmarks, which allowed Josef Goebbels to gloat that at last the Nazis had enough money to control all forms of communication in Germany. But this wasn't enough to satisfy Hitler. On 27 February 1933, the Reichstag was set afire by persons unknown. Göring blamed the Communists, resulting in Hitler having thousands of them arrested and sent to concentration camps.

Adolf Hitler now had absolute power, and he decreed that the Nazis party would be the only party allowed in Germany. When the union leaders protested, Hitler sent them to the camps as well.

By then the SA had become a force larger than the German Army, and Hitler believed Ernst Röhm, as head of the SA, could be a threat to his own position. Hitler responded by expanding his personal body-guard unit, the *Schutzstaffel*, or SS, which was commanded by Heinrich Himmler. In the meantime, he had Himmler and his assistant, Reinhard Heydrich, prepare a dossier showing examples of Röhm's disloyalty.

With each move, Hitler's grip on the government tightened. He'd made it clear that air power would be vital in Germany's renewed military strength, and to Messerschmitt that meant greater opportunities for BFW. To expand the Luftwaffe, Hitler appointed Hermann Göring to head the Air Ministry, which was called the *Reichsluftfahrtministerium*, or RLM.

Therefore on 1 May 1933, Messerschmitt joined the Nazi party. From then on he was never seen without a swastika pin in the lapel of his business suits. His membership number was 342354.

But developments did not turn out as Willy had hoped. For his deputy in the RLM, Göring chose the man who had sworn never to order a design from Messerschmitt again. The new State Secretary for Air, Göring announced, would be Erhard Milch.

8.

Though Milch didn't trust Göring, he performed with his customary efficiency. Göring came to consider him indispensable. When Messerschmitt complained that Milch was blocking him from securing government contracts, Göring looked the other way.

In June 1934, Adolf Hitler decided it was time to dispense with Ernst Röhm. Many of Röhm's top SA commanders were homosexual, and Hitler used that as an excuse to have them executed. Röhm was arrested and taken to a prison cell in Munich, where he was shot by SS officers. Hitler then announced that as leader of the SS, Heinrich Himmler would report only to the Führer. Reinhard Heydrich was promoted to general.

That summer Milch directed BFW to build 30 Dornier Do-11 twin-engine bombers and 24 Heinkel He-45 reconnaissance airplanes under license. Naturally this was humiliating to Messerschmitt, as Milch knew it would be. But the revenues enabled BFW to emerge from bankruptcy, and the company again became profitable; its outlook brightened.

BFW was then selling M27 and M29 trainers to Spain, Italy and Austria. Messerschmitt once more concentrated on designing superior lightplanes. One of his best was the M35, a low-wing, single-seat monoplane built for aerobatic competition.

BFW produced 15 of the type. Powered by a 150 hp Siemens SH 14A radial engine, the M35 was highly responsive and light on the controls, with a top speed of 230 kph. Rudolf Hess flew an M35 to win the Zugspitz Trophy of 1934.

This led Major Wimmer of the Air Ministry to ask Messerschmitt why BFW wasn't manufacturing military aircraft based on his own designs. Willy replied that he'd been shut out by Milch, and as a result was forced not only to undertake work from other German companies, but also from other countries.

That last bit of news set off a furor within the German Government, and Messerschmitt was forbidden to take any more orders from foreign customers. The RLM then awarded BFW a contract to design a lightplane that would compete in the Challenge de Tourisme Internationale.

Messerschmitt realized that what the RLM wanted was an airplane that could be used for courier purposes by the military. This was the opportunity he'd been waiting for. He created his most successful lightplane of all, the M37.

The design was revolutionary. The aircraft was built entirely of metal, and the fuselage was of monocoque construction. The cabin was glass-enclosed. A pilot and copilot sat up front and shared dual controls, with two passengers behind them. The landing gear was retractable, and the cantilevered low wings could be folded. And to give the aircraft a slow landing speed, the wings were fitted with large flaps and Handley Page slats. Contributing to the development of the M37 was Robert Lusser, an outstanding young engineer Willy had recruited to BFW. Lusser was one of his ablest assistants.

The RLM then ruled that all German aircraft must have a prefix that would identify the builder. The prefix would be followed by a number, which could be used only once. In compliance, the M37 became the Bf-108.

The new airplane was far more advanced than any other in the Challenge de Tourisme Internationale. It won first prize, and the Air Ministry ordered BFW to build 34 of them. The finished product was the Bf-108B. The engine was an Argus 10e V-8 of 270 hp, and the airplane's top speed was 350 kph.

The Bf-108B became an immediate favorite of German government officials. Ernst Udet had one, and so did Rudolf Hess. Generals Koller and Sperrle flew them as well. Josef Goebbels' Propaganda Ministry proclaimed the Bf-108B as a further example of German technical superiority. Because of its speed, it was called the Taifun.

In another stroke of good fortune for Messerschmitt, his friend Ernst Udet was made head of the RLM's *Techniches Amt*, its Technical Office. When the RLM decided the Luftwaffe needed a new standard fighter, Udet proposed that BFW be given a chance to compete for the contract.

Milch claimed BFW was not qualified. And besides, General Göring had already directed Heinkel, Arado and Focke-Wulf to vie for the assignment.

But Udet enjoyed tweaking his bosses' noses, and insisted on including BFW in the competition. The former fighter pilot could get away with such conduct because he was a great favorite with the German people. An authentic hero in the war, Udet had later appeared in a number of movies in the U.S. as well as in Germany. In Hollywood he'd been friendly with Spencer Tracy and Clark Gable and other stars. And he'd had affairs with many glamorous women.

While in America Udet had become enthusiastic about dive bombers, having seen the U.S. Navy's Curtiss-Wright F9C Hell Divers. He bought two of them for $15,000 apiece and shipped them to Germany, and their performance convinced the High Command of their value as ground support aircraft.

That led to the development of a new dive bomber for the Luftwaffe, the Ju-87 *Sturzkampfflugzeug*, or Stuka. Udet boasted that the Stuka was built as a result of his foresight.

Göring had his own pet project. He directed Messerschmitt to design a twin-engine aircraft he called a *Zerstörer*. Heinkel, Focke-Wulf, and Dornier were also to submit designs. Göring claimed the aircraft could be used as a fighter or as a light bomber, but in Messerschmitt's opinion, that meant it would be ineffective in either role. And he thought calling it a destroyer was fatuous.

Meanwhile, Udet continued to press Göring and Milch, and finally they allowed BFW to compete for the standard fighter contract. Milch thought Messerschmitt's entry had no chance.

Assisted by Walter Rethel, Willy designed a prototype that embodied everything he'd learned about constructing a fast, highly maneuverable aircraft. The result was the Bf-109.

Heinkel was considered likeliest to win the contract. The company had built many different types of aircraft, and Germany's current standard fighter was the Heinkel He-51 biplane. Arado and Focke-Wulf also designed prototypes, but their fighters offered nothing new. As far as Ernst Heinkel was concerned, the competition was a mere formality.

A heavyset, balding man, Heinkel looked down his imperious nose at BFW, fully aware that the small firm in Bavaria had recently been bankrupt. He had little respect for its chief designer, whom he regarded as a builder of gliders.

Unlike Messerschmitt, Heinkel had never joined the Nazi party. He considered Hitler dangerous, and was resentful that the new government had forced him to fire a number of his best engineers and designers because they were Jews.

Heinkel assigned the job of creating the new fighter to the firm's top designers, the twin brothers Siegfried and Walter Günter. The He-112 they produced was the first Heinkel of all-metal monocoque construction. It was also the company's first low-wing monoplane, and the first with retractable landing gear. It had an open cockpit, and elliptical wingtips.

The flight trials began at Travemünde on 8 February 1936. The Focke-Wulf design was soon rejected, and Arado dropped out. That left only the Heinkel and the Bf-109 as contenders.

Alongside the He-112, the Messerschmitt design looked small and almost fragile. It had too long a nose, and stubby, square-tipped wings. The landing gear splayed out, making the fighter seem knock-kneed. Its cockpit was glass-enclosed, which surely would hinder visibility.

Yet it soon became clear that Willy Messerschmitt knew exactly what he was doing. The lighter Bf-109 had a better rate-of-climb, and was faster at any altitude. It was more maneuverable, and could pull out of a dive more quickly. Its proportions had also been carefully thought through. The short, trapezoidal shape of the wings enabled it to attain higher speeds, and the slats and large flaps permitted slower landings. The blunt wings also helped the aircraft make tighter turns.

But the most unusual design feature was a strong firewall forward of the cockpit to which all structural elements were connected, including the wing spars, engine mounts and landing gear. This was a radical departure from the conventional practice of mounting them at different points of an aircraft, in order to distribute the load. An advantage of joining the gear to the fuselage, rather than to the wings, was that the wings could be removed for repairs without cradling the airplane.

By the time the trials ended, there was no doubt as to which was the better aircraft. The Bf-109 had totally outperformed the He-112. Additionally, its simpler design would make it cheaper to build.

A demonstration for Hitler was held at the Rechlin test center. The Führer saw that Germany now had a superior new fighter, and congratulated Messerschmitt. For the designer, it was the greatest triumph he had yet experienced in his career. Hitler wasted no time in exploiting his new weapon. In 1936 the Olympic Games were held in Germany, and among the more than 100,000 spectators were officials from many different countries. They had been primed in advance by Joseph Goebbels' propaganda to expect a surprise.

The surprise came when a Bf-109, marked with black crosses and a swastika, flew low and fast over the huge stadium. All eyes were on the small, nimble fighter, its engine roaring as it flashed across the blue sky and disappeared. Seconds later the airplane reappeared and this time it performed a slow roll as it passed overhead, sunlight glinting on its metal wings. Observers were amazed. They had no idea the Luftwaffe possessed such an aircraft. It was obvious that the fighter was far more advanced than those of other air forces.

British officials in the audience realized that the German aircraft was outstanding, but the RAF was quietly developing a fighter of its own. Built by Supermarine, it had first flown as a racer and was a superb performer. It was called the Spitfire. The Russians were also impressed. They too had been working in secret to develop a modern fighter. Nikolai Polikarpov was designing one at his aircraft works in Moscow.

But Hitler had made his point. Germany was now a leader in aeronautical technology, and the Bf-109 was a prime example of the nation's prowess. Naturally, none of the observers knew that the fighter they'd seen was only a prototype.

Messerschmitt was told to start mass-producing the Bf-109 as quickly as possible. To accommodate the orders, he began construction of a second factory at Regensburg. And despite his misgivings about the twin-engine destroyer, he won that competition as well. The machine was designated the Bf-110.

Then came an event that would have grave implications not only for Messerschmitt, but for Germany and the world. On 17 July 1936, civil war broke out in Spain.

9.

The war began after the Popular Front, a coalition of the Communist party and three other political groups, won the election and took power in the Second Spanish Republic. Opposing the newly formed government was the Falange, a party of Fascists. Most people in Great Britain, France, and the U.S. sympathized with the Spanish Government Loyalists.

Spain's army officers were members of the Falange, known as Nationalists. To keep them from rising up against the government, they were banished to outposts in North Africa. One of these officers was General Francisco Franco Bahamonde.

On 18 July, army garrisons on the mainland rebelled, and their forces occupied parts of northern Spain. For help in putting down the rebellion, the Spanish government turned to the Soviet Union and France. The U.S.S.R. in particular was eager to assist, hoping to expand its Communist empire. Dictator Joseph Stalin sent personnel, aircraft, tanks and artillery. French Prime Minister Léon Blum sent airplanes and crews.

General Franco wanted desperately to return to Spain with his troops, but he had no way to transport them. He asked Germany and Italy for aid. Benito Mussolini was willing to help, and so was Adolf Hitler, who was obsessed with hatred of Communism. The Führer ordered his military commanders to assist Franco, and Germany provided 20 Ju-52 tri-motor transports. Six Heinkel He-51 fighters were sent as well.

The aircraft were shipped on the 22,000-ton freighter *Useramo*, which sailed from Hamburg to Cadiz in August 1936. Accompanying them were Ju-52 aircrews, six fighter pilots, and a dozen mechanics. The group traveled as vacationers on a cruise booked through the fictitious Union Travel Agency. The Heinkel fighters were sent to the Tablada airfield at Seville, and the Ju-52s began hauling Franco's troops back from North Africa.

Meanwhile the Soviets shipped large numbers of heavy tanks and artillery pieces to Cartagena. They also sent 50 Polikarpov I-15 fighters and 150 pilots and maintenance personnel to the Carmoli and Los Alcazares airfields.

The Polikarpov I-15 was a small, open-cockpit, gull-winged biplane with a radial engine. An excellent aerobatic performer, its top speed was 315 kph. It was armed with four 7.62mm machine guns and was called the *Chato*, Spanish slang for snub-nosed boy.

Germany then sent additional aircraft and pilots. The air force was named the Condor Legion. General Hugo von Sperrle was its commander, and his chief of staff was Oberst Wolfram Freiherr von Richthofen, a cousin of the World War I ace. Italy also bolstered the Nationalists by sending thousands of troops, along with aircraft, tanks and artillery.

German pilots soon encountered an aircraft that was different from any they'd seen before. This was the Polikarpov I-16, a truly modern fighter. It was a low-wing monoplane with retractable gear and an enclosed cockpit, and was powered by a 1,000 hp Ash-62 9-cylinder radial engine. The I-16's maximum speed of 490 kph gave it a great advantage over the much slower He-51 biplane, and it was also more heavily armed. It carried two wing-mounted 20mm ShVAK cannons, and two 7.62mm ShKAS machine guns on its cowling.

The Russians called the I-16 the *Ishak*, which meant donkey, while to the Spanish Loyalists it was the *Mosca*, or fly. The Nationalists called it the *Rata*, or rat. But by any name, it was a formidable opponent.

In one engagement, nine He-51s were escorting five Ju-52s and three He-46 reconnaissance aircraft when they were jumped by sixteen Chatos and eight Ratas. In the ensuing battle the Germans shot down four of the I-15s, but they were unable to catch the Ratas. Whenever an He-51 pilot tried to maneuver into position to fire at one, the pilot of the stubby little monoplane simply opened his throttle and pulled away.

Göring then had 50 more of the outmoded biplanes sent to Spain. He failed to understand that it was the ability of the German pilots, and not the quality of their aircraft, that enabled them to hold their own in dogfights. The German High Command believed air power should be used to support ground forces. For that reason Stuka dive bombers were also sent to the Condor Legion, along with a number of He-70 light reconnaissance bombers and He-111B medium bombers. In a typical attack the bombers would drop their explosives on enemy positions while fighters provided top cover. Following the aerial assault,

Nationalist armor and infantry would overrun the battered enemy. As Luftwaffe pilots were rotated back to Germany, they reported on engaging the Polikarpov I-16 fighters in combat. Göring finally realized that the situation was different from what he'd thought, and ordered Messerschmitt to send some Bf-109s to Spain so the Condor pilots could evaluate them.

The only examples Willy had were hand-built prototypes. He shipped three of the aircraft to Cadiz on the *Useramo*.

10.

The first time Condor Legion pilots saw a Bf-109, they were not impressed. The bow seemed overly long, because it housed a liquid-cooled V-12 engine. And the wings looked too short. The pilots thought the Bf-109 would probably be nose-heavy, and have insufficient lift. Hardly an ideal design for a fighter.

Their doubts notwithstanding, the pilots underwent training in the prototypes. The airplanes were hard to control on takeoffs and landings, and the Jumo 210B engine tended to overheat. A pleasant surprise, however, was the fighter's performance. It was fast and highly maneuverable, with an excellent rate of climb. After a few weeks the Bf-109 prototypes were sent back to Germany, with recommendations for improvement. The pilots were ordered to continue operations with their biplanes.

As the air battles continued, a number of German airmen became noted for their bravery and skill. One of the most effective arrived in the spring of 1937. He was Oberleutnant Adolf Galland, the Staffelkapitän of 3.J/88.

Galland was unorthodox in his personal style. While the airmen in his command wore carefully tailored olive-brown uniforms, his consisted of mismatched odds and ends. When he flew in warm weather he wore swim trunks. A cigar was always clenched in his teeth, even in the cockpit. Painted on the side of his biplane's fuselage was Mickey Mouse brandishing a hatchet.

Galland had a broken nose and was nearly blind in his left eye, the result of a flying accident in 1935. His black hair was slicked back, and a thick mustache adorned his upper lip. Women found him irresistible.

But Galland was no showboat. He relished bombing Loyalist tanks and troops, never flinching as he and his pilots were met by blazing ground fire and attacks by enemy aircraft. He flew more than 300 missions in Spain.

In addition to his leadership, Galland contributed two innovations to the Condor Legion. One was a special train called a *wohnzug*, which acted as a home for the pilots. It had sleeping quarters, a mess room, a briefing room, an office, a kitchen, and bathrooms. The train made it possible for a staffel to be shifted quickly from one location to another.

The second innovation was a drop tank filled with a 25-gallon mixture of gasoline and used engine oil. Attached to the tank were two 22-pound bombs. When the tank was dropped among enemy troops the bombs exploded, dousing the soldiers with sticky flaming liquid, a precursor of Napalm. Galland called the device *das teufelsei*, the devil's egg.

Generals Sperrle and Richthofen informed Göring that the Condor Legion pilots were anxious to receive better equipment. Göring's response was to put more pressure on Messerschmitt. Working night and day, Willy's team hand-built a dozen more of the improved Bf-109s and shipped them off.

The question remained—how would they perform in combat? What would happen when they came up against a well-equipped enemy that was firing real bullets?

11.

When the new Bf-109s arrived in Spain, they were assigned to 2.J/88, whose recently appointed Staffelkapitän was Oberleutnant Günther "Franzl" Lützow.

The fighters were the Bf-109B model, dubbed the Bertha. The engine was the Jumo 210D, an inverted V-12 of 770 hp. It produced a 20-kph increase in speed, which the pilots welcomed.

Lützow was anxious to test the new Messerschmitts in combat. A trim young man with close-cropped brown hair and a strong jaw, Lützow was a member of an illustrious Prussian military family. His father was an admiral in the German Navy.

On 6 April 1937, General von Richthofen ordered Lützow to lead his charges in support of an attack by Franco's tanks and infantry at Ochandiano, in the Cantabrian Mountains. Tactics called for sweeping the skies clear of Red aircraft while He-111 bombers went in at low altitude to hit the enemy. Heinkel He-51 biplanes from 1.J/88 and 3.J/88 would take part in the attack as well, and so would Italian fighters and bombers. No aerial charts were available, so Lützow located the target on an old road map and briefed his pilots. He then went out to the flight line.

A row of Bf-109s stood there with noses high, like hounds eager to begin the hunt. The aircraft were painted gray with a black disc on the fuselage and wings, and a black St. Andrews cross on the white rudder. The staffel's insignia, a top hat, was below the cockpit.

Lützow carried out a ground check of his fighter. He made sure mechanics had topped off the fuel tank, which was just behind the pilot's seat and held 88 Imperial gallons. When he was satisfied that all was in order he climbed onto the left wing and got into the cockpit, sliding down onto the narrow seat with his parachute beneath him. It was a tight fit. The seat was like that of a race car, with the pilot in a semi-reclining position. A ground crewman helped strap him in, and he pulled the side-swinging canopy into place. Lützow locked it as the man gave him a thumbs-up and jumped to the ground.

To start his engine, Lützow flicked the switches that turned on the electric power and the boost pumps. He pushed the plunger that would send a shot of primer to the engine, then cracked the throttle and energized the starter.

The sound began as a soft whine, which rapidly increased in volume. When it became a shriek he pressed the starter button. The prop spun and the stacks belched flame and blue smoke, and the engine came to life with a roar. He checked the oil pressure to be sure it was rising, then eased in more throttle, bringing the rpm from 700 up to 1,000.

The aircraft was vibrating and shaking now, as if again showing its eagerness. The red control tab indicated the radiator flaps were closed, and he opened them to slow the rise of the coolant temperature.

After waiting a minute or so for the engine to grow warmer he added still more power, taking the rpm up to 1800. The fighter began rolling, and he pushed the stick forward a little to lighten the tail. With a touch of brake he taxied toward the place where he would do his runup, looking from side to side because he had no view directly ahead. The other fighters followed him.

Once in position he applied his brakes, his gaze flicking over the panel: oil temperature 50 degrees Celsius, coolant 70. He opened the throttle until the gauges read 2100 rpm and 76 centimeters of manifold pressure, and then exercised the prop twice, each time letting the rpm fall to 1800. A magneto check showed a slight drop on one side, an equal drop on the other. The coolant temperature continued to rise.

Next he cranked the flaps 20 degrees down, and trimmed the elevator to plus one degree. He tightened the throttle friction and made sure the boost pumps were on, and that the primer was locked and the radiator flaps were wide open. The gauges showed temperatures and oil pressure all in the green. Coolant was up to 105 degrees. Now he had to get going, before the engine overheated.

The fighters would take off three at a time, with his trio first. Glancing at the other pilots, he got a nod from each of them. He released the brakes and opened the throttle until the manifold pressure rose to 102 cm. The airplane again began moving, and as it gained more speed he brought the tail up, which gave him forward visibility.

The surface of the grassy meadow was rough. As the fighter bounced along on the takeoff roll, Lützow hoped the undercarriage would hold together until he was airborne. He knew the other pilots would have similar concerns.

When the airspeed indicator showed 160 kph he put in a bit of left rudder to offset the torque and eased the stick back. One more bump, and then the airplane rose into the air. The sensation of leaving the ground never failed to thrill him.

He pressed the electric undercarriage control, and the gear retracted with a resounding *clunk, clunk*. Airspeed read 230 kph. With his left hand he quickly turned the wheel to raise the flaps. He adjusted the elevator trim, and as his speed increased he closed the radiator intakes and powered back to 90 cm and 2,300 rpm for the climb. The airplane soared upward.

After reaching an altitude of 3,500 meters he leveled off. The Bertha was equipped with an FuG-7 radio, and he called his pilots through the throat mic, telling them to follow him in flying a circuit of left turns. The bombers were already up there, waiting for them.

This morning it took only a few minutes for the aircraft in Lützow's Staffel 2 to form up and move into position above the twin-engine Heinkels. As soon as they were assembled, he led them off on a heading of 010 degrees. He kept his power settings at slow cruise so as not to outrun the bombers.

It was a fine spring day. Visibility was about 20 km, and the only clouds were a few thin patches of cirrus. Beneath him the fields and the groves of trees formed a pattern of rich greens and browns.

As he drew closer to the battle site the scene changed. Here the terrain was mountainous, and in the passes he saw torn earth and shell holes and soldiers' corpses and burned-out trucks and wrecked cannons and dead horses. And then through streaming smoke the ragged front lines came into view: Nationalist armor and infantry pressing an attack, and Reds firing back at them with tanks and rifles and horse-drawn artillery.

Down there were hundreds of machines, and thousands of men. Muzzle flashes were visible in the smoke, and shells were bursting in bright yellow blossoms of flame. Tanks crawled like so many bugs over the rugged landscape.

Above the action on the ground, a large number of aircraft wheeled at low altitude, strafing and dropping explosives. Lützow recognized many of them as Soviet Tupolev bombers, with mottled camouflage and red bands on the fuselage, tail and wingtips. Among them were similarly marked Polikarpov fighters, both I-15 Chatos and I-16 Ratas. Some of the Russian aircraft were engaged in dogfights with He-51 biplanes.

It was the Polikarpovs that Lützow and his pilots were after. If the fighters were taken out the bombers would have no protection. He flicked off his guns' safety and radioed his pilots to attack: *"Angriff! Angriff!"*

Opening the throttle, he dove toward the enemy airplanes, rapidly building speed. A Rata was the closest, so he turned to line up on it, noticing that the pilot seemed unaware of the impending danger. Lützow waited until he was so close that the outline of the Russian monoplane loomed in the 109's reflector gunsight. But as he was about to press the firing button, the Rata banked sharply to the left.

Too late! Lützow swore as he flew by, angry with himself for failing to turn quickly enough to prevent the enemy's escape. That was the difficulty in flying a fighter with great speed; an advantage could easily be thrown away. Certainly he should have fired sooner. He hauled back on the stick, gravity forces pressing him down in his seat, and climbed again. At this point the sky was full of whirling aircraft. Some of the Ratas and Chatos had begun attacking the Heinkel bombers, and his 109s were busy holding them off. Several airplanes were streaming black smoke and spinning down out of control.

Lützow's gaze flicked back and forth. In addition to dealing with the enemy, he knew he also had to be watchful to avoid a collision. More than once in a crowded sky he'd seen airplanes slam together and burst into flames.

The Heinkel bombers were doing good work. Lützow could see them dropping sticks of bombs on the Red ground forces, the fiery explosions flinging up dirt and shattered metal and the broken bodies of soldiers. There were also a few Ju-87 Stukas in action. The new dive bombers were ideal for such a mission.

Once more he picked out a Loyalist fighter and went after it. This one was another I-16, and the pilot was alert to the pursuing 109. The enemy airman rapidly turned one way and then another in an effort to lose him. Lützow was aware that both Polikarpov types could turn in a short radius, and the Rata appeared to be flown by a skilled pilot—Lützow would have to be extremely sharp to catch him. He maneuvered carefully, left hand on the throttle, right hand on the stick and the firing button.

Before he could close on the target, a stream of fiery balls suddenly streaked past his cockpit and he realized that now he was the one under attack. He shoved the stick forward, taking the Bertha into a dive. The fighter hurtled downward, standing on its nose.

When Lützow pulled out he was only a few meters above the battlefield. G-forces jammed him down into his seat once more, and this time his vision was blurred. He blinked and shook his head. His body felt incredibly heavy. As he regained altitude his sight cleared, and he saw that he'd lost his pursuer. He went on climbing, and when he leveled off he chose still another enemy fighter and flew toward it.

This one was a Chato. It too began a turn, but instead of trying to stay with it Lützow pulled up still higher. Then he put his aircraft into a steep bank and dove on the biplane. He aimed at a point just ahead of its nose and opened fire.

It was a perfect deflection shot. His tracers tore into the Chato, and the aircraft broke up.

Again Lützow looked at the sky around him, and to his surprise he found the other enemy fighters had run off. The Tupolev bombers had fled as well. Only two aircraft were visible, and both were members of his staffel. He called to them, and the three maneuvered to form a loose formation. A glance at his gauges told him he was getting low on fuel, so he turned south, and with the others following, headed back to the Condor Legion's airfield at Vitoria.

On the way he felt a surge of pride. This was his first experience in combat, and he'd achieved a victory. His kill would be the first ever recorded by a Bf-109. He'd learned that the fighter was faster than the Polikarpovs, and could turn at least as tightly. It could also out-dive and out-climb them. All this meant he had his hands on a weapon that would enable him to become an ace. Or an *experte*, a name used by the Luftwaffe to denote fighter pilots who'd scored ten victories.

But far more important than the impact on his own career, was the effect the Bf-109 would have on the war. With airplanes like this, the Condor Legion would rule the Spanish skies.

12.

When word of Lützow's victory reached him, Willy Messerschmitt was elated. Subsequent reports described the Bf-109 completely outfighting its opponents, scoring kill after kill. Its exploits in combat confirmed to the Air Ministry that Messerschmitt had been right all along.

Adolf Hitler was also delighted to hear of his new weapon's achievements, boasting that Luftwaffe fighter squadrons were all fully equipped with Bf-109s. While that wasn't true, it soon would be. Messerschmitt finally got the BFW assembly lines rolling at both Augsburg and Regensburg, and the factories began turning out Bf-109s in quantity. Yet so great was the demand that the Fieseler company, another manufacturer of aircraft, was issued a contract to produce more of them under license.

Typically, Willy Messerschmitt continued to make improvements. The wooden propeller was replaced with an all-metal variable-pitch type, and new versions of the Jumo engines, the 210G and 210Ga, featuring fuel injection and two-stage superchargers, were installed. Armament was beefed up by mounting two additional machine guns in the wings.

To display the airplane's superiority in as many ways as possible, Messerschmitt decided to try for a new world's speed record. The current record had been set by Howard Hughes in his Hughes H-1 at Santa Ana, California in September 1935.

For the attempt, a Bf-109 was specially prepared. Although press releases claimed it was a normal version, the airplane was in fact stripped down to make it much lighter. It also mounted a unique Daimler-Benz DB-601 engine that would produce 1,650 hp. The engine would run for only a short time before it burned out.

On 11 November 1937, Dr. Hermann Wurster, BFW's chief test pilot, took off from the field at Augsburg and flew the aircraft over a measured course at a speed of 620 kph. It was a new world record, and the press showered Messerschmitt with praise. He did not, however, disclose that the record-setting Bf-109 was a one-off that would never fly again.

The actual production model could come nowhere near such performance, but it was still faster than any of its opponents. Designated the Bf-109C, or Clara, it was in service only a short time before it was overtaken by the Dora, which in turn was followed by the Emil. With each new version, the Bf-109 became more effective. And the Condor Legion produced more heroes.

Oberleutnant Werner Mölders became the leading experte, with 14 kills. He also devised the *schwarm* formation, which consisted of two pairs, called *rotte*, each with a leader and a wingman. The formation proved so effective it would soon be adopted by the RAF, whose pilots called it the finger four.

By the summer of 1938, the war in Spain was all but over. Generalissimo Franco's Nationalist forces had cut off Madrid from outside aid, and the Loyalist army faced certain defeat. For some Spanish citizens, this was a cause for rejoicing, but to the Loyalists and Joseph Stalin, it was a great disappointment. Despite the Soviet dictator's military support, the defense against Franco's Nationalists was ending in failure.

However, within Germany there was great pride in the prowess of the Condor Legion. Thanks to Joseph Goebbels' propaganda, its pilots had become famous. Celebrated as brave German warriors, they were awarded the *Spanienkreuz* in gold.

Willy Messerschmitt's fame increased as well. High-ranking officers of the RAF and the Imperial Japanese Air Force, among others, came to Augsburg to inspect his Bf-109.

One visitor was the legendary American pilot Charles Lindbergh, the first man to fly solo across the Atlantic. When he arrived in Germany, Lindbergh was given a formal reception by Hitler. Afterward he asked for a tour of the BFW factory.

Messerschmitt was pleased and honored. He showed Lindbergh and the other officials around their facilities, and entertained them with a banquet in the company's executive dining room. Following the last toast, Lindbergh asked to fly a Bf-109. Willy did not grant the request, but he did permit his guest to fly a Bf-108. After putting the airplane through strenuous aerobatic maneuvers, Lindbergh pronounced the Bf-108 better than any light aircraft in the U.S. He also said there was no question in his mind that Germany had the best air force of any nation.

Lindbergh's comments were not appreciated by the American military, nor by many U.S. citizens. And President Franklin Roosevelt became furious when they were reported to him; in his view Lindbergh was being disloyal.

Roosevelt then spurred Congress to increase its appropriation of funds to the military. He too understood the growing importance of air power, and was determined that the United States would not be left behind. Aircraft manufacturers such as Boeing, Lockheed and Curtiss were urged to step up their development of new fighters and bombers.

And yet, if the American president had known about a project that was about to get underway in Germany, he would have made even greater demands on the U.S. firms. The endeavor would lead to a revolutionary change in aircraft design.

PART II

BIRTH OF THE JET AGE

13.

The project began in October 1938, a few weeks after Lindbergh's visit to the BFW factory. Executives of the Bayerische Motoren Werke drove the 60 kilometers from Munich to Augsburg for a secret meeting. Messerschmitt had been doing business with BMW for years, using its engines to power many of his aircraft. But today the relationship was to take on new significance.

The visitors were shown into a conference room. They were welcomed by Messerschmitt and Walter Rethel, and also by Robert Lusser, who by then was head of the company's project bureau. Present for BMW GmbH were Dr. Kurt Lohner, Dr. Miller Berner, and Dr. Hermann Ostrich. When Messerschmitt saw Ostrich, he sensed the reason for secrecy—Ostrich had been involved in experimental work on jet engines since 1928.

A steward brought in coffee, and left the room. The men lighted cigarettes and cigars, and Dr. Lohner opened the meeting by saying the Air Ministry wanted the two firms to establish a special partnership. It would be called The South German Development Focal Point, and its objective would be to produce a jet-powered warplane.

Messerschmitt felt a spark of excitement. He had long maintained that speed trumped virtually every other factor in a combat aircraft, a conviction borne out by the achievements of his Bf-109 in Spain. To get speed, it was necessary to minimize weight and drag and increase thrust. That called for a sleek machine with as much power as possible, and no other form of propulsion could match the potential power of a jet engine.

46

Lohner said he and his associates were confident the goal would be achieved. It was also fitting, he added, that the partnership would be formed by two Bavarian companies, a sentiment Messerschmitt agreed with. Even though the Iron Chancellor, Otto von Bismarck, had forged a united Germany from a loose confederation of city-states some 40 years earlier, there was still a strong rivalry among the various regions. Messerschmitt said he was sure that as Bavarians, they could outdo the Prussians. The remark inspired chuckles all around, but it also struck the right note, as he'd known it would.

Dr. Berner then admitted they were not alone in the race. Groups in several countries were already striving to produce jet aircraft engines. The British in particular were hard at work, their government financing a former RAF pilot named Frank Whittle to develop his engine in a company called Power Jets. The Italians were also busy, backing the engineer Secondo Campini in a similar venture.

In Germany, Junkers had started jet engine development the previous year. Directing the effort was the company's chief structural engineer, Herbert Wagner. From what BMW had learned, Junkers hadn't made much progress thus far. A more sophisticated program, Berner said, was underway at Heinkel. Messerschmitt had heard about his rival's experiments with jets, and questioned Berner on the status of Heinkel's efforts. Berner explained that Ernst Heinkel had hired Hans von Ohain, a young engineer who'd built a jet engine of his own design while still an engineering student. Heinkel had set up Ohain in the Hirth Motorenwerke, a company Heinkel bought for the purpose. Supposedly Ohain was quite far along in building an engine that could successfully power an aircraft.

Berner maintained that BMW was also making progress. Dr. Ostrich was heading the project, and offered a description of the firm's efforts. Ostrich said BMW engineers had experimented with many different concepts. One was a motor jet, which was a supercharged piston engine with a jet exhaust. Eventually, however, that approach had proved unsatisfactory. The engine hadn't delivered much more thrust than a conventional internal combustion type, and it tended to break down.

They'd also worked on development of a centrifugal-flow jet, which used a turbine to compress air and force it into combustion chambers that formed a ring around the engine. That had also been rejected.

Among its drawbacks, the engine was highly unreliable. One or more of the combustion chambers frequently malfunctioned, and as a result it would not deliver power consistently.

Finally the BMW engineers decided that the way of the future would be an axial-flow turbofan. That was what the company was developing now, but it was also the type a number of other engine manufacturers were working on as well. Messerschmitt knew quite a bit about jet power, having studied engineering journals on the subject for several years. He'd also been given reports on jet engine development by the RLM. He listened carefully as Ostrich explained the project.

Essentially, Ostrich said, an axial-flow jet engine had three main parts: a centrifugal compressor, a single combustion chamber, and a two-stage turbine. At the front end a large fan sucked in air and sent it into the compressor. The greatly compressed air then entered the combustion chamber, where fuel was burned. That created a high-speed rush of hot gasses, which caused the turbine to spin. Some of the resultant energy was used to power the compressor, and some of it kept the fan turning, so as to continue sending air to the compressor. The exhaust from the gasses had great force, and that provided thrust.

Ostrich said BMW believed their design would be superior to other axial-flow engines because of certain unique features, such as newly perfected bearings made of stainless steel and an air induction fan that turned at much higher speeds. Additionally, there was the company's ability to build power plants of better overall quality.

Messerschmitt asked about the engine's weight. Ostrich replied that surprisingly, it would have a better power-to-weight ratio than a piston engine, yet it would provide at least half again as much thrust. And as BMW continued development, the favorable ratio would be increased still further.

Rethel asked what type of fuel would be used. The most promising, Ostrich replied, was a highly combustible liquid similar to kerosene. Propane and natural gas converted to liquid form had been tried, but they hadn't given as good results, and gasoline was too volatile.

The metals used in construction of the combustion chamber were another problem. They had to be extremely durable, and also able to withstand great heat from the exhaust gasses. Messerschmitt said it seemed to him that the heat could be hazardous, which Ostrich admitted was true.

And yet, as Messerschmitt noted, the superheated exhaust gasses were what provided the thrust that would enable the plane to fly. A powerful engine was one thing, but it would not be very practical if it burned up the airplane.

His associates agreed, and Lohner quickly replied that BMW was testing various metals. Thus far the material showing the most promise was an alloy that combined titanium, for strength, and molybdenum for its ability to withstand great heat. Molybdenum was also extremely hard and durable, and yet it had the high melting point of 2,623 degrees Centigrade. They were also testing osmium, which had an even higher melting point.

Berner said that though development of BMW's turbojet was still in the early stages, they were making good headway. He was confident they could compete successfully in the race to produce an engine that would be both practical and reliable. For the winner, he went on, the prize would be enormous. An airplane powered by a jet engine could attain speeds far beyond that of anything in the air. No one knew better than Messerschmitt what an advantage that would be. Nor did anyone doubt that this was exactly the kind of project the Führer was exhorting the aircraft industry to pursue. They were all aware that Hitler wanted Germany to have the most powerful military forces of any nation, and that he was especially enamored of secret weapons such as super bombs and monster armored vehicles and silent submarines. To him, an aircraft of unsurpassed speed would be a fabulous war machine.

Lusser said that as his firm's project manager, he'd need an approximate timetable. Could BMW give him an idea as to when they hoped to have a working engine?

Lohner replied that it was too soon to say, but he'd send a tentative schedule as quickly as possible. Dr. Berner said that in the interim he hoped Messerschmitt would be thinking about the type of aircraft his company would design for the engine.

Messerschmitt replied that he'd already thought about it. "It will be a fighter," he said. "The world's first jet fighter."

14.

By this time many Germans were firmly behind Adolf Hitler, believing that within a few short years he'd accomplished miracles. They held him responsible for lifting the country out of depression, producing a strong economy and creating millions of new jobs, and bringing Germany back to world importance. Though he was acclaimed as a truly great leader throughout much of Germany, not everyone agreed. There were Germans who considered him a power-mad adventurer, and a danger to peace. Multiple assassination attempts were made, though none succeeded. Yet it seemed nothing could stop Hitler from building up Germany's armed forces and preparing them for war, and all at a rapid pace.

In addition to the firms constructing aircraft, companies such as Daimler-Benz and Auto Union were turning out tanks, armored cars and self-propelled cannons. Shipyards in Hamburg and Bremerhaven were building U-boats and battleships. Firearms makers such as Sauer, Krupp and Mauser were producing artillery, rifles and machine guns. Additionally, there were hundreds of other manufacturers busy making all types of military equipment.

By early 1938 more than two million young men were in the German armed services, with more being added once they reached the age for induction. Emboldened by his sense of destiny, the Führer announced that he would provide more *liebensraum*, or living space, for the German people. Obviously there was only one way to achieve this— it would require taking additional lands from neighboring countries through armed aggression.

Having endured the misery brought about by the First World War, many people were not anxious to ignite another. Their fears were heightened when in March 1938, Hitler's troops seized Czechoslovakia. This was a direct contravention of the Munich Agreement, which had been signed by the British Prime Minister Neville Chamberlain and the French Premiere Édouard Deladier, as well as by Hitler and Benito Mussolini. The agreement was lauded by Chamberlain as a guarantee of "Peace in our time." It permitted Germany to occupy the Sudetenland, as long as the Nazis promised they would not take the rest of Czechoslovakia.

Sure that his appeasement-minded enemies would not dare to wage war, Hitler ignored the agreement and sent in his army to occupy the entire country. And he was right. The Allies issued protests, but beyond that did nothing.

By that time BFW was enjoying unprecedented prosperity. On 11

July 1938, the directors voted to change its name to Messerschmitt AG. Thereafter, the designation of any new aircraft the firm produced would have the prefix "Me," rather than "Bf." And though he held no advanced academic degrees, Willy would be called Professor Messerschmitt.

In the design center, plans for the jet fighter were being made and revised. Messerschmitt had put forward the overall concept, but the team working on the project was largely under the direction of Dr. Woldemar Voigt.

For the aircraft to achieve maximum possible speed, Voight proposed to power it with two engines, rather than one. For best airflow, the engines would be mounted in the wings. Considering that BMW was already behind schedule in delivering prototypes, the team went as far as possible with the design.

The following spring the war in Spain ended. By then Mussolini and Hitler had officially become allies, signing a treaty they called "The Pact of Steel." Thanks to their aid, Generalissimo Franco's Nationalist forces were victorious.

It was also a victory for Willy Messerschmitt. Some military leaders were saying that Franco could not have won the war without the Condor Legion, and the Condor Legion could not have won without the Bf-109. The Nazi government awarded Willy the German National Prize for Art and Science during a ceremony that was led by Chancellor Adolf Hitler.

Messerschmitt was now receiving a flood of orders from the Air Ministry, not only for the Bf-109 but for many other types as well. The most important such assignment from the RLM called for the development of a long-range, heavy bomber. At Messerschmitt AG, planning began as Project P1061.

The Messerschmitt entry would be huge. It would be powered by four engines, and would carry an enormous load of explosives. When built, it would be designated the Me-264.

15.

Heinkel was already ahead in the race to produce a heavy bomber. The company had built a prototype, the He-177, and was preparing to test-fly it. Mounting two Daimler-Benz DB-610 engines of 2,950 hp each, the airplane's range would be 5,200 km. The bomb load would be 6,200 kg, and the armament six machine guns. The Air Ministry was solidly behind it, and was awaiting results of the flight tests.

Nevertheless, Messerschmitt was confident his entry would surpass the Heinkel. He contended that the Me-264 would be lighter and faster, and still capable of carrying a larger load of bombs. Willy knew that many of the world's aviation experts subscribed to the theories of Giulio Douhet, an Italian general who predicted that future wars would be won by strategic bombing. The RAF's General Hugh Trenchard and the American Colonel Billy Mitchell also embraced Douhet's ideas.

Though Hermann Göring was enthralled by Douhet, he did not accept the concept of heavy bombers. Instead, the Luftwaffe's commander believed that priority should be given to medium bombers and dive bombers, since two of those machines could be built for the cost of one heavy bomber. And as Göring put it, "The Führer does not ask me how big my bombers are, but how many I have." This led to friction between Göring and the RLM. Milch argued that strategic bombing could only be successful through the use of the largest machines possible. However, in the end Göring prevailed, and the RLM cancelled its orders for heavy bombers.

Messerschmitt was irritated by the change of direction, especially because he'd already begun building a prototype of his bomber. He was ordered to develop a schnellbomber instead, a medium bomber with a maximum speed of at least 500 kph.

Willy then went about improving the Bf-109E. He upgraded the armament, retaining the cowl-mounted machine guns while installing 20mm Oerlikon cannons in the wings. Although Messerschmitt was producing the Emil in both its Augsburg plant and the factory at Regensburg, the company could not fill all the orders. So in addition to Fieseler, Focke-Wulf was given a contract to manufacture the fighters under licence.

Messerschmitt was also dealing with a vexing problem. Göring's obsession with the Bf-110 had induced him to order construction of a successor model, even before the flaws inherent in the so-called destroyer could be corrected. The new version was the Me-210, and the RLM directed Messerschmitt to build 1,000 of them, based on nothing more than the plans.

The decision was a rash one, and it would have far-reaching implications for the Messerschmitt firm. In fact, the 210 would become the worst fiasco in the history of the company, though no one, least of all Willy, would realize that at the time. Messerschmitt also lost out in a competition that was won by Gerhard Fieseler, when his *Storch* became the standard STOL airplane of the Luftwaffe. As always, such a defeat stuck in the Professor's craw.

Fieseler's machine was aptly named, because a stork was what it looked like. It was a high-winged monoplane, and the legs of its landing gear were long and slender. Powered by a 240 hp Argus As-10 engine, it carried a two-man crew. Most remarkable was its short take-off and landing capability. A Storch could be throttled back to fly at the remarkably slow speed of 50 kph—pilots claimed you could land it on a postage stamp.

Then Fieseler came up with another extraordinary idea. This was a flying bomb that would be powered by a pulse-jet engine. It was designated the V-1. Willy had to admit the flying bomb was a brilliant concept. If it worked, a V-1 could be produced at a fraction of the cost of a bomber. He wished he'd thought of it himself.

The next setback occurred when Heinkel hired away Robert Lusser. Highly annoyed by Lusser's disloyalty, Willy replaced him by promoting Woldemar Voigt to Bureau Chief.

On top of those headaches, Messerschmitt was endlessly criticized by Erhard Milch. The Bf-109, Milch asserted, was not as reliable as it should have been. The aircraft was too fragile, and too difficult for the average pilot to fly. A better choice for the Luftwaffe's front-line fighter would be the new airplane being developed by Kurt Tank at Focke-Wulf.

At last Messerschmitt submitted plans for a jet fighter to the RLM. This was project proposal P1065. BMW was to supply the engines as soon as the kinks were worked out. Despite Milch's skepticism that such a project would ever come to fruition, the Air Ministry approved the plans and agreed to underwrite the cost of further development. Inspectors were sent to Augsburg to monitor progress.

Working on the project under Messerschmitt's direction were Bureau Chief Voigt, engineers Wolfgang Degel and Karl Althoff, and aerodynamicists Walter Eisenmann and Riclef Schomerus. The airplane would be a single-seater, with two jet engines in the wing roots. Maximum speed would be 900 kph at 3,000 meters.

The airplane would have fixed landing gear and a tail wheel. The cockpit would be pressurized, and endurance would be 55 minutes at 85% thrust. Armament would be two 30mm cannons. The RLM officials authorized Messerschmitt to proceed.

The team produced a mockup, and after a number of postponements, BMW finally delivered the engines. But to Messerschmitt's dismay, the 003 turbojets were both heavier and considerably greater in diameter than the designers had been led to expect. Therefore it would not be possible to place them in the wing roots, and the aircraft would have to be redesigned.

At first the engineers thought the solution might be to suspend the engines in nacelles beneath the wings. That was judged impractical, however, because the weight of the engines shifted the center of gravity too far forward. And Messerschmitt hated the idea, inasmuch as the arrangement would increase drag. He instructed the team to search for an alternative answer.

Still another problem arose when bench testing revealed that the maximum thrust of each engine was only 350 kg, which was less than half of what BMW had promised. Therefore the engines would have to be improved as well, and once again Messerschmitt was faced with delays he could do nothing about.

A week later, an event took place that baffled him. On 23 August 1939, a non-aggression pact between Germany and Russia was signed in Moscow by the Nazi foreign minister, Joachim von Ribbentrop, and his Soviet counterpart, Vyacheslav Molotov. This meant that in spite of Hitler's deep hatred of Communists, he was now on what appeared to be amicable terms with Joseph Stalin.

Messerschmitt could hardly believe it. Shortly after the Propaganda Ministry announced the news, he got in touch with his contacts in the government, and picked up enough secret information to piece together the truth.

The pact was not what it seemed. Actually it was an agreement for the two countries to invade Poland and divide the land between them. Germany would take the western third, and the U.S.S.R. would have the eastern two-thirds. Poland as a nation would cease to exist.

Naturally, officials in other countries, especially the British and the French, were hailing the pact as an assurance of peace. The Germans knew those countries would be outraged when Poland was invaded, yet the Nazis believed that, just as when Hitler seized Czechoslovakia, the

Allies would do nothing about it.

Messerschmitt discussed the situation with the Baroness. He felt that, contrary to the German government's stated belief, there was a good chance there would be war. Lilly was shaken, partly because she realized the potential danger to Germany, but also because she feared for her son Eberhard. Now 21 years old, the young man had become a trained engineer and an accomplished pilot. He was working in the factory on the next version of the Bf-109.

Messerschmitt tried to reassure her. But at the same time, he could not help contemplating what a major war would mean to his company. Demands for his airplanes would be raised to a level beyond anything he had ever imagined.

16.

Four days after the signing of the pact between Germany and Russia, Messerschmitt was stunned to hear another piece of news.On 27 August 1939, a tiny monoplane made the first jet-powered flight. The aircraft was the He-178, built by Heinkel.

The engine was the work of Hans von Ohain, who'd graduated from Goettingen University only three years before. It was a turbojet that used a centrifugal-flow compressor. The airframe was designed by Heinrich Hertel, Karl Schwarzler, and the twin brothers Siegfried and Walter Günter. The aircraft was constructed in the Heinkel works at Marienehe, and was smaller than most sport airplanes of the time. Its shoulder wings spanned a mere seven meters, and the fuselage was only a bit longer. The pilot's seat was in the nose. The engine was mid-mounted, with a curved duct under the belly for air intake. An exhaust pipe extended beyond the tail.

Ohain's engine weighed 795 pounds and produced 1,110 pounds of thrust. With that narrow power-to-weight ratio, test pilot Erich Warsitz found the airplane needed a long takeoff roll to leave the runway. Once aloft it was easy enough to handle, but when he tried to accelerate, the engine cut out and he was fortunate to land without crashing. Nevertheless, the He-178 had been the first jet aircraft to fly.

Now Messerschmitt put more of his energy than ever into the development of his design. If he couldn't build the first flying jet, he would be the first to put a jet fighter into service. As always, he believed that the key to success lay in building in as much power as possible. That was why two engines were needed, not one. But where was he to get engines that were both reliable and of acceptable size and weight? As he wrestled with the problem, he received nothing from BMW but excuses.

By this time, Hitler was ready to invade Poland. Brimming with confidence, the Führer told Colonel General Keitel, chief of the High Command, and Army Commander Colonel General von Brauchitsch, to unleash the German forces.

To justify the attack, an incident was staged by SS General Reinhard Heydrich on 1 September 1939. At his direction, a dozen inmates of Buchenwald prison were dragged from their cells before dawn. They were forced to put on Polish Army uniforms, and were taken to a radio station that was close to the Polish border. An SS operative yelled over the radio that Polish forces were attacking. Heydrich then had the prisoners shot.

Later that morning Hitler told the members of the Reichstag that Poland had attempted to invade Germany, and that the Wehrmacht was returning fire. Joseph Goebbels' propaganda arm published photos of the dead prisoners as proof. By that time five German armies had launched an all-out attack across Poland's northern, western and southern borders.

There was great disparity between the opposing forces. Germany sent in 1,800,000 troops against a Polish army less than half that size. The German Panzer divisions had 2600 tanks, the Poles 180. German artillery was mechanized, while most of Poland's big guns were horse-drawn. The Luftwaffe as well had a considerable advantage. There were 1,939 German warplanes, while the Polish Air Force had fewer than 800, with only about 400 fit for combat. Moreover, the Polish fighters were mostly obsolescent PZL P11 low-wing monoplanes, built in Warsaw by the state-owned Polish Air Works. With their open cockpits, low speed and light armament, they were markedly inferior to the German Bf-109s.

The German attack was based on the new concept of Blitzkrieg. Devised principally by General Erich von Manstein, it had first been employed in Spain, and was a complete departure from the static trench warfare of 1914–1918.

Blitzkrieg tactics were based on coordination between air and ground. Under cover provided by Bf-109s, dive bombers shocked the enemy's defenses. Then tanks charged in and together with motorized infantry destroyed the encircled enemy.

As in Spain, the Luftwaffe had the ideal machine for such work. It was the Junkers Ju-87, the *Sturzkampfflugzeug*, or Stuka. Few aircraft in the history of aviation were as ugly, or as well-suited to their role in combat.

A rugged monoplane with gull wings and fixed gear, the Stuka was powered by a Junkers Jumo 211D engine that gave it a top speed of 385 kph. It had a crew of two, a pilot and a rear gunner. Armament consisted of three 7.9mm machine guns, and either one 500 kg bomb or four 50 kg bombs in racks under the wings. It was painted black, and a siren was affixed to the left leg of the landing gear. The siren was Udet's idea.

To begin an attack, the pilot picked out a target and trimmed the aircraft. He set the altitude for the bomb release, closed the engine's cooler flaps, and deployed the dive brakes. That put the Stuka into a dive. After bomb release the airplane automatically retracted the dive brakes and pulled out of the dive. The pilot opened the cooler flaps and climbed away. According to Stuka pilot Leutnant Weiniki:

> The prescribed altitude for bomb release was five hundred meters, but I found that the lower I dove before letting go, the better my chances of getting the desired result. So I'd often go as low as three hundred meters before I released my bomb. The only trouble was that this made me a good target for the enemy on the ground. With all the fire from cannons and machine guns and rifles coming up at me it was like diving into a hornet's nest. One way of knowing how much enemy fire I'd taken was when our mechanics checked the damage to my Stuka after I returned to base. Once there were twenty-eight holes in it. A bullet had ripped away part of my right boot, but I hadn't realized it at the time.

Not only were some of the Stukas hit by ground fire, but others fell victim to attack by Polish fighters that evaded the Bf-109s. Although their aircraft were obsolescent, many pilots of the Polish Air Force were excellent combat fliers. Göring could hardly believe the reports of Stuka losses.

Nevertheless, the Bf-109s had a field day. Using the tactics devised by Werner Mölders in Spain, they easily shot down the Poles' old PZL P11s whenever they engaged them. The Bf-110 destroyers, on the other hand, were largely ineffectual as fighters. Therefore it was decided to use them as low-level bombers. Riggers hastily fitted them with wing racks, but unless they were protected by the Bf-109s, they weren't much good at bombing, either.

By the third week of the invasion the Polish forces were in a hopeless situation. In some battles the Poles sent cavalry units against tanks, and their infantry had to move on foot while being outflanked by German armor. Their airfields were bombed relentlessly, and many of their airplanes were destroyed on the ground. The others were shot down by Bf-109s, which virtually wiped out the Polish Air Force.

Along with all the other punishment dealt by the Luftwaffe, Göring ordered his bombers to hit Poland's rail centers and its communication systems. These were reduced to smoking ruins by Heinkel 111s and the Do-17s.

France and Britain had declared war on Germany on 3 September, but that was the extent of their involvement. As far as military help was concerned, very little was provided.

The Soviets finally made their move on 17 September, sending two army groups across Poland's eastern borders. They met only slight resistance, and more than 200,000 Poles surrendered to the Russians. Many of the soldiers agreed to serve in the Red Army and fight against the Germans. But because Joseph Stalin did not trust Polish officers, he had twenty thousand taken to the Katyn Forest, where the Soviets shot and buried them in mass graves. At the end of World War II the Russians would blame the atrocity on the Germans.

On 6 October the Polish forces surrendered. On that date 17,000 soldiers put down their arms and become prisoners of the Wehrmacht.

Despite the vaunted "Pact of Steel" between Germany and Italy, Mussolini had contributed neither troops nor materiel. Hitler felt Il Duce had been cowardly and duplicitous. Victory, the Führer asserted, had been won by Germany alone.

But that victory did not come as cheaply as the High Command expected. According to General Milch's tabulation, 285 German aircraft had been destroyed. A total of 239 airmen had been killed, and 88 others were missing. On the ground, the losses were far worse. During the six weeks of war more than 48,000 Germans had become casualties, with 16,000 dead. Some 700 tanks were lost to Polish defenses.

Nevertheless, Hitler was pleased by the outcome of the campaign. He believed it proved he had the strongest army in the world, and was sure his enemies could never stand up to it. Adding to that conviction was their failure to act. In the months following the Polish surrender, the Allies continued to be more or less passive. During the lull the British press labeled the situation, "The Phony War."

But as the world waited for the other shoe to drop, development at Messerschmitt AG continued at a rapid pace. The Professor thought that sooner or later hostilities would escalate, and he was confident that when they did, his aircraft would again serve with distinction in combat.

He also wished fervently that the problems with jet engines could be overcome, so that he could speed up development of the Me-262. Such a fighter would give the Luftwaffe an enormous advantage. There had to be a way to acquire serviceable engines, and he would do his best to find it.

17.

Although it was called the Phony War, there was nothing phony about Hitler's plans. Convinced that German victory was inevitable, he ordered his generals to prepare for a major attack on the Allies as soon as possible. However, members of the High Command did not share the Führer's exuberance. For all its success in Spain and Poland, the Wehrmacht could hardly be expected to prevail everywhere. At the moment it was sorely in need of rest and refitting.

But Hitler was not to be denied. After bad weather caused delays, he insisted on setting the attack for 17 January 1940. On that date Germany would invade Belgium, Holland and France.

The operation was to begin with an airborne assault on Belgium. There Luftwaffe Chief of Staff Jeschonnek would establish bases from which to launch raids on Britain. Fighter squadrons stationed at the bases would also protect the Reich from counterattacks by air.

Then a new problem arose. The Soviets had attacked Finland the previous fall, and in March 1940 the battered Finns signed a peace treaty with the U.S.S.R. As a result, Finland was now occupied by a Russian army, a situation the British used as an excuse to move troops into neutral Sweden as a buffer.

To Adolf Hitler, it was an intolerable development. Germany needed the iron ore that was shipped through ports in Norway. The Führer had no doubt that the Allies intended to cut off the supply, so to prevent that from happening, he made plans to invade both Norway and Denmark.

The Royal Navy anticipated such a move, and began mining the Norwegian coast. On 8 April a British fleet of three battleships, four cruisers, and 12 destroyers sailed for Norway from Scapa Flow. With them were a number of French warships.

Hitler sent two German divisions into Denmark on 9 April. In only 12 hours of fighting Copenhagen was taken, and Danish resistance ended.

At the same time, a German naval force consisting of three pocket battleships, four cruisers, 14 destroyers, and dozens of torpedo boats and supply vessels sailed to Norway. Aboard the ships were thousands of German troops. The ships were accompanied by 30 U-boats.

Despite running battles with the Allies, the Germans succeeded in landing their assault forces in the key Norwegian ports of Oslo, Narvik, Bergen, Trondheim, Kristiansand and Egersund. British and French units were sent to aid the Norwegian Army, but they failed to stem the German onslaught.

The Luftwaffe played an important role in the invasion. While Bf-109 fighters protected the ships and their human cargos, paratroopers jumped from Junkers Ju-52s. This was the first use of paratroopers in combat, and at Oslo they quickly captured the airport, thus giving the Luftwaffe a base from which to harass the Royal Navy throughout the campaign.

The RAF fought valiantly, with Whitleys, Beauforts, and Wellingtons bombing German vessels and ground forces; Fairey Swordfish biplanes attacked the ships with torpedoes. But the Luftwaffe destroyed many of the bombers, and Bf-109s chewed up the British Hurricanes and Gladiators.

On 8 June the German battleships Scharnhorst and Gneisenau sank the aircraft carrier HMS Glorious, with a loss of 1,519 men. Only 45 sailors survived. On the ground the British and French also suffered defeats. Eventually they withdrew completely, leaving Norway secure in German hands.

In all, the operation was another triumph for Germany. Her casualties were light, with 3,800 dead and roughly twice that number wounded. The Luftwaffe lost about 100 aircraft. For the Kriegsmarine, however, the losses were much more severe. Three German cruisers, 10 destroyers and six U-boats were sunk, which would prove a considerable handicap later on when Hitler planned the invasion of England.

The Royal Navy, on the other hand, had done well in the sea battles. It lost the one aircraft carrier, along with two cruisers, seven destroyers and one submarine. Thus the British came away in better shape than their foe.

Nevertheless, Hitler believed the way was now clear for him to launch the assaults on Belgium, Holland and France. Again he ordered his generals to prepare for the invasion of those countries. As before, some of them grumbled among themselves, but they dared not disobey.

One of the German officials most troubled by the planned attacks was Erhard Milch. He knew that the French Air Force, unlike the Polish, had large numbers of modern aircraft. He also knew the British were rapidly building up the RAF. And both France and Britain were buying airplanes from the U.S.

Milch further realized that war would hamper the development of German aircraft by causing shortages of vital materials, including oil, rubber and aluminum. The strength of an air force, like that of any other armed service, greatly depended on the viability of its equipment.

Did Hermann Göring comprehend the demands that would be made on the Luftwaffe? Milch doubted it. Göring was full of bluster, constantly boasting to Hitler that his air force was indomitable. But he made no provisions for contingencies. For that matter, the Führer was even less likely to be deterred by logistical problems. When they were pointed out, his usual response was to brush them aside. To a man like me, he was fond of saying, there is no such word as "impossible."

Milch, on the other hand, was a realist. The invasion had been pushed back several times, but he was sure there would be no more postponements. The operation would be launched the following spring, and the aircraft manufacturers had better be ready to answer the Air Ministry's demands.

He ordered them to expand their output, and to continue development of new models. Every builder was subjected to increased pressure, including Professor Willy Messerschmitt.

18.

In response to demands from the Air Ministry, Messerschmitt AG was running at full throttle. Although work on the Me-262 was hampered by the lack of suitable engines, teams were busy developing a wide range of other aircraft. And as usual, the Professor was making changes to airplanes already in service, including the Bf-109.

The landing gear had continued to cause problems. With its narrow track, the fighter was still difficult to handle on the ground. If the pilot was at all careless with brakes or rudder, he'd ground loop the airplane.

Many did. So many, in fact, that Milch ordered General Udet to undertake a study by the Technical Office. It showed that Bf-109s had been in hundreds of ground looping incidents, often resulting in significant damage to the aircraft. To correct the problem, Messerschmitt and his engineers stiffened the gear and splayed it at a wider angle. They also put a lock on the tail wheel to prevent castoring. Although these changes helped, the fault was never completely overcome.

Nevertheless, the next generation of the renowned fighter was hurriedly prepared for production. Designated the Friderich, this version would have a reconfigured tail, with a cantilever design that obviated the need for external bracing. It would also have a retractable tail wheel, smaller and more streamlined radiators under the wings, and a supercharger intake that was repositioned to increase the ram-air effect.

There would be changes in the armament as well. Although the cowl-mounted machine guns would be retained, the 20mm cannons in the wings would be eliminated. Pilots had complained that their recoil caused too much vibration and could even throw the fighter off course. Instead, in the Friderich, a single cannon would fire through the shaft of the airscrew. This idea had been abandoned earlier because it caused the engine to overheat, but now the engineers believed they had overcome the problem.

The greatest improvement would be the fighter's new engine, the Daimler-Benz 601E-1. With 1200 hp, it promised to boost the fighter's speed dramatically. And instead of carburetors, it used fuel injection, so it would not cut out when inverted.

Messerschmitt was also working on a rocket-propelled airplane. Experiments with machines of this type had begun as far back as 1928, when the engineer Alexander Lippisch built a glider powered by a rocket motor that burned hydrogen peroxide fuel. Later he used similar motors to boost takeoff in Henschel and Focke-Wulf aircraft.

At Peenemünde, yet another designer was also experimenting with rocket-powered airplanes. This was Werner von Braun, who would later become famous for his development of missiles. Von Braun had installed a rocket in an airplane that had a piston engine. The idea was that after reaching a high altitude, the pilot would switch off the piston engine and fire the rocket. In tests the concept proved impractical.

Officials of the Air Ministry believed Lippisch's work offered the most promise. Therefore they funded his development of a rocket-powered airplane that would be constructed by Heinkel. The airframe did not meet Lippisch's specifications, however, so he left Heinkel and joined Messerschmitt to carry on the project.

The Professor was not enthusiastic about rocket power; he considered the fuel unstable and much too volatile. Nevertheless he agreed to have his firm take on the assignment, and the resulting aircraft became the Me-163. It was a strange machine, shaped like a bullet with swept-back wings, and with a tail that featured a large fin and rudder but no horizontal stabilizer. In an effort to circumvent the shortage of metals, much of the airframe was built of wood. In early tests the Me-163 lacked sufficient power to achieve an unassisted takeoff. An additional fault lay in the design of the wings, which were too small to provide sufficient lift. Much time would pass before the Me-163 was ready for more test flights.

Meanwhile, Messerschmitt was absorbed in developing the Me-262. Despite all the delays, he was determined that the project would be successful. The main problem continued to be the lack of proper engines. Although BMW had assured him that more powerful ones would be delivered soon, they failed to materialize. Willy then learned that the new Junkers 004s might be available. He told the design team that if BMW did not come through he would try to obtain the Junkers turbojets.

Messerschmitt was also acutely aware that when at last he did have the right engines, he'd need to have an airframe ready. He had the design team conduct wind tunnel tests of the mockup, and though the tests were encouraging, another unresolved question was where to position the engines. He thought they probably would be too heavy to place in the wing roots. Putting them in nacelles under the wings wouldn't be satisfactory either, because of the resultant forward shift of the center of gravity and the increase in drag.

Then one of the engineers, Wolfgang Degel, proposed a solution. Why not try mounting the engine nacelles under the wings after all, but sweep the wings back from a point just beyond the location of the nacelles? That would move the center of gravity rearward, without sacrificing strength.

Messerschmitt resisted the idea. What I want, he said, is speed. That is why we're building a jet fighter. And what is the impediment to speed? Drag, of course. So how can maximum speed be attained with those huge pods interrupting airflow?

Degel retreated, but Voigt and the others embraced the concept. They pointed out that even with heavy engines, the arrangement would achieve the balance called for by the laws of aerodynamics. The argument went back and forth, with Messerschmitt continuing to oppose Degel's suggestion. But he had no better solution, and at last he reluctantly gave his approval.

The team then made further refinements to the aircraft. The wings would be tapered, with slats on the leading edges. The ailerons would be the Frise type. When a Frise aileron was applied, a small portion of its leading edge moved down into the airflow. The result was increased drag on that side, which offset drag on the other aileron and thus reduced adverse yaw. To shorten the landing roll, a fist parachute would be installed in the tail. The radio would be a FuG-17 with a homing device. Also, the aircraft would be slightly larger than originally planned. Its wingspan would now be 12.35 meters, and its length 10.46 meters.

The project team made modifications to the fuselage as well. A cross-section view in a report written by Voigt on 21 March 1940 showed a nearly triangular shape that increased the aircraft's resemblance to a shark. The weapons were now to be three MK108 30mm cannons, contained in a hinged nose compartment.

As time went on, an air of excitement pervaded the team of designers. Imagine building a fighter that would be as much as 150 kph faster than anything else in the air. It was mind-boggling! So stirred were they by the airplane's potential that they thought nothing of spending 18 hour days in the project center, laboring to bring it to life. They knew there would soon be all-out war, and the Me-262 had to be made ready for it.

19.

Messerschmitt's contacts kept him informed as to what was going on at the highest levels of the Nazi government. He was told that the Führer would soon order an attack. The French and the British, Hitler believed, were incapable of stopping the Wehrmacht. The war was as good as won. Some senior officers still had reservations, but they were reluctant to express them. The few who did were ignored. The Führer wanted warriors, not cowards—he listened only to men who shared his convictions.

There were plenty of those. In fact, most members of the *Oberkommando der Wehrmacht*, the German High Command, were now pressing to begin the assault. The OKW believed the Panzers would rip through the enemy defenses with ease, and that the Luftwaffe would make short work of the weak aerial opposition.

The French were equally confident. In the early 1930s, to protect their border with Germany, they'd built the Maginot Line. Named for the French war minister Andre Maginot, the defenses consisted of anti-tank emplacements and pillboxes, with bombproof artillery casements behind them. They ran all the way from Luxembourg to Switzerland, and were considered impregnable. In addition, the French Army comprised 85 divisions, compared with the Germans' 62, and its commanders were seasoned veterans who had prevailed in the last war. They insisted a German invasion could not succeed.

Officers of the French Air Force shared that view. The FAF had 4360 aircraft versus the Luftwaffe's 3270, and the French airplanes were of the latest design. Joining them were 12 British squadrons. Any German attack, the FAF officers said, would fail.

Thus the mind-set of the French was entirely defensive. Even though they'd declared war eight months earlier, they had undertaken very little offensive action. Instead, they simply sat tight and waited for the Germans to make their move.

During this brief period of calm, the Commander in Chief of the French Army, General Maurice Gamelin, reviewed his plan with Prime Minister Édouard Deladier. Gamelin realized the Germans heavily depended on the use of armor. But if they tried to breach the Maginot Line their tanks would be impaled, and the French guns would destroy them. And if they attacked in the Ardennes? The rocky land and the steep hills and dense forests would prevent them from using their armor. So once again the Germans would be denied the use of their most effective weapons.

Their armies might also attempt to go through Central Belgium, as they had in the last war. But they would be stopped there as well. The Belgians had 23 divisions of their own, and the British Expeditionary Force would provide eight more. Deladier was satisfied, and the meeting ended. But there were blind spots in Gamelin's assessment.

The first mistake was the general's faith in the Maginot Line. Its fortifications had been designed for the wrong war. France was prepared for the battles it had fought in 1918, not those it faced in 1940.

The second flaw was Gamelin's analysis of where and how the Germans would attack. The enemy had a plan of their own, devised by General Erich von Manstein.

At dawn on 10 May the German field commander, General Gerd von Rundstedt, sent seven Panzer divisions, led by Generals Heinz Guderian and Erwin Rommel, to spearhead an attack in the Ardennes. The Panzers quickly cut a swath through the rugged territory, and German divisions stunned the French by roaring into southeastern Belgium and northern Luxembourg. Others invaded the Netherlands.

Once again, Blitzkrieg proved unstoppable. Stukas bombed enemy positions, fast-moving tanks overran them, and mechanized infantry mopped up. The roads were clogged with wrecked equipment and people trying to escape. The Luftwaffe added to the havoc by strafing both troops and civilians.

On 14 May, 60 Luftwaffe He-111 bombers attacked Rotterdam. Meeting no opposition other than sporadic antiaircraft fire, they destroyed the center of the city. Holland quickly surrendered. Meanwhile General Guderian's Panzers crossed the Meuse River near Sedan. Some French units put up strong resistance, notably the 4th Tank Division led by General Charles de Gaulle, but they were unable to halt the German advance. Meanwhile, the Allies in Luxembourg and Belgium continued to retreat.

On 21 May, Guderian's Panzers reached the Channel Coast, with Rommel's division arriving soon after. They captured the port cities of Cherbourg, Caen, and Le Havre, and then closed the trap on the isolated Allied forces in the northeast.

French generals claimed the defeat of their army was due to lack of support from the French Air Force, but this was an attempt by the generals to cover up their own failures. In fact, the French pilots fought bravely and with skill. For example, the squadrons flying the Curtiss 75A-3 shot down 98 German aircraft, and the squadrons equipped with the Bloch-152 and the Dewoitine D-520 destroyed 86 more.

But despite their courageous efforts, the Luftwaffe outfought them. With a kill ratio of better than two to one, the Germans broke the back of the French Air Force. Flying the Bf-109, aces such as Wolfgang Schellmann, Herbert Ihlefeld, and Günther Lützow ran up their scores.

So did Adolf Galland, who later would become General of Luftwaffe Fighters. Galland had respect for the French airmen. He reported a dogfight with a pair of Moranes:

> I banked steeply and closed in on one of the enemy airplanes. The pilot flew well, but his aircraft was inferior to mine. I got in a broadside in a climbing turn. He burst into flames and spun down into a forest not far from Meaux, north of Paris. I then closed in on the other one. He went down vertically, trailing black smoke.

On the French side, Captain Marcel Albert, who became an ace flying the Bloch-152, said:

> The Messerschmitts were faster than any of our aircraft. The only way I could shoot one down was to dive on it and fire before the pilot knew I was there. The leaders were very good, probably had flown in Spain.

On 25 May British Intelligence gained an invaluable tool when cipher experts at Bletchley Park, 50 miles northwest of London, broke the Luftwaffe Enigma code. From then on, the British were able to decipher communications between the Luftwaffe and the German High Command.

Göring knew nothing of this. He refused to acknowledge any weakness in the Luftwaffe, and his arrogance led to one of the great blunders in the war. It took place when the German divisions stood poised on the Channel Coast just outside Dunkirk, ready to obliterate what remained of the enemy forces. The port was in shambles, and on the beach some

350,000 British and French troops, commanded by General Lord Gort, were holding out. Low on ammunition, short of food, water and medical supplies, they were determined to fight as long as possible. Confronting them were four Panzer divisions.

Guderian was eager to attack, but his superiors, General von Rundstedt and General von Kleist, called a halt. They claimed it was necessary in order to bring up the infantry, which had lagged behind the fast-moving Panzers. Guderian was furious. He argued that his tanks had a golden opportunity to finish off the enemy. Yet, the senior officers insisted that he wait until the infantry arrived.

It was left to Hitler to settle the dispute. He listened to both points of view, and hesitated. He felt that Rundstedt and Kleist might be right, that acting precipitously could jeopardize the success of the campaign.

But then Göring spoke up, displaying his usual hubris. "My Luftwaffe can handle this," he said. "We'll complete the encirclement and close the pocket from the air. Whatever enemy troops are left alive will surrender. There is no need to send in the Panzers. They can sit back and watch."

Hitler regarded Göring as his most trusted confidante and commander. He told him to go ahead.

The Luftwaffe was ill-prepared for the task. The squadrons of bombers and fighters not only needed repairs and replacements, but also had to operate from airfields far from the coast. That would restrict the time they could spend over Dunkirk before having to return for more fuel and ammunition.

Heavy fog then set in over the beach and stayed there for three days, preventing the Germans from flying. The delay gave the British a valuable respite. When at last the fog lifted and the Luftwaffe was able to attack, its aircraft were met by RAF fighters coming across the Channel from England.

The short distance to Dunkirk enabled the British to stay and fight much longer than their adversaries, and they could quickly return to base for a fresh supply of petrol and ammunition. Not only that, but many of the British airplanes were Spitfires.

Before this, the Germans had encountered only a few of them, because the RAF had held its best fighters in England to defend the homeland. But now the Germans realized that the Bf-109 was not the only great fighter in the war.

Luftwaffe Leutnant Peter Beyer said, "This was the first time I had encountered Spitfires. I got into a scuffle with one, and found I could not out-turn it. While I was trying to get a shot at him, another Spitfire fired a burst into my tail. I went into a spin and managed to bail out when I was only a few hundred meters from the ground."

As the battle raged in the sky, the Royal Navy made a valiant effort to rescue what remained of the battered troops. But the warships were unable to sail close enough to the beach, because the water was too shallow. A call went out for smaller vessels.

In response, an armada of small boats, many of them manned by civilians, put out of English ports and headed across the Channel. Motor yachts, launches, lifeboats, car ferries, a paddle steamer, anything with a shallow draft, took part. On the beach at Dunkirk British Army engineers built jetties with wrecked trucks so the boats could dock and take on soldiers.

Nearby, attacks by Stuka bombers had ignited oil storage tanks. Ironically, light from the fires acted as beacons for the boats to home in on, while at the same time smoke obscured the rescue operation. As a result, German pilots often were unable to see their targets.

For the next five days and nights, the small craft braved the roiling seas and attacks by the Luftwaffe to rescue the haggard troops, many of them wounded. More than a hundred of the boats were sunk, along with some 30 British naval vessels.

In the end, a total of 338,226 men were rescued. It became obvious that Göring's egotism had played a vital role in allowing the enemy to escape. The nucleus of the British Army was returned to England, where it would be rebuilt into a powerful fighting force. As Sir Winston Churchill proclaimed, this was "The miracle of Dunkirk."

Though France was now all but defeated, Paris was still holding out. On 3 June, 300 German bombers conducted a raid on the city, inflicting more than 900 casualties. The British knew the raid was coming, but rather than reveal that they'd cracked the Enigma code, they chose not to warn their French allies.

The following day, remnants of the French Air Force retaliated against Germany by attacking Munich and Frankfurt with Farman F-222s and Bloch-131 bombers. The raids caused only slight damage, and most of the French aircraft were shot down.

Then the Germans lost one of their best pilots. On 6 June, Hauptmann Werner Mölders led squadron III/JG 53 into battle against a flight of French fighters over Compiegne. Mölders was still the Luftwaffe's leading ace, with 25 kills to his credit.

In the dogfight, Mölders engaged a Dewoitine D-520. A fast, low-wing monoplane, the D-520 was the best fighter in the French Air Force. As Mölders tried to get into firing position, a second Dewoitine, flown by Lt. René Layragues, sent 20mm shells into the engine of the Bf-109. Nearly blinded by oily smoke, Mölders made a crash landing and was taken prisoner.

On 7 June, the French Air Force struck once more, this time achieving what Göring had boasted would be impossible: they bombed Berlin. The damage was not extensive, with less than 200 casualties reported, but the Luftwaffe's commander-in-chief was both embarrassed and outraged.

On 10 June, Italy declared war on Britain and France, and on 22 June, the French finally admitted that their situation was hopeless. They signed an armistice with Germany.

For the Allies, the defeat was devastating. More than 1,500,000 soldiers had been captured and made prisoners. Three hundred thousand others were killed, while the Germans lost only 35,000 dead.

On 23 June the dream Adolf Hitler had been nurturing for more than two decades at last became reality. Standing in the front of an open Mercedes, the victorious Führer toured Paris. As the huge black car rolled down the Champs Elysees, accompanied by goose-stepping Waffen SS troops, French citizens lined the boulevard. They gaped at Hitler with a mixture of awe and hatred, but he was oblivious to their reactions. He was already planning his next bold stroke, the invasion of England.

20.

At the end of June, 1940, Willy Messerschmitt was invited to a ceremony at the Imperial Chancellery in Berlin. The Führer wished to express his appreciation for the Professor's contributions to Germany's victory over the Allies.

Messerschmitt packed a bag and told Lilly he'd be back the following day. He then flew his personal Bf-108, which bore the registration D-IMTT, to Berlin. When he landed at Schoenfeld Airport a car was waiting for him, and he was driven the 20 kilometers into the city. There he checked into his favorite hotel, the grand old Adlon on Unter den Linden, near the Brandenburg Gate. After a change into fresh clothing, he had the car drive him to the Chancellery.

The enormous structure was located at Vossstrasse 6, in the heart of the capital. Constructed of stone and marble, it stretched the length of a city block. The austere facade contained banks of tall windows, with four lofty Doric columns at its entrance. Above the columns, a stone relief depicted a stylized German eagle clutching a swastika.

The Chancellery was the work of Hitler's favorite architect, 35-year-old Albert Speer. Incredibly, Speer had designed and built it in only one year. When it was finished, the Führer was delighted, saying it would give visitors a taste of the power and grandeur of the German Reich.

Messerschmitt was saluted by black-uniformed Allgemeine SS guards as he went through the massive doors. An official greeted him with the Nazi salute and had him sign in. Then the official escorted him to the reception gallery. It was a long walk—the corridor took up some 220 meters, and the rooms along the way were richly decorated with paintings and mosaics. Busy people were everywhere, some in civilian clothes, but most in the uniforms of Army and Navy officers.

The reception gallery was another 145 meters long. Red banners emblazoned with the swastika hung from the high ceiling, and on the walls colossal oil paintings in gilt frames depicted scenes from German mythology. There were also portraits of such figures as Charlemagne, Siegfried, and Frederick the Great.

Many of the people in here were prominent members of the Nazi regime. Messerschmitt knew most of them. They nodded and expressed greetings as he moved about.

Reichsmarschal Hermann Göring was on hand, as were Admiral Erich Raeder and Deputy Führer Hess. Both Heinrich Himmler and Reinhard Heydrich of the SS were also there, along with Foreign Minister Joachim von Ribbentrop. And off to one side, wearing a black uniform and looking over the crowd was the head of the Propaganda Ministry, Joseph Goebbels.

Of the many sycophants and manipulators who made up Hitler's innermost circle, none was more fearsome than this man. It was Goebbels who ran the campaign urging the extermination of all enemies of the Reich, especially Jews. It was hard to reconcile so puny a creature with his reputation as a ruthless operative. Goebbels was physically slight, with a club foot. His hair and eyebrows were jet black, and in his narrow face his eyes darted constantly, like those of a ferret.

The minister's personal life was as dark as his public one. His wife Magda had been married to Günther Quandt, the principal owner of BMW, when Goebbels stole her away. Since then he'd fathered six children by her, which did not hinder his activities as a womanizer. He maintained several mistresses.

Today's event was probably Goebbels' idea. It's likely that the propagandist staged it to generate favorable publicity for the Führer and the war against the Western Allies.

Looking around, Willy spotted his rival Ernst Heinkel, and also Ferdinand Porsche, the brilliant automotive engineer who now designed tanks for the Panzer divisions. Their presence meant he wouldn't be the only one praised by Hitler today.

Hermann Göring greeted him, and offered congratulations. The Reichsmarschal was attired in one of his resplendently gauche uniforms, this one pearl gray with gold epaulets and festooned with medals, including the Pour le Mérite that he'd won in the last war.

Göring was now a very rich man. He'd been demanding payoffs ever since the Nazis seized power, calling the bribes consulting fees. He collected them from everyone who did business with the Luftwaffe, including BMW, Junkers, Heinkel, Focke-Wulf, Arado and many others, as well as Messerschmitt. It enabled him to live in splendor at Karinhall, his estate north of Berlin.

At that moment the doors at the end of the gallery opened, and the Führer entered. His appearance had an instant effect on the assembly. He was greeted by shouts of "Heil Hitler!" and by thunderous applause.

Hitler stepped onto a raised podium and waited for a few moments, letting the applause roll over him. Unlike the fancy uniforms of the generals and admirals in the gallery, his was a plain brown tunic and black trousers. On his left sleeve was a red armband with a black swastika against a white background.

The Führer quieted the crowd by raising his hand. Then he began to speak with his rough Austrian accent.

His voice rising, Hitler spoke of the magnificent victory the Wehrmacht had won over the ineffectual Allies. It was a victory of the strong and noble over the devious and corrupt, of the brave over the cowardly. He said Germany would now take its rightful place as leader of the civilized world, because the German people would not be denied. Germans were pure Aryans, and that fact would enable the nation to become ever stronger. The Third Reich was destined to last a thousand years.

He went on for more than an hour, stimulating himself as well as the members of his audience. And then at last he came to the subject of today's ceremony. The men who were being honored today, Hitler said, embodied Germany's leadership in the realm of science and technology.

He lauded the work of Professor Willy Messerschmitt and that of Ernst Heinkel, exclaiming that their aircraft had swept the skies of all opposition. And he praised the work of Dr. Ferdinand Porsche, whose tanks had spearheaded the Panzers' drives through enemy defenses. These men, Hitler said, were as important to the German war effort as the military commanders whose forces fought on the battlefields and in the air.

When he finished speaking, the crowd again burst into applause. Sieg heil, they shouted. Sieg heil!

Hitler left the podium, and stepped over to a place where photographers were waiting. Messerschmitt, Porsche, and Heinkel were presented to the Führer, who shook their hands and uttered a few words of praise as the flashbulbs popped.

Hitler later said to Heinkel and Messerschmitt that victory would be achieved by rendering the enemy incapable of resistance, and the way to do that would be through relentless air strikes by bombers. Therefore he was thankful that brilliant aeronautical designers like Dr. Heinkel and Professor Messerschmitt were working on such aircraft.

Long after Messerschmitt left the Chancellery, he was euphoric. Hitler had thanked him personally for his contributions, a great honor. Of course, he'd had to share the spotlight with Porsche and with his detested rival Heinkel, but that aside, it had been a wonderful day.

One point, however, had slipped by him. The Führer had made it clear that by air power, he was referring to bombers. Willy did not realize that would eventually lead to trouble for his company—and that it would be disastrous for Germany.

But at the moment, the future looked radiant. And there was much work to be done. The invasion of England would take place any day now, and Messerschmitt was sure his airplanes would play a key role.

21.

The invasion plan was code-named Operation Sea Lion. It called for an assault on a 40-mile stretch of the English coast by 160,000 German troops. For it to succeed, two preliminary objectives had to be met.

The first was destruction of the Royal Air Force by the Luftwaffe. Control of the skies would make it possible to achieve the second objective, the clearing of the English Channel by the combined efforts of the Luftwaffe and the Kriegsmarine. Once the Channel was clear, the invasion fleet could get safely across.

As usual, Göring assured the Führer his air force would prevail, yet he chose not to reveal the damage sustained during the six weeks of combat in France. The Germans had lost 1,469 aircraft, and the Luftwaffe was in need of a complete overhaul. The looming Battle of Britain would be far more difficult than the Reichsmarschal thought, but thanks to Goebbels' propaganda, most German citizens had no idea of the true situation. News stories said the Luftwaffe had swatted the enemy like so many flies. The French Air Force had been conquered, and the RAF soon would be as well.

At this time the Messerschmitt Design Center in Augsburg was moving forward with the Me-262 project. A report by Woldemar Voigt was sent to the Air Ministry on 21 March, and representatives of the Technical Office went to the factory to inspect the mockup.

The officials were favorably impressed, and a contract was issued for 20 trial aircraft. They were to be equipped with the new BMW P3302 turbojet engines, which Messerschmitt was assured would soon be ready for delivery. The RLM also specified that the airplanes were to be fitted with ejection seats, dive brakes, and armor-protected fuel tanks. Messerschmitt continued to have reservations as to the feasibility of the new engine arrangement, but he pressed ahead. He'd already built assembly jigs and components for the construction of the aircraft.

Willy tended to rush his projects while leaving financial details to others. With that in mind, the board of directors voted to have the banker Friedrich Seiler officially become business manager of the company. Messerschmitt was irritated, but there was nothing he could do about it.

Seiler was wary of allowing the firm to move too quickly with the Me-262. His view of the project was that developing a revolutionary new type of aircraft was all well and good, but nothing should be done to erode the sales volume of the Bf-109. That airplane was the company's cash cow.

To assuage Seiler, Messerschmitt said the Me-262 would not replace the Bf-109, but would complement it. Jet engines, he pointed out, consumed fuel so rapidly that the new aircraft could only be effective as a short-range fighter.

Meanwhile, the question remained as to when the English Channel would be cleared so that German vessels could make it across.

The attempt began on 10 July 1940, when Feldmarschal Kesselring launched a raid on British shipping in the Channel. Taking part were 60 German aircraft, most of them Dornier Do-17 and Heinkel He-111 bombers, accompanied by Bf-110s. The Kriegsmarine was busy as well. Its U-boats attacked merchant ships carrying supplies from Canada, Australia and the United States. Many merchantmen were sunk, despite being escorted by cruisers and destroyers of the Royal Navy.

The British often used aircraft to defend against the U-boat attacks. The RAF dropped depth charges from bombers such as the Vickers Wellington and the Armstrong Whitworth Whitley. Even the Short Sunderland, a ponderous four-engine flying boat, was pressed into anti-submarine service.

RAF fighter squadrons were also in action, attacking the Luftwaffe aircraft. The Germans soon learned that gaining control of the skies would not be as easy as Göring had claimed. And clearing the Channel would not be a simple matter, either.

22.

From the outset, the Luftwaffe was faced with a number of handicaps. One was that many of Kesselring's aircraft had to fly to the Channel from bases in northwest Germany, and others from Norway. That left them with enough fuel to spend only a short time over their targets.

Another problem was that the distance was too great for the bombers to be escorted by Bf-109s. Only the twin-engine Bf-110s had the range to make such a trip, and then only when they were carrying an auxiliary fuel tank under the fuselage. Göring had dubbed the Bf-110 the *Zerstroyer,* but with a 264-gallon tank strapped beneath it, pilots nicknamed it the *Dackelbauch*—the dachshund-belly. And the aircraft was not meeting the Reichsmarschal's hopes.

Göring envisioned the Bf-110 as capable of flying deep into enemy territory, where it would accompany his bombers and defeat opposing fighters. In addition, the aircraft itself could be utilized as a bomber. This was a fallacy, but he held on to it with typical stubbornness. Flown by a brave pilot and an alert gunner, he insisted, the Bf-110 would be a potent weapon.

Events proved him wrong. The aircraft was too slow to be effective as a fighter, and it was still slower when carrying the auxiliary tank. Worse, it was too ungainly to contend with agile British Hurricanes and Spitfires.

When the German Heinkel and Dornier bombers reached the Channel they were attacked by RAF fighters from Biggin Hill, Croyden and Tangmere, and the Bf-110s provided scant protection. Within a few days 68 German airplanes were shot down, while the RAF lost 30. Both the Germans and the British had air-sea rescue services, yet many of the aircraft crews that survived the crashes drowned in the rough waters of the Channel. Meanwhile the Luftwaffe commanders rushed to establish bases closer to the French coast. The stations were set up in the Pas de Calais area, directly across from the Straits of Dover, the narrowest part of the Channel.

The Luftwaffe now had 2,500 serviceable aircraft. The RAF had 1,200, including 800 fighters, but only 660 of the Hurricanes and Spitfires were combat-ready. Also, some of Britain's best pilots had been killed in France, and still others were lost in the encounters over the Channel.

The RAF did have several important advantages, however. One was an elaborate radar system. The British had built 51 radar stations in southern England, and their scanning was coordinated by central control. Germany had nothing like it.

Another advantage was that the British were fighting over their own territory. When one of their fighters was low on petrol or out of ammunition, the pilot could land and replenish his stocks and be back in the air within minutes. But when the Germans ran short, they had no choice but to go home.

Commander of the Luftwaffe's III/JG 26 was Hauptmann Adolf Galland. He knew the British pilots were tough and courageous, and had some fine airplanes. Though the Hawker Hurricanes could not match the Bf-109 in speed or rate of climb, the Spitfires were every bit as good as the German fighters. Still, Galland claimed the Bf-109s were faster than the Spitfires by a few kph and could out-climb them as well. Also, the German engines were fuel-injected, while the British were still using carburetors.

"So our engines didn't conk out as theirs often did," Galland said. "In my first encounter with them, I was with my squadron over the Thames Estuary. We made a surprise attack from a favorably higher altitude. I glued myself onto the tail of the airplane flying outside on the left flank and fired a long burst. The Spitfire went down almost vertically. I followed it until the cockpit cover came flying toward me and the pilot bailed out. His parachute failed to open and he crashed into the water. In all, I'd say our Bf-109 was slightly superior to the Spitfire."

Galland may have thought so, but there was another factor bearing on a comparison of the two aircraft, and he and other Luftwaffe pilots were soon made aware of it. Although the Bf-109 had a marginal edge in speed and rate-of-climb, a Spitfire could make tighter turns. And that was crucial in a dogfight.

RAF Sgt. Pilot James Long said, "The Messerschmitts were a bit faster, and if one got the jump on you, you were in trouble. But the Spit's turning ability was fantastic. So the thing to do was turn hard and keep on turning, try to get behind him. I got my first kill that way. A 109 surprised me and I took hits in my left wing. I banked toward him, and after we went 'round a couple of times I was able to get in a burst. My tracers must have hit his fuel tank, because his airplane exploded. When I landed my ship had nicks in it from the debris."

As the German losses increased, the pilots were vilified by Göring, who accused them of shirking. The pilots found the uninformed criticism infuriating, but the truth was that the Luftwaffe's strategy was not panning out. The Germans scored many victories, but the RAF kept putting up more fighters. And as their pilots gained experience, they became more proficient.

One of the most memorable dogfights occurred on 28 July, at 18,000 feet above Folkestone. It was fought by two outstanding fighter pilots, though neither knew who the other was.

Flying a Spitfire was Flight Lieutenant "Sailor" Malan, a South African so nicknamed because he'd shipped out as a merchant seaman at the age of 15. He now had a dozen kills.

Opposing him was Werner Mölders. After the surrender of France, Mölders had been released from a prisoner-of-war camp and rejoined the Luftwaffe. He was promoted to Major, and given command of JG/51. His record had grown to 25 victories.

Leading his squadron in a Bf-109E, Mölders attacked Malan's formation of Spitfires and shot one down. The sailor pulled up above him and dove, firing as he went. His tracers raked Mölders' fuselage, but did no vital damage. The two began scissoring, the series of circling maneuvers in which fighter pilots try to get into position on one another's tail. Neither was successful, until Malan rolled onto his back and caught Mölders as he made a turn. Once more Malan's tracers hit the Bf-109, and this time sent it spinning earthward.

Mölders was badly wounded. Bleeding heavily and barely conscious, his legs pierced by .303 machine-gun bullets, he nursed the Bf-109 back across the French coast before crash-landing. He was pulled from the wreckage and taken to a hospital, where he spent the next two months.

"The bugger was a hell of a pilot," Malan said, "whoever he was. But a lot of them were. There was another chap I saw a few times who was also bloody good. He shot down several of our people. I never got a crack at him, though. I could recognize him because he had Mickey Mouse painted on his airplane."

The pilot who flew with that insignia was Adolf Galland, of course. Galland's record of 50 kills became the highest among Luftwaffe pilots in the Battle of Britain.

Many other German airmen also ran up impressive scores, and by the end of July the British had only about 200 front-line fighters still in condition for combat. Fortunately for the British, the Luftwaffe commanders were unaware of this.

Angry and frustrated, Göring ordered a change in strategy. It was based on the principle that the purpose of air power was to bomb the enemy. If bombers were fast and well armed, they would be impervious to attack. Fighters were of limited value. The Do-17, the He-111, and the Ju-88 were all perfectly suited to such a strategy, Göring concluded, because they were quick-strike aircraft that could also be used as dive bombers. And the Ju-87 Stukas had already demonstrated their value in one campaign after another.

Ignoring the earlier losses over the Channel, Göring was sure his medium bombers would be the key to victory. England would be defeated, and much of the glory would go to him.

The veterans of the *Geschwaders* did not share his optimism. Instead, they cited Baron Manfred von Richthofen, who in World War I said, "The fighter pilots have to rove in the area allotted to them in any way they like, and when they spot an enemy they attack and shoot him down. Anything else is rubbish."

Orders, however, were orders. And on 15 August, proclaimed "Eagle Day" by Göring, the Luftwaffe launched its largest attacks to date. More than 1,000 German bombers and fighters took part, flying 1,485 sorties. They succeeded in destroying a number of British radar centers and airfields, and inflicted heavy damage on several aircraft factories.

Yet many of the attackers were lost. Oberleutnant Karl-Heinz Krahl, Staffelkapitän of 3/JG2, said the fighter pilots were ordered to stay with the bombers at all costs. They were to fly close to them, like dogs guarding a flock of sheep. The pilots tried to make Göring understand it was a mistake, that the proper tactic would be for the fighters to fly well out in front. That way they could shoot down the enemy planes before they ever got near the bombers.

But Göring, Kesselring, von Doring and the rest of the old pilots couldn't see it. They still thought in terms of how they'd protected reconnaissance aircraft in 1918. And apparently they'd forgotten Richtofen's principles and the freedom they'd had in flying patrols. They had very little understanding of what modern aerial combat was like.

During the battles, the weaknesses of the Bf-110s became still more obvious. Not only were they unable to protect the bombers, but they themselves had to be protected by the Bf-109s. The Spitfires and Hurricanes destroyed scores of them.

Even less well suited to the task were the Stukas. Vulnerable while making their dives, they were mauled by the British fighters. By late August, so many Stukas had been lost that the Luftwaffe withdrew them altogether.

And as always, range was a problem for German aircraft. The endurance of a Bf-109 was 80 minutes. Forming up took 10 minutes, and flying to England took 30, which left a maximum of 10 minutes for combat before it was necessary to return to base. Bombers were at a similar disadvantage, though He-111s did a lot of damage to the targets they could reach. Some airfields were put out of commission altogether. Biggin Hill, for example, had so many bomb craters it became unusable. Many of the radar towers were also destroyed.

As the losses mounted, it became clear that the Luftwaffe was again failing to achieve its objectives. The RAF had been battered, but its pilots were unbowed. In a speech before Parliament, Prime Minister Winston Churchill said, "Never in the field of human conflict was so much owed by so many to so few."

And then on the night of 24 August an event took place that changed the course of the war. As so often happened, it began with a mistake. A Ju-88 pilot became disoriented in fog and decided to jettison his bombs into the Channel.

He did not realize he was over the center of London.

23.

The misdirected bombs killed more than a hundred Londoners and wounded many others. Men and women were blown to pieces as they emerged from a theater, and others died in a pub. In Carnaby Street the air was filled with flying chunks of metal and shards of glass. Parts of a taxi—and its passengers—splattered the walls of a bank.

Reaction from the British was unbridled fury. The public demanded revenge, and in retaliation, 43 Wellingtons from RAF Bomber Command made a raid on Munich a few nights later. The bombing did much damage, and dozens of Germans were killed.

Now it was Hitler's turn to be outraged. He vowed that from then on the Luftwaffe would bomb British cities night after night, until they were leveled. Civilian casualties? Good—the British would be punished without mercy. The main target was London, which was England's largest port and the site of its military headquarters. With its population of 7,000,000 people, and its political and commercial importance, it was the heart of the British Empire. Destroying it, Hitler believed, would shatter Britain's will to fight.

The first of the great raids on the capital took place on 7 September. At 4 pm that day, 348 German bombers, escorted by 617 fighters, dropped 500 tons of explosives on the city. The British had ringed the area with barrage balloons and antiaircraft guns, but neither proved effective.

The damage was horrendous. Countless buildings were destroyed, and fires engulfed the city. More than 177,000 people crowded into the underground stations to escape the onslaught, though many others were killed before they could find shelter. The raid finally ended, but two hours later the Luftwaffe struck again.

This time the attacks went on throughout the night. British defenses were even less capable than in the daytime, because the RAF had no night fighters. Piccadilly, Bond Street, and Park Lane were all in flames, as were many other parts of the city. The fire brigades were overwhelmed. In places no water was available, because the pipes had been ruptured. And there simply were not enough firemen to cope with the emergency. Those who were on hand worked ceaselessly.

Compounding the problems were heaps of rubble that blocked badly damaged roads and streets. The obstacles made it difficult for firefighting equipment to get through, and hampered ambulances as well. Police carried many of the wounded on stretchers to hospitals that were soon overcrowded.

As Hitler had promised, the bombers returned the next night, and the next. They dropped bombs ranging from 150 to 2,500 pounds. And in addition to the high-explosive type, they hit the city with incendiaries. Fires ravaged the capital.

As the attacks went on, deaths and injuries steadily increased, yet very few people left the city. Many volunteered as medical workers, sentries, and air raid wardens. The Luftwaffe was also busy in the daytime. With newly devised larger fuel tanks, they attacked Bristol, Cardiff, Swansea, Liverpool and Manchester. More buildings were destroyed, and more civilians were killed and injured.

Nevertheless, the British factories were turning out greater numbers of aircraft than ever, and the RAF was sending more pilots to the operational squadrons. The pilots were not as well trained as their German counterparts, but they lacked nothing in determination and courage.

By late September the Spitfires and Hurricanes were creating havoc among the Luftwaffe raiders. After one attack on the seaports in Wales, only a handful of Ju-88s and Do-17s returned. And in a raid on the Westland Aircraft factory in Yeovil, the Luftwaffe lost 43 aircraft to 16 by the RAF. Because of the growing losses, Göring decided to stop the daylight attacks altogether. Instead, he ordered the Luftwaffe to concentrate entirely on night bombing.

There was no letdown in the dedication of the German fighter forces. After Mölders and Galland each scored their fiftieth kill, they were called to Berlin and awarded Oak Leaves to the Knight's Cross, at that time Germany's highest military decoration. Trautloft, Lützow, Krahl and many other Luftwaffe pilots also added to their long lists of victories.

The Luftwaffe generals then realized how wrong they'd been in failing to recognize the need for heavy bombers. Orders went out to Junkers, Heinkel, and Focke-Wulf to produce aircraft capable of carrying far larger loads than the twin-engine airplanes currently in service. And Messerschmitt went back to work on his huge Me-264. The latest version would be powered by four Junkers Jumo liquid-cooled 12-cylinder engines of 1340 hp, and would carry a bomb load of 3968 lbs.

Messerschmitt was handicapped, however, by shortages of critical materials as well as limited factory space. When he importuned the Air Ministry to help clear the bottlenecks, Milch turned a deaf ear. It would be some time before a prototype could be produced.

Showing more foresight than the Germans, the British had introduced a number of heavy bombers shortly before the war began. The most effective were the A.V. Roe Lancaster and the Handley-Page Halifax. These heavy, high-capacity aircraft now began operations, striking objectives deep in Germany. Flying at night, they bombed Frankfurt, Hannover, Stuttgart and Cologne. But with no sophisticated navigational equipment, they had to find their way by dead reckoning, and they sometimes missed their targets entirely.

The Luftwaffe, on the other hand, had no trouble locating London. Although the city was blacked out, the Thames Estuary was visible from the air on all but the foggiest nights. And after the first loads of bombs were dropped, fires and searchlights guided the following flights of raiders.

As the Germans continued to pound the capital, the RAF's need for an effective night fighter became desperate. It was at this point that the Bristol Beaufighter made its debut. With its twin engines, the aircraft bore some resemblance to the Luftwaffe's much-maligned Bf-110, but was faster and more maneuverable, with more firepower. Mounting four 20mm cannons in the nose, and eight .303 machine guns in the wings, with another .303 manned by the rear gunner in the dorsal position, the Beaufighter was a fearsome weapon. No other aircraft of its size was so heavily armed.

As one Beaufighter pilot put it, "The German bombers were the most vulnerable in the belly, because they had only one machine-gun turret there. I would slide in underneath and then haul back on the controls and open up. Took no more than two or three seconds to kill the turret gunner and tear the aircraft apart. You had to watch out, though, because if it hadn't yet dropped its bombs the ruddy thing would go up in a huge flash, and that could take you with it. Some crews in my squadron were killed like that. So we were careful not to get too close before firing."

For all their effectiveness, Beaufighters also sustained a considerable number of losses. The German bombers were escorted by hundreds of Bf-109s and Bf-110s, and though the destroyers were as ineffectual as ever, the Bf-109s exacted a heavy toll on the night fighters.

Meanwhile the Axis nations formalized their relationship. On 27 September, 1940, the Tripartite Pact was signed by Germany, Italy and Japan. Two weeks earlier Italy had invaded Egypt, and Il Duce was already pressing Hitler to send troops in support.

At the beginning of October the British announced that civilian casualties for the prior month were 6,954 dead, and 10,615 injured. The Luftwaffe raids did not abate. On 5 October a hospital in Kent was hit, killing patients and nurses. Even Buckingham Palace was damaged by exploding bombs. And on 26 October, in the largest raid to date, a Catholic orphanage in London filled with children was wiped out by a direct hit.

The RAF knew the Germans had assembled an invasion fleet in French and Belgian ports. Handley Page Hampdens attacked the sites and destroyed many of the vessels. Four bombers and three fighters were lost in the raids.

Elsewhere the Wehrmacht was again on the move, as German troops entered Romania. Hitler was now looking eastward, and his enthusiasm for Operation Sea Lion waned. Although he would not admit it, the RAF had won the Battle of Britain. In November the Führer ordered his generals to shelve the Sea Lion plan for the time being, telling them the invasion of England would take place in the spring. No one believed him.

Also in November, a bold action took place against the Italian Navy. At the time, most of its fleet was anchored in Taranto, a well-defended harbor on the instep of the Italian boot. The British thought it might be possible to strike the enemy warships a mortal blow, whereupon the Royal Navy would gain control of the Mediterranean Sea.

A task force consisting of the aircraft carrier *Illustrious*, two heavy cruisers, two light cruisers, and four destroyers sailed into the Gulf of Taranto. At 2100 hours on the night of 10 November 1940, when the British ships were 170 miles from the harbor, the *Illustrious* launched a flight of 12 torpedo bombers. An hour later, the carrier launched nine more.

The aircraft were Fairey Swordfish, antiquated open-cockpit biplanes called "string bags" by the three-man crews because of their wire bracing. They were powered by Bristol Pegasus nine-cylinder radial engines, and their maximum speed was less than 100 knots when they were carrying a 1600-pound torpedo.

The Italians had no radar, but were alerted by an audio system that picked up the sound of the Swordfish engines. When they arrived, the raiders were met by blazing antiaircraft fire from the Italian ships and shore-side batteries. The Swordfish crews dropped magnesium flares that flooded the harbor with light, and as shells exploded around them, the biplanes made their torpedo runs at an altitude of less than 50 feet. Several were hit, but they kept on.

The damage they did crippled the Italian fleet. Three torpedoes struck the battleship *Littorio*, while others blasted holes in the *Caio Duilio* and the *Conte di Cavour*. Seven other ships were sunk or put out of commission.

Miraculously, only two Swordfish were lost. Although many of the remaining 21 aircraft were badly shot up, they made it back to the *Illustrious*. The task force then set sail for Gibraltar, leaving the Italian Navy in ruins.

Benito Mussolini was deeply humiliated by the disaster, and Hitler's reaction was anger tinged with contempt. It was not the first time the Führer had expressed disdain for his ally Il Duce and the Italian armed forces, and it would not be the last.

Nor did Hitler's hatred for the British diminish. Later in October the RAF again bombed Munich in a night attack that caused extensive damage. Munich was the birthplace of the Nazi party, and the raid sent the Führer into another violent rage. He ordered Göring to avenge the bombing.

The Reichsmarschal chose Coventry, a major manufacturing center 85 miles northwest of London, as the target. Many factories vital to the British war effort were located there, including Armstrong Whitworth, GEC, Daimler and Dunlop. The plants turned out everything from machine tools and aircraft to scout cars and tires.

By then the Germans had developed the X-Gerat navigational system, which would guide airplanes to an objective by means of intersecting radio beams. On the night of 14 November Göring sent 449 bombers and 350 fighters on the raid, with the objective of totally destroying the city. The Luftwaffe dropped 500 tons of both high-explosive and incendiary bombs, and by morning Coventry was an inferno. Attempts to quell the flames were beyond the capabilities of the firefighters, and most of them died in the raid.

Along with 21 factories, the homes, schools, theaters, and virtually all other buildings in the city were obliterated. The hospital became a tomb for patients and the medical staff. Coventry's 14th Century cathedral was wrecked, with only its spire left standing. More than a thousand people were killed, and twice that many injured.

Hitler congratulated Göring and the bomber crews. He said it was the kind of punishment the British deserved.

After the war there was speculation that because the riddle of the Enigma machine had been solved and British Intelligence could read the Luftwaffe's messages, Churchill knew of the raid in advance. It was said that rather than reveal the decoders' secret, he chose not to warn the city, and instead sacrificed it. The charge was never proven.

Following the raid on Coventry the attacks on other British cities continued. In December Churchill held a meeting of his cabinet at which the casualty figures were reviewed. There had been 15,029 in October, and 10,790 in November.

Churchill declared that in light of what the Luftwaffe had done to England, it was time to conduct the war with no show of remorse. The Germans should be hammered to oblivion by unrelenting aerial bombardment.

24.

Messerschmitt made sure to stay well informed on the struggle between the Luftwaffe and the RAF. General Udet often visited the factory and posted him on developments, and so did a number of combat pilots and commanders.

By now Messerschmitt realized that the Führer's grand plans for the invasion of Britain were foundering, if not dead. Although the Luftwaffe continued its campaign of bombing targets in England, its efforts were outpaced by the steadily increasing attacks on Germany by the RAF. Each night, large fleets of British bombers dropped their deadly loads on German cities, and as the RAF attacks intensified, many Nazi officials concluded that greater emphasis should be placed on defense. Yet little was done to strengthen the Luftwaffe fighter squadrons responsible for guarding the homeland.

The main reason for the neglect was Adolf Hitler's thirst for vengeance. He was adamant that his forces must always be on the offense, aggressively carrying the fight to the enemy. To him, defense equated with retreat, and retreat was for cowards. The Luftwaffe's role was to attack.

None of his top commanders dared to challenge his views, least of all Hermann Göring. Instead, the Reischsmarschal went on berating the fighter pilots, accusing them of failing to show the correct spirit, and of lacking courage. So the airmen assigned to protect German cities from the RAF raiders were failing their mission? That was because they were fearful of the bombers' machine guns! It was shameful!

This was the same sort of abuse he'd heaped on the pilots who fought the Battle of Britain, and it produced the same results. The airmen were bitter and frustrated at being subjected to false and defamatory accusations by the man they referred to as *Der Dicke*, the fat one.

Another part of the problem that was never properly addressed concerned the organization of the Luftwaffe. Its operations at that time were divided among four *Luftflotten*, or air fleets, spread across Germany. Luftflotte I covered the northeast; II the northwest; III the southwest; and IV the southeast. Each Luftflotte was self-contained, with its own bomber, fighter, reconnaissance, and training units.

Each also had its own commander, who ran his show according to his personal ideas. The system was grossly inefficient, because there was no central coordination among the fleets. The commanders competed for honors by sending their best units into battle over the British Isles, often shortchanging the units assigned to home defense. Göring further complicated the situation by frequently changing the commanders.

As a consequence of these shortcomings, the RAF met less resistance than expected, and continued to expand the frequency and scope of its raids. In February 1941, Frankfurt, Hanover and Hamburg were bombed, and so were targets in France, including Brest and Le Havre. In early March the RAF struck Cologne and a dozen other cities, and two weeks later the unthinkable took place: British bombers raided Berlin.

Hermann Göring had publicly boasted that such an event would never occur. If the RAF ever reached Berlin, he said, "then my name is Meyer." Predictably, Luftwaffe pilots took him up on it, and referred to him as Meyer as well as Der Dicke.

Hitler's response to the raid was also predictable. Instead of instructing Göring to shore up German defenses, he ordered more attacks against cities in Britain. Clydebank, Bristol and Plymouth were all hit, and night after night bombs were dropped on London. British civilian casualties in March totaled 4,259 killed and 5,557 injured.

During this time, RAF Fighter Command continued to add strength. Increasing numbers of aircraft were built, and pilots gained further combat experience. Spitfires, Hurricanes and Beaufighters exacted a punishing toll on the German attackers. As more Luftwaffe bombers and fighters took part in the raids, more of them were shot down.

In Germany, bitter criticism was heaped on the Luftwaffe by the Air Ministry for wasting aircraft and personnel. The Luftwaffe countered by accusing the Air Ministry of not providing the proper equipment. Where were the heavy bombers needed to achieve victory, Göring demanded. Why had the Luftwaffe failed to sweep the skies clear of the RAF, the Air Ministry shot back. Intrigue and recriminations were rampant, and relations between Göring and Milch became icy. The Reichsmarschal undermined Milch as much as possible, but he dared not fire him. Milch was not only vital to the management of the Air Ministry, but his talents were recognized by Hitler.

Messerschmitt avoided entanglement in such matters. He had enough political problems as it was, dealing with the RLM. His job was to turn out the best aircraft he could design and manufacture, and that's what he focused on. Among the many tasks occupying the Professor was the next stage of Project P 1065: building the jet-powered trials aircraft. Although at first he'd resisted hanging the engines beneath the wings, he now saw a number of advantages.

For one, the concept simplified construction of the main wing spar. And for another, the hanging nacelles would make maintenance of the engines much easier, which would be especially important in aircraft undergoing trials. As the work went on, the members of the design team thought the swept-back wings resembled those of a *Schwalbe*, or swallow. So they began calling the airplane by that name. It wasn't as dramatic as the names the Professor usually favored, but he permitted its use.

Then a new dilemma arose, as usual involving the engines. The BMW P3302s had still not arrived, and in desperation Messerschmitt asked Junkers for Jumo 004s. Junkers promised to send them, but those engines were not delivered, either.

In late March, while Messerschmitt and his designers were casting about for some way to power the Me-262 for high-speed testing, another jolting piece of news reached Augsburg. The rival Heinkel works had launched the world's first jet fighter.

At a glance, the twin-engine Heinkel He-280 bore some resemblance to the Me-262. Its engines were suspended in nacelles beneath the wings, and it had a long, low profile. A major difference was that unlike the single vertical stabilizer of the Messerschmitt aircraft, the He-280 had two.

But just as with the Me-262, the Heinkel had engine problems. Its He-S8 turbojets put out only 720 kg of thrust between them, and with test pilot Fritz Schaefer at the controls the aircraft was unable to attain a maximum speed greater than 650 kph. Thus its performance was not much different from that of piston engine aircraft, including the latest Bf-109.

The Heinkel engines were also unreliable, and difficult to service. At times they would not start, and on subsequent test flights one or the other cut out. During one test, both engines failed and Schaefer was lucky to make a dead-stick landing.

Although Milch encouraged further development, Udet advised Ernst Heinkel that the Air Ministry had little interest in his jet airplane. Despite these contradictory messages, work on the Heinkel continued. Obviously, political wheeling and dealing was once more a factor.

To Willy Messerschmitt, the news of Heinkel's jet was extremely troubling. Unless he could find a way to hurry progress of the Me-262, the rival firm might find ways to overcome the He-280's faults. And if the Heinkel were to become operational, the Air Ministry would abandon his own project.

Therefore, not wanting to hold up development any longer, Messerschmitt authorized the design team to modify one of the trial airplanes by mounting a piston engine in its nose. This would at least permit testing of the airframe before the turbojets were installed.

The aircraft was designated the Me-262V-1 (V for *Versuchs*, or experimental), and the engine selected was a Junkers Jumo 210G, a liquid-cooled V-12 of 700 hp. The engine was favored because of its relatively light weight, but it turned out to be a poor choice. The Jumo would provide barely enough thrust to achieve lift from the airplane's thin wings. It was a case of combining two elements not meant for each other.

Nevertheless, test pilot Fritz Wendel was assigned to make the flight. Wendel was a highly trained engineer as well as an accomplished flier who'd logged nearly four thousand hours in the air. He knew the lack of power would make it difficult to get the V1 off the ground, but thought that once at altitude, it would be easy to test the V1's aerodynamics and control responses. He was right, on both counts.

The machine needed every bit of the long runway at Augsburg to lift off. Wendel nursed it into the air at the last moment, barely clearing the hedges that lined the field. He raised the flaps and slowly climbed to an altitude of 5000 meters.

Once up there, the prototype performed as he and the design team had hoped. It was light on the controls and very stable. And so clean was it that even with the piston engine he was able to attain a speed of 600 kph in level flight. It was, he reported, a delight to fly.

Later, two other pilots, Karl Baur and Lukas Schmid, also flew the new aircraft, and after putting it through extensive testing they all agreed that it was a fine machine. Just wait, they said, till it was fitted with proper jet power plants. Messerschmitt and his designers were highly gratified. But where were the turbojets Junkers had promised?

Adding to the Professor's frustration was the introduction of designer Kurt Tank's Focke-Wulf 190. The first of the firm's new fighters had been delivered to the Luftwaffe, and pilots were unstinting in their praise.

Messerschmitt heard the reports, and was skeptical. As the standard fighter of the Luftwaffe, his Bf-109 was being built in great quantities.

Could the Fw-190 really be its equal, or even superior? To Messer-schmitt that seemed highly unlikely. Kurt Tank was a competent engi-neer, but as far as Messerschmitt was concerned, that's all he was.

The facts suggested otherwise.

25.

There are aircraft designers, and there are test pilots. Kurt Waldemar Tank was both. He flew every airplane he designed at least once, and often he was the first to fly them.

One would never take him for a daredevil. He had sparse blond hair and a bland face that usually wore a cheerful expression. He rarely displayed anger. Tank's big opportunity came through Erhard Milch, whose enmity toward Willy Messerschmitt never subsided. Milch placed an order with Focke-Wulf that specified its fighter must outper-form not only Britain's Spitfire, but the Bf-109 as well.

Tank led a team of his best designers in working on the Fw-190. Tank called it the *Würger,* or Butcherbird. Many of his ideas did not mesh with those of Messerschmitt.

For one thing, Tank's experience as a soldier in the First World War had taught him that military equipment should always be sturdy, reli-able, and uncomplicated to use. Therefore his fighter must be as easy to fly as possible. He designed the Fw-190's gear to have an extremely wide track, so that takeoffs and landings would be no problem.

More important, Tank wanted the pilot to be relieved of distracting chores so he could concentrate on defeating the enemy. An ingenious invention called the *Kommandogerat* automatically adjusted propeller pitch, fuel mixture and engine boost, plus the oil cooler flaps. Above 7,000 meters it automatically shifted the two-speed supercharger. No other fighter was as simple to fly.

The pilot would also be protected by excellent armor. The curved seatback was shaped from 8mm steel, and there were 13mm plates of head and shoulder armor, and 8mm plates on either side. Armament was better that that of the Bf-109. There would be at least four wing-mounted 20mm cannons, and two machine guns in the cowl as well. For maximum visibility, the cockpit canopy was a bubble of armored glass.

Tank submitted two proposals to the RLM. One called for use of the Daimler-Benz DB-601 liquid-cooled engine, and the other would use the BMW 801 air-cooled radial. Although radial engines were not in favor as power plants for fighters because of their weight and their questionable reliability, General Udet directed Focke-Wulf to install the BMW.

In many respects, the engine was highly advanced. It had two banks of seven cylinders each, displaced 41 liters, and generated 2,000 hp. But it tended to overheat, and BMW's engineers were slow to improve the cooling system. As a consequence, development of the Fw-190 lagged behind schedule.

Tank solved the weight problem by moving the cockpit farther aft, and extending the fuselage. Even with the heavy engine, the change in center of gravity gave the airplane perfect balance. BMW then got the overheating under control, and thereafter the big radial was very dependable. After priming, the engine would fire immediately and run smoothly throughout the flight.

When the prototype was shipped to the Rechlin Test Center, Tank was the first to fly it. He sent the airplane into a series of power dives from 6,000 meters, and had not the slightest difficulty in pulling out. Its rate of climb was 16 meters per second, and it also had a very rapid roll rate—both were faster than those of the Bf-109. After that, Tank and other test pilots ran the gamut of aerobatic maneuvers: loops, Immelmann turns, spins, hammerheads, slow rolls, barrel rolls, snap rolls, tail slides. In every one of them the Fw-190 performed splendidly.

There were a few problems, of course, as in any new airplane. Most were relatively minor, such as the canopy release not working at speeds above 500 kph. The solution was the installation of two 20mm cartridges that would blow the canopy open far enough for the slipstream to carry it away.

A far more serious drawback involved maneuverability. Although the Fw-190 was faster than any contemporary fighter, it could not turn in quite as short a radius as a Bf-109. And if the pilot tried forcing it, the airplane would snap into a spin.

That did not trouble Tank. He said the aircraft could climb faster than an enemy, and therefore would be in position to attack from above. Superior height, he pointed out, had been an advantage from the earliest days of aerial combat.

Deliveries of the Fw-190 to the Luftwaffe began in early 1941, and its outstanding capabilities were quickly recognized. Pilots were eager to fly it, and the Air Ministry, led by Milch, urged that it be put into operations at once. The Bf-109, Milch said, would be gradually phased out.

During a visit to the Test Center at Rechlin, Messerschmitt saw Kurt Tank's new design for the first time. He had to admit the Fw-190's lines were exceedingly graceful. And he could see why the wide track of the landing gear would appeal to pilots.

Most impressive, however, was the aircraft's performance. There was hardly anything the Fw-190 couldn't do well. And to find out whether Milch's threat to replace his fighter with the Fw-190 was true, Messerschmitt questioned the Technical Director of the Air Ministry, his old friend General Ernst Udet.

Don't worry, Udet told him. The Fw-190 was a fine aircraft, and large numbers were being ordered for the Luftwaffe, but not in the same quantities as the Bf-109. Tank's new fighter was more complicated to build, and more expensive.

And there was one other thing. Not all pilots were as enthusiastic about the Fw-190 as Milch claimed. Combat veterans had learned it could not turn as tightly as either the Bf-109 or the Spitfire. Having tangled with the renowned RAF aircraft, they considered that a major fault. Therefore many of them had decided to stick with Professor Messerschmitt's fighter.

Willy was relieved, but he knew Udet well enough to be suspicious; the general was a wily politician whose word could not be trusted. Sure enough, new orders called for three times as many Fw-190s as Bf-109s to be constructed for the Luftwaffe.

When they heard that, both Messerschmitt and the company's business manager, Fritz Seiler, were stunned. But Seiler then discovered that members of Udet's staff had submitted false information on the performance of the two aircraft. The orders were reversed.

So Udet's maneuvering, aided by Milch's hatred for Willy Messerschmitt, had not succeeded. Moreover, the Fw-190 had yet to undergo the critical test of engaging the enemy in combat.

Messerschmitt responded by concentrating on the two projects that were most important to his future. One was improving the Bf-109. The other was developing the fighter that could revolutionize aerial warfare. Somehow he had to overcome all obstacles, and get the Me-262 ready to go to war.

PART III

A CRUCIAL MISTAKE

26.

The Air Ministry urged Messerschmitt to equip the Me-262 with a tricycle landing gear. He resisted, since that would add weight. The RLM pointed out that the Heinkel jet used such an arrangement, because it provided better visibility on takeoffs and landings. That only made Willy dig in his heels.

One change he did agree to was strengthening the cockpit, inasmuch as specifications called for it to be pressurized. The aircraft would then be ready for more flight testing. Yet still, there was no word on delivery of the Junkers Jumo 004 engines.

While the design team waited impatiently for the turbojets to arrive, Deputy Führer Rudolf Hess asked Messerschmitt to make a Bf-110 available to him. Willy was happy to do so. Hess had done him many favors, and was a strong supporter of his designs.

Recently gossip had circulated about Hess's mental health—some within the Nazi hierarchy whispered that he was emotionally disturbed. The rumors might have originated with jealous rivals, such as Joseph Goebbels, Martin Bormann, and Heinrich Himmler. Göring was another who resented Hess's relationship with the Führer.

Messerschmitt ignored the gossip. When Hess asked for extra fuel tanks to be installed in the Bf-110, and for the cockpit heating system to be improved, the changes were made. Hess also wanted to know what radius curve should be flown if the autopilot was not in use. He asked for a calibration of the static pressure and an associated set of curves showing what a reading of 450 kph at various altitudes would be

93

in reality. Messerschmitt had technicians supply the information.

On 10 May 1941, the Bf-110 was rolled out onto the ramp. Hess wore the uniform of a Luftwaffe officer and carried with him a leather dispatch case containing a set of aerial charts. Also in the case was a photograph of his four-year-old son, Wolf Rüdiger Hess, and a letter in a sealed envelope.

The Deputy Führer had told no one at the factory, including Messerschmitt, what his intentions were. The closest he'd come was mentioning that he wanted to test the Bf-110's long-range capabilities. He'd also hinted that he might be flying to Norway on official Nazi business.

Hess had good weather for his flight. The sky was mostly clear, showing only a few high cirrus clouds. He took off and set a course of 315 degrees, and after climbing to 4,000 meters began breathing oxygen through his mask. He made no radio contact with ground controllers, and did not switch on the transponder. The German radar system would show him only as a single blip, if at all.

He crossed the coast near Emden, and from there flew over the East Frisian Islands and on out over the North Sea. Then he changed course, turning a few degrees farther to the northwest. He switched fuel tanks, and just as the factory had assured him it would, the system worked perfectly.

With no earthly features beneath him, the flight became monotonous. There was nothing to see but a seemingly endless gray-green ocean and a distant horizon that at times was obscured by clouds. With the autopilot not engaged, he had to pay close attention to his instruments.

According to the studies he'd made of the weather at this latitude and time of year, the wind would be out of the northeast at 30 kph. Judging from the pressure on the right side of the airplane, that forecast was accurate. He adjusted his heading to account for drift, and again switched tanks. As the hours passed, he frequently calculated his position and made further course adjustments. According to his estimate, he should be in sight of land by now. Yet nothing was visible ahead of him but the sea and the sky, stretching to infinity.

Then at last, some five hours and 1500 kilometers after taking off from Augsburg, he saw a thin line on the horizon. It was the coast of Scotland. He throttled back and descended to 1,200 meters. Ahead was the large bay called the Firth of Forth. He'd be crossing the coast just to the south of the bay, and that would give him a bearing for Glasgow.

After passing over the bay he turned westward, and flew another 50 kilometers. Reducing the power further, he again descended. At 700 meters he brought the nose up and held it there. When the slow-flying aircraft was close to stalling he turned on the autopilot and set it, unfastened his seat belt, and pushed the canopy open.

Holding his dispatch case tight against his chest, he stepped over the side onto the wing root. As the wind tore at his uniform, he took a deep breath and jumped. He counted to ten and pulled his parachute's ripcord.

As he dangled beneath the yellow blossom of the chute, he looked down and saw a farmhouse and barns set among gently rolling fields where sheep were grazing. When the ground came up to meet him he landed hard, tumbling head over heels.

A sharp pain told him his ankle had been injured. But he got to his feet and unhooked the parachute harness. The house wasn't far; he'd walk to it. He'd hobbled no more than a dozen steps when a man appeared from behind one of the buildings. The man was holding a pitchfork, and he shouted at Hess to stop and put up his hands.

Hess obeyed. "Good evening," he said in heavily accented English. "I have an important message for the Duke of Hamilton. The Duke knows me. I must deliver my message to him at once."

The man stared at him, and finally said, "Come with me."

Hess lowered his hands and retrieved his case. Moving slowly because of his injured ankle, he followed the man to the house. He was told to sit on the back steps.

A woman came out, and the farmer whispered something to her. She looked wide-eyed at Hess and went back inside. The man stayed with Hess, continuing to hold the pitchfork.

Minutes passed. Then a large black Wolseley sedan drove onto the property and came to a stop near the house. Two men got out and stepped over to Hess and the farmer.

One of the men said to Hess, "Get in the car."

27.

That night Britain's Prime Minister Winston Churchill was informed that Rudolf Hess had flown to Scotland from Germany. Hess had with him a letter he wanted to deliver to the Duke of Hamilton. Churchill asked how Hess knew Hamilton, and was told they'd met in 1936 at the Olympic games in Berlin.

The letter requested Hamilton to arrange for Hess to meet King George. Hess said Hitler was planning to invade Russia, but before that happened, Hess was sure he could persuade the king to make peace between Britain and Germany. The two countries could then join together in a war on Russia—but if the offer were refused, Germany would blockade the British Isles until the people starved to death.

Churchill thought Hess's proposal was ridiculous. He was told Hess was in a military hospital near Glasgow, where he was being treated for a broken ankle suffered when he bailed out of his aircraft. Churchill sent an order to the British Foreign Secretary, Sir Anthony Eden, instructing that Hess be brought to the Tower of London and held as a prisoner of war.

The Prime Minister's order was carried out. Hess underwent lengthy psychiatric evaluation, during which he claimed astrologers had read in the stars that he was ordained to bring about peace. The doctors concluded that he was delusional.

Churchill's reaction was mild compared with that of Adolf Hitler. When the news of Hess's flight reached the Führer, he flew into one of his violent rages.

How could this happen? Hitler howled. How could someone so high in the Nazi government have become such a vile traitor? Striding back and forth in his study at Berghof, the Führer kept pointing to his head and shouting that Hess was insane. Göring was quick to agree.

People throughout Germany, as well as those in every other country, soon got the news as well. Joseph Goebbels' Ministry of Propaganda did its best to twist the truth, announcing that Hess had gone mad because of injuries sustained in the First World War. But the reports fooled no one. They were contradicted by BBC broadcasts from London, which said Hess had flown to Britain to beg for peace.

Hitler ordered the execution of anyone who'd helped Hess make his flight, and if Hess were somehow to return to Germany, he was to be shot at once. The sinister Martin Bormann replaced him as Deputy Führer.

In Augsburg, Willy Messerschmitt was as shocked by the news as everyone else. Soon afterward two of Himmler's Gestapo operatives paid him a visit, where they questioned him relentlessly. He was able to convince them that he'd known nothing of Hess's intentions, and was warned to tighten security. After that he heard no more about the Hess defection.

A few days later, Germany suffered another disaster. It began with a running sea battle in which the newly launched German battleship *Bismarck* sank the British cruiser *Hood*. Of the cruiser's 1,418 crewmen, only three survived.

Determined to avenge the *Hood*, other British warships hunted and attacked *Bismarck*. In one of the most incredible events in the history of military aviation, an antiquated Fairey Swordfish from the carrier *Ark Royal* launched a torpedo that jammed the battleship's rudder, rendering her unable to steer. The British then closed in and rained shells on the crippled German ship until she sank beneath the waves. Nearly 2,100 of the *Bismark's* crew lost their lives.

Germany was plunged into mourning. Citizens expressed grief and outrage at the demise of their prized warship. And Goebbels' propaganda inspired even greater hatred of the enemy.

In Augsburg, Professor Messerschmitt felt sorrow as well. But at the same time, pressure from the Air Ministry for him to increase aircraft production indicated something else was afoot.

By that time Germany was fighting on many fronts. The Afrika Korps was battling the British in Tunisia, and the Wehrmacht had invaded Yugoslavia and Greece. German airborne forces had invaded Crete. And though the Luftwaffe continued to bomb cities in Britain, that campaign had never achieved its original objective.

Yet Hitler was planning an operation that would dwarf any of his past campaigns. The Führer issued orders to the general staff, and on 22 June, 1941, Germany attacked the Soviet Union.

28.

In Germany's long history of warfare, one of her greatest military leaders was King Frederick I, who ruled in the 12th century. A fierce, powerfully built man, he was called Barbarossa because of his flaming red beard. According to legend he never died, but lay asleep in a mountain cave in Thuringia. One day, it was said, he would awaken and lead Germany to victory over her enemies.

That legend was what inspired Adolph Hitler to call his attack on Soviet Russia Operation Barbarossa. He was confident that a war with the Soviets could be won in ten weeks.

Once again, a number of senior officers were opposed to his plans. Commander in Chief of the Army Walther von Brauchitsch urged finishing Germany's other campaigns before mounting an assault on the Soviets. But the Führer overruled him. Reichsmarschal Göring also demurred, pointing out that the bombing of Britain was still ongoing. Then too, he'd sent units to Greece and Crete, and to North Africa to support General Rommel's troops. Engaging the Russians could be too taxing for his already stretched-thin forces. Hitler overruled him as well.

At 0300 hours on 22 June, 1941, 148 German divisions smashed through the Russian defenses and drove eastward, joined by fifteen Finnish divisions. Altogether some three million troops took part in the invasion. The Red Army had almost the same strength as the Germans: 130 divisions, 2,900,000 men, though by contrast, the Russians were poorly organized and communications were haphazard.

A theoretical Russian advantage was that the Soviets had three times as many aircraft. But while some were Yak-1 and Polikarpov I-16 fighters, and Ilyushin Il-4 and Tupolev-58 bombers, others were old biplanes that would be no match for the modern Luftwaffe machines. Additionally, many of the Russian Air Force commanders had been assigned their positions because of party loyalty rather than military expertise. Paranoid as always, Stalin had sacked many of the best senior officers and had them shot. Thus, Russian pilots had few competent leaders, and as a result they flew with scant discipline. They were often peasant youth with little education, and they had even less aptitude for flying. Training had long been neglected.

In addition to supporting the panzers, the Luftwaffe was ordered to demolish the enemy's air force. The Germans put up 1200 operational aircraft, and on the first day of the invasion they destroyed more than 2,000 Russian airplanes, most of them on the ground. But one of the Luftwaffe's other goals was not met at all. That was the eradication of Soviet engine and aircraft factories. Again the Germans failed because they did not have long-range bombers capable of reaching the most distant targets.

The Stukas, however, were as powerful a weapon as they had been in Poland and France. They now often carried SD-2 and SD-10 fragmentation bombs that flung hot shrapnel in all directions when they exploded. The bombs savaged Red Army ground troops. But unlike the men in the bomber and fighter squadrons, the Stuka crews were rarely given leave. They flew sortie after sortie, until they were either wounded or killed. Relatively few members of the original crews survived the war.

The most successful of all Stuka pilots was Hans Ulrich Rudel, whose exploits became legendary. In a raid on 23 September 1941, his squadron attacked Soviet ships in Kronstadt Harbor, near Leningrad. Rudel dove through withering flak to drop a 500 kg bomb on the Soviet battleship Marat. Her magazine exploded, and within minutes she went to the bottom. On later missions Rudel sank two Russian cruisers and a destroyer. Those were amazing feats for a pilot flying a slow, single-engine airplane.

Most of the time the Stukas attacked elements of the Red Army. The Russians fought back by putting up heavy fire with their 7.62mm Maxim-Sokolov machine guns and 85mm cannons. For the pilots, flying just above ground level in unfamiliar territory was extremely hazardous.

"We'd be down there," Rudel recounted, "bombing and machine-gunning the enemy, when suddenly we'd find ourselves in a closed canyon, with nothing but rock walls ahead of us. All you could do then was make the tightest turn possible, which didn't always work. We often lost aircraft that smashed into the cliffs."

Rudel flew a world-record 2,530 missions. In addition to the enemy warships, he destroyed almost 2,000 other targets, including 519 tanks, 70 landing boats, and more than 150 artillery emplacements. Eventually he became the most highly decorated member of the German armed forces. Stalin offered a bounty of 100,000 rubles to any Russian who could kill him, but no one was able to collect.

The Luftwaffe's Chief of Intelligence was Major Rudolph Loytved-Hartegg. He determined that the Red Air Force had about 15,000 aircraft, and that there were approximately 2,000 airfields in the western part of Russia. When the report was presented to Göring, the Reichsmarschal refused to accept the data. It was impossible, he said, for the primitive Soviets to produce so many airplanes and airfields. Nevertheless, fleets of Ju-88 bombers were ordered to attack.

Major Robert Poetter was in command of I Group of Bomber Wing

76. His Ju-88s flew in low and riddled the parked Soviet aircraft. Maintenance sheds and storage tanks went up in flames, and runways were pocked with so many bomb craters they became unusable. Bodies littered the area. Many German bombers were also lost, as fire from the ground intensified. And attacks by Russian I-16 fighters took an additional toll. If the German crews survived a crash, they were tortured and killed by Russian soldiers.

Major Klaus Haberlen, commander of the 2nd Squadron, Bomber Group 51, described an attack as similar to flying into a display of fireworks. On one raid, his Ju-88 was hit more than 30 times. According to Haberlen:

> The shells would be exploding all around you and there would also be thick small-arms fire. The smoke made the target hard to see. Many of my comrades were so badly shot up in those dives they were unable to pull out.
>
> If you went down in enemy territory, you had to hold off the Russian soldiers as long as possible. When the bomber's machine guns were no longer operable, you'd use your pistol. Our Walther PPKs carried seven rounds, and you wanted to make sure you saved the last one for yourself.
>
> Surrender was out of the question, especially if the soldiers were Mongols. Often we found the wreckage of a bomber with the remains of the crew nearby. The enemy had cut off their genitals and their ears and noses before finishing them with bayonets.

Luftwaffe fighter pilots, meanwhile, ran up impressive scores. Staffelkapitän Hans Philip said that in the early days of the operation, the Russians were not only clumsy pilots but seemed to have no concept of fighter tactics.

"They would fly in a kind of loose gaggle," Philip recounted, "and when you attacked they would scatter in all directions. You picked one out and closed in on him, and shot him to pieces. Then you looked for the next one."

Red Air Force bomber units attempted to counterattack, but without much success. One of their problems was that only the Russian squadron leader would know what the objective was, and only he would have a map. So if the leader was shot down, the other pilots would continue on aimlessly until they too became victims of the Luftwaffe fighters.

Yet a few of the Soviet pilots were outstanding. One was Lt. Alexander Pokryshkin. Flying a MiG-3, he got his first kill on 23 June 1941.

The battle began at 4,000 meters over the village of Iasi, when Pokryshkin and his wingman spotted a schwarm of Bf-109s. To the surprise of the enemy pilots, Pokryshkin attacked one head-on. Anticipating a left turn by the German, Pokryshkin swung around behind him. But before he could fire, two of the other Bf-109s dove on him and he was forced to break off. At the same time his comrade was also under attack, and he went to give aid.

The pursuer became the pursued. Pokryshkin got onto the German's tail and fired a long burst, and the enemy fighter went down trailing a plume of black smoke. Pokryshkin then made a classic beginner's mistake. Thrilled by his victory, he banked his airplane and watched the burning Bf-109 fall. As he did, the remaining fighters pounced on him and ripped his MiG with cannon fire. One of the shells blasted a hole in his right wing, and another lanced the cockpit, barely missing his head.

The MiG went into a vertical spin. Choking and half-blinded by smoke, Pokryshkin struggled to regain control. He pulled out when the badly damaged airplane was only a hundred meters above the earth.

But the MiG was finished. Pokryshkin flew a short distance and crash-landed. When he climbed out of the wreck, he found he'd suffered only minor injuries. During the following years he flew 550 sorties and shot down 58 more German aircraft, becoming the leading Soviet ace to survive the war.

Pokryshkin was an exception, however. More often the Russians were sitting ducks for the disciplined and experienced Luftwaffe pilots.

On the first day of Barbarossa, for example, Werner Mölders shot down an I-153 and two SB-2 bombers. On 30 June he surpassed von Richthofen's WWI record of 80, and on 15 July he became the first pilot in history to reach 100 victories. By that time Mölders held the rank of Oberst, or colonel. He was awarded the knight's cross with oak leaves and diamonds and ordered to stop flying in combat, but he ignored the order and added several more kills to his record.

The German High Command thought it would be impossible for the

Soviets to sustain their losses, and Hitler concurred. Russia was defeated, he declared; Barbarossa was a triumph.

But the Führer's euphoria was premature. Josef Stalin found a way to stem the tide—fortunately for him, a few able commanders had avoided his purges. One of them was General Georgi K. Zhukov, who Stalin put him in charge of the western front. Another was Colonel General Ivan S. Konev, assigned to lead the Red Army in the north. And to command the Soviet forces in the south, Stalin appointed General Semyon K. Timoshenko.

The generals began to refit and reorganize the army. Officers were ordered to stay behind the troops in the field, and to shoot any soldier who refused to fight. A scorched earth policy was employed. The Russian forces continued to retreat, but now they inflicted heavy losses on the Germans.

For that reason, the Wehrmacht did not move as rapidly as originally planned. Although Minsk and Smolensk were captured by summer's end, a siege of Leningrad was not begun until 15 September. And Kiev was not captured until a week later.

Meanwhile Russian factories, far from the battle zones, stepped up production. They poured out equipment, ammunition, and supplies, and rushed the materiel to the beleaguered Red forces. Nearly a million more Soviet youth were conscripted and pressed into service.

The German generals then became aware of another threat. They knew that soon the autumn rains would turn the roads and fields into seas of mud. And not long after that, all of Russia would be seized in winter's icy grip.

Hitler realized it as well. But again he would not listen to his commanders, who wanted to halt the attack until spring. Instead he ordered an all-out drive on Moscow.

29.

Following Hitler's orders, the Wehrmacht continued to drive eastward. But the Russian winter was as formidable an enemy as the Red army. With temperatures falling to minus 20 degrees Celsius, firearms and other equipment froze and became useless. Men froze as well. Most German soldiers were still wearing summer uniforms because they had not been sent winter gear—it was an unforgivable blunder. Many died from the cold, and many more from pneumonia and other diseases. The attack on Moscow bogged down, and the army was forced to wait for conditions to improve before resuming the offensive. Hitler was irate, but even he realized there was no other option.

The Luftwaffe, however, went on battling the Soviet Air Force. Most of the Bf-109s in combat against the Russians were the latest version, the Friderich, and reports extolled the fighter's performance. The German aircraft was faster and more heavily armed than the enemy's Ratas, Yaks, and MiGs, and in dogfights it was almost always victorious.

Especially gratifying to Messerschmitt were the exploits of pilots who were flying the Bf-109. Mölders and Galland were two of his favorites, though the men were nothing alike. Mölders was always impeccably dressed in a hand-tailored gray-blue uniform, while Galland continued to wear non-regulation gear and was never without a cigar. In fact, Galland's fighter was the only Bf-109 with an ashtray built into the cockpit.

Messerschmitt's troubles with Erhard Milch did not let up. In September the Air Ministry issued another of its inexplicable orders: the Me-262 must now be built as a reconnaissance aircraft. It was to be equipped with cameras, and should have greater range. And it was to carry no armament.

Messerschmitt found this baffling. German Intelligence had learned the British had successfully flown a jet, the Gloster Meteor, only a few weeks earlier. Thus the race between the two sides to produce jets for combat operations was at high pitch. And now Milch wanted him to concentrate on building an Me-262 for reconnaissance? Incredible.

Dutifully, Messerschmitt began the modifications. Because he still had no reliable jet engines, he suggested powering the aircraft with Walter rocket engines or Schmidt-Argus pulse jets. The RLM turned down the idea.

But at last the Junkers 004 turbojets arrived, and tests on them were begun. To Messerschmitt's relief, early results were encouraging. Perhaps he could soon have the Me-262 flight-tested with proper engines.

Then in another reversal, the RLM again pressed the development of long range bombers. Messerschmitt, Focke-Wulf, and Junkers were ordered to produce them; Heinkel had already test-flown its He-177. There were several reasons for the change. One was the ability of the

RAF to raid targets deep in Germany with their Lancasters and Halifaxes. The big British bombers were doing extensive damage to German cities and killing thousands of civilians, and with its thin homeland defenses the Luftwaffe was unable to stop them.

Another reason was the belief that sooner or later the United States would enter the war. German spies reported that the USAAF was testing its own long-range bombers, such as the Boeing B-17 and the Consolidated B-24. And also, the leaders' shortsightedness was taking a toll on the Wehrmacht's campaigns. In the Battle of Britain and now the fighting in Russia, far-flung enemy factories could go on producing war materiel with impunity.

Hitler berated Göring for failing to equip the Luftwaffe with heavy bombers. The Reichsmarschal in turn blamed Milch, who said the mistake was due to the incompetence of Udet. In fact, the problem with Udet was much more severe. The Technical Department of the RLM, which he headed, was a haven for irresponsible bureaucrats. Its staff had swollen to more than 4,000 planners and engineers, and they produced little more than make-work. Göring knew it, and so did Milch.

Allegations notwithstanding, the need for heavy bombers was deemed critical. At Augsburg, the Me-264 project had long been put aside, yet now it was to be given high priority.

Furthermore, the Air Ministry wanted the bomber to be capable of flying much greater distances than to Britain or Russia. The Me-264 should be able to carry a large load of bombs across the Atlantic and drop them on New York! The theory was that nothing would be more harmful to American morale than seeing Manhattan's tall buildings blasted to bits and many of its citizens killed. People in the U.S. would lose all enthusiasm for involvement in the conflict.

Cooler heads in Germany realized this was nonsense. If the Luftwaffe did succeed in bombing New York, Americans would be outraged. Their desire to defeat Germany would be greatly increased, not lessened.

Nevertheless, Messerschmitt pressed ahead. His plan called for the bomber to have a wingspan of 35 meters, and carry a bomb load of 1,798 kg. It would be manned by a crew of ten, and armed with eight machine guns. Four Junkers Jumo V-12 engines would provide 1340 hp each. In order for the aircraft to reach New York and return, the tanks would hold 4,329 gallons of fuel. Unofficially, the Me-264 was known as the Amerika Bomber.

Messerschmitt was also ordered to develop a huge glider for use as a transport. The aircraft was designated the Me-321 and called the Gigant. It would be big enough to carry a self-propelled assault gun plus the gun crew and a towing vehicle, as well as a battle tank and crew. The glider would be towed by four Ju-52s connected to it by a special harness.

After many setbacks, prototypes of both aircraft were built and test-flown, but the Me-264 was never put into service. And though 200 of the gliders were produced, they did not become operational, either. A powered version of the Gigant would later be built, and used to fly supplies and ordnance across the Mediterranean to the Afrika Korps.

Another project at the Augsburg factory was the Me-209 fighter. Thus far it had not tested well, and Milch wanted to kill the project. But for the moment it stayed alive.

Messerschmitt was also working on another new fighter, designated the Me-309. Plans called for it to be faster and more maneuverable than the Bf-109, and capable of performing at much higher altitudes. Willy felt there was good reason for him to push the project: the Fw-190 had at last flown in combat. Four of the new German fighters had engaged a flight of eight Spitfires over the Channel, and two of the enemy were shot down. The Fw-190s returned to their base in France without a loss.

That news also inspired Willy to step up his attempts to build successful prototypes of the Me-262. But constant interference by the Air Ministry made the work especially difficult, and Messerschmitt often lost his temper. Only Lilly could soothe him, and even she sometimes failed to restrain him from erupting at Milch and the fools in the RLM. He was most troubled by the order to build the Me-262 strictly as a reconnaissance aircraft. This, while German Intelligence was reporting that both the British and the Americans were rushing to produce operational jet fighters!

Yet Messerschmitt and his engineers modified their plans. Instead of guns in the nose, the aircraft would carry both still and motion-picture cameras. It would be stripped of armor, and additional fuel tanks would be installed to increase its range.

At the same time, Willy carried on a parallel project in secret. He planned a version of the jet he believed was the only correct one: the

Me-262 as a heavily armed pure fighter.

But first he had to produce a prototype of the aircraft that could be measured in actual flight tests.

30.

While working on the Me-262 prototype, the designers ran into a familiar stumbling block. Again the trouble lay with the engines, as the new Junkers 004 turbojets turned out to be another disappointment. Although at first they bench-tested well, the engines would run only a short time before quitting. And once they cut out, they could not be restarted.

The reason, Junkers engineers ascertained, lay with the materials used in their construction. Because of critical shortages of durable, heat-resistant metals such as cobalt, nickel and chromium, alloys of softer metals had been substituted. When great heat was generated in the combustion chambers, the alloys melted.

Efforts were made to repair the engines, but the damage was too extensive. Therefore orders were sent to Junkers for new engines, built of sturdier materials. This meant more delays.

Meanwhile the RLM was urging further development of the Me-163, the rocket-powered Komet. Messerschmitt remained ambivalent about the prospects of such a machine, because of the volatility of the fuel. Many of his designers agreed with him, referring to the 163 as "the flying firecracker."

Despite their doubts, the Messerschmitt firm built several prototypes and sent them to Peenemünde, where they were fitted with the Walter HWK R II-203B motor for flight testing. Because the aircraft's fuel supply would enable it to remain airborne for no more than a few minutes, one of the prototypes was towed to an altitude of 4,000 meters by a Me-110. The tow line was then cast off and the rocket motor fired.

Piloted by Heini Ditmar, the Komet reached a speed of 1100 kph. But as soon as its fuel was exhausted, the aircraft went into a steep dive. Ditmar was unable to recover until he was only a short distance from the earth. The RLM ordered design changes.

Messerschmitt attempted to have work on the Me-163 given a lower priority, yet his requests to the Air Ministry were denied. He also asked Ernst Udet for help, but his sometime friend no longer had much influence. In fact, Udet was being deliberately bypassed in the making of decisions. His enemies in the RLM had seen to it that he was vilified for failures to procure the heavy bombers needed by the Luftwaffe, and labeled him an inept bungler. His overstaffed department was looked upon with contempt.

Propaganda Minister Josef Goebbels was careful to keep all this from becoming public, because he felt it important that Udet remain a hero in the eyes of the people. But to those who knew him well, it was obvious that Udet was deeply depressed. A talented artist, he had for years drawn caricatures and sent them to his friends. In the drawings he poked fun at high-ranking officials, including Milch and Göring. Significantly, one of his cartoons showed Udet himself chained to a desk while dreaming of flying over the clouds and happily smoking a cigar. But these days he no longer drew them.

Nor did he do much of anything else. He spent very little time at his office, and was more often holed up in his Berlin apartment. He began drinking heavily, and using drugs.

Once admired for his unfailing good cheer and his boundless energy, Udet became increasingly morose. On 17 November 1941 he telephoned his mistress. He told her he'd taken too much abuse from people he did not respect, and that he'd stand for no more of their lies. Then he put the muzzle of his old 9mm Luger pistol into his mouth and pulled the trigger.

When his body was discovered, it was surrounded by empty cognac bottles. In his safe was a letter addressed to Göring, in which Udet poured out vitriolic comments about Milch, blaming the Air Minister for betraying him.

Goebbels handled the incident deftly. Newspapers and radio reports announced that the brave General Ernst Udet had died in a plane crash while testing a new design, but the pilot's friends soon learned the truth. Preparations were made for a state funeral, and Willy Messerschmitt planned to attend. So did Werner Mölders.

As the Luftwaffe's leading ace, Mölders' score stood at 115 confirmed kills, and his exploits were closely followed in Germany. He was one of only twelve men to hold the Knight's Cross with Oak Leaves, Swords and Diamonds.

Like many of his fellow airmen, Mölders revered Ernst Udet. To attend the funeral he arranged to fly from the Crimea to Germany as a passenger in an He-111 bomber. Only Mölders and the pilot were aboard for the long trip, and they encountered bad weather most of the way. They were relieved when at last they reached Breslau and began descending through the clouds.

Suddenly they were buffeted by a heavy rainstorm and violent wind gusts. They were short of fuel, and the pilot felt he had no choice but to attempt a landing. He throttled back and dropped gear and flaps, but his final approach was blind. Far short of the runway the bomber hit telephone wires and crashed. Mölders and the pilot were killed.

Germans everywhere grieved, and Willy Messerschmitt was especially affected. In less than a week, he'd lost two friends. Both Mölders and Udet had played important roles in his professional career, and both had meant much to him personally. With a heavy heart, he went to their funerals.

And the momentous events of 1941 did not end there. The following month a military operation once again changed the course of history. On 7 December, Japan conducted an attack on the United States Naval Base at Pearl Harbor. The conflict that had begun with the invasion of Poland was now truly a World War.

31.

News reports by both the BBC and German media told the same story: America had suffered heavy losses in the raid. A task force of the Imperial Japanese Navy had approached Hawaii at dawn and launched torpedo bombers, dive bombers and fighters from its carriers. The aircraft sank twelve US warships, including four battleships, three cruisers and two destroyers. Some 200 planes were destroyed, and almost 3,000 Americans died.

The attack had been planned by Commander of the Combined Fleet Admiral Isoroku Yamamoto, and was carried out by task force commander Admiral Chuichi Nagumo. Japanese losses were light; only a handful of their airplanes were shot down.

The reaction in Germany was jubilation. Before this, only Italy had provided the Nazis with military support, and lately even this support had become ineffectual.

Now in sharp contrast, Japan had shown the world that she was a potent force. With one blow she'd virtually wiped out the U.S. naval forces in the Pacific. It would be impossible, German radio broadcasts proclaimed, for the weak Americans and the feeble British and Australians to stop her. Soon all of Asia would be under Japanese control.

In the U.S., President Franklin Roosevelt called 7 December 1941 "a day that will live in infamy," and the United States declared war on Japan. Germany then declared war on the U.S.

That news was also heartening to German audiences. America, they were told, could not possibly wage war on both Japan and Germany at the same time. Tied down in the Pacific, and with her navy in tatters, the U.S. would no longer be a threat to Germany.

Now it would be open season on the American freighters and tankers that were hauling desperately needed fuel and supplies to Britain. Hundreds of German U-boats were prowling the North Atlantic seas, and the obsolete American naval vessels escorting the convoys would provide little protection. The wolf packs would devour the merchant ships and the old Navy tubs as well.

Hitler and his commanders had been aware of Japan's intentions long before the attack took place. For years prior to the raid, Germany had sent technical advisers to Japan, many of them transported by U-boat.

Professor Messerschmitt knew several aeronautical engineers who went to Japan during that time. Torpedo experts were also sent, and no one knew more about such weapons than the specialists in Germany's Kriegsmarine. In fact, other nations lagged behind in the development of torpedoes. The U.S. Navy, for example, was plagued by torpedoes that inexplicably turned off course, or if they did strike home did not explode. Some even turned around and hit the submarine that had fired them.

But German torpedoes were rarely defective. And following their Axis partners' advice, the Japanese built dependable ones as well. These were the Type 95 that accounted for most of the damage to U.S. ships at Pearl Harbor.

Another area in which the Germans contributed was the construction of bombs that could penetrate the decks of warships and explode deep inside the hulls. To accomplish this, the German ballistics experts recommended the use of modified 356mm and 381mm naval artillery shells. Loaded with at least 1,000 kilograms of explosives and fitted with fins to ensure accuracy, the bombs could pierce the armor of a battleship when dropped from an altitude of 3,000 meters.

Years earlier, the American General Billy Mitchell proved that bombers could sink a battleship. He also predicted that eventually the U.S. would go to war with Japan, and that the conflict would begin with a Japanese attack on Pearl Harbor. He was court-martialed and shortly afterward, resigned from the service.

Some U.S. military authorities, however, took Mitchell's views seriously. In 1932, Admiral Harry Yarnell conducted joint Army-Navy exercises in which aircraft from a naval task force attacked Pearl Harbor. Theoretically the bombers sank a number of ships before successfully making their escape. Despite this, the Joint Chiefs of Staff dismissed the maneuvers as having no basis in reality, and ridiculed the results. An actual assault would fail, they said, because U.S. battleships would quickly destroy the attackers. Ironically, Yarnell's feigned raid took place at dawn on a Sunday morning. The date was 7 December 1932.

Leaders of the Imperial Japanese Navy, on the other hand, took careful note of the U.S. exercises. And later they were interested in the assault by the British on the Italian fleet at Taranto, when the ancient, torpedo-carrying Fairey biplanes crippled Il Duce's navy. Afterward, Admiral Yamamoto sent delegates to Italy to study the operation and report on how its lessons could be applied to an attack on Pearl Harbor.

The success of the Japanese action inspired Adolf Hitler. He said in a speech that while Japan crushed all resistance in the Pacific, Germany would destroy the Communist hordes in the east. As always, the Third Reich would be victorious.

Once again, a few German leaders were not as optimistic. Willy Messerschmitt recalled what he'd learned about U.S. industrial capacity. The Americans had invented mass production, and their resources were virtually unlimited. There was also the fact that U.S. factories were far beyond the range of bombers. It might be possible for his Me-264 to reach New York, but sprawling plants in places like Detroit and Seattle could go on producing tanks and airplanes and other equipment while completely safe from attack.

But Messerschmitt had more immediate problems to deal with. He still had no idea when he might receive dependable turbojet engines, and until that time, little progress could be made on the Me-262. He and his designers continued to work on a number of other projects.

Then an old problem resurfaced. The ill-fated Me-210, the fighter-bomber originally slated to be the successor to the Me-110 destroyer, continued to bedevil the company. Although every test pilot who flew it said the 210 was poorly designed and not fit for service, Messerschmitt had produced hundreds of them and sent them to Luftwaffe units.

True to their reputation, the airplanes were trouble from the outset. Some underwent structural failure in the air, and a number of fatal accidents occurred. Finally Luftwaffe commanders refused to order their pilots to fly the airplane. Göring and Chief of Air Staff Jeschonnek heaped blame on Messerschmitt and called for his head.

Naturally, Erhard Milch was only too happy to oblige, and ordered Messerschmitt to report to RLM headquarters. Willy flew to Berlin and went to the huge brownstone building on Leipzigerstrasse.

After a perfunctory exchange of Heil Hitler greetings, Milch read off a long list of complaints concerning the troublesome aircraft. The Professor did not argue about the charges. He said he regretted the mistakes, and that he and his designers were already making changes in the aircraft to overcome its faults. Test results were encouraging.

Such efforts would not be necessary, Milch said. The Me-210 program was to be shut down at once. And Messerschmitt would no longer be managing director of the firm.

Willy was staggered. He was not to lead the company he'd built? That was unbelievable.

The decision had been made, Milch went on, because it was in the best interests of the Third Reich. The company was a valuable producer of aircraft, and the Professor was to continue with his design duties. But, even though he was the major stockholder in the firm, he would have no executive authority. The new managing director would be Theodor Croneiss. All this had been approved at the highest levels of the government.

Milch then handed Messerschmitt a document formalizing the changes. The meeting, he said, was over. Heil Hitler!

32.

Milch's decision to end production of the Me-210 was extremely heavy-handed. The production line was shut down, and hundreds of skilled workers lost their jobs. The cost to the government in wasted materials and man-hours was enormous. The company suffered as well, financially and in prestige, resulting in a loss of 30 million Reichsmarks. No doubt Messerschmitt's rivals in the aircraft industry enjoyed a fair amount of schadenfreude.

Some men would have slunk away in disgrace, but not Willy Messerschmitt. Instead, he simply went on with his design work, while the financial and operating decisions were made by two of the company's executives, Friedrich Seiler and Kakan Kokothaki. Messerschmitt gave them input via a steady stream of memos. Theo Croneiss played almost no part in the management of the company, and rarely went to the Augsburg plant. Prior to his appointment as managing director, he had been chairman of the stockholders' committee, a position he continued to hold.

A few weeks later another surprising event took place, again involving the Me-210. After Milch had forced the company to stop production, flight tests were conducted. With an extended fuselage and powered by the new DB-603 engines, the aircraft performed remarkably well.

After reviewing the tests, the RLM reversed itself and ordered the fighter-bomber to be put into full production. To avoid association with the Me-210, the new version would be designated the Me-410. However, this did not bring any change to Messerschmitt's diminished authority.

Willy could only shake his head. He decided that as soon as he could find dependable turbojets, he would put the Me-262 through flight tests as well.

At the beginning of March, 1942, the long-awaited BMW P3302 engines finally arrived at Messerschmitt AG. But just as with the Jumos, the big BMW axial flow turbojets failed to deliver acceptable thrust. They also frequently quit because of the extreme internal temperatures. BMW's top engineers came from Munich to work on the engines, and practically lived in the factory. It took them weeks to get the turbojets operating with any degree of dependability.

Hence it was not until the end of March that Messerschmitt, Woldemar Voigt, and the other members of the design team were ready to undertake the next flight test. This would be the first time the aircraft would fly with jet power, and the men were understandably apprehensive.

After one more bench test, the engines were fitted under the wings of the aircraft. They were rated to provide just over 700 kg of thrust, but the engineers feared they might not perform as promised. So as a precaution, the Jumo piston engine was left in the nose, resulting in a machine with a very odd appearance.

As in the first test flight, Flug Kapitan Fritz Wendel would be at the controls. On the evening of 25 March, the Me-262 V-1 was towed out to the end of the grass runway at Augsburg. Wendel and the designers and engineers made a thorough ground inspection, and mechanics used a gasoline-powered external motor to start the jet engines. Protective wire screens were placed over the air intakes.

Next, the mechanics hand-propped the Jumo. When it caught, Wendel ran it up and checked the magnetos. Finally he stood on the brakes and slowly and carefully eased in power to all three engines. A gradual increase was important in a piston engine, but doubly so with turbojets. Rapidly advancing the throttle of a jet would be sure to cause a failure.

Satisfied that the engines were running properly, Wendel released the brakes and the V-1 began moving. At takeoff the Jumo would provide 730 hp, and together with the thrust of the turbojets, that should be more than adequate. The wind was at 20 kph, which might help as well.

But to Wendel's surprise, the airplane did not accelerate as rapidly as he would have liked. Instead it seemed to lumber along the grass strip. The airspeed indicator slowly crept past 100 kph, and not until he was more than halfway down the runway did he experience any feeling of lightness.

If he wanted to shut down, now was the time; seconds later it would be too late. He decided to keep going. When a short distance from the airfield boundary he pulled back the stick, and the V-1 lifted off. It cleared the fence by one meter.

When he retracted the gear the airplane picked up speed, but not as much as it should have. Acutely aware of the V-1's sluggishness, Wendel maintained a gradual rate of climb and flew straight ahead, the Jumo running at 2600 rpm. The instruments indicated the turbojets were providing maximum thrust, though his instincts told him otherwise. The power-to-weight ratio was clearly inadequate.

Compounding the problem, he surmised, was the V-1's wing. It had been designed with a very thin chord to help the airplane reach high speeds, but at the moment there was a much greater need for lift. So he'd wait until he'd reached an altitude of 400 meters before reducing the Jumo's rpms and adjusting the fuel mixture and propeller pitch.

Without warning, the right-hand turbojet flamed out. The airplane lurched and dropped the wing on that side, and Wendel used aileron to correct. Then the turbojet on the left also failed. Again there was a lurch, and again he tried to correct. But the V-1 had undergone an extreme change in flight characteristics. The nose fell sharply, and he knew at once why that was happening: the turbojets had become two dead weights beneath the wings. The airplane headed for the earth at a 60-degree angle.

There was no elevator trim control on the V-1. Regaining a level attitude now could only be achieved by hauling back on the stick. He reduced power on the Jumo and pulled the stick hard with both hands. It wouldn't budge.

Bracing his feet against the cockpit floor he tried again. The effort took every ounce of his strength, but gradually the stick came back and the aircraft's nose lifted toward the horizon. The V-1 continued to sink, albeit in a flat attitude.

Wendel shoved the throttle of the piston engine wide open, and with full power the aircraft began flying almost level. But by now it was only about 50 meters above the field, which made use of the ejection seat impractical; before his parachute opened, he'd hit the earth.

Struggling to hold what little altitude he had, he realized that if the Jumo were to fail there would be no way he could avoid a crash. He had to return to the runway. Trying to land downwind was out of the question; the V-1 was too heavy to attempt it. He'd have to go back to the threshold.

It seemed to take forever to reach the point where he could turn final. When at last he got there he banked again until he could line up on the runway, heading into the wind. He'd have to reduce speed to land, but cutting the power would cause the airplane to drop like a rock. At least he could add drag by lowering the gear, and that would slow him down a little. He pressed the handle, and a moment later the lights on the panel glowed green; the wheels were down and locked.

Still too fast. He knew the technique for landing a hot airplane was to get its nose up and set it down on the mains. So he closed the throttle farther and pulled the stick all the way back, hoping the slats on the leading edges of the wings would add sufficient lift as the airplane settled. But the V-1 refused to cooperate.

Now the runway was rushing up to meet him, and the controls had become virtually useless. He switched off the ignition and closed the fuel cock, and crossed his arms over his face.

The airplane hit hard. As it skidded down the runway the gear was ripped away, and the turbojets dug into the turf, producing shrieks and groans in the airframe. The propellor bent and the Jumo's crankshaft broke, stopping the engine. There was a danger of the V-1 flipping over onto its back, which would crush Wendel like a bug. But eventually the airplane slid to a halt.

Badly bruised, Wendel unfastened his safety harness, opened the canopy, and climbed out of the cockpit. He waited quietly for the ground crew to reach the wreck.

33.

The reaction from the Air Ministry was predictable. It decreed that in light of the crash of the V-1, Messerschmitt was to curtail the program. Construction would be limited to Prototypes V-I through V-5. Further work on the Me-262 would be authorized only if tests of turbojet engines were successful.

To Messerschmitt, this was ridiculous. Crashes of innovative new aircraft were common. Every company experienced them; accidents were virtually unavoidable. The Luftwaffe needed new and better weapons if it was to prevail against the enemy, and here the RLM was throwing up obstacles. Willy had few illusions about who was behind such an asinine directive.

He then learned that Junkers was developing new engines. Otto Mader, the head of Junkers' research laboratory, claimed the company's improved 004 turbojets were rugged and dependable. The metals used in them were much more durable and would not break down under high temperatures.

Messerschmitt was not convinced, yet he felt he had to take Mader at his word. He ordered the Junkers turbojets, and continued to work on his many other projects at the same hectic pace. The RLM was pressing him to speed up production of the Me-410, and he was also busy refining the intended successor to the Bf-109. The Air Ministry considered those projects more important than work on the Me-262, which was an attitude shared by the Luftwaffe commanders. The jet had shown little promise so far, and few officers, including Reichsmarschal Göring and Chief of Air Staff Jeschonnek, actually believed it had much of a future.

Messerschmitt AG was now producing 250 Bf-109s per month at its Regensburg factory, but the design was more than six years old. Clearly new models were needed. The point was emphasized when Göring made one of his periodic visits to Augsburg. He was flown to the company's field in a Ju-52, accompanied by three of his staff officers and his chief of Intelligence, Colonel "Beppo" Schmid. Heavier than ever, the Reichsmarschal wore one of his fancy light blue uniforms, his feet encased in gleaming black boots.

He spent a long time examining the latest variant of the Bf-109, the Gustav. Like the Friderich, the fighter had the DB-601 engine, but the modified engine would now provide 1475 hp. And to improve high-altitude performance, it was fitted with nitrous oxide injection. The Gustav also had a pressurized cockpit, as well as a stronger airframe and a sturdier undercarriage.

Another project that got the Luftwaffe commander's attention was the Me-410, the twin-engine schnellbomber that was back in production. It was being produced as a destroyer as well, and that version would succeed the Me-110.

Inspecting these and other projects took up most of the Reichsmarschal's time, and he showed little interest in the Me-262. As far as he was concerned, the jet was not to be taken seriously, certainly not any more so than the Me-163, the rocket-powered Komet. In his view, fast, piston-engine fighters and bombers were what the Luftwaffe needed, not experimental contraptions.

The Reichsmarchal also tweaked his host by remarking about the success that pilots were having with the Focke-Wulf 190. It was a great fighter, he said, and its record in combat was proving it. He questioned whether the Bf-109G could keep pace, and Messerschmitt assured him it would. He said the reason the RLM had urged development of the Gustav, was because the Fw-190 did not perform well at altitudes above 5,000 meters. And in dogfights with Spitfires, that was a serious disadvantage. The Bf-109G, on the other hand, would hold its own at any altitude. Göring shrugged off the remarks.

Later the two men talked about the war in Russia. The Wehrmacht was sure to defeat the Soviets at Kharkov, Göring said, and would soon take Sevastopol. As for the Luftwaffe, combat with the Russians was like shooting pigeons. Fighter pilots Otto Kittel, Walter Nowotny and Heinrich Ehrler, to name but a few, were rapidly running up their scores. Willy replied that he too was happy to see such dominance over the enemy in the air. Especially because all three of the men mentioned by the Reichsmarshal were flying the Bf109F, the Friderich. Göring ignored that comment as well.

In his opinion, the Reichsmarschal said, the Russians could not hold out much longer. They were terrible soldiers, and their pilots were worse. Just as the Führer had said, Germans were a far superior race. Messerschmitt was relieved when Göring and his officers left for the trip back to Berlin.

As more time went by, the Junkers engines still had not arrived. So except for minor alterations, no further work on the Me-262 could be undertaken. Meanwhile, a number of portentous events took place in other parts of the world.

On 18 April, Mitchell bombers, launched from the U.S. Navy aircraft carrier Hornet, attacked Tokyo and other cities in Japan. The raiders were led by Colonel James H. Doolittle. This was the first strike on the Japanese homeland, and though Goebbels' Propaganda Ministry made no mention of it, Germans learned of the raid by listening to the BBC. Tuning into the broadcasts from Britain was against the law, but many civilians and military personnel did it anyway.

The next event was much more significant. Over four days in early June, a great sea battle at Midway Island pitted U.S. forces against a fleet of the Imperial Japanese Navy. It was the first major naval engagement in history to be conducted by warplanes rather than surface ships. Unlike the Doolittle raid, there was no way the news of the battle could be suppressed, but interpretations by the various media were markedly dissimilar.

According to the BBC, American dive bombers had inflicted a mortal blow on the Imperial Navy. Four Japanese aircraft carriers were sunk, while the U.S. lost only one. Commentators said it would be difficult, if not impossible, for Japan's navy to recover from a defeat of that magnitude.

In Germany, the Propaganda Ministry described the action as a victory by the Japanese. Newspaper and radio accounts said the Imperial Navy had completely outfought the enemy, and only a few badly damaged U.S. warships had survived. Sentient people were accustomed to Goebbels' twisting of facts, and concluded that his description of the battle was bogus.

The implications were clear. Only six months after the Japanese triumph at Pearl Harbor, the tide had turned in the Pacific. Although the Japanese army had won a number of victories on land, the reigning sea power in that theater of war was now the United States Navy. The situation for Japan would not improve, but only grow worse.

Some high-ranking Wehrmacht officers began to have doubts about the war. By now Britain, Free France, the Soviet Union, China, and the United States were all allied against the Axis powers. Germany, the officers said, was fighting on too many fronts. The campaign in Russia was meeting stiffer resistance, and the Afrika Korps was losing its campaign.

There were also increasing acts of rebellion in areas that were under Nazi occupation. In Prague, SS General Reinhard Heydrich was injured when a bomb, set off by partisans, exploded under his car. He was taken to a hospital where he died from septicemia. In retaliation, Himmler's SS forces arrested and shot more than 13,000 people. Heydrich was given a state funeral attended by Adolf Hitler.

At this point it was no longer possible to deny Germany's vulnerability to air raids. Under the new Chief of Bomber Command, Air Marshal Arthur "Bomber" Harris, the RAF was attacking many targets in the fatherland. On the night of 30 May, the first thousand-bomber raid was launched against Cologne. Tons of explosives were dropped, causing the deaths of more than 1,200 people and the destruction of 250 factories and 18,400 houses.

The problem, according to those German commanders bold enough to speak out, was that most of the Luftwaffe's aircraft were in offensive action, rather than defensive. General Galland said Germany needed at least three times as many fighters to combat the RAF bombers, but repeated requests for them were denied. Hitler refused to face reality.

Willy Messerschmitt would not allow such thoughts to erode his confidence. So the RLM was making shortsighted decisions regarding the Me-262? He would prove them wrong. Besides, whether or not pigheaded Nazi officials could grasp its importance, a new development was taking place. German Intelligence reported that the USAAF was preparing to set up operations in England. To Messerschmitt, that made the need for a superior interceptor still more critical.

It was not until the beginning of July that the new Junkers Jumo 004A turbojets were at last delivered to the plant at Augsburg. Engineers Degel and Helmschrott wasted no time in setting them up for tests, and the RLM was advised that if all went well, the next flight of the Me-262 would soon take place. After a week of rigorous bench testing, Degel reported that the engines were performing satisfactorily. Now they would be put to the ultimate test, powering a prototype in the air.

Willy Messerschmitt knew very well how much was at stake. This would be the first time the aircraft had flown under pure jet power. There would be no piston engine as a backup, no reserve should the turbojets fail. If the test ended in another crash, it could mark the end of the program.

And it could also be the end of his best test pilot, Flug Kapitan Fritz Wendel.

34.

The Jumo 004A turbojets were larger and heavier than the BMW engines, and new nacelles had to be built to accommodate them. The Me-262V3 prototype was modified to carry the nacelles, and its rear fuel tank was moved farther aft to compensate for the shift in the center of gravity. When the nacelles were ready, Messerschmitt supervised as Degel, Helmschrott, Voigt and Schomerus installed the engines. Once in place, they again ran well.

The test would take place at the nearby Leipheim Airfield. The runway there was longer and paved in concrete, which would provide a better chance for a trouble-free takeoff and landing. Police closed the roads, and the aircraft was transported to Leipheim on a flatbed truck.

On the morning of 8 July 1942, the skies over southern Germany were hazy and the winds light as the V-3 was rolled onto the taxiway. The airplane had been painted in a mottled blue scheme on its upper surfaces and plain light blue on the underside, with straight black crosses on the fuselage and wings and a black swastika on the vertical stabilizer.

Fritz Wendel and the designers and engineers undertook a thorough ground check of the aircraft. They had made a similar inspection before the V-3 left Augsburg, but now they did it all over again. Wendel looked at every inch of the airplane with a critical eye. Nothing seemed amiss.

The Flug Kapitan was calm and dispassionate as always. He wore casual clothing, with no helmet. When the inspection was completed, he climbed into the cockpit and fastened his harness. He switched on the fuel pumps, applied the brakes, and mechanics used a portable four-stroke motor to start the turbojets. Screens were placed over the intakes.

Wendel slowly advanced the throttles, running the engines up to 8,000 rpm. To compensate for their added weight, he adjusted the trim to make the aircraft less nose heavy. As he sat there, his gaze flicked back and forth over the instrument panel. Except for gauges showing tailpipe gas temperature and fuel injection pressure, and the turbojets' slightly different tachometers and fuel gauges, the instruments were not much different from those in piston airplanes. Altimeter, airspeed indicator, rate-of-climb, artificial horizon, turn-and-bank, radio, compass, all were more or less standard.

So was the cockpit layout. The throttle, flaps, and landing gear controls were on the left side, along with indicators showing the position of the landing gear legs. The levers for activating the newly installed elevator and rudder trim mechanisms were on that side as well, as were the fuel shutoff and selector valves, and the valve that regulated the flow of oxygen for breathing.

On the right side were the canopy release lever and the master switch, along with a bank of individual switches for the battery, fuel pumps, radio, pitot heat, windshield heat, and the generator for each engine. There was also a dial for earphone volume, and a lever for the manifold drains.

In some ways the 262's flight controls were simpler than those in most aircraft, because in a jet the pilot would not have to adjust propeller pitch or fuel mixture. The stick felt comfortable in Wendel's right hand, and his feet rested easily on the rudder pedals. Thanks to the sloping nose, forward visibility would be excellent, once the tail was raised.

The tailpipe gas temperature was normal, but Wendel had to be thinking about his last experience in an Me-262 prototype, and about how capricious turbojet engines could be when hot. No radial or inline power plant he'd ever known had failed so abruptly and so often as these. The jets would not give a warning, either. They didn't slowly lose power or sputter roughly before quitting, they just flamed out. Would the Junkers turbos perform faithfully today, or would they, too, fail at the worst possible moment?

That would likely mean a complete loss of the airplane, and in an emergency he might not be able to get out in time. But he wasn't paid to worry about his personal safety. He was a test pilot, which meant he put his life on the line each time he stepped into a new, untried aircraft. He checked the gauges once more, released the brakes, and with the engines at full power began his takeoff roll.

It started well enough, but then to his surprise he encountered the same difficulty he'd had on the grass at Augsburg. As the V-3 was moving down the runway it was still in a three-point stance. There was insufficient airflow over the elevators, and as a result he was unable to raise the tail. Thus he had no forward visibility, and at the rate he was moving, he'd never have enough speed for takeoff.

As he kept on, the problem persisted. There was a possible solution, though it would risk setting the aircraft onto its nose. He tapped the brakes, and to his relief, the tail unstuck. As the fuselage came level he could see ahead.

Now, however, he'd once again used up much of the runway. Beyond the end of the pavement were storage buildings and a parked truck. Hit those with full fuel tanks and the airplane would become a ball of fire.

The airspeed indicator read 200 kph and both engines were running strongly. There were only a few meters of concrete left as he gently pulled back the stick. At that point he still wasn't sure whether the aircraft would lift off.

But it did. He retracted the gear and the V-3 climbed out smoothly. At first the rate of climb was not remarkable, but once he began to gain altitude, the jet accelerated more rapidly. The experience was different from anything he'd known in a piston aircraft. Even though he was holding it at a steep upward angle, the Me-262 continued to increase speed.

And of course there was no tendency to veer, because turbojets did not produce a torque effect. He was aware, however, that if they failed this time, there was no piston engine in the nose that would enable him to land safely. Abruptly the altimeter showed him at two thousand meters, then three, then four. He leveled off, marveling at the aircraft's performance. The speed! Eight hundred kph indicated, with no effort. It was breathtaking.

He was wary of overtaxing the engines, so even though the airplane was still accelerating, he eased the power back a bit. He also wanted to learn how the 262 would handle at this airspeed, which turned out to be another revelation. Gently he banked left, then right, then left again more steeply, bringing the airplane around in a 180-degree turn. Now another steep climb, followed by a shallow dive. Nose up again, repeat the maneuvers.

Wendel was captivated. The jet was stable and light on the controls, and remarkably easy to fly. He wished he could put it through more rigorous moves, but he'd be a fool to press his luck.

A glance at his watch told him it was time to land. He'd been in the air for twelve minutes, but it seemed more like twelve seconds. Regretfully, he came back to the airfield, and gradually reduced power as he flew a long downwind leg.

After turning into the wind, he dropped the gear and lowered the flaps. Still cautious, he decided to make a wheel landing rather than try for a three-pointer. With the ASI showing 175 kph, the airplane touched down. He let it go on with its landing roll for some distance, not applying the brakes until it was almost at a stop. Then he slowly taxied to the ramp.

When he opened the canopy and climbed out, he saw grins on the faces of the observers. Messerschmitt and the others surrounded him, eager to shake his hand. And for once, Wendel grinned widely himself.

When he returned to the design center, he wrote one of his extensively detailed reports. In addition to its value to the designers and engineers, the account would be of great help to pilots who would follow him in flying the Me-262. He covered everything from preflight inspection and taxiing to handling the aircraft in the air. He addressed the harmony of the flight controls, the airplane's stability characteristics, and the individual components. Special attention was paid to the principle of treating the turbojets gently and with great respect.

In summary he wrote, "My jet engines ran like clockwork. It was a pure pleasure to fly this new machine. In fact rarely have I been so enthusiastic about a first flight with a new aircraft as I was with the Me-262."

35.

If Professor Messerschmitt was expecting praise from the Air Ministry for the Me-262's first successful flight under pure jet power, he was mistaken. Instead, the RLM simply authorized additional flights at the Rechlin Test Center.

Over the following weeks a test pilot at Rechlin, Heinrich Beauvais, made six flights in the V-3 with varying results. Unlike the coolly deliberate Fritz Wendel, Beauvais was rash and impetuous. When making his seventh flight, he crashed the airplane on takeoff. He sustained only slight injuries, but the jet was badly damaged. Beauvais attributed the accident to warm air temperatures preventing the engines from delivering full thrust. Neither the Junkers nor the Messerschmitt engineers thought that plausible, but the RLM accepted the pilot's explanation.

For the Messerschmitt team, the incident was yet another setback. The V-3 could be repaired, but it would take time, and none of the other prototypes were in condition for testing.

Then politics intervened once again. In one of his surprise moves, the Führer appointed Albert Speer State Minister of Armament. Before this, the onetime architect had been the Minister of Munitions, and had long impressed Hitler with his organizational skills and his ability to get things done. Now he'd become the overlord of all armament production. When his promotion was announced, it was Erhard Milch's turn to experience sharp disappointment. Milch had wanted the job for himself.

Speer wasted no time in asserting his authority. He issued orders to increase efficiency in the manufacture of all war materials, including everything from tanks and armor plate to cannons and U-boats. And also, of course, aircraft.

Milch was nothing if not shrewd. While Göring sulked at this latest development, Milch promised Speer his complete loyalty and devotion. The two men formed a cordial working relationship, though they made a strange pair. Speer was tall and urbane, Milch short and feisty, but there was no question as to who was boss. So when Speer saw the potential in jet-powered warplanes and ordered greater efforts to build them, Milch hurried to obey the command. Milch was not about to favor only Messerschmitt, however. Heinkel and Arado were also encouraged to step up their jet programs.

Nevertheless, new life had been breathed into the Me-262 project. And in another turnabout, the RLM decreed that now the Me-262 was to be built as a fighter, and not for reconnaissance. Messerschmitt was pleased, of course, by the decision. The company was ordered to build five more trials aircraft, plus ten machines with certain modifications. These versions of the 262 were to have tricycle undercarriages, pressurized cockpits, FuG 25A radios, armor to protect both the pilot and the fuel tanks, and dive brakes. They would also carry the new 30mm MK 108 cannon in the nose and two machine guns in the wings.

As work on the airplanes was undertaken, the situation on many fronts continued to deteriorate. In North Africa, Feldmarschal Erwin Rommel's forces were seriously weakened by a lack of supplies and replacements. The RAF was destroying most of the German air transports that attempted to fly over the Mediterranean, with fewer than 30% of them getting through. Although the Afrika Korps had won nearly all of the earlier battles, combat losses and sickness had reduced their ranks to about 100,000 men. The British commander, General Bernard Montgomery, had more than twice that number.

In addition, the Americans had provided Montgomery with 300 Sherman tanks. Shells fired from their 75mm cannons could easily pierce German armor as well as the light tanks inherited from the Italian Army. And the Americans were preparing to invade Africa with a large force of their own.

Then in the second battle of El Alamein, Rommel suffered his worst defeat of the desert war. German losses were 13,000 killed, and 46,000 taken prisoner. A total of 450 German tanks were destroyed.

This was a disaster from which the Afrika Korps could not recover. Although the Luftwaffe had fought bravely and effectively, it too suffered from attrition. When the Germans lost an aircraft or a pilot, there was no way to replace them. And that fall the man considered by many to be the greatest fighter pilot of the war was killed.

He was Hans Joachim Marseilles, and at 22-years of age he was the Luftwaffe's youngest hauptmann, or captain. He was also a free spirit, hardly the sort considered ideal by the Nazi military. Thumbing his nose at discipline, he broke every rule. He wore his hair long, and was a fan of American jazz. Next to flying, his chief interest was girls. But he was without equal in the cockpit of a Bf-109.

After training he was assigned to 4/JG52, a fighter staffel in the geschwader commanded by Johannes "Macky" Steinhoff. During the Battle of Britain he shot down seven British aircraft.

"Marseilles was remarkably handsome," Steinhoff recalled. "He was a gifted pilot, but he was unreliable. He had girlfriends everywhere, and he was often too tired to be allowed to fly. His irresponsibility was the primary reason I sent him packing."

Marseilles was transferred by Steinhoff to 1/JG27 in North Africa, commanded by Major Eduard Neumann. Perhaps because there were no women around, Marseilles began to take combat seriously. Yet on one of his first sorties, he was shot down by an RAF Hurricane. He climbed out of the wreck with nothing injured but his pride, and the event seemed to motivate him.

From then on, Marseilles experimented with unorthodox aerobatic maneuvers. Using these techniques against pilots of the Desert Air Force, he achieved a rapid run of victories. After only a short time his score rose to 50, then to 75. Soon he had 101, and 26 of them were scored in a period of thirteen days. On 15 June 1942 he shot down four aircraft in three minutes.

It was said that his eyesight was so keen he could see his opponents before they saw him. As soon as he did, he would climb for the most advantageous position and attack. Diving on an enemy formation, he would knock down one or two airplanes before the pilots knew what was happening.

In a dogfight, one of his unconventional methods involved abruptly throttling back and lowering his flaps so that he could tighten his turns. As soon as he came around he'd shove the throttle open and the pilot who'd been chasing Marseilles would suddenly find the German behind him. Before the enemy could react, he'd be dead.

In order to protect their less agile fighter-bombers, the Allies sometimes formed a Lufberry circle, which meant that if an enemy attacked the tail of a fighter-bomber, he would be exposed to fire from the next airplane in line. At times it was an effective tactic, until the Desert Air Force ran into Marseilles.

His approach was to begin his attack from about 300 meters above, and one kilometer to the side. At full power he'd dive beneath the circle and then zoom up, standing the Bf-109 on its tail and firing a short burst into an enemy aircraft as it passed over his head. He almost always set the target afire, and often killed the pilot. The speed of his fighter would then carry him back up above the enemy formation, whereupon he'd again dive and repeat the attack.

Other Luftwaffe pilots tried to emulate Marseilles' methods, but they couldn't match his skills. They flew with him and fought in many battles alongside him, and had only admiration for the man who became known as "The Star of Africa." Despite his youth, he was awarded Germany's highest decoration, the Knight's Cross with Oak Leaves, Swords and Diamonds.

Of all his feats, those on a sweltering day in September 1942 were perhaps the most incredible. In three sorties, Marseilles shot down 17 Allied aircraft. Feldmarschal Albert Kesselring was visiting the squadron at the time, and as a pilot himself, was flabbergasted by Marseilles' success.

But the strain was taking a toll. Marseilles became uncharacteristically tense, and at night after a day of fighting he drank increasing amounts of brandy. He lost weight, chain-smoked cigarettes, and found it hard to sleep. The end came soon after. On a mission in which no enemy aircraft were sighted, Marseilles and his pilots headed home, and while still over enemy territory, a faulty pump in the engine of his Bf-109G caused an oil fire.

His comrades urged him to hold on, radioing that he would soon be over German-held terrain. But the fire grew more intense, and Marseilles replied that he couldn't stand the heat and the smoke any longer. He opened the canopy, rolled the 109 inverted, and bailed out. As he did, he was struck by the vertical stabilizer. His fellow pilots watched in horror as his limp body fell earthward.

There is no way to know whether the impact killed him, or if he was still alive during the long fall from 4,000 meters. He landed face down in the desert.

Hans-Joachim Marseilles' record shows a total of 382 sorties. In his short career he shot down 158 enemy aircraft, among them 101 P-40s, 30 Hurricanes, 16 Spitfires, and four bombers.

Willy Messerschmitt had known the young man and liked him. Marseilles had visited the factory at Augsburg, and the Professor admired him for his outstanding flying ability. Word of his death was depressing.

But more ominous than the bad news coming out of Africa were reports from Russia. Luftwaffe veterans returning from combat kept

Messerschmitt well informed, and the truth was very different from the lies put out by Propaganda Minister Goebbels.

36.

In Russia, another harsh winter began with snow falling heavily on the Caspian plains. The enemy had regrouped under Marshal Zhukov, and his forces stubbornly resisted the German invaders. Whereas the Afrika Korps was fighting eight divisions of the British army, on the Eastern front the Wehrmacht was engaging 250 divisions of Soviet troops.

Adolf Hitler then made one of his monumentally foolish decisions. Against the advice of his generals, he ordered Colonel General Friedrich von Paulus to lead the Sixth Army in an attack on Stalingrad. Von Paulus was to take the city, and after that, the Führer declared, the Germans would go on to capture the desperately needed oil fields in the Caucasus.

Members of the High Command thought the plan was both hazardous and unnecessary. German forces were already poised to seize the oil fields, and there seemed to be no reason to chance becoming bogged down at Stalingrad. But Hitler insisted, probably because of his hatred of the Soviet dictator for whom the city was named.

As the Sixth Army battled its way through the Red defenses, some of the fiercest hand-to-hand combat of the war took place. The Germans eventually occupied much of the city, but never fully succeeded in securing it. If they took a few streets during the day, the enemy would take them back in savage fighting at night.

Stalingrad became a hellish place. Civilians huddled in cellars while artillery, mortars and small arms fired ceaselessly, destroying buildings and combatants. A pall of smoke blackened the sky, and the cries of the wounded mingled with the ear-shattering roar of explosions. Bodies, body parts, wrecked equipment, and rubble littered the city. As the battle raged on, many German soldiers were killed in combat, and almost as many others died from exposure and disease. The Soviets sustained staggering losses as well, but unlike their foe, they were able to bring in large numbers of replacements. The fighting went on for months, with no decisive gains made by either side.

With the conflict seemingly at a stalemate, Zhukov suddenly launched a counter-offensive. Under his direction six Soviet armies, numbering more than a million men, surrounded the area, trapping some three hundred thousand German troops in the ravaged city.

Von Paulus requested permission to punch out and retreat to the west, but Hitler would have none of it. Instead, the Führer ordered General Hoth's Fourth Panzers to go to von Paulus's aid. Hitler also asked Göring whether the Luftwaffe could carry in supplies by air, and with typical hubris, Göring said of course it could. Göring directed General Richthofen to have Junkers Ju-52 transports begin shuttling supplies to airfields a few miles from Stalingrad. Hitler thought once a corridor was opened by the Fourth Panzers, supplies could be delivered from the airfields to von Paulus. And once this was accomplished, the Sixth Army would again go on the offensive.

It was a fatal miscalculation. The Luftwaffe had nowhere near enough transports to carry out the mission. Although German fighters dominated the skies, Soviet MiGs and Ratas managed to shoot down many of the lumbering Ju-52s.

Erhard Milch, by now a feldmarschal, rushed from Berlin to the battle site, but before he could reorganize the forces attempting to deliver supplies, his vehicle overturned and he was badly injured. Nevertheless he refused to leave, and did his best to improve the delivery system.

It was too late. General Hoth's Panzers were stopped by the Soviet armies, and only a paltry amount of supplies ever reached the airfields, and much of that fell into the hands of advancing Red troops. The relief effort was an abject failure.

Von Paulus knew his soldiers were doomed. Half-starved, frost-bitten, many of them wounded and suffering from illness, they had no hope of holding off the relentless Soviet attacks. The remaining officers urged von Paulus to surrender. In an attempt to save at least some of his men, he radioed for permission. Hitler sent the following reply:

Supreme Commander to 6th Army, 24 January 1942:
Surrender is forbidden. 6th Army will hold their positions to the last man and the last round and by their heroic endurance will make an unforgettable contribution towards the establishment of a defensive front and the salvation of the Western world.

Thus military professionals were again overruled by the former lance corporal. But in the end, von Paulus surrendered anyway. Fewer than one third of his troops remained alive to be captured by the Soviets, and many of those would die of cold and starvation in Soviet prison camps. Hitler ordered a day of national mourning, not for the fallen German soldiers, but for the shame brought on Germany by von Paulus's cowardice.

Many of the nation's military leaders were disgusted by the Führer's refusal to accept responsibility for the debacle. Obviously, the loss of the entire Sixth Army at Stalingrad was an enormous catastrophe. But far worse was the feeling that the loss might deny Germany the strength, in men and materiel, to stem attacks on the fatherland waged by the Soviet hordes.

Willy Messerschmitt realized full well what such events portended. And if those signs weren't clear enough, he could see firsthand the results of the enemy's growing strength. The Allied bombing of Germany was taking a toll on the production of war materials, and he was sure that sooner or later his own company would be a target.

He was also revolted by Hitler's blaming others for the Stalingrad disaster, and by his declaring that the German soldiers who fought and died there were cowardly. Willy refused to honor the proclamation, and kept his men working far into the night.

37.

As the new year began, the aerial attacks on Germany intensified. Whenever the winter weather permitted, the RAF sent large numbers of aircraft on bombing missions, and with each day British Intelligence added new targets.

By this time the U.S. 8th Air Force, commanded by Major General Carl "Tooey" Spaatz, had established bases in England with only a handful of aircraft and personnel on hand. Getting organized was a struggle. The 8th had flown its first mission the previous summer, when crews of the 15th Bomb Squadron borrowed six twin-engine Bostons from the RAF. With the 15th's commander Charles C. Kegelman leading, the Americans joined RAF 226 Squadron in a low-level attack on Luftwaffe airfields in Holland. Two of the American-crewed bombers were shot down by Bf-109s.

The next mission involved twelve B-17s of the 97th Bomb Group, which attacked the Sotteville railroad yards at Rouen, France. The mission commander was Colonel Frank Armstrong, and the lead pilot was Captain Paul Tibbets, who three years later would fly the B-29 Enola Gay to Hiroshima and drop the first atom bomb. The damage at Rouen was slight. Many bombs missed the yards altogether, and while several B-17s were hit by flak, none were lost.

The Americans continued to expand operations, bringing more aircraft and more personnel to England. General Spaatz was transferred to the Mediterranean theater, and replaced by Major General Ira C. Eaker.

The new commander of the 8th was a square-jawed Texan who'd won his wings in 1918. In the attack on Rouen, Eaker had flown the B-17 "Yankee Doodle." Gruff and demanding, he chafed at being tied to a desk by administrative duties. His headquarters as CO of the 8th were at High Wycombe, 30 miles northwest of London.

Like many other military leaders, Eaker was a disciple of the Italian Air Force General Giulio Douhet. In his 1921 book "Command Of The Air," Douhet claimed bombing both industrial centers and their civilian populations would break down the material and moral resistance of the enemy. And since the bombers would be heavily armed, enemy fighter planes could not stop them.

General Eaker's counterpart in the RAF, Air Vice Marshal Arthur "Bomber" Harris, also agreed with Douhet. Harris had been a fighter pilot in World War I, and in the 1920s gained notoriety when he put down rebellious tribesmen in Iraq by dropping bombs on them that dispersed poison gas. "The only thing an Arab understands," Harris said at the time, "is the heavy hand."

Harris brought the same attitude to his new position, when in February 1942 Winston Churchill selected him to run Bomber Command. "The enemy," the prime minister said, "must be made to burn and bleed." Often reviled as a merciless killer by civilian officials, Harris engendered admiration and unwavering loyalty among British air crews. There were conflicting opinions, however, between Harris and Eaker.

Harris favored area bombing, rather than attempting to pinpoint objectives, reasoning that it would result in widespread destruction and kill many civilian workers. Also, bombing should be carried out at night, because experience had shown that daylight raids cost unsustainable losses of aircraft.

Most important, Harris believed the 8th Air Force should be

brought under control of the RAF, with his Bomber Command running the show.

Eaker rejected Harris's ideas. The USAAF would direct the 8th's operations, he said, not the British. And instead of area bombing, he advocated precision bombing of key targets, such as the factories that produced tanks and aircraft and munitions. What's more, Eaker said, tight formations of heavily armed bombers should conduct the raids in daylight to insure accuracy. His boss, USAAF commander Lt. General Henry "Hap" Arnold, shared his convictions.

Harris declared that Eaker's concepts of strategy and tactics were dead wrong. He also favored aircraft that could drop huge amounts of explosives. British manufacturers built several types, but the best were the Handley Page Halifax and the Avro Lancaster.

The Halifax Mk II carried a bomb load of 13,000 pounds. Its crew consisted of seven men: pilot, engineer, navigator, bombardier, radio operator, topside gunner, and tail gunner. The upper gunner had twin .303 machine guns, the tail gunner had four, and there was another .303 in the nose. The aircraft was 71 feet 7 inches long, and had a wingspan of 104 feet. Powered by four 1280 hp. Rolls-Royce Merlin engines, it had a maximum speed of 265 mph, and a range of 1,860 miles.

As good as the Halifax was, the Lancaster was better. It was about the same size as the Halifax: 69 feet long, and with a wingspan of 102 feet. It too had a crew of seven, and was powered by four Rolls-Royce Merlin engines. Its top speed was 275 mph. But the Lancaster's lifting capability and its range were unmatched by any other aircraft. It weighed 36,900 pounds empty, but could carry 33,000 pounds of fuel, bombs and crew, or nearly its own weight. Its maximum range was 2,250 miles, so it could drop its 22,000 pounds of bombs on targets deep inside Germany.

The USAAF also had a pair of outstanding heavy bombers, the Boeing B-17 Flying Fortress and the Consolidated B-24 Liberator. Both were comparable to the British planes in overall dimensions. The B-17F had a wingspan of 103 feet 9 inches and a length of 74 feet 4 inches; the span of the B-24D was 110 feet, and its length was 66 feet 4 inches.

Both were powered by four engines, 14-cylinder air-cooled Pratt & Whitney radials rated at 1,200 hp. Maximum speed of the B-17 was 287 mph, and its range was 2,000 miles; for the B-24 maximum speed was 303 mph, range 2,300 miles.

But when it came to crews and armament, the American bombers were quite different from the British. The B-17 was crewed by ten men, including a copilot, and carried eleven .50-caliber machine guns: two in the top turret, two in the tail, two on each side of the fuselage, two in the belly turret, and another in the nose. Later a chin turret would be added, bringing the number of machine guns to thirteen. The normal bomb load was 6,000 pounds.

The B-24 also had ten in crew, and carried eleven .50-caliber machine guns. There was no belly turret, but it had three .50s in the nose. Maximum bomb load was 8,000 pounds.

To Harris, the differences between the British and American aircraft proved his point. The American planes carried more crew and more guns, but far fewer bombs. He was particularly contemptuous of the B-17. Calling it a Flying Fortress, he said, was typical American boastfulness with little foundation in fact. The gun stations were poorly designed and the bomb load too small.

Furthermore, he believed the American idea of daytime missions was completely wrong and would only result in a high loss of bombers. He said the Yanks were fine chaps and all that, and surely they meant well. But they had no clue when it came to the proper way of running an air force in a war.

Eaker's rejoinder was just as blunt. He said Harris's methods were wasteful. Area bombing simply meant flying in the dark and dumping bombs indiscriminately, hoping they might do some damage. It was a dumb way to conduct air raids.

The matter came to a head in late January 1943 when Prime Minister Churchill and U.S. President Franklin Roosevelt held a summit conference in Casablanca. Eaker and Harris both attended, along with other top military commanders.

At the conference Churchill and Roosevelt had their chiefs of staff issue a directive calling on the Allied air forces to form one all-powerful strategic air arm. The RAF and the 8th Air Force were to work together along the lines Vice Marshall Harris wanted.

Though Eaker had lost, giving up was not his style. In a last-ditch ploy, Eaker presented his views directly to Churchill. Reading aloud from a one-page memo, he summarized his argument: "If the RAF continues night bombing and we bomb by day, we'll bomb them round the clock and the devil shall get no rest."

With his appreciation for a stirring catchphrase, Churchill was intrigued by the sound of "round the clock bombing." And the more he thought about it, the more he liked both the phrase and what it represented. Reversing himself, the prime minister gave his blessing. So in the end, Eaker got his way.

Harris was extremely disappointed, of course, but he was also a pragmatist who possessed a coldly calculating mind. He decided to endorse day and night bombing, though he would do so in a way that would work to his advantage.

38.

Two days after the conference in Casablanca ended, the U.S. 8th Air Force carried out its first attack on a target in Germany. On a cold, damp morning, sixty-four B-17s took off from their bases in England. They were drawn from the 91st Bomb Group at Bassingbourn, the 303rd at Molesworth, the 305th at Chelveston, and the 306th at Thurleigh. After forming up they crossed the Channel on a northeasterly heading, accompanied by Spitfires and P-47s. As they flew over Holland, their escorts rocked their wings and left them.

The bombers then continued on to northern Germany. The mission called for them to strike Bremen, a major manufacturing and shipbuilding center. But as the flight of aircraft approached the city at an altitude of 23,000 feet, they found the area blanketed by fog.

Forced to divert to their alternative target, they swung northwest and flew to the naval port of Wilhelmshaven, where the Kriegsmarine's U-boats were built. The weather there was somewhat better. Ships were visible in the harbor, and so were the submarine pens. The B-17 bombardiers crouched over their Norden bombsights and guided the aircraft as they prepared to release their loads.

Having learned a harsh lesson in the Battle of Britain, the Germans had greatly improved their radar technology. The country was divided into Himmelbett zones, each containing a Wurtzburg radar station that covered a radius of about 22 miles.

Despite this, the attack caught the defenders by surprise. The radar operators had misread the intentions of the American aircraft until the bombers were well within range of the target. Luftwaffe fighters were alerted, but not in time to intercept.

Wilhelmshaven was far from defenseless, however; the port was ringed by antiaircraft batteries. The 88s opened up with a vengeance, firing hundreds of rounds of flak. One of the shells caught a leading B-17 with a direct hit and the bomber exploded. There was a ball of flame and a jarring concussion and then nothing remained but bits of smoking wreckage falling through the mist.

A following B-17 succeeded in dropping its bombs, but a moment later it too was struck, the blast tearing off its right wing. The stricken aircraft rolled over and slowly fell out of the sky, spinning like a dead leaf in the wind until it crashed in the center of the city.

Two engines of another bomber burst into flames, and the pilot dived in an attempt to put out the fires. The maneuver failed. He could not pull out of the dive and the airplane plunged into the waters of the harbor.

The surviving B-17s headed back to England, but on the way they were harassed by FW-190s. The Germans made passes from above and behind the ragged formation, firing their 20mm cannons. The shells killed and wounded several members of the bomber crews and damaged their aircraft, yet no additional bombers were lost. B-17 gunners claimed seven enemy fighters were shot down.

Exactly how effective the bombing had been was impossible to gauge, though General Eaker was pleased by the crews' reports of the mission. The B-17s had damaged a vital target, bomber losses were only two percent, and the gunners had destroyed a number of Luftwaffe fighters. He felt the results confirmed his belief that American bombing methods were correct.

In drawing this conclusion, Eaker made two crucial mistakes. The first was assuming that unescorted US bombers could fly successful raids and return without suffering crippling losses. Later experience would demonstrate the folly of that idea.

The second error was accepting the aerial gunners' word on victories. Eventually it would be seen that such claims were wildly inflated. The gunners didn't intentionally twist the truth; they were brave men who fought in brutal conditions. And in the heat of battle they honestly thought they were knocking great numbers of Bf-109s and FW-190s out of the sky.

But they were often wrong. They scored hits, and sometimes did destroy German fighters, though they made nowhere near as many kills as they claimed. Thus the bombers weren't getting the protection from their gunners that Eaker thought they were.

Air Marshal Harris did not share Eaker's optimistic conclusions. Nor did British critics have much faith in the ability of the USAAF to fly successful missions in the future. They foresaw heavy American losses.

Eaker ignored the criticism and carried on. And as Harris had predicted, many U.S. bombers were lost in subsequent raids on targets in France and Holland. Finally in the spring of 1943 Eaker admitted he'd miscalculated. His bombers then raided additional targets in France, but with a significant difference: they were escorted by fighters.

Some of the escorts were RAF Spitfires. And some were an American aircraft that was arriving in England in large numbers. This was the P-47 Thunderbolt, and it was like no other fighter in the world.

For one thing, the P-47 was big. In fact, it was the biggest single-seat, piston-engine fighter ever built. Parked alongside a Spitfire, its wingtip was higher than the British aircraft's canopy. The P-47 was also more than twice as heavy, coming in at an operational weight of 16,200 pounds vs. 6,622 for the Spitfire. No wonder pilots called it the Jug.

When they first saw one, RAF airmen joked that if a P-47 were attacked, the pilot could evade the enemy by running around and hiding inside the cockpit. Joking aside, it wasn't long before the new fighter would prove its worth in combat.

The P47's creator was as unusual as the airplane. He was Alexander Kartveli, who had emigrated to America from the Soviet state of Georgia. A brilliant aeronautical designer, he became the chief engineer of the Republic Aviation Company at Farmingdale, Long Island, New York. Kartveli's approach was the opposite of that followed by most designers. He believed that the key to success for a fighter was to build in as much power as possible. So instead of first conceptualizing the airplane, he began with an engine.

The one he chose was the new 2,000 hp turbocharged Pratt & Whitney Double Wasp, the XR-2800-21. The most powerful of all U.S. aircraft engines, it was a radial with two rows of nine cylinders each. The only other radial-engine fighter in the ETO was the Fw-190, and to distinguish the P-47 from the German aircraft, its engine cowling and tail were painted white.

Because of the size and power of the Double Wasp, Kartveli had to design an airplane large enough to handle it. The resulting P-47 was not only huge, but incredibly rugged. It was also not as maneuverable as most contemporary fighters, though it was surprisingly fast. Top speed of the P-47D was 428 mph. And it had other advantages as well.

Lt. John Phillips, a pilot who was also an aeronautical engineer with a degree from MIT, had this to say about flying the P-47 in combat:

> First thing we learned was not to try to turn with a Messer-schmitt 109 or a Focke-Wulf 190. Instead, the trick was to gain altitude and then dive on them. If the enemy pilot tried to escape by diving, you had him. No other fighter could stay with a P-47 in a dive. You could reach 550 miles per hour diving, and there was no problem. Also the Jug had eight .50-calibers in the wings, and it was a great gun platform, steady as a rock. My first kill was a Focke-Wulf that was attacking a B-17. I came at him from above, and didn't fire until I was very close, no more than two hundred yards. My guns tore him apart. As far as I'm concerned, the P-47's only negative was range. It had a 375-gal-lon tank, so you could only go part way with the bombers before you had to leave them. Later on we had drop tanks, and that was a big improvement. And talk about a Jug's ability to take punishment? Once I came back after a mission and part of my engine had been shot away. But it kept right on running, got me home. The P-47 wasn't what you'd call an elegant airplane, but it was as tough as they come.

Now that his bombers had fighter escorts, Eaker was planning more ambitious attacks. General Arnold wanted raids to be made on key German industries such as aircraft and ball bearings, and Eaker was eager to carry them out.

Meanwhile RAF Bomber Command went on sending large flights of its own heavy aircraft to Germany. In night raids the British struck such centers as Oberhausen, Essen, Dortmund, and Frankfurt. Fleets num-bering from 250 to 600 bombers took part in the attacks. And by way of further infuriating the enemy, the RAF also flew Mosquitos over enemy territory virtually as they pleased. On 30 January, 1943, the Nazi leadership held a rally in Berlin to celebrate the tenth anniversary of Hitler taking power. As the festivities began, six Mosquitos of 105 and 139 Squadrons roared over the city at low altitude and dropped bombs.

Hitler, Speer, Milch, Göring, Goebbels and the others ran for cover, and more than a hundred people were killed. Adding to the Nazis' humiliation, German fighters and flak batteries failed to touch the raiders. The RAF aircraft had thumbed their noses at the German officials and got away clean.

Hitler had a fit, spewing most of his vitriol at Göring. The enemy, screamed the Führer, had better bombers and better pilots and the Luftwaffe was again shown to be worthless. Deeply embarrassed, the Reichsmarchal left the city and slunk away to Karinhall, his sumptuous estate northeast of Berlin.

But Bomber Command was not without its own problems. After several of the RAF's heaviest raids, reconnaissance aircraft took photos that showed the enemy had sustained little damage. In an attack on Munster, not a single bomb landed closer than five miles from the target. Instead, most of the explosives struck farmers' fields.

Prime Minister Churchill and the top British commanders reviewed such failures with dismay. To make matters worse, the photos were also shown to Parliament, where there were calls for Harris's removal. One member of the House of Commons said it was ridiculous to send all those bombers to blow up a few cows.

But British scientists were developing some remarkable new devices. One was H2S radar, and another was a radar-jamming device code-named Window. Still another was Oboe, the radio-guidance system that sent Mosquito pathfinders and bombers on course toward their targets.

When the Mosquitos reached an objective they dropped brilliant, brightly-colored pyrotechnic flares. As the sky over the target became bathed in eerie light, pilots of the Lancasters, Halifaxes and Wellingtons were able to pick out their targets even from a great distance. The pilots then adjusted course at the Initial Point, and when over the city released their explosives. The result was much greater accuracy.

Nevertheless, Harris was more set than ever on the principle of area bombing. The pathfinder system simply made it more efficient. As far as he was concerned, the more German civilians killed, the better.

"Terror bombing!" howled Goebbels' media. "An inhuman practice by the filthy British," intoned German radio announcers. "The Terror Bombers are deliberately killing innocent people!"

Overlooked, of course, were the raids that the Luftwaffe had carried out on cities in Britain. In London alone, from September 1940 to May

1941, 43,000 civilians were killed. And the raids continued, as Luftwaffe bombers struck targets in southern England and Wales almost every night. Many civilians were being killed in those attacks as well.

The British knew that German radar stations in France monitored RAF bombers from the moment they were airborne. The radar operators would plot the bombers' progress, and then pass the information to General Kammhuber's night fighter squadrons. As a result, German night fighters sometimes attacked the bombers shortly after they took off, and when bombers did succeed in reaching Germany, the Luftwaffe would be waiting for them. Flak batteries would also have been alerted, and often the RAF was greeted with a hot reception.

So to negate the effectiveness of German radar, the British proposed using a new technique they called Window. RAF bombers would drop large quantities of foot-long strips of aluminum foil, called chaff. Instead of seeing blips on their radar screens, the German operators would suddenly be looking at images that resembled a snowstorm.

Vice Marshal Harris wanted to introduce Window as soon as it was developed. When used in conjunction with the recently perfected H2S radar and the Mosquito pathfinders, it would be like arming the RAF with a deadly new weapon.

But the British authorities were opposed. The use of Window would be too risky, Harris was told, because the Germans would catch on and introduce a similar system of their own. Then the Luftwaffe would jam RAF radar, and British defenses would suffer.

For the moment, therefore, Bomber Command made do with putting additional numbers of heavy aircraft into service, and stepping up both the frequency and the intensity of the raids. With each attack, Harris tried to wreak more death and destruction than the one before.

As the bombing of the German homeland escalated, the news from other fronts continued to worsen. The Soviets were counterattacking, driving the Wehrmacht back and reclaiming territory. In another key battle following the German surrender at Stalingrad, the Red army retook Kursk.

Then, for the first time, the American forces in North Africa went into action. Led by the 1st Armored Division, they attacked General Erwin Rommel's Panzers in the battle of Kasserine Pass. The green Americans had little chance against the seasoned German veterans, and were routed.

Nevertheless, that was the last victory for the Desert Fox. Short of food, ammunition and medical supplies, his exhausted troops had no hope of stemming the powerful Allied offensive. A week later, the Germans began withdrawal from Africa.

Willy Messerschmitt, in his race to introduce the Me-262 as the first operational jet, received disturbing news. Added to the pressure to prove his aircraft superior to the Heinkel 280, it was recently reported by German Intelligence that in England, on 5 March 1943, the Gloster Meteor, powered by two Halford H1 turbojets, had made its maiden flight.

39.

Messerschmitt's reaction to the news of the Meteor was to try harder than ever to get his Me-262 ready for operations, knowing that Germany had a critical need for improved homeland defense. His efforts were blunted, however, by orders from the RLM to concentrate on the Me-410, and also on development of a new version of the Me-209. This was the Me-209II, which bore hardly any relationship to the original. The RLM hoped the piston-engine fighter would eventually replace the Bf-109.

Meanwhile, as the Allied bombing gained momentum, the short-comings of the Kammhuber Line method of deploying fighters became increasingly apparent to the German High Command. Yet nothing was done to improve it, because General Kammhuber was a longtime favorite of Göring.

One area that did improve was aircraft production. Under prodding from Reichsminister Speer, the program was greatly expanded. The RLM also instituted the Vulcan program, calling for stepped-up development of jet and rocket-powered airplanes.

Yet Milch had no enthusiasm for the Me-262, claiming that tests had revealed many weaknesses. Albert Speer, on the other hand, saw the jet's potential. He was also aware that Adolf Hitler had respect for Messerschmitt, and that the Führer was intrigued by the prospect of equipping the Luftwaffe with an airplane of surpassing speed. Pressured by Speer, Milch reluctantly moved the Me-262 up to priority level DE, the highest in the Vulcan program.

Messerschmitt did his best to keep the ball rolling. The V-3 was still undergoing repairs, so flight tests were conducted with other proto-types, chiefly the V-2. A problem emerged when the aircraft developed vibrations in the wings, preventing it from being flown at speeds greater that 690 kph. Engineers overcame the fault by strengthening the wing ribs, and in subsequent tests the V-2 was able to reach 800 kph.

The Führer then issued an edict. From that point on, all fighter air-craft must be *Jagdbombers*, or *Jabos*, equipped to perform the role of both fighter and bomber. There would be no exceptions.

Naturally Messerschmitt found this disconcerting. The Me-262 was an extremely fast, heavily armed, short-range aircraft. As such, it was a fighter with great potential for use as an interceptor. It was not a bomber, nor a fighter-bomber.

But when asked by the Air Ministry whether the Me-262 could carry bombs, Willy said it could, probably thinking that a negative reply would jeopardize the program. And he also might have recalled the dis-cussion at the Reich Chancellory, when the Führer had expressed enthu-siasm for bombers.

Now with this order it was obvious that as always, Hitler was less interested in defense than in carrying out offensive action against his enemies. He wanted aircraft that could be used to punish as well as van-quish them, and the way to do that was by bombing. Whether or not it made sense for the Me-262 to be converted to a fighter-bomber didn't matter—the Führer had spoken. Messerschmitt had engineers Wolfgang Degel and Woldemar Voigt prepare a proposal for the new version of the Me-262.

The jet's armament would consist of a nose bay housing four MK-108 30mm cannons. The bombs would be either one of 500 kg, or two of 250 kg each, or the aircraft could carry one 700 kg torpedo. When carrying a torpedo it would have two fewer cannons in the nose. There would be two armored 900-liter fuel tanks, and one 300-liter tank with-out armor. The undercarriage would be the tricycle type. Accommoda-tion would be made for rocket-assisted takeoffs.

In other changes, the slats would be extended along the entire lead-ing edges of the wings. The speed brakes would be eliminated, as well as the pressurized cockpit and ejection seat. Takeoff weight would be 6,000 kg. The engineers also designed a mechanism by which the tailplane could be adjusted in flight after the bombs were dropped, to accommodate the change in CG. The device was fitted at the junction of the fuselage and the vertical stabilizer.

The Messerschmitt proposal was accepted by the RLM. The officials also concluded that the Me-262 project was more advanced than that of the Heinkel He-280 jet fighter. As a result, the He-280 was dropped from the jet development program. But experimental work on pure jet bombers, such as the Arado 234, the He-343, and the Ju-287, would continue.

Despite the order to convert the Me-262 to a fighter-bomber, the win meant a lot to Professor Messerschmitt and his design team. When the decision was announced, there was rejoicing in the center at Augsburg.

Naturally the opposite reaction took place at Heinkel headquarters. Ernest Heinkel was angry and disappointed, believing his He-280 was better than the Me-262, and that it had not been given fair consideration. He railed publicly against the RLM officials and others in the Nazi government, a rash move that led to his being isolated and often ignored.

Still another strange twist took place when someone, either an enemy of Messerschmitt or a competitor, secretly told Milch that the Me-209 would be inferior to the Bf-109G and the FW-190D fighters currently in service. The rumormonger said that even with the new Daimler-Benz 603 engine, the Me-209 would be slower, would have a lesser rate of climb, and would be less maneuverable than the other aircraft.

Without waiting to learn whether the information was true, Milch ordered work on the Me-209 curtailed. Yet he was hesitant to put all his chips on the Me-262, as there was no evidence that the jet would hold its own in combat. So how could it replace the fighters that were flying now?

Messerschmitt and Seiler also had reservations. They believed that while the Me-262 would have no equal as an interceptor of bombers, it was not suited to become the Luftwaffe's standard fighter, especially since it might also be expected to carry bombs. They urged more testing before the RLM made a final decision to abandon the Me-209. And of course, Messerschmitt and Seiler continued to resist any plan that would curtail production of the Bf-109. That fighter was much more versatile, as well as being a vitally important money-maker for the company.

Until then the Luftwaffe General Staff had paid little attention to the Me-262. But stories of its speed generated new interest, and as a result, Hauptmann Wolfgang Spate of Erprobungskommando 16 was ordered to test-fly a prototype.

Spate was a fighter pilot with a particular fondness for the Fw-190. To him, a jet was a newfangled, untried machine. Moreover, he knew nothing of the Me-262's history, including the political wrangling that had gone on during its development.

By then some of the work on the airplane had been transferred to Lager Lechfeld, a Luftwaffe base not far from Augsburg. The V-3 had been repaired, and when Spate arrived at Lechfeld and first saw it, he was surprised. The jet didn't look to him like a fighter; in some ways it appeared quite graceful, especially with the sloping nose of the fuselage. But he was taken aback by the large engine pods under its wings. The airplane was also larger and heavier than either the FW-190 or the Bf-109.

Spate listened carefully when the engineers explained that the throttles of the turbojets had to be handled with care, and that the aircraft would require an unusually long takeoff roll. The tricycle undercarriage had not yet been installed, so he'd need to use the toe-taps to unstick the tail. Also, the aircraft should be treated gently in turns. By the time he was strapped in and ready to take off, Spate wasn't sure what to expect.

Once he was airborne, however, his uncertainty gave way to exhilaration. The airplane performed like nothing he'd ever experienced. Its speed was breathtaking, and it was remarkably easy to fly. But recalling the engineers' advice, he conducted maneuvers cautiously. When he landed, he voiced strong approval for the airplane and asked to make a second flight.

Unfortunately, with his second flight he'd become overconfident, and a bit careless. After taking off, he put the V-3 through more vigorous maneuvers, and tried a steep side-slip. Stick over to the right, hard left rudder. The resulting change in airflow prevented the turbine blades from turning properly, and both engines flamed out. His heart in his mouth, Spate descended rapidly. The move restarted the engines, and he again landed safely.

Spate then sent his report to the General Staff. It praised the Me-262 profusely—the airplane, he stated, was ready for operations, and should be put into service at once.

General Galland read the report with raised eyebrows. Could the machine really be that good? As one of the Luftwaffe's top aces, Galland had been a loyal proponent of the Bf-109, and now he was being given the opinion of another pilot that the Me-262 could out-perform any other fighter. Intensely curious, Galland decided to find out for himself just what this new type of aircraft was all about.

But before he could arrange to check it out, another mishap occurred. The V-2 crashed at Hiltenfingen on its 48th flight, killing test pilot Willy Ostertag. When the wreckage was examined, it was determined that the cause of the accident was jamming of the tailplane mechanism. It would not be the last such incident.

Undeterred, Galland went to Augsburg a few weeks later, where he was greeted warmly by Willy Messerschmitt. On 22 May 1943, the Luftwaffe general got his first look at an Me-262. When he beheld it, Galland's reaction was the same as Spate's. With its large size and its two underslung engine nacelles it certainly bore no resemblance to other fighters.

However, when he flew the airplane, as usual chewing on a cigar, he too was dazzled by its speed and ease of handling. And being Galland, he put it through a much more strenuous series of maneuvers than Spate had dared to undertake. He looped, rolled and dove it, and with his superb flying skills, the general experienced no problems.

The Me-262, Galland concluded, was years ahead in performance. It was faster by far than anything he'd ever flown, and without a reciprocating piston engine driving a propellor, there was no need to compensate for torque. As soon as he landed, he rushed to a telephone and called the Air Minister at his office in Berlin.

When Erhard Milch came on the line, Galland expressed enthusiasm for every aspect of the new airplane. Like Spate, he believed it should be put into service at once, and summarized his evaluation with a remark that would become legendary. "It felt," Galland said, "like angels were pushing."

He then wrote a one-page report, in which he said:

1. The aircraft represents a great step forward, which assures us an unimaginable advantage should the enemy adhere to the piston engine.
2. The flying qualities of the airframe make a good impression.

3. The engines are completely convincing, except during
    takeoff and landing.
4. The aircraft opens completely new tactical possibilities.

Lastly he wrote, "The aircraft could be our biggest chance. The Me-209 project should be cancelled, and all production facilities assigned to it should be turned over to the Me-262."

Milch mistrusted Messerschmitt, but he had great faith in Galland's judgment. He decided to make the change, depending on approval by Göring. The Reichsmarschal agreed, and work on the 209 was stopped. The RLM then authorized production of the first series of 100 Me-262 aircraft.

Willy Messerschmitt hoped he'd be permitted to build the jets without further interference. He also would see to it that they were equipped as fighters. The Luftwaffe's need for effective home defense could not be more urgent.

That was brought into sharp focus a few days later, when the RAF launched its greatest offensive of the war. The objective was to destroy as much of Germany's industrial capacity as possible. The target was the Ruhr.

40.

The Ruhr Valley in northwestern Germany was one of the largest coal-mining regions in the world. Most of the nation's steel mills were located there, as well as many manufacturers of materiel vital to the war effort. Using coal as an energy source, the factories turned out everything from machine tools to locomotives. One of the largest firms was Thyssen Industries, and another was Krupp, maker of munitions.

The valley took its name from the Ruhr River, whose waters originated in the Sauerland mountains and then flowed 217 kilometers west to the Rhine. Tributaries such as the Möhne, Eder, and Sorpe rivers emptied into the Ruhr. The rivers had been dammed to create vast artificial lakes, so that hydroelectric plants at the sites could also provide power.

RAF planners, led by Vice Marshal Harris, theorized that destruction of the cities in the Ruhr would cripple Germany's ability to supply its armed forces. Harris therefore ordered massive raids by heavy bombers. The attacks began in March 1943, and reached their peak in May and June.

Night after night, flights of RAF aircraft dropped high explosives onto targets in the valley. Dortmund and Düsseldorf were hit with two thousand tons of bombs, and another thousand tons fell on Bochum. Duisburg and Essen and Witten were also ravaged. In a raid on Wuppertal, 2,450 civilians were killed and 118,000 lost their homes.

As the attacks went on, Air Minister Milch decried the Luftwaffe's inability to stop them, which was mainly due to the Luftwaffe's limited numbers of night fighters. As a result, the German people in the target areas suffered greatly, with no relief in sight.

Reichsmarschal Göring blamed much of the problem on the conveniently dead Ernst Udet. Göring said that Udet had failed to provide the Luftwaffe with aircraft that were properly equipped to counter the attacks. He also considered the Luftwaffe fighter pilots cowards.

Milch was outraged. As one of the few who dared refute Göring to his face, he reminded him that the Reichsmarschal himself had approved Udet's production plans, and that the pilots were in fact brave men.

A cooler appraisal was made by Major Joachim "Hajo" Hermann. The major believed the problem was the Kammhuber Defense Line. Too few night fighters were being sent to the scene of the raids, he said, or else they were sent too late. In a conference of Luftwaffe commanders held by Göring, Major Hermann described the methods used by the RAF. "The first aircraft releases its markers over the target, and then even the stupidest pilot can see the signal from as far away as the Thames Estuary. After they dump their bombs, it looks as though the whole area is one huge sea of fire."

Still, Vice Marshal Harris was not satisfied. In keeping with his theories of how air war should be conducted, he wanted to bring about total destruction. He contended it was necessary to break the German peoples' spirit.

Harris's point of view was strange. Britain had been bombed more or less constantly for three years by then, and thousands of civilians had been killed and wounded. Countless buildings had been damaged beyond repair, and yet the British people resolutely held fast. Why should German civilians react differently?

But Harris was adamant. While studying maps of the region, another idea occurred to the RAF planners. What if some of those dams on the reservoirs were breached? That would flood the valley, wiping out much of the hydroelectric power. The rampaging flood waters would ruin the manufacturing plants, drowning great numbers of workers.

Further study showed that 70% of the valley's water storage capacity was in the Möhne, Eder, and Sorpe reservoirs. The Möhne alone held 30,016,000,000 gallons of water, and the Eder was even larger, with 45,218,000,000 gallons. Yet because they were so massively constructed, the dams would be impervious to damage by conventional bombs. Was there a scientist in Britain who could devise a solution?

There was. A noted inventor, Dr. Barnes Wallis, was working at the National Physics Laboratory at Teddington. Wallis contrived a bomb that contained 6,600 pounds of Torpex explosive. Code-named "Upkeep," it was to be carried under a Lancaster and connected by belt drive to a motor in the aircraft. The belt would rotate the bomb at 500 rpm.

When dropped at low level over a reservoir, the rapidly rotating bomb would bounce across the surface of the water like a flat stone skipping over a pond. After striking the dam it would roll down to a predetermined depth and explode. Wallis believed shock waves would then burst open the dam, and millions of gallons of water would flood the valley.

The RAF decided to try an attack using the unorthodox devices. A squadron designated 617 was secretly formed by Bomber Command and staffed with 133 handpicked aircrew. For six weeks, the crews carried out practice attacks on the Uppingham and Durwent reservoirs in England. The runs were conducted mostly at night, with the Lancasters flying low and dropping dummy bombs.

The mission was called Operation Chastise, and the pilot chosen to lead it was Wing Commander Guy Gibson. Only twenty-four years old, Gibson had already won the Distinguished Service Order with bar and the Distinguished Flying Cross with bar. Painted on the bow of his bomber was the cartoon character Popeye.

Nineteen Lancasters, each with a rotating bomb slung beneath it, would take part in the raid. The plan called for them to fly in three waves.Nine aircraft in the first wave, led by Gibson, would attack the Möhne dam. If they succeeded in breaching it, the Lancasters that still had bombs would go on to hit the Eder.

The second wave would be led by Flight Lieutenant J.C. McCarthy, an American who'd joined the RAF at the outset of the war. McCarthy's five Lancasters were to fly a more northerly route, so that the Germans would be unable to guess their true objective. They would attack the Sorpe dam.

The third wave consisted of the remaining five Lancasters, which would depart a few minutes after the others. If the first two waves failed, they were to attack any dam they could reach.

Bomber Command ordered Operation Chastise to be launched from the RAF base at Scamton on 16 May 1943. At 2130 hours, the Lancasters took off in pale moonlight. To avoid detection by enemy radar, they flew across the North Sea just above the waves. They were so low that one of them caught its belly on a whitecap, tearing the bomb loose. The pilot turned back.

The others flew on, crossing the Dutch coast and then swinging toward the Ruhr. By then the German gunners had been alerted, and the flak was even heavier than expected. Five of the Lancasters were hit by shells from the 88s and crashed. Another was badly damaged and limped back to England.

Gibson continued to lead, and most of his remaining bombers made it to the Möhne reservoir. As they swooped over the water, the sky was ablaze with fire from the enemy batteries. Several more Lancasters were hit, but they managed to stay in the air.

Three of the attackers dropped bombs that skittered over the surface of the lake and struck the dam. The bombs rolled down and exploded, but the wall held. Then a fourth Lancaster, flown by Flight Lieutenant D.J.H. Maltby, drew close and let go. That bomb caused a mighty explosion that breached the dam.

Shrapnel had torn holes in the wings and fuselage of Gibson's airplane, though miraculously, neither he nor any of his crew had been hit. With his bomb still intact, he flew 40 miles farther up the valley toward the Eder reservoir; three other Lancasters were still with him.

When the aircraft reached the lake, the flak gunners were ready for them. The batteries put up thousands of rounds of cannon and machine-gun fire. Gibson told his navigator to pull him out of his seat if he was killed. Then fly the airplane, he said, and make the drop.

As he approached the target, the pilot was half-blinded by the flashes of exploding shells. But up ahead he could see the huge dam in the swirling mist.

At the last moment, Gibson released his bomb. The device bounced across the water and hit the wall of the dam and sank. The 6,600 pounds of Torpex exploded, and a white tower of water, mixed with chunks of concrete, shot into the air.

They'd done it. First the Möhne had been breached, and now the Eder. Exhausted, but thrilled by their feat, Gibson led the survivors toward home. They again flew through heavy flak, and by another miracle, eleven Lancasters made it back to Scamton. Fifty-three crew members had died carrying out the mission.

The BBC and newspapers in Britain reported the raid with great pride, and paid tribute to the courageous RAF airmen. For his bravery and determination, Wing Commander Gibson was awarded the Victoria Cross. Thirty-four others were also decorated.

The torrents of water set loose by the ruptured dams drowned nearly three thousand Germans. Twenty miles of land in the Ruhr valley were flooded, and damage to the factories and workers' homes was severe. None of the steel mills were in operation for the rest of the year, and boat traffic on the rivers was halted. It took months to repair the railroads.

And still, Harris wanted to inflict more damage. He sent RAF bombers on additional raids of cities in the area, and thousands more tons of explosives were dropped on Oberhausen, Krefeld, and Gelsenkirchen. Further attacks on Wuppertal brought the total number of deaths there past 8,000.

As usual, Hitler's response was full of rage and bluster. He ordered a buildup of defenses in the Ruhr, but that was largely paying lip service to the situation—what he wanted most was revenge. Therefore, he instructed Reichsmarschal Göring to increase Luftwaffe attacks against cities in England, and also demanded that both Fieseler's flying bomb and von Braun's rocket be made ready for strikes on London.

Milch knew this was muddled thinking. He was convinced that the buildup of fighters for home defense should be given the highest priority. And he too rejected the concept of the Kammhuber Line, which called for fighters to stay within their assigned areas. Instead, he believed in the principle of *Schwerpunkt*, which called for a heavy concentration of forces wherever they were needed.

Major Hermann was in complete agreement. A veteran of more than 300 missions, Hermann based his ideas not on theory, but on combat experience. Rather than argue with the wooden-headed General Kammhuber, Hermann handled the problem his own way.

The major assembled a group of experienced German bomber pilots, and began scrounging equipment from various fighter squadrons. He acquired two dozen Bf-109s and Fw-190s, and instructed the pilots to attack RAF bombers from a flak-free zone high above, using the searchlights and the fires and bomb flashes to illuminate the enemy aircraft.

Hermann called his unit "Wilde Sau." The term is usually translated as "Wild Boar," but is actually German for "Wild Sow." Why he wanted to name the outfit after a wild female pig is anyone's guess.

41.

On the night of 2 July 1943, 600 RAF heavy bombers attacked Cologne. Located near the western end of the Ruhr valley, the city was the site of a number of important factories, including the Siemens chemical works. The British aircraft reached the area without encountering fighter opposition.

Once over the target, however, they ran into a hail of flak. The bombers illuminated the city with their pyrotechnic devices, and began dropping tons of explosives. The detonations, together with the flares and the searchlight beams and the bursting antiaircraft shells, made the night sky weirdly bright.

As a result, the bombers were clearly visible, just as Hajo Hermann knew they would be. The major was flying an Fw-190, and in the flashing light he could see the enemy machines' mottled camouflage and their red-white-and-blue roundels. They were mostly Lancasters, though there were some Halifaxes as well.

Leading his Wilde Sau pilots over the bombers, Hermann kept just above flak range until he was ready for the fighters to make their firing passes. Then at a signal from him they descended like banshees, firing their cannons and machine guns. Three of the British aircraft blew up before the crews realized they were under attack, and within minutes four more bombers were ablaze and spinning toward the earth.

Hermann picked out a Lancaster and closed in on it. The pilot tried to evade him, but he couldn't shake the Focke-Wulf. Hermann got in several bursts, and after finishing off the enemy aircraft, he saw to his satisfaction that other RAF raiders were being shot up as well. As they made their bomb runs, more of them fell prey to the Wilde Sau fighters' guns.

The following day, in a conference with Milch and other officers at the Air Ministry, the major described the action: "I opened fire on this one bomber, which began to burn at once but carried on flying, though it was on fire. So I let him have it again from one side, right in the cockpit, and then it went down like a stone. The pilot must have been hit."

Milch asked whether the flak gunners knew what was happening. Hermann said they had no idea. Were they surprised when the bombers started dropping like flies?

The major laughed. "They were astounded to find ten or eleven down, when they had shot down only two the day before."

Encouraged by Hermann's report, Milch went to Göring and tried to convince him that the Wilde Sau defense should be widely employed. But the Reichsmarschal dismissed the idea with a flick of his hand. To him, one such incident meant little. And besides, the request was coming from Milch.

By then most Nazi officials, including Hitler and Speer, realized that the real brain behind the Luftwaffe belonged to Milch, and not to Göring. Apparently the Reichsmarschal was also aware of it. Resenting his subordinate's favorable reputation, Göring did everything he could to undermine him.

Nevertheless, the RAF's plan to destroy the industries in the Ruhr was obvious to everyone. Many of the cities had been laid waste, with factories and homes in ruins and thousands of civilians dead. A raid on Essen had not only badly damaged the Krupp steel works and armament factories, but had also wiped out more than half the labor force. The British attacks were seriously disrupting Germany's ability to produce war materiel.

Finally, Göring was forced to concede. The Luftwaffe changed the procedures of the Kammhuber Line, and concentrated more night fighters in the area. Together with the flak batteries, they began taking a heavy toll on the British attackers. In a subsequent raid on Krefeld, 44 bombers were shot down.

Surprisingly, one of the most effective night-fighters was Messerschmitt's much maligned Bf-110. Although it had failed as a day fighter and as a fighter-bomber, the aircraft was well suited to its new role.

Equipped with Lichenstein C1 radar, the Bf-110 chewed up a growing number of RAF heavy aircraft. The Ju-88 also performed well as a night fighter, though it was not as successful as the Messerschmitt. But the problem remained that there were insufficient numbers of both types, a problem compounded by the Luftwaffe's failure to coordinate the defenders.

As this went on, the war on the eastern front reached yet another turning point. The Germans began a new offensive, based on a plan conceived by Hitler's best military strategist, Feldmarschal Erich von Manstein.

At the time, the Soviets occupied a bulge in the German line south of Orel and north of Kharkov. The bulge was 200 km wide and 150 km deep, and at its center lay Kursk. The battered city had been lost by the Russians in November 1941, and then retaken by them in February 1943.

Von Manstein proposed tricking the Soviets into launching an attack through the bulge. The Germans would fall back beyond Kharkov, and when the enemy was overextended, von Manstein would counter with a classic Blitzkrieg flanking thrust. That would trap the entire southern wing of the Soviet Army against the Sea of Azov, where the Reds would be destroyed. It was a bold plan, and one that could lead to a victory great enough to restore the German army's momentum. But for Hitler, the plan was too bold. He rejected it.

Perhaps after the defeat at Stalingrad, the Führer was no longer as certain of his military brilliance. Or perhaps he just failed to grasp that a large opportunity lay before him. As von Manstein put it in a notable understatement, "In spite of having a certain eye for tactics, Hitler lacked the ability of a great captain."

The High Command then devised an alternative plan. It called for Central Army Group, under Feldmarschal von Kluge, to attack Kursk from the north, while von Manstein's Southern Army Group attacked the city from the south. The plan was code-named Operation Zitadelle. On 15 April, Hitler gave his approval.

The operation was to begin in May, but Hitler put it off until June, and then July, maintaining that by then the Germans would have more tanks to send into the battle. Von Manstein considered the delays a grave mistake. He knew the enemy would become aware of the Germans' intentions, and would have plenty of time to prepare. He also believed

Hitler was afraid of the risks in the Zitadelle plan as well.

The Führer admitted as much. When General Guderian advised that it would be better not to attack Kursk at all, Hitler replied, "I know. The thought of it turns my stomach."

But the operation would go forward, and the Germans had amassed a powerful force. It included 800,000 infantry and 2,700 tanks, among them the new Tiger, King Tiger and Panther types, and also the new Ferdinand self-propelled gun. The latter was named for its designer, Dr. Ferdinand Porsche, but troops called it *Der Elefant*. Used primarily as a tank destroyer, it mounted a 105mm cannon, with armor was as thick as a battleship's.

New aircraft had arrived as well. These included the Focke-Wulf 190 fighter, and the latest variant of the Bf-109, the Gustav. Another new machine was the single-seat Henschel HS-129, built for ground attack. The Henschel was powered by twin 550 hp Gnome-Rhône engines, captured from the French. It was heavily armored and heavily armed, with two 7.92mm machine guns, two 20mm cannons, and one 30mm cannon. It carried a 350 kg bomb load. However, the aircraft's performance was poor. The cockpit was so cramped there was no room for the Revi gunsight, which had to be mounted out on the bow. The much older Stuka was a far better machine for attacking tanks.

The Luftwaffe had also assembled a large fleet of Heinkel He-111 and Junkers Ju-88 bombers. Altogether the Germans had 2,000 aircraft in place for the offensive. Tons of bombs had been stockpiled, and millions of rounds of ammunition.

By the time he finally gave the order to launch the attack, Hitler had regained his confidence. After all, the Russians had already suffered more than four times more casualties than the Germans. His army, he was sure, would again be victorious.

But the Soviets were aware of the Germans' plans. Members of the Lucy spy ring in Switzerland, and subversives in the Nazi government called The Red Orchestra, had informed the Soviet High Command as to when and where the offensive would begin.

With this knowledge the Russians were able to gather an even greater force than that of the Germans. Led by Generals Georgy Zhukov, Konstantin Rokkossovsky, and Nikolai Vatutin, an army of 1,300,000 infantry, 3,600 tanks, and 2,800 aircraft were in place. The Soviets had also laid a vast minefield outside Kursk, and used 300,000 civilians to dig miles of trenches.

At 0200 hours on 5 July, the Germans were surprised when Russian artillery opened up with a heavy barrage. This was the first sign to German army commanders that the enemy knew their plan. But there would be no turning back now; at 0430 they responded with a barrage of their own, and an hour later the armor and infantry jumped off under air cover.

Von Manstein's Panzer divisions spearheaded the drive. At the forefront were Panther and Tiger tanks, as well as the Elefant self-propelled guns. Stuka dive bombers and Ju-88s supported the armor, with Bf-109 and FW-190 fighters overhead. Behind the tanks were masses of infantry. It was a classic Blitzkrieg attack.

At first the Germans made good progress, penetrating ten kilometers the first day, though at a cost of 25,000 casualties. As time went on, the going became more difficult than expected. Slowed by exploding mines, the Germans were targeted by thousands of Ilyushin rockets and by the 76.2mm cannons of the Russian tanks.

They were also harassed by great numbers of Red aircraft. The Russians had a good ground attack bomber of their own, the two-place Ilyushin IL-2 Stormavik. It mounted a pair of 7.62mm machine guns and two 23mm cannon firing forward, and a 2.7mm machine gun manned by the gunner in the rear seat.

Russian fighters were also in abundance at Kursk. They were mostly Yak-1s and Yak-7s, along with some of the newer Yak-9s. Small and nimble, the Yaks were lightly armed, with one 12.7mm machine gun and one 20mm cannon, but they were the most effective of the Soviet fighters. Apparently in designing them, the Russians had borrowed a page from Willy Messerschmitt.

Yet the German aircraft could outfight the Yaks, simply because the Luftwaffe pilots were better trained than the Russians. Also, the Yaks had a weakness; they did not perform well at higher altitudes. Airmen such as Wolf-Dietrich Wilke and Gerhard Thyben and Kurt Tanzer, flying the Bf-109G, shot down dozens of them.

During the battle the most notable combat record of all was that of Oberfeldwebel Hubert Strassl, of JG51. Over the course of three days, Strassl shot down 30 Soviet aircraft, raising his score to 67. But on 8 July, after he'd achieved the last three of his kills, Strassl's Fw-190A, "Black 4," was bounced by Russian fighters. In the ensuing dogfight,

Strassl's airplane was heavily damaged, and he was forced to bail out. His parachute failed to open, and he fell to his death 60 km north of Kursk. He was posthumously awarded the Ritterkreuz.

Unlike the siege of Stalingrad, the action on the ground took place in warm summer weather. But the scene was no less hellish, with thousands of tanks maneuvering on both sides and frequently exploding as they were hit by bombs and cannon shells. Rockets screamed over the masses of infantry and burst among them, and artillery pieces often fired at point-blank range. It was the largest tank battle in history.

The explosions smashed equipment and men's bodies and ripped gaping holes in the earth. Dogfights took place all over the smoke-darkened sky, and many aircraft crashed in flames. Bombs were dropped continuously onto the battlefield.

No soldier who survived the conflict would ever forget the noise. It was a nerve-shattering cacophony that burst eardrums and made it almost impossible to think. While many combatants were killed by bullets and shrapnel, many others died from the effects of concussion. In the July heat the atmosphere was infused with an acrid stench of cordite, mixed with that of burning rubber, melting metal, oily smoke and human blood. And there was also the stink of feces, as dead mens' bowels evacuated.

The Luftwaffe's Stukas were as effective as ever, yet the Soviets kept bringing up more tanks and artillery. Ju-87 pilots such as the famous Hans Rudel fired their cannons with uncanny accuracy, blowing apart dozens of enemy tanks each day, but still there were countless others.

In the end the German armor was able to penetrate the enemy lines for a gain of about 15 kilometers, but eventually the Panzers' advance was brought to a halt. The Soviets then mounted a determined counterattack—led by their powerful T-34 tanks, they drove the Germans back.

Thousands of Russian infantrymen flooded the battlefield. They hit the German armor with saddle charges and Molotov cocktails, and the tank crews were riddled with bullets as they tried to climb out of their burning machines.

Many of the Russian soldiers were as young as 14, though they had not been drafted according to age. Instead, if they were big enough to carry a rifle and a pack, they were given a week or two of training and sent to the front lines. Behind them were officers brandishing pistols, ready to shoot any soldier who failed to charge when ordered.

Against them were some of the Wehrmacht's best divisions, including three of the Waffen SS, but still, it was all they could do to hold up the determined Soviet forces. The Germans dug in and formed a defensive line, hoping they could stave off the waves of advancing armor and infantry.

Despite what was happening in the field, Hitler stubbornly insisted that Zitadelle would eventually succeed. The Russians would be stopped, he claimed, and then cut up by flanking attacks. The reality, however, was that no matter how many Soviet tanks were destroyed, or Soviet aircraft shot down, or Soviet infantrymen killed, there was an endless stream of replacements. Far more than the defeat at Stalingrad, the battle for Kursk would turn the tide against the Germans on the eastern front. After that the Wehrmacht would never again mount a major offensive against the Russians.

As the fighting ground on, another crucial event took place, this one in the Mediterranean. On 10 July, the Allies invaded Sicily, their ships and landing craft supported by three thousand aircraft.

Hitler's reaction was irrational. He called off Zitadelle, and ordered the transfer of dozens of Luftwaffe units from both Russia and Germany to southern Italy, in order to counter the Allied attack. Sicily, he declared, must not be lost.

The army commanders were horrified, as were Milch and Speer. Not only would the German forces at Kursk now have far less air cover, but Germany itself would be made more vulnerable to bombing attacks. The advisers protested, yet Hitler would not budge. Göring, of course, merely carried out the Führer's orders.

As it turned out, the capricious move led to still another link in the chain of disasters.

42.

The invasion was code-named Operation Husky. The plan called for the British 8th Army, under General Bernard Montgomery, to land at Pachino on the east coast of Sicily, while the American 7th Army, under General George Patton, would land at Gela on the west coast. The Canadian 1st Infantry Division, under General H.L.N. Salmon, would be part of the British forces. Overall commander of the combined Allied armies was General Dwight D. Eisenhower.

The defenders were 365,000 Italian troops commanded by General Alfredo Guzzoni, and 40,000 Germans under General Albert Kesselring. Most were veterans of the failed campaign in North Africa, and equipped with several hundred tanks and artillery pieces.

The Axis forces were supported by Luftwaffe bombers and fighters flying from bases in Southern Italy. Most of these were the units that had been transferred from Russia and Germany on orders from Hitler. They were outnumbered two-to-one by the Allies, who sent 3,000 aircraft into action.

Ignoring the odds, on the night of 9 July the German planes attacked both prongs of the invasion forces. Despite stiff resistance from RAF Spitfires and American P-38s, they destroyed a number of the Allied ships and landing craft.

One of the cargo transports was the 20,000 ton USS Robert Rowan, carrying ammunition and supplies. Making a low-level run, a Ju-88 scored a direct hit on the American ship. The Rowan was torn open by a fiery explosion and sank almost at once, its grave marked by a column of black smoke rising from a burning oil slick. Among the crew of 550 sailors, only a handful were rescued.

Just after midnight on 10 July, the U.S. 82nd Airborne Division made its first combat jump. Strong winds blew most of the paratroopers far from their intended landing places. Casualties were light, however, and at dawn the men rallied and defended against a counterattack by Italian troops.

Allied armor and infantry then swarmed onto the beaches and moved inland, despite heavy artillery fire by Italian shore batteries and strafing by the Luftwaffe. British and American forces both made sizeable advances. The following night, four airborne operations were carried out. In two of the operations the British hauled troops in 144 gliders, but only 12 of the gliders reached their objective. Many of the others crash-landed in the sea.

General Patton ordered his reserve paratroop regiments to be flown in by 150 Douglas C-47 aircraft and dropped as reinforcements. But as often happens in the heat of battle, there was a communications failure. The Royal Navy did not get the word, and gunners on its ships mistook the transports for German bombers and shot down several of the American planes.

Patton also had problems with his Allied counterpart. He and

Montgomery were fierce rivals, and Patton felt the British commander enjoyed an inflated reputation. He characterized Montgomery as "that little fart."

Both men were eager to capture Palermo, the capital of Sicily. German troops under General Kesselring slowed Montgomery, but the poorly led Italian forces opposing Patton crumbled, and the Americans took the city. Montgomery then attempted to reach Messina before Patton, but again the Americans moved faster. In his high-pitched, squeaky voice, Patton shouted, "This is a horse race with the prestige of the U.S. Army at stake!" And once more his Third Infantry Division soldiers beat the British to the prize.

But as the Americans entered the city, the veteran German troops put up strong resistance. Patton tried flanking them in three amphibious landings, but, unable to breach the enemy's defenses, he mounted a head-on assault, and that succeeded.

By the time the U.S. troops broke through, they found that most of the surviving Germans and many Italians had been evacuated by ships that would take them across the Straits of Messina to Italy. Allied fighters attacked the transports but the Luftwaffe held them off, and the ships succeeded in reaching Reggio di Calabria on the Italian mainland. A total of 100,000 men and 10,000 tanks and other vehicles managed to escape.

Tempering the Allies' disappointment was the surrender of General Guzzoni's remaining forces, along with the final tally. Axis casualties were 29,000, and 140,000 were captured. The Americans suffered far fewer casualties, with 2,237 dead and 6,544 wounded. British losses were 2,721 dead, and 10,122 wounded. Canadian casualties numbered 2,310.

To the Italian government, the defeat in Sicily made it clear that the war was lost. Benito Mussolini, the boastful dictator and staunch ally of Germany, was paralyzed with fear. He had reason to be. The Fascist Grand Council, one of whose members was Mussolini's son-in-law, Count Galeazzo Ciano, voted to take away Il Duce's power and transfer it to King Vittorio Emanuele III.

The king replaced Mussolini with Pietro Badoglio, who proclaimed that Italy would continue to fight shoulder-to-shoulder with Germany. But behind the scenes Badoglio was secretly negotiating a surrender with the Allies, and had Mussolini arrested and imprisoned.

Hitler regarded the loss of Sicily as intolerable. As always he blamed others for the debacle, fuming that his staff had underestimated the strength of the Allied invasion forces, and that General Kesselring had mishandled defense of the island. He never admitted that he himself had made a mistake by pulling Luftwaffe units from both Russia and the German homeland, and sending them to fight in a lost cause.

Now the Führer was in a much worse position than he had been before. Both the army and the Luftwaffe had sustained yet another defeat that had cost them men and materiel. And Sicily was not only lost, but would serve as a stage from which the enemy forces could invade Italy.

Rubbing salt in the wound was Badoglio's perfidy. The new Italian leader was a committed antifascist, and Hitler loathed him. It was obvious that the Italian government was on the verge of collapse, and when that time came, the Germans would have to defend Italy alone.

As for the downfall of Mussolini, Hitler considered it a personal affront. For all his bumbling, Il Duce had been a partner in the Axis alliance. The Führer vowed to rescue him.

Meanwhile the British saw the weakening of Germany's homeland forces as a golden opportunity. Vice Marshal Harris made plans for a bombing attack that would be more horrific than any other.

Above: Willy Messerschmitt at age 17 along with a French prisoner of war who helped him build the S5 glider, September 1915. *Photo: EADS Corporate Heritage*

Messerschmitt upon graduation as an engineer from the Technische Hochschule in Munich, 1923. *Photo: EADS Corporate Heritage*

M17 lightplane built by Messerschmitt in 1926. He stands at the bow, holding propeller. *Photo: EADS Corporate Heritage*

Willy Messerschmitt's personal Bf-108 over the Bavarian Alps. The author has owned similar aircraft. *Photo: EADS Corporate Heritage*

Adolf Hitler visits a Messerschmitt factory, November 1937. From left: Theo Croneiss, Professor Messerschmitt, Adolf Hitler, F.H. Hentzen, R. Kokothaki. *Photo: EADS Corporate Heritage*

Messerschmitt's chief test pilot, Dr. Hermann Wurster, familiarizes Charles Lindbergh with controls of a Bf-108 prior to his October 1938 flight. *Photo: EADS Corporate Heritage*

A Bf-109-E, powered by a Daimler-Benz 601A 1,100hp engine.
Armament: two 7.9mm machine guns, three 20mm cannons.
Photo: EADS Corporate Heritage

Two of the Luftwaffe's most celebrated *experten:* Lt. Col. and later Lt. Gen. Adolf Galland (104 victories) and Col. Werner Molders (115 victories).
Photo: EADS Corporate Heritage

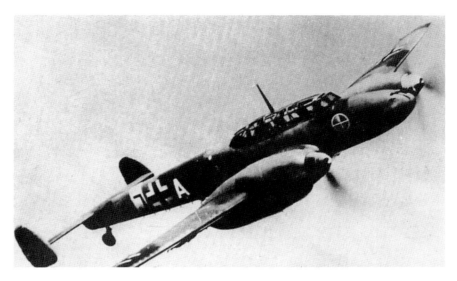

A Bf-110. Unsuccessful as a fighter or fighter-bomber, later very effective as a nightfighter against Allied bombers. *Photo: EADS Corporate Heritage*

Professor Messerschmitt with engineer Wiedekind outside the flight-test hangar at the Augsburg plant in April 1940. *Photo: EADS Corporate Heritage*

Ernst Heinkel, Willy Messerschmitt, and Ferdinand Porsche are honored by Adolf Hitler at a ceremony in Berlin. *Photo: EADS Corporate Heritage*

Board members at Regensburg, August 1940. From left: Friedrich Mayer, F.H. Hentzen, Baroness Lilly Stromeyer, Willy Messerschmitt, Theo Croneiss, R. Kokothaki, F.W. Seiler. *Photo: EADS Corporate Heritage*

The Me-210 fighter-bomber, a disastrous failure. Worst mistake in Willy Messerschmitt's career. *Photo: EADS Corporate Heritage*

Robert Lusser, aircraft engineer, designer and pilot. At Messerschmitt, he worked on development of the Bf-108, Bf-109, and Bf-110. He later left to join Heinkel. *Photo: EADS Corporate Heritage*

Hermann Goring and Erhard Milch at demonstration of new aircraft, 1942. Chief of Air Staff Hans Jeschonnek stands behind them.
Photo: EADS Corporate Heritage

Fritz Wendel with the Me-262 V3. He piloted this aircraft on its maiden flight, 8 July 1942. *Photo: EADS Corporate Heritage*

Bf-109-G fighters flying in *schwarm* formation on escort mission over the Mediterranean, May 1943. *Photo: EADS Corporate Heritage*

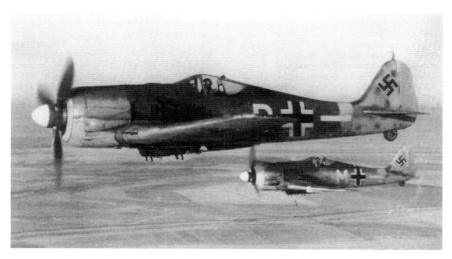

Focke-Wulf FW-190 fighters powered by aircooled BMW 801 engines over France, 1943. *Photo: EADS Corporate Heritage*

Me-262 A-1a (WNr. 130 167) first flew on 30 May 1944. This aircraft made almost 300 test flights during development of the type. *Photo: EADS Corporate Heritage*

Test pilot Fritz Wendel inspecting an Me-262 at Luftwaffe air base Lager Lechfeld, October 1944. *Photo: EADS Corporate Heritage*

An Me-262 fighter serving with Kommando Nowotny. After Major Nowotny's death on 8 November 1944, the unit became JG7.
Photo: EADS Corporate Heritage

The Me-163 B Komet rocket interceptor. Conceived by Dr. Alexander Lippisch, it was developed and produced by Messerschmitt. 300 were built, but were never effective in combat. *Photo: EADS Corporate Heritage*

Luftwaffe test pilot Heinz Suhrbeer (r) with mechanic making preflight inspection of an Me-262 at Lager Lechfeld in early 1945. Suhrbeer later flew the Me-262 in combat. *Photo: EADS Corporate Heritage*

Me-262 built in a factory hidden within a forest near the Salzburg-Munich Autobahn.
Photo: EADS Corporate Heritage

Me-262 A-1a fighters of III.EJG2 take off from Lager Lelchfeld in February 1945 to intercept a U.S. bomber fleet attacking Munich.
Photo: EADS Corporate Heritage

Cockpit of Me-262 A-1. Throttles are on left side. Note safety
device over trigger on top of control stick.
Photo: EADS Corporate Heritage

Above: The rack under each wing of an Me-262 held 12 R4M rockets. The blast from one rocket could bring down Allied bombers. *Photo: EADS Corporate Heritage*

Left: Col. Hajo Herrmann, creator of the *Wilde Sau* nightfighter unit, and later proponent of *Sonderkommando Elbe,* whose pilots were directed to ram Allied bombers. *Photo: EADS Corporate Heritage*

Lilly and Willy Messerschmitt in July 1965 at the International
Transport Exhibit in Munich. Prof. Messerschmitt is wearing
the "Golden Windrose" neck chain awarded him for his
pioneering work in aviation.
Photo: Professor Gero Madelung, Willy Messerschmitt's nephew

PART IV

REAPING THE WHIRLWIND

43.

A s conceived by Harris, this would be the first joint mission flown by the RAF and the U.S. 8th Air Force. They were to hit the same target with round-the-clock bombing over four days, the British attacking at night and the Americans in daylight. The operation was code-named Gomorrah. Until now the RAF had carried out all the large-scale raids on Germany, with the 8th Air Force mainly attacking targets in France, Holland, and Belgium. The raid on Wilhelmshaven, and a few others, had been exceptions.

As the British had predicted, the Americans' B-17s and B-24s were being mauled by German fighters. But the Yanks refused to abandon their methods, insisting that precision bombing, and not area bombing, would do the most damage to German war industries. Therefore, they went on flying by day in tight formations, the bombers depending on massed fire from their machine guns to hold off the enemy. Sometimes that succeeded, but increasingly it did not. American losses mounted.

The target Harris and the RAF planners had chosen was Hamburg. Located 80 kilometers down the Elbe River from the North Sea, it was Germany's largest seaport, and its second largest city. An important business and cultural center, Hamburg was more than a thousand years old, with a population of about two million people. As a port, Hamburg was vital to Germany's ability to wage war. This was where ships carrying much-needed raw materials discharged their cargos, including iron ore from Scandinavia. Without that ore, the nation's steel industry could not function. Hamburg was also the site of large shipyards, which

159

were situated near the confluence of the Elbe, Alster, and Bille rivers. The battleship Bismarck and more than 200 U-boats had been built there.

Numerous manufacturers were in the area as well, producing aviation parts and engines, machine tools, military uniforms and boots, medical supplies, chemicals, textiles, and electrical components. Nearby storage barns were filled with grain.

In planning Gomorrah, Harris showed no pity for Hamburg's inhabitants. His views were summed up when he quoted from the bible, saying of the Germans, "They have sowed the wind, and so shall they reap the whirlwind."

The initial attack was scheduled for 24 July 1943. By then the RAF's new Window idea was ready for service, and British authorities granted Harris permission to use it.

On the evening of the 24th, Mosquito pathfinders took off from their base in England and crossed the Channel, guided by the Oboe navigational aid. Once over France the crews began releasing chaff, and kept it up all the way into Germany. As the aluminum-clad paper strips fluttered downward, they rendered the German Würzburg radar system useless. The operators' screens showed nothing but blizzards of white dots, making it impossible either to identify or to track the fast twin-engine aircraft.

Shortly after the pathfinders took off, 791 heavily loaded Lancaster, Halifax and Wellington bombers followed. They too dumped chaff into the night sky, compounding the Germans' confusion. The only evidence of the impending raid came from the thunderous roar of more than two thousand British aircraft engines passing overhead.

Without radar, the German defenses were blind. No data could be sent to the flak gunners and searchlight crews, or to the Luftwaffe pilots. And though the chaff was jamming the enemy's radar, it had no effect on the H2S radar aboard the Mosquitos. Nor did the Germans have any means of countering it.

When they looked at their screens, the Mosquitos' navigators saw what an incredible technological advance the new H2S radar system was. There before them were images of every feature of the city. It was easy to pick out the shipyards and the factories and other buildings, as well as the rivers and the canals and the nearby lakes. Even the stone flak towers with their antiaircraft guns were visible.

And of course, the residential neighborhoods could also be clearly seen. Electronic probing had laid the city bare.

At the sound of the Mosquitos' engines, searchlight beams swept the sky and flak gunners sent up 88mm shells. But at the height the aircraft were flying, the searchlights merely moved back and forth and the AA shells burst harmlessly. The pathfinders then began dropping flares.

The pyrotechnic devices lit up the area. So bright were the red and green and yellow markers that crews of the lead RAF bombers could see them from a distance of many miles. The pilots simply adjusted course and headed for the target.

They arrived at the stroke of midnight. Most of the aircraft were carrying 4,000-pound high-explosive blockbusters, while others had 500-pounders in their racks. Keying on the objective, the crews opened their bomb bay doors, and a cascade of the huge finned missiles rained down on the hapless city, striking with colossal force. They exploded by the hundreds, and hundreds more followed. Within minutes many of the largest buildings were smashed, and people unlucky enough to be inside them were crushed to death.

The shipyards were wrecked, and so were vessels tied up at the docks. Streetcars, trucks and automobiles were flung into the air like toys, trees were vaporized, houses shattered. Anyone out on the street was killed instantly.

With the German radar cancelled out by Window, not only had the flak and searchlight crews been given short notice, but so had the civilian population. Now with the earth trembling from the shock of the explosions, survivors left their homes and rushed down into the concrete subterranean shelters, while others huddled in their cellars. Many were caught outside by the horrendous bomb blasts.

In addition to the HE types, some of the aircraft dropped incendiaries packed with white phosphorus. Upon landing, the phosphorus ignited fires that were almost impossible to extinguish. Soon the fires were burning all over Hamburg, but with an effect not only on buildings. When white phosphorus touches human skin, it can burn down to the bone. If that doesn't kill the victim, the chemical can still do irreparable damage to the heart, liver and kidneys. While many people in Hamburg were annihilated that night by exploding bombs, many others died in excruciating pain from phosphorus burns.

Another property of burning phosphorus is that it produces dense smoke, which was why it was often used to make smoke screens. In little time, a choking, poisonous smoke obscured much of the area. People also died from inhaling it.

A full hour passed before the last of the bombers made its run. During that time the Luftwaffe, its home defenses weakened by Hitler, sent only a few night fighters to the site. The radar in those machines had been nullified by the chaff as well, but because of the fires and the few searchlight beams still operating, the pilots could see the bombers plainly. Yet, there weren't enough of the Bf-110s and Ju-88s to make much of a dent in the bomber stream. The British aircraft remained in formation, and their gunners shot down a number of enemy planes.

Occasionally a fighter managed to evade the defensive fire and zero in on a bomber, usually from beneath it. The German pilot then poured machine gun and cannon fire into the bomber, sending it down in flames. But such victories were few. In the end, only 12 RAF bombers were lost.

Meanwhile, on the ground, the reeling defenders did what they could to tend to the wounded and deal with the fires and the wreckage. It was a herculean task, especially since many of the firemen and rescue workers themselves had been killed, and many of the fire stations had been demolished. Getting help to where it was needed was often impossible—the streets were either piled high with blazing rubble or pocked with bomb craters.

"Terror bombing!" Goebbels' news media again shouted. "Proof that the British are inhuman! History will condemn them!"

But to the RAF, Operation Gomorrah was very nearly perfect. The damage to the target was enormous, and bomber losses were less than two percent. Harris was thrilled with the results.

That had been only the opening round. More blows would soon strike Hamburg. And it would be the Americans' turn to deliver them.

44.

The day after the RAF raid, Hamburg's surviving firemen, medics, police, soldiers and laborers struggled to cope with the devastation. Many of the city's largest buildings had been smashed to rubble, and the shipyards were a tangle of twisted steel and wrecked vessels and machinery. Some of the fires were brought under control, while others continued to burn, and the air was filled with poisonous smoke.

Human suffering was widespread. Thousands were dead, and thousands more had been wounded. People fortunate enough to have found shelter crept out to assess the damage. Bulldozers had cleared a few of the streets, enabling aid workers to take the injured to where they could be treated, but treatment was hard to come by. There was a shortage of doctors and nurses, because many of them had been killed in the bombing. The hospitals also had been hit, and though damaged, they were filled to capacity. Temporary aid stations were equally crowded

The only way to treat phosphorus burns was to immerse the skin in water, and then if possible remove the hot particles. If the patient lived, the wounds had to be bathed with copper sulfate solution, though often people died in agony.

In the late afternoon the city was subjected to a grim surprise. It was the second phase of Harris's Operation Gomorrah. Two wings of the U.S. 8th Air Force made the attack, with nearly 200 bombers reaching Hamburg. Yet, when they tried to find their assigned targets, all the crews could see was a huge column of smoke. In addition, strong winds aloft over the North Sea had prevented the aircraft from holding proper formation. Many had become stragglers.

In broad daylight the bombers were clearly visible to flak gunners. The batteries began firing, and the American aircraft were met with a barrage. The Luftwaffe had also been alerted, and though short of fighters, several staffeln of Bf-109s were sent to intercept.

There were other problems that confronted the bomber crews. Lt. Philip P. Dreiseszun, navigator in the "Lethal Lady," a B-17 of the 381st Bomb Group, recounted that his aircraft's assignment was to bomb the Klockner engine factory. However, with the smoke and the flak there was no hope of picking out a specific target. So instead, the aircraft's bombardier released the load of ten 500-pounders somewhere over the city, guided only by the thick black cloud rising thousands of feet into the air.

The B-17 was then rocked by bursting antiaircraft shells. Dreiseszun's B-17 was heavily damaged, and as the pilot tried to hold the airplane steady, it was attacked by fighters firing 20mm cannons. The projectiles tore through the bomber.

Dreiseszun was wounded by shell splinters in his arms and legs. Bleeding profusely, he saw that the bombardier had suffered a deep chest wound. He dumped sulfa powder into the gaping hole, and then tried to apply a bandage, but it was too late. The man was already dead.

There was no possibility that the B-17 could continue to fly. Its control surfaces had been shot up, and one of the engines was on fire. The pilot ordered the crewmen to bail out. Although several of them had also been wounded, they were able to exit the burning aircraft.

Dreiseszun kicked open the nose hatch and jumped into the icy air. He pulled his ripcord after falling an estimated two thousand feet, wincing from the pain when the parachute opened and the harness bit into his crotch. He had removed his gloves when trying to treat the bombardier, and now his hands suffered chilblains. Hanging limp and semi-conscious in his parachute, he floated down for 20 minutes before reaching the earth.

He landed hard, and almost immediately was surrounded by German soldiers who were pointing their weapons at him. They dragged him to his feet and took him to a nearby village, where his wounds were treated. After interrogation he was sent to Stalag Luft III, where he spent the rest of the war; other survivors in the crew were sent to Stalag Luft XVII. The copilot and one of the waist gunners weren't so lucky, and were beaten to death by enraged civilians. Apparently the civilians believed Joseph Goebbels' story of American airmen, who were all Chicago gangsters paid to commit atrocities against helpless German citizens.

After completing their bomb runs, the remaining B-17s turned back to the coast. They were further harassed by fighters and fired on by flak batteries, but most of them made it home to their bases in England. Fifteen American bombers were lost.

Again, Harris was pleased. Because of the smoke there was no way to reconnoiter the damage Hamburg had sustained, but he was sure the situation on the ground was chaotic. The great city would be a shambles, blasted to ruins by the bombs. It would also be swarming with firemen and workers trying to put out fires and contend with the damage. Police and soldiers would be attempting to restore order, and medics would be treating countless numbers of injured. The city would be full of dazed, homeless civilians.

To the Vice Marshal, that made the situation ideal for launching the final phase of Gomorrah. He scheduled it for 27 July. The raid would be the most ferocious of all.

That night Mosquito pathfinders again took off in the darkness and led a great fleet of RAF bombers to Germany. There were 787 of the heavy aircraft, including 353 Lancasters, 244 Halifaxes, 116 Stirlings, and 74 Wellingtons.

Once more the fleet of bombers reached Hamburg at midnight, homing in on the brightly colored markers that had been dropped by the pathfinders. As before, chaff had nullified the German radar, thus handicapping the searchlight and flak crews. Nevertheless, the gunners fired thousands of 88mm shells up into the night sky, and the Luftwaffe, having suspected yet another attack on the city, scrambled a large number of night fighters. Yet none of this stopped the bombers from making their runs as planned.

Beside HE, many of the RAF aircraft were also loaded with even more diabolical incendiaries. These were tall brass cylinders called small-bomb containers, or SBCs. Each was packed with 236 white phosphorus bombs. When dropped, an SBC opened up at 1500 feet above the target and scattered the phosphorus bombs.

First, the aircraft carrying HE dumped their loads, causing more destruction among the already shattered buildings. The new piles of rubble blocked the streets and prevented firefighting vehicles from getting to where they were needed most.

Then came the cascade of incendiaries. Each of the phosphorus bombs started an intense, white-hot fire—it was as if a million savage fireflies had attacked Hamburg. In all, the RAF dropped 2,326 tons of both high-explosive and incendiary bombs on the doomed city.

The atmospheric conditions were ideal for the RAF's purposes. The air at ground level was unusually warm, with a temperature of 30 degrees Celsius, and humidity was only 30 percent. Since there had been no rain for days, the region was extremely dry.

Many of the firebombs landed in the densely populated working-class districts of Borgfeld, Hamm, and Hammerbrook. Within minutes the entire area was ablaze, with temperatures reaching as high as 1,000 degrees Celsius. The atmosphere was so hot it sucked surrounding air toward the center of the fire at enormous speed. The superheated air carried with it flaming wreckage, including uprooted trees. The flames consumed everything in their path and then spread out, until Hamburg was totally engulfed.

Protection of any kind was impossible. People who had crowded into the underground concrete shelters or gone down to their cellars were incinerated. Some tried to flee the city, but anyone above ground was snatched up by the fiery hurricane winds. Women trying to run away had children torn from their arms, and then they too were vaporized.

Fighting the fires was equally hopeless. Fire trucks melted, and whole cadres of firemen were either suffocated or burned to death. Many medics and aid workers died from breathing toxic smoke or the billowing fumes of carbon monoxide. In addition to factories and shipyards, 1,620 apartment houses were destroyed by the fires, as were countless small homes. In fact, hardly any building in Hamburg escaped damage. Many were wiped out as if by a giant hand.

The Luftwaffe night fighters fought the bombers as well as they could, but again they were too few in number to cope with the great fleet. RAF losses were relatively light, with only 17 aircraft shot down.

The following day, Hamburg was a nightmarish landscape. Fires continued to burn everywhere, and among the huge piles of rubble were scores of blackened, unrecognizable human corpses. The smoke was visible a hundred kilometers away.

Not only did Vice Marshal Harris consider Gomorrah a splendid operation, but in fact, viewed it as a model for future attacks on Germany. It also confirmed his belief that area bombing was the most effective way to use air power.

Clearly, Hamburg had been rendered a ghost city. It would no longer be able to make its former contributions to the war effort, and whether it could recover was doubtful. Fifty thousand of its citizens were dead, and more than a million others, many of them injured, had fled the city.

Most German leaders understood the significance of the attacks. Albert Speer said that if similar raids were made on six other major cities, Germany would be unable to continue the war. Obviously, there was a desperate need to strengthen the nation's defenses.

Hitler, however, saw matters differently. As always, the Führer was obsessed with a desire for revenge. He insisted that Germany's response should be to intensify its bombing of Britain. "The only way to fight terror," he proclaimed, "is with terror!"

Erhard Milch had no such illusions. Like Speer, he knew that Germany could not endure more bombing on the scale of the Hamburg raids. He urged that homeland defense be given priority over everything else. Fighter production had to go up to at least 3,000 a month, he said, or the war was lost.

As for Messerschmitt AG, the company was to deliver increased numbers of the Bf-109, and at the same time, rush development of new aircraft. The Luftwaffe needed as many Me-262 jets as the firm could produce.

45.

Messerschmitt knew that constructing the Me-262 in any meaningful quantity would be difficult. There were still unresolved engineering problems, and the firm was heavily preoccupied with other projects. By now it employed more than 16,000 workers, including slave laborers, and was building its products in 25 different locations in Germany and Austria.

Following standard procedure, a schedule was presented to the Air Ministry. This was Production Program 223, and after some grumbling the RLM agreed to it. The schedule called for delivery of the first production-run jet aircraft in January 1944. In February, eight more would be produced, then twenty-one in March, forty in April, and in May, sixty. Thereafter, sixty Me-262s per month would be delivered.

Even those modest numbers were optimistic. The company's jig and tool department was overburdened, and at the same time Program 223 was to be implemented, Messerschmitt was also preparing for series production of the Me-309 piston fighter. Additionally, the firm was short of skilled labor.

One part of the dilemma was solved by pulling experienced machinists away from other companies. There were howls of protest, but Messerschmitt got away with it.

To keep the Me-262 program on track, he decided the fuselages and tails would be produced at the Regensburg plant, while the wings and assembly of the aircraft would take place at Augsburg. To make room, some of the Bf-109 production was moved to Wiener-Neustadt.

The jet's most pressing engineering problem was that of the undercarriage. It still consisted of the mains plus a tail wheel, though General Galland had strongly recommended that the aircraft be equipped with tricycle gear. He said the brake-tapping procedure on takeoffs was crude and dangerous, and would be too much for the average pilot to handle.

Messerschmitt had agreed to change the undercarriage to a tricycle type, but it had yet to be built. So for a test flight, a nose wheel borrowed from an Me-309 was bolted onto a prototype Me-262, the V5. The aircraft was flown by Karl Baur on 6 June 1943. It required the usual long takeoff roll, and because the makeshift nose wheel was not retractable, the V5 was sluggish and nose heavy once it was in the air. The team concluded that for a satisfactory test, the Jumo 004 A-O engines would need assistance. To provide it, a pair of Borsig RI-502 rockets were mounted under the fuselage. They were rated to provide 1,100 pounds of thrust for six seconds.

On the next flight, Baur began his takeoff roll and waited until the aircraft reached a speed of 175 kph before he ignited the rockets. When he did, the reaction was more abrupt than he'd expected. The nose rose sharply, and the V5 began to lift off.

Baur knew the danger: if the aircraft left the runway before it had sufficient flying speed, it would stall as soon as the rockets' six seconds of assistance expired. The result would be a nasty pancake crash. Hastily he shoved the stick forward. The V5 touched down and continued its roll.

When Baur finally did take off, he found that the roll had been shortened by almost a hundred meters. That did nothing, however, to improve performance once the V5 was aloft. It had the same undesirable characteristics as in the earlier test, and if anything the added drag of the rockets made matters worse.

Messerschmitt then directed Voigt to stop everything and install a hydraulically powered retractable nose wheel. To adjust the CG for proper balance, the main wheels were moved one meter back toward the tail. The Borsig rockets were eliminated.

The next problem concerned the armament, which consisted of three machine guns in the nose and two Mark-108 30mm cannons in the wings. General Galland had considered that inadequate as well. In Galland's opinion, machine guns were of little use against bombers. So it was decided that the production aircraft would be armed with four cannons in a nose bay.

Other changes were also made. Since the cockpit would not be pressurized, an oxygen tank was provided. Pilots would breathe through a mask, and wear electrically heated clothing.

As these refinements to the Me-262 were carried out, one of the Air Ministry's many orders ironically called for producing greater numbers of the Bf-110. A special version, the F-4, had been developed expressly for night fighting. It was equipped with a Telefunken radar intercept system, and the rudders were enlarged for greater stability. The aircraft was fitted with exhaust flame dampers, and the paint scheme was light blue, which made the F-4 hard to see against the night sky.

But the most important improvement was in its armament. Two MK-108 30mm cannons were placed in the rear cockpit, facing forward and slanted upward at a 15-degree angle. Luftwaffe pilots called the brace of cannons Schräge Musik, which literally meant slanted music, but was also slang for jazz. The arrangement was designed to take advantage of the vulnerable bellies of the RAF Lancaster and Halifax bombers.

Neither of the British aircraft had guns in that position, so the pilot of an F-4 would slip in from below and behind. His gunner would open up at close range, and even one or two hits were often enough to destroy an enemy bomber. Long regarded as an ugly duckling, the aircraft had blossomed into a swan, thanks to its newfound prowess. The RLM wanted more of them.

More day fighters were wanted as well, and therefore larger quantities of Bf-109s would also be built. Although many pilots considered the Fw-190 a better fighter, one-third more Bf-109s were being produced than Focke-Wulfs. A total of 6,379 Bf-109s would be manufactured in 1943, all of them the Gustav version. They were powered by the new Daimler-Benz DB-605 engine, which provided 1,800 hp.

Because of General Galland's view that machine guns alone weren't enough when attacking bombers, a number of different armament schemes were used in the Gustav. A few were fitted with MK-108 30mm cannons mounted in underwing pods, which proved unsuitable because of the added drag. Pilots called the pods bathtubs, and hated the way they downgraded performance. Eventually the idea was abandoned.

The need for greater firepower persisted, however, and the Gustav was then equipped with two cowl-mounted MG-131 7.9mm machine guns, a MK-108 30mm cannon that fired through the spinner, and two MG-151 20mm cannons in the wings. It was an awesome combination, and necessary, because the Bf-109G's role in attacking American bombers was critically important.

There was plenty of action for them, with Flying Fortresses and Liberators pounding German cities on a daily basis. Many U.S. bombers were shot down by pilots flying the Gustav. Yet despite the losses, the American commanders were as convinced as ever that their methods were correct. After the experience in Operation Gomorrah, General Eaker was not eager to take part in any further joint missions with the RAF. Instead, Eaker and the 8th Air Force planners concentrated on precision bombing of targets that they, and not Vice Marshal Harris, selected. The Yanks clung to their principle of flying in tight formation, with bombers putting out formidable amounts of fire to hold off enemy fighters.

Luftwaffe pilots favored approaching the *viermots* from above, swooping down at an angle for a quick firing pass and then climbing out of range of the bomber's machine guns. The tactic didn't always work, because the pass was so brief that there was little time to aim with the fighter's reflector sight. The angle further reduced the pilot's chances for getting hits.

Attacking directly from astern was even less effective. The fighter would not only be targeted by the bomber's tail gunner firing twin .50-calibers, but also by others in the formation. Too often the hunter would be destroyed by his prey.

Considering this, the Germans came up with a bold new idea. They'd observed that the American B-17 had no forward-firing guns in its nose. Then why not attack it head-on? Hauptmann Egon Mayer, the commander of the Luftwaffe's 2nd Fighter Geschwader, elected to try such an approach.

Over Magdeburg on a cool, clear day, Mayer and his pilots intercepted a formation of three hundred bombers. The enemy aircraft were coming toward the Germans at 7,000 meters, and Mayer leveled off his Bf-109G at the same altitude. He picked out a B-17 and flew directly at it.

As the oncoming four-engine aircraft rapidly grew larger in his gunsight, Mayer could make out the pilot and copilot. He fired his cannons and machine guns and saw tracers smash into the cockpit. At the last instant he pulled back the stick, and his Bf-109G zoomed upward, barely missing the B-17. The bomber spun down out of control, mortally wounded.

After that, Luftwaffe pilots were encouraged to try the same tactic.

Using Mayer's approach, they attacked other B-17s on subsequent occasions, and though sometimes achieved similar success, they did not always. More than once an overly eager young fighter pilot made a head-on run at an enemy bomber and failed to pull up in time. The *Gustav* and the *viermot* then illuminated the sky with a fiery explosion.

The USAAF took steps to correct the problem. Chin guns were added to the B-17s, a pair of .50-calibers that would be fired by the bombardier when he wasn't busy with his Norden bombsight. It was enough to discourage head-on attacks, and most Luftwaffe pilots then reverted to their earlier methods.

Nevertheless the fighters achieved a growing number of kills, and the Americans realized they could not sustain such losses. The only answer would be to introduce a fighter with sufficient range to escort the bombers all the way to the target. German Intelligence reported that the U.S. had recently built such a long-range aircraft, and was testing it.

Meanwhile, at the design center in Augsburg, Messerschmitt was dealing with a heavy workload. Along with fine-tuning the Me-262 and the Bf-109G, and increasing production of the Bf-110F4 night fighter, he was busy with the ongoing development of heavy aircraft, in particular the Me-264. He also oversaw further experiments with the rocket-powered Komet, the Me-163. The Komet had never held much interest for him. He regarded the fat, bullet-shaped lines as a contradiction of everything he thought an aircraft should be. But doubts notwithstanding, he supervised a redesign. The result was the Me-163B.

The new version had more or less the same ugly shape as the original, but now with more sharply swept-back wings. Covered with plywood, the wings were fitted with slats to help prevent spinning. To add strength, the fuselage was reinforced with lightweight alloys. In another change, the 163B mounted a much more powerful engine. This was the Walter RII-211, which produced 3,750 pounds of thrust. The fuel was T-Stoff, an 80% hydrogen peroxide-based liquid. In addition, C-Stoff, a solution of hydrazine hydrate in methanol, was used as a catalyst.

The Walter engine had a ravenous appetite, consuming fuel at the rate of 11 pounds per second. For that reason, the aircraft carried 229 gallons of T-Stoff in the main tank behind the cockpit, plus 26 more gallons in tanks on either side of the cockpit, plus two 16-gallon tanks of C-Stoff in the wings.

Even with all that fuel, the Komet could remain in the air no longer than six minutes. Trailing a stream of white smoke, it would zoom to an altitude of 10,000 meters. And after performing a maneuver or two, it would come down for a hot landing. The aircraft's undercarriage consisted of a trolley with large wheels, and a belly skid. As the Komet left the runway, the trolley and wheels would be left behind. When landing, the aircraft would touch down on the skid and slide to a stop.

The RLM had ordered six prototypes of the Komet, and 70 pre-production aircraft, hoping the design would become an effective interceptor of enemy bombers. Testing was bedeviled with mishaps from the outset. In one of them the veteran test pilot Heini Ditmar was at the controls.

Ditmar took off, circled high above the field, and brought the Komet in to land. When he was four meters above the runway, the engine cut out. The aircraft slammed down, and Ditmar's spine was fractured in several places. Lucky to have survived, he spent the next two years in a hospital.

Test pilots doubted the Komet would ever be fit for combat. Messerschmitt shared their misgivings.

With so many activities occupying the Professor's time, Fritz Seiler and Rakan Kokothaki were nominally in charge of the company's day-to-day business operations. Even so, the man who made most of the key decisions was Willy Messerschmitt. And as a result, he found himself suffering physically from the strain. He wasn't sleeping well, often getting less than four hours a night, and his blood pressure was much higher than it should have been. His eating habits were erratic, and he chain-smoked cigarettes.

Lilly urged him to get more rest and to change his lifestyle, but he refused to slow down. He was anxious to fulfill the RLM's orders on schedule, because he knew as well as anyone what was at stake.

His anxiety was well-founded. For Germany, the war news was nearly all bad. The recent battles on the eastern front had been disastrous, and the Wehrmacht was losing ground to the Soviets. In Africa, General Rommel's forces had been defeated, and the Allied armies in Sicily were preparing to invade mainland Italy. The news from the Pacific was equally grim. The defeat at Midway had crippled the Japanese Imperial Navy, and the Emperor's ground forces had lost Guadalcanal. And now, the United States Marines were in control of the

Gilbert and Marshall Islands, as well as New Guinea.

Messerschmitt was not alone in worrying about these events and what they meant; any perceptive German official had to be deeply concerned. Not only did the setbacks of the armed forces indicate what was happening, but increasingly, the enemy was bringing the war to the German homeland.

The facts surrounding the destruction of Hamburg had been too great for the Propaganda Ministry to distort. Many people in Germany had friends and relatives who'd been in Hamburg during the firebombing, and the survivors' horror stories spread rapidly. Other cities, such as Frankfurt, Stuttgart and Munich were also hit repeatedly, and later that summer, Augsburg was bombed for the first time. Damage was relatively slight, and Messerschmitt AG was unscathed. The Professor realized, however, that sooner or later the factory would suffer serious damage. With that in mind, he ordered his staff to prepare for a move to Oberammergau, a small Alpine village farther south in Bavaria. The development bureau would be the first to leave.

Before the move could be made, the Americans took aim at an industry Germany could not afford to lose—in fact, it was more vital than any other. Keenly aware of the target's value, the USAAF planned a daring attack. The operation would be extremely hazardous, and might result in great losses of bombers and aircrews. Yet despite this, the American commanders concluded the attack would be worth the risk.

46.

A modern army cannot function without machines. And machines cannot function without oil. Although Germany was rich in coal, she had no oil deposits. Some of her oil was imported, and some of it was synthetic.

The Germans had learned to make synthetic oil by liquefying coal. Invented by Professor Franz Fischer and Dr. Hans Tropsch in 1925, the process used metal catalysts to combine carbon monoxide gas and hydrogen at temperatures above 900 degrees Celsius, thereby reducing hydrocarbons to liquid.

The Fischer-Tropsch process enabled Germany to produce 125,000 barrels of synthetic oil a day from coal. In addition to supplying lubricating oil, the process provided the Wehrmacht with both diesel fuel and petrol for aircraft, ships, tanks, trucks and other vehicles. The volume was crucial for keeping the machines of war running, but much larger amounts of natural oil were needed as well.

One of Germany's chief sources of natural oil was an area 50 kilometers north of Bucharest, in occupied Romania. Seven refineries were located there, five of them in the town of Ploesti. Another was 18 miles to the northwest at Cimpina, and the seventh was at Brazi, five miles south. Together the refineries produced an estimated million tons of oil a month, and supplied 35 percent of Germany's aviation fuel. It was obvious to leaders of the USAAF that knocking out those refineries would deal Germany a severe blow.

The USAAF had attacked Ploesti once before. On the night of 11 June 1942, thirteen B-24s of the 9th Air Force took off from an RAF field at Fayid, Egypt and headed north. The inexperienced crews had no lead navigator, and did not fly in formation. Instead, each aircraft had to find its own way to Romania, and then to Ploesti. One B-24 was forced to turn back with engine trouble, but the others flew on.

Incredibly, all twelve of the remaining bombers reached the oil fields shortly before dawn. The pilots had difficulty identifying the targets, but they dumped their bombs on the refineries and started fires in the storage tanks. Ultimately, the raid did little damage to the complex, and none of the bombers were shot down. Six of them landed in Iraq, two in Syria, and four in Turkey. Their crews were interned.

Now in the summer of 1943, the USAAF planned another raid. The objective this time was to completely destroy the refineries. The plan was devised by the 9th's Col. Jakob E. Smart, and was code-named Operation Tidal Wave. Some U.S. officers were opposed to it, warning that losses could be as high as 50 percent. But eventually, the top-secret plan was approved by General Arnold, and by the Supreme ETO Commander, General Dwight D. Eisenhower.

The mission would be no milk run. The Germans were well aware of the refineries' importance, and in the year following the first raid they'd beefed up defenses. A great number of flak batteries were now in the area, and several Luftwaffe fighter squadrons were based at nearby airfields.

Another problem was distance. A task force starting from North Africa would have to fly just over 1,200 miles to reach the target, and then fly home. No Allied fighter had anything like that range, so the bombers would be without escorts.

Success would depend heavily on two factors. One, of course, was surprise. The bombers would have to hit the objective before its defenders had time to react. That meant approaching at low altitude, to evade detection by enemy radar.

The other factor was striking power. This time a large, well-organized force would be required. There would be but one raid, with no possibility of a second chance.

Therefore, the task force would consist of five groups. Two of them, the 98th and the 376th of the 9th Air Force, were already based in North Africa. The other three were the 44th, 93rd, and 389th Groups of the 8th Air Force, based in England, who would be moved to Africa to take part in the raid. A total of 177 aircraft would fly the mission, all B-24s. The planners chose the Liberator because it had great range and was considered more rugged than the B-17. It also carried a larger bomb load, up to 8,000 pounds.

The raiders would depart from fields near Benghazi, Libya. It was a bleak site. The North African desert was arid and desolate and subject to extreme fluctuations in temperature. Even in summer the nights were cold, and yet by midday the thermometer often registered 120 degrees Fahrenheit. The ground crews and the airmen lived in tents, ate poor food, and developed rashes. They shivered when the sun went down and sweated when it came up, and were bitten mercilessly by large black flies. Shoes had to be shaken out to dislodge scorpions. And now and then, unexpected sandstorms blew with such force that paint was ground off airplanes and trucks.

Maintaining the B-24s was a tough job, and the sand made it worse. Tiny particles of it got into oil and grease; it damaged moving parts and constantly fouled carburetors. In the extreme heat engine gaskets and hoses dried out and cracked, and even in the shade of tarpaulins, tools were blistering hot to the touch.

Flying was equally difficult. Heat shimmers made it hard to judge distance, which could result in overshooting a runway or else setting down short of it. The heat also caused instruments to give quirky readings or fail altogether. And at times, an engine would quit for no apparent reason.

On 31 July 1943, mechanics and armorers worked far into the night to prepare the B-24s. Each aircraft was loaded with ten M43 high explosive 500-pound bombs, plus eighty M50A1 incendiaries of 41 pounds apiece, packed in clusters. Machine guns were given a last check, and belts of ammunition put aboard. Takeoff was scheduled for 0400.

The bombers of the 376th Group would lead the mission. One B-24 of the 376th would be flown by Col. Keith K. Compton, and the mission commander, Brig. Gen. Uzal Ent, would be in Compton's airplane. The 93rd, 98th, 44th, and 389th Groups would follow in that order. Each group was assigned specific targets.

The idea was that attacking all six refineries at once would saturate the defenses. With so many bombers hitting them the flak gunners would be confused, and the Luftwaffe fighters would barely have time to become airborne before the bombers had destroyed their targets and left the area.

It was a simple plan, and a good one. But in war nothing is ever simple, nor does a plan ever go exactly as intended. Certainly that was true of Operation Tidal Wave.

47.

The bombers took off as the dawn's first yellow rays streaked the eastern sky. The 177 B-24s formed up, and Brig. Gen. Ent and Col. Compton led the groups on a heading of 355 degrees. They held an altitude of 500 feet and a cruising speed of 215 mph.

Trouble started early on. While over the Mediterranean, three of the groups fell behind. Next, a bomber in the 376th apparently experienced engine failure as it neared Corfu. The B-24 rolled over at low altitude and crashed into the sea, its bombs exploding when it hit. The mission's route navigator was in that airplane. The pilot of another bomber in the 376th made the mistake of circling over the crash site, looking for survivors. All he saw was black smoke rising from bits of burning wreckage, and by then the other aircraft had flown on. Knowing his overloaded bomber could never catch up and rejoin them, he turned back to Benghazi.

Now a new hazard confronted the groups. As they approached the mountains, they found the peaks shrouded in lofty white towers of cumulus. There was nothing to do but climb and pray. They did both, and plunged into the clouds.

The bombers avoided the granite tops by only a few feet. As they made their way through the dense vapor, crews lost sight of one another, and broke formation. When the 44th, 98th, and 389th Groups emerged from the gloom, the bombers were widely scattered. By the time they'd reformed and were again on course for Pitesti, there was no sign of the 93rd or the 376th Groups that had earlier been some distance ahead.

Meanwhile, in the lead aircraft, Gen. Ent and Col. Compton saw that, though the 93rd was still with the 376th, they'd lost the other three groups. Because of radio silence, they were unable to try contacting them. The two officers decided the others might have turned back, or perhaps some of them had crashed into the mountains.

It was decision time. Making the attack with only two groups would not only be extremely hazardous, but probably suicidal. Ent and Compton did not hesitate. They headed straight for the first Initial Point at Pitesti. From there they'd go on to the final IP and commence their bomb run. They'd hit the targets as hard as they could, and if they were unable to get away afterward, so be it. What they did not know was that the other three groups were still following, and would also attack the targets. But by then the stragglers would be more than 20 minutes late, and would encounter a fully alerted defense.

After reaching Pitesti, Ent and Compton turned on course for the second IP, but mistook the town of Targoviste for Floresti. Too soon, they turned southeast and descended to start their bomb run.

In accordance with the plan, the other aircraft of the 376th and the 93rd closed up, line abreast on Ent and Compton's bomber. They flew for several minutes without spotting the refineries, and suddenly found themselves approaching the outskirts of a large city. Ent realized with a shock they were wrong, that this was Budapest, the capital of Romania.

At that juncture the general felt he had no choice but to break radio silence. He shouted into the mike that they'd made a mistake. He ordered all pilots to turn north for Ploesti, and to bomb targets of opportunity.

By then there was no possibility of achieving surprise. Moreover, the defenses were even heavier than expected. As the fleet of B-24s roared on to the sprawling oil fields, they were met with a firestorm of flak. More than 230 German 88s were lofting shells at them, and other gunners were firing 40mm Oerlikons. At the level the bombers were flying, it was hard to miss them.

Flak was not the only problem. The refineries were surrounded by a forest of barrage balloons, tethered to the ground by steel cables. Snagging one could rip the wing off a bomber. And to make things still worse, the Germans had ignited hundreds of smoke pots that were streaming thick black clouds, obscuring much of the area.

Col. Compton steered his B-24 directly at one of the refineries, a great sprawl of machinery, pipes, storage tanks and tall chimneys, that was issuing still more smoke high into the air. The bombardier opened the bomb bay doors, and in the nose the navigator fired the .50-calibers. It was the first time a heavy American bomber was engaged in low-level strafing.

Holding the B-24 steady took all of Compton's strength and concentration. The flak bursts and the smoke and the waves of concussion made it almost impossible for him to make out the target. But then he ordered bombs away, and the heavy load of explosives left the Liberator.

Compton banked hard, and the tail gunner yelled that they'd hit the target dead on. When he completed the turn and looked back, the colonel saw that the refinery had become a vast cauldron of flames and explosions.

The question now was whether they'd make it home. The odds were not good; swarms of Bf-109s and Bf-110s appeared, and began diving on the bombers with all guns firing. The B-24s were especially vulnerable because they were not in a mutually protective formation. Instead they were all over the area, most of them mistakenly bombing targets that had been assigned to others.

One was the bomber of the 93rd Group flown by Maj. John Jerstad. Alongside him in the cockpit was the Group's leader, Lt. Col. Addison E. Baker. Jerstad had volunteered for the mission, even though he'd already completed his combat tour and was eligible for rotation back to the States.

Baker spotted a refinery he could not identify, but under the circumstances he decided it was as good as any and told Jerstad to attack it. The refinery was actually the Columbia Aquila, a target that had been assigned to the 44th Group. As Jerstad headed for it, flak set his airplane afire. The pilot might have been able to pull up to an altitude that would permit his crew to bail out, or perhaps he could have turned away from the refinery and crash landed on open ground. Instead, with the B-24 continuing to take withering hits, he flew on course for the target.

The bombardier released his load of sixteen 500-pounders, and the refinery erupted in a series of violent explosions. The low-flying B-24 was caught in the inferno and blew up, vaporizing Baker and Jerstad and the other crew members.

Now bombers were attacking any refinery they could reach. Two refineries that had been targets for the 93rd were destroyed by bombers of the 98th, and similar mistaken attacks were made by other pilots.

In one of those, Major Norman C. Appold led five B-24s of the 376th in a run on the Concordia Vega refinery. The installation had been assigned as a target for 93rd, but Appold did not even attempt to identify it. By that time, he was too busy trying to fly his aircraft while his gunners were fending off attacks by German fighters.

Jinking was impossible if he and the others hoped to score hits; they had to hold their B-24s as steady as possible. Despite the pounding from 20mm shells and bursting flak, the bombers blew the Concordia Vega into a million pieces of flaming wreckage. All five of Appold's charges survived the run and turned for home.

Meanwhile, the 389th Group, led by Col. Jack Wood, at last reached the IP at Pitesti and turned northwest for the refinery at Cimpina. That target, too, was surrounded by flak batteries, and by then the gunners had been on alert for some time. When the B-24s began their bomb runs, the sky became a hellish cloud of bursting shells. But Wood's group plastered the refinery with HE, wrecking the entire installation and setting fire to thousands of tons of oil. A gigantic trail of black smoke rose from the blaze as the attackers pulled away.

Col. Wood was surprised to find himself still alive. The target had been totally destroyed and somehow his battered airplane, and most of the others in his group, had made it through.

However, four of them had not. One was flown by 2nd Lt. Lloyd H. Hughes, a 21-year-old graduate of Texas A&M who was on his fifth combat mission. As Hughes wheeled his B-24 toward the refinery, shrapnel from bursting flak shells punctured his aircraft's fuel tanks. With streams of gasoline pouring from the tanks he flew on, he refused to turn away, even when his left wing caught fire. He dropped his bombs squarely on the target.

There was a lake bed not far from the refinery, and beside it was a narrow beach, where Hughes hoped to crash-land the airplane. He banked his blazing B-24 and headed for it—though by now, flames had reached the cockpit. Nearly blinded by smoke, the pilot failed to see that there was a steep bank near the lake. The B-24 clipped the bank with a wing and exploded.

The last two groups to reach the refineries at Ploesti were the 44th, commanded by Col. Leon W. Johnson, and the 98th, led by Col. John R. "Killer" Kane. A 1936 graduate of West Point, who also held a degree in advanced engineering from MIT, Col. Johnson was a quiet man, and a scholar. Col. Kane, on the other hand, was large and brash. The son of a Texas preacher, he'd played football at Baylor before the war. A highly skilled pilot himself, he demanded topnotch performance from the officers in his command, and was a stickler for discipline.

The two groups had made the correct turns at the first and second IP, and as they approached the target area they were greeted by an awesome sight. The oil fields were a mass of blazing storage tanks and wrecked machinery that was sending up a pall of black smoke. Bombers were wheeling through flak bursts, some of them crashing even as the two commanders watched. No sane man would fly into that. But Johnson and Kane did just that, and led their groups straight for the target.

As Johnson entered the chaos, he was startled to see several other B-24s flying head-on toward him. They were members of the 376th that had just completed their runs on the Columbia Aquila refinery, leaving it in flames. The other pilots must have been as surprised to see Johnson as he was to see them. At the last possible moment, they pulled up, missing the colonel and the aircraft following him by a narrow margin.

Undeterred, Johnson flew on, intending to unload his bombs on the burning refinery and finish the job. The flak was terrible, but what he hadn't anticipated was the explosions of bombs with delayed-action fuses that had been dropped by the 376th. Now those explosions rocked his airplane and sent up huge sheets of flame.

Still he held course, and dumped his bombs into the blazing tangle of wrecked machinery. More fiery eruptions took place, and when his B-24 completed its run, it had been blackened from nose to tail. He had to squint through the smudges on his windscreen to see where he was going.

The group had paid a price for its bravery. Of the 16 bombers that made the final attack on the Columbia Aquila, seven had crashed in flames. The nine survivors were all damaged.

Meanwhile, 21 others in Johnson's command, led by Lt. Col. James Posey, flew to the refinery at Brazi. No doubt the Germans had concentrated their defenses at Ploesti, because at Brazi there were fewer flak batteries. Posey's B-24s made a perfect run, dropping their bombs squarely on the target and completely demolishing it. As they left the area, nothing was left but fire and a column of smoke that could be seen as far off as Bucharest.

But Bf-109s caught up with Posey as he proceeded to lead his pilots home. Using good defensive tactics, the bombers stayed close together as their gunners sent streams of machine-gun fire at the German fighters. Only two bombers were lost.

Now it was Killer Kane's turn. As he made his approach, his earphones were full of chatter from other pilots, and he noticed that many of the voices were German. Kane roared, "Shut up, you bastards!" And surprisingly, they did. He led his 41 followers toward the nearest refinery.

Their bombs slammed into the refinery and destroyed it. Kane then circled the oil fields, looking for another target. By that time his airplane was riddled with flak, and the number four engine had been shot out. The colonel feathered the prop and went on circling until he picked out a second refinery.

His group bombed that one as well, and then with more than 30 holes in his wings and fuselage, Kane decided it was time to leave. Fifteen of his B-24s had been lost.

However, the circling had used up so much fuel that there was no chance for him to make it all the way back to Benghazi. And the Luftwaffe wasn't through with him, either. Over Bulgaria, three more of his Liberators were shot down.

The colonel's battered bomber, the "Hail Columbia," made it as far as Cyprus. There, Kane spotted an RAF airfield and brought his B-24 in for a crash landing. Both he and his crew lived through it, but the airplane was totally destroyed.

Col. Kane and Col. Johnson were awarded the Medal of Honor for their exploits. That brought the total to five, the most ever awarded for a single action.

Many others who took part in the epic raid were also decorated. Ent, Compton, Appold, Wood, Posey, and Capt. William R. Cameron of the 44th Group were all awarded the Distinguished Service Cross.

Of the 177 bombers that took off from Benghazi, 44 were lost in combat. Five hundred brave men did not return.

48.

In spite of the sacrifices made by the Americans in Operation Tidal Wave, the damage to the Ploesti oil fields was not permanent. New derricks were constructed to pump crude oil, and more than a thousand laborers were put to work rebuilding the refineries. Within six months the complex was back in business.

Nevertheless, Air Minister Milch and Arms Minister Speer were convinced that aircraft production had to be given top priority. Although manufacturers were already straining to meet demand, they were pressured to increase their output still further.

Messerschmitt was ordered to speed up the delivery schedule for the Me-262. Yet confusing directives from the RLM ordered that in addition to the fighter, he was to continue work on three other versions: a reconnaissance model, a two-seat trainer, and a highspeed bomber.

Obviously, the only version that made sense was the one that was being rushed into production. The Me-262 had been conceived from the beginning as a fighter, and the Professor and his design team were busy testing and refining it.

As work on the Schwalbe went forward, the war continued to go against Germany. Adolf Hitler was infuriated by the collapse of the Italian government, and by the deviousness of the new prime minister, Pietro Badoglio. On 3 September the Allies invaded mainland Italy, and that day Badoglio secretly signed an armistice. Hitler did not learn about it until a week later.

Defiant as always, the Führer sent additional Wehrmacht divisions into Italy. And on 10 September 1943 they occupied Rome. Hitler also ordered his army commanders to find a way to rescue Mussolini. He believed that if Il Duce were freed, Italian troops would go on fighting alongside Germany. However, Badoglio's government was determined not to let that happen. After Mussolini's arrest, he was moved from one location to another so as to foil any rescue attempt. Hitler decided a commando operation was called for, and took a personal hand in selecting an officer to lead it.

At the Führer's orders, six candidates were called to Wolfschanze, his heavily armed command center in the Prussian forest. All were tough, resourceful combat veterans.

Hitler asked each man whether he knew Italy. Only one did, having traveled there by motorcycle with his bride on their honeymoon. A thirty-five-year-old captain, he had a reputation for carrying out daring exploits. Hitler dismissed the others and appointed him. His name was Otto Skorzeny.

Tall and muscular, with black hair and a small mustache, Skorzeny had been born into a military family in Austria. While a student in Vienna, he was a noted fencer who won 15 duels. Souvenirs of those days were saber scars on his cheeks and jaw.

In 1931 Skorzeny had joined the Austrian Nazi party and become a storm trooper. When the Germans took over Austria, he drew the attention of party officials by saving the life of Austrian President Wilhelm Miklas. On 12 March 1938, Nazi thugs tried to kill Miklas, and Skorzeny stopped them.

Later he joined the Waffen SS, the elite troops of the German army, and served with distinction in the notorious Das Reich Division. He was badly wounded in a battle on the eastern front, and awarded the Iron Cross for bravery under fire. Sent back to Germany on a hospital train, he eventually recovered.

Once he'd regained his strength, Skorzeny was recommended by a fellow officer to lead a new commando force, the SS Special Unit Friedenthal. He did an excellent job of training his soldiers to fight behind enemy lines, and that was another reason Hitler chose him to rescue Mussolini.

To keep his true purpose a secret, Skorzeny was assigned as an adjutant to Luftwaffe General Kurt Student, the commander of Germany's Paratroop Corps. The two worked together on the mission, which was code-named *Unternehmen Eiche*, or Operation Oak. As a first step, they had to locate Il Duce.

Word came that he was hidden away on the island of Ponza, near Naples. Before the Germans could act, Mussolini was moved again, this time to La Maddalena, an island north of Sardinia and 250 kilometers from the Italian coast. Informants had reported seeing him there.

Skorzeny had an He-111 bomber fly him over the island, so that he could reconnoiter and take photographs. As the Heinkel circled, it was spotted by RAF Spitfires and shot down. Skorzeny and the pilot were picked out of the sea by an Italian destroyer.

Mussolini was moved once more, and days went by with no clue as to his whereabouts. The Germans then learned through radio intercepts that he was being held in a hotel 140 kilometers northeast of Rome. This was the Albero-Rifugio, a ski resort on the Gran Sasso d'Italia, located on a mountain peak in the Apennines. The hotel was guarded by a special contingent of Italian troops, and was accessible only by a cable car that ran up 3,200 meters from the valley floor below. An assault by the Germans was considered impossible.

But not by Skorzeny. Again, he carried out aerial reconnaissance, taking photographs of the hotel from a Heinkel bomber. Later, he and Student were joined by Major Harald Mors, a paratroop battalion commander, in planning an attack.

They considered dropping paratroopers onto the hotel grounds, but rejected the idea because the men would be scattered by wind swirling about the peak. Instead, they decided Skorzeny and a force of commandos would be flown in on gliders. At the same time, Major Mors' men would arrive by truck at the base of the mountain and secure the cable car. Once Mussolini was freed, he would be flown off the peak in a Storch.

Skorzeny knew that reaching the Albero-Rifugio would be difficult. The mountain fell off steeply on all four sides, and the only possible place for landing was a small triangular patch of ground near the hotel. The guards would be heavily armed, and getting Mussolini out would be even more challenging. But Skorzeny was determined to succeed.

On 12 September, Skorzeny's men seized Italian General Fernando Soleti in Rome and compelled him to join the venture. Then, in perfect weather, twelve DFS-230 assault gliders, each carrying a pilot and nine troops, were towed aloft by Ju-52s from Rome's Practica Di Mare airfield.

When the flight reached the mountain peak, the gliders were released from their towing cables. As Skorzeny's pilot descended, he saw that the level area near the hotel was strewn with rocks. He was lucky to make a bumpy but safe landing.

Skorzeny leaped out, and ran to the hotel entrance, shoving General

Soleti ahead of him with a Schmeisser submachine gun. At Skorzeny's urging, Soleti told the guards to throw down their arms. They obeyed, and the German commandos stood watch over them while Skorzeny entered the hotel and bounded up the stairs.

When he burst into the room where Mussolini was found cringing, he saw that there were two officers with the dictator, both holding pistols. Skorzeny pointed his Schmeisser at them, and they too dropped their weapons. Turning to Mussolini, Skorzeny saluted and said, "Duce, the Führer sent me. You are free!"

Mussolini hugged his benefactor, blubbering that he knew his friend Adolf would not desert him. Skorzeny led him back down the stairs.

By this time the other gliders had landed, but not all of them safely. Several crashed into boulders on the peak, injuring the men in them. Meanwhile, the Storch had appeared overhead and was preparing to land. The pilot of the single-engine airplane was Captain Heinrich Gerlach. Maneuvering to miss the gliders, he set it down on the rocky ground with a landing roll of only 20 meters. At his direction, commandos then pulled the Storch back to the edge of the patch, facing it into the wind. Now the problem would be getting it loaded and off again.

Skorzeny bundled Mussolini into the passenger seat of the aircraft and fastened his safety belt; he then began climbing in as well. Gerlach shouted to him to get out, he could never take off with the three of them aboard.

Skorzeny well understood the airplane might crash and kill them all. But he reasoned that if he stayed behind, and the Storch crashed anyway, the mission would have failed. And for this, Hitler would never forgive him—he'd be expected to shoot himself. So why let the pilot fly off with the prize and get the glory? Better to take his chances.

Ignoring Gerlach's protests, Skorzeny squeezed into the small luggage compartment behind Mussolini. He pulled the door shut and told the pilot to go. Gerlach saw he had no other choice. He opened the throttle and the Storch began its takeoff roll. With three big men aboard, it seemed too heavily loaded to make it, but when Gerlach eased back the stick, the Storch sailed off the mountain. To avoid any enemy fighters that might be in the area, Gerlach flew down to treetop level. The engine began running roughly, probably because rocks had damaged the prop on takeoff, yet the aircraft kept going, even as its gear was clipping leaves from the trees.

Saying a prayer, Gerlach gradually regained altitude until the Storch was at 300 meters. Then it was flaps up, and a gentle turn to a heading of 195 degrees. A little over an hour later, the Practica Di Mare airfield was in sight. Gerlach checked the windsock and banked the Storch around to the active runway. The Storch settled gently, and the wheels kissed the asphalt.

A tumultuous crowd of Germans greeted the three men. When Skorzeny clapped Gerlach on the back, the pilot merely shrugged. Nothing to it.

From there Skorzeny and Il Duce were flown to Vienna in an He-111. Skorzeny was dropped off, and Mussolini was flown on to the Wolfschanze late that same day. He and Hitler had an emotional meeting, with Il Duce thanking the Führer profusely.

Skorzeny's gamble had paid off. He was promoted to major and awarded the Knight's Cross. And thanks to Goebbels' propaganda, he immediately became famous. Stories in the German newspapers and on radio proclaimed him "The most dangerous man in the world."

Captain Gerlach was awarded the Knight's Cross as well. So was Major Mars, for having successfully blocked resistance by Italians at the base of the mountain. Many others among the pilots, commandos and paratroopers who had taken part in the operation also were decorated and promoted.

There was another result that was less sanguine. The success of Unternehmen Eiche reinforced Hitler's belief in himself as a brilliant commander and a political genius. He set up Mussolini in a puppet Italian government, and made plans to battle the Allies with renewed fervor.

One of the millions of people who would be affected by Hitler's views was Willy Messerschmitt. The Führer's obsession with offensive action would have an unforseen bearing on development of the Me-262

49.

Problems arose with the jet's hydraulically operated nose gear. The engineers had to try a number of different pressures and activating devices before they got it to retract properly. To Messerschmitt the tricycle undercarriage was just one more encumbrance on an already heavy aircraft, but by then he was resigned to using it.

His concerns were heightened when the gear proved fragile in flight tests. Pilots were urged to keep the nose high when landing. As the aircraft slowed down, the nose would settle by itself without imposing undue strain on the forward wheel.

Failure to observe the rule resulted in an accident. On 4 August 1943, the Me-262V5 landed hard on all three wheels. The impact caused extensive structural damage, and as the aircraft began taxiing back to the flight line, the gear collapsed.

While repairs to the V5 were under way, the Allies launched Operation Pointblank. The objective was to weaken German aircraft production before the planned D-Day invasion of Europe.

First, the U.S. 8th Air Force bombed the Messerschmitt factory at Augsburg, resulting in fifty people being killed and many more injured. A number of aircraft were destroyed, but no Me-262s were damaged. Bf-109s from Reim airfield at Munich shot down two of the B-17s.

Then on 13 August a much larger raid was carried out on the works at Wiener-Neustadt. One fourth of all Bf-109s were being produced there at the time, and the plant was also constructing jigs that would be used in the series production of the Me-262.

Major General James Doolittle led B-17s and B-24s to the target from Foggia airfield in southern Italy. Their bombs destroyed the plant, and 185 workers were killed. Another 150 were wounded.

To Willy Messerschmitt, the events were deeply painful. He knew personally many of the people working in the two factories, and some of them had been with him since the earliest days of his company. Now they were either hospitalized or dead.

Hitler's reaction was to accuse the Luftwaffe of failing to provide an effective defense. But instead of berating Göring, he blamed General Jeschonnek. Too few fighters had been sent to intercept the terror bombers, he snarled, and those that did were not properly led.

Göring responded to the raid by heaping scorn on the fighter pilots, calling them cowards. He also blamed Milch for not producing sufficient numbers of fighters, which was absurd. Milch's position had always been that the Reich not only needed more fighters, but that the Luftwaffe should assign more of them to homeland defense. He'd also defended the pilots to Göring's face.

Hitler then made two rash decisions. First he countermanded

Milch's order and insisted that the Me-209 be put into production at once. Then he ordered a cutback of the Me-262 program. What the Luftwaffe needed, he said, were more piston fighters. Despite being sorely frustrated, Milch issued a directive to Messerschmitt AG to reduce work on the Me-262 and begin producing the Me-209. The Professor's objections were overruled.

Four days later, the U.S. 8th Air Force conducted another massive raid, this time launching a double strike against the Messerschmitt factory at Regensburg, and the plants at Schweinfurt that were producing vitally important ball bearings.

The Regensburg raid was carried out by 146 bombers, led by Col. Curtis LeMay, commander of the 4th Bombardment Wing. Over Germany, the B-24s and B-17s were attacked by 160 fighters, with Bf-109s, Bf-110s, and Fw-190s boring in from all sides. Fifteen bombers were shot down, but the remaining 131 reached Regensburg.

The raiders hit the Messerschmitt plant with 298 tons of bombs. The buildings, machinery, and Bf-109s under construction were all destroyed. Four hundred workers were killed and nearly 500 wounded. Once again, Willy Messerschmitt lost many friends.

The bombers then turned south and flew over the Alps. Two damaged B-17s landed in Switzerland, and one went down in Italy. Five others crashed in the Mediterranean. A total of 24 bombers were demolished; the rest reached North Africa.

Meanwhile, the second force struck Schweinfurt. Its leader was Brigadier General Robert B. Williams, commander of the 1st Bombardment Wing. There were 230 B-17s in the attack, and 300 Luftwaffe fighters ripped into them. Cannon fire sent a dozen of the bombers down in flames.

The B-17s that were still flying made it to Schweinfurt. They dropped 549 tons of HE and incendiary bombs on the Kugelfischer Werke, the Vereingte Kugellager, and the Fichtel & Sachs factories. The workshops were destroyed, and 203 workers were killed. Flak knocked down three more bombers before the battered survivors began the trip home.

As they flew toward Brussels, German fighters hit them again. Navigator Elmer Bendiner saw fires burning brightly on the ground below and didn't understand what they were, until he realized the fires were the funeral pyres of B-17s. To the relief of the bomber crews, 93

Spitfires and 85 Thunderbolts met them to provide cover as they approached the North Sea. But the Luftwaffe was not yet through with them.

Spitfire pilot James Long: "We were at twenty-two thousand feet when we made contact with the B-17s. I'd say there were more than a hundred enemy fighters making firing passes at them. The bombers were in rough shape. One poor bugger had half his tailplane shot away, and there were big holes in many of the others. We got right into it, and the Germans put up a hell of a scrap. I caught one Messerschmitt from behind and gave him a burst, and he went down smoking. Quite a number of Germans were shot down, but still they got some of the B-17s."

Long was correct; German fighters downed eight more bombers, and three others crashed into the sea. The Allies claimed 20 kills. In all, 36 bombers of the Schweinfurt force did not return. A staggering total of 60 bombers were lost on the double strike. Missing were 552 crewmen.

That same night RAF bombers struck the rocket production center at Peenemünde, with a result that was nothing less than a catastrophe for the Germans. Total deaths among scientists and workers was 750, and the rocket program was set back by months.

On this occasion Jeschonnek was indeed at fault. He'd issued the wrong orders to Luftwaffe fighter units, sending them to Berlin instead of Peenemünde. The aircraft had circled aimlessly over the capital, waiting for an attack that never came. When Hitler was informed of the mistake, he again turned his wrath on Jeschonnek, shouting abuses at him for an hour. After he was dismissed, Jeschonnek retired to his quarters and shot himself in the head.

Meanwhile RAF Vice Marshal Harris was eager to subject Berlin to the same level of destruction that had been sustained by Hamburg. The German capital had been bombed many times, and thousands of its inhabitants had been killed. Now Harris planned to totally demolish it.

But the Germans had plans of their own. It was obvious to the Luftwaffe leaders that the Kammhuber defense was incapable of stemming the RAF attacks, and that only *Schwerpunkt* had been proven effective. Therefore, the techniques devised by Major Hermann and his *Wilde Sau* night fighters would be put to use. The Major instructed the flak batteries to fire star shells, and the searchlight operators to direct their beams to the cloud layer. That would flood the area with light, and the

German pilots would have no trouble picking out the enemy aircraft.

On the night of 29 August 1943, RAF Bomber Command launched a massive attack on Berlin. Six hundred Lancaster and Halifax bombers took part, and when they arrived over the city they found the sky almost as bright as day. They were then set upon by Hermann's fighters. The result was a terrible loss for the British, with fifty-six bombers shot down and many others so badly damaged they could not be repaired. Almost all the aircraft that returned had dead or wounded crew members aboard.

On 31 August, Harris staged the second raid. Again 600 bombers were in the raiding force, and again Major Hermann's night fighters put on a savage defense. Forty-seven bombers were lost.

With grim determination, Harris ordered still another attack the following night. This one was flown only by Lancasters, and 22 of the bombers were destroyed. Finally compelled to admit defeat, the Vice Marshal called off the raids.

Milch exulted. Now there was proof, he said, that given sufficient numbers of fighters, the Allied attacks on Germany could be so costly in men and machines that both the Americans and the British would give up on them. How he wished Hitler and Göring had understood this earlier.

Somehow Germany had to build more fighters, and the right type of fighters. Milch would do everything he could to kill the Me-209, and get the Me-262 program back on track.

50.

In September German Intelligence sent a report to the RLM that said the British were forging ahead with their jet program. According to spies, the De Havilland Vampire had made its first flight, with Geoffrey De Havilland Jr. at the controls. The single-seat aircraft was described as having an egg-shaped fuselage and twin tail booms. It was powered by a D.H. Halford H-1 turbojet engine, mounted abaft the pilot. The report provided no information on performance.

Messerschmitt was sure that despite orders to cut back on the Me-262 program, he could still beat the British in bringing his jet fighter to operational status. After all, the British had produced the Gloster Meteor, and then nothing more had been heard of it. Who could say the new De Havilland would be any better?

His confidence was given a further boost when Gerd Lindner made a test flight in the Me-262V3 at Lechfeld. Lindner took the V3 to 5,000 meters and attained a speed of 960 kph in level flight. Messerschmitt hoped that would induce the Führer to reconsider his order, but there was no reaction from Berlin.

In the meantime many other matters demanded Willy's attention, among which was moving designers and engineers to Oberammergau. In light of the recent raid on Augsburg, as well as those on Wiener-Neustadt and Regensburg, he was anxious to protect them from harm.

He also wanted to protect his wife. In the last Augsburg bombing, the Baroness had been at home when shrapnel badly damaged the house. Although uninjured, she was terrified. Her son, Eberhard von Stromeyer, was working at the plant at the time as an assistant designer. The young man had graduated from the University at Darmstadt with a degree in aeronautical engineering, and was also a highly accomplished pilot. Both he and the Professor were in the factory when the bombs fell, and though neither was injured, the need for the move to Oberammergau became all the more urgent.

A small village, Oberammergau was about 80 kilometers south of Munich. The new Messerschmitt facility would be located in a complex of old army barracks. It was surrounded by meadows and a pine forest, and offered spectacular views of the Bavarian Alps. Proximity to the mountains would make it difficult for bombers to attack the complex, which was one of the reasons for choosing the site. The old barracks would provide plenty of room, with one section used as quarters for the 1500 workers who would move from Augsburg.

The Professor and Lilly also needed a place to live in the area. They found a large unoccupied villa in Murnau on the shore of Lake Staffelsee, about halfway between Oberammergau and Munich. The house was called Hochried, but did not come without complications. Messerschmitt's lawyer, Dr. Langbehn, made inquiries and learned that Hochried was owned by a German citizen who had emigrated to America and was living in New York. The German embassy in Switzerland reported that there was a heavy mortgage on the house, and that the owner would be willing to sell if the buyer would meet his price. He would also want the proceeds to be paid in Swiss francs.

At that point the Baroness's financial acumen came into play. A major stockholder in Messerschmitt AG and a member of the board of directors, Lilly proposed that the company pay off the mortgage. She would then provide the balance of the selling price from her own funds.

The board gave its approval, and with Dr. Langbehn's help, Lilly negotiated with the owner through lawyers in Switzerland. Finally Hochried was sold to the Messerschmitts for the bargain price of 150,000 Swiss francs. The amount was equal to the mortgage, which was paid off by the company. Thus all the money for the purchase came from the firm.

The move of workers and equipment to Oberammergau was well under way by mid-October. Assembly lines were set up, and materials and parts were organized in storage sheds. The RLM was assured production would be running full force by year's end.

During this time Willy Messerschmitt was hospitalized briefly at Murnau hospital. The official reason was an asthma attack, but in fact he was exhausted from overwork; he was probably also suffering from the effects of chain-smoking his favorite Juno cigarettes. Nevertheless, within a few days he was back at his desk.

Meanwhile, arguments took place concerning the type of materiel Germany's factories should be producing. Milch, of course, was convinced that more fighters were needed. Speer agreed, but he was reluctant to send workers and materials into aircraft manufacturing at the expense of weapons for the army and navy. And as always, Hitler was adamant that only an offensive strategy was acceptable, convinced that the vital need was for more bombers. And he insisted that they must be *schnell* bombers, not the long-range type.

The Führer knew the Allies were preparing to invade Europe from the west. He believed that when enemy troops and equipment were massed on the beaches of France, fast bombers could destroy them, leaving the Allies unable to gain a foothold. The issue was raised once more on 14 October, when the 8th Air Force again struck Schweinfurt. Reconnaissance photographs revealed that the factories had been repaired, and now the U.S. commanders were determined to crush Germany's ability to produce ball bearings once and for all.

A force of 291 B-17s was assembled for the raid. RAF Spitfires escorted them across the Channel, and over France the British fighters were relieved by 50 P-47 Thunderbolts. Twenty-five Fw-190s then attacked the raiders, and a short time later 20 more arrived. Within minutes several of the B-17s were on fire, and two of them exploded. The Germans lost six fighters.

One of the Thunderbolts went down in flames, and two more were badly damaged. By then the P-47s were at the end of their range, leaving the bombers to fend for themselves. For the next three hours, the B-17s were raked over by Bf-109s and Fw-190s. The Germans had learned that an effective tactic involved forcing a bomber to leave its protective combat box. Luftwaffe pilots called this *Herausschuss*. Once a bomber had been cut out, it became a lone straggler and easily shot to pieces by the fighters, like a wounded stag harried by wolves.

Only 226 B-17s made it to Schweinfurt. In all, 59 were shot down. One crashed in the Channel on the way home, five more crashed in England, and 12 others were so badly damaged they would never fly again. Of the 2,900 men who flew the mission, 650 were killed.

Although the damage the bombers inflicted was extensive, it was not as severe as the planners had hoped. Although 350 workers died in the raid, Armament Minister Speer claimed the ball bearing factories' output was reduced by only 50 percent. However, the raid taught Speer a lesson. From then on he would see to it that all production facilities were dispersed as widely as possible. Never again would so critical an industry be concentrated in one location.

In addition, he now shared Milch's resolve that no matter what Hitler decreed, the building of fighters, and not bombers, had to be the number one objective of the aircraft manufacturers.

51.

Because of Hitler's orders, the Me-209 program was still alive in November 1943, and was still taking workers and factory space away from the Me-262. Series production of the much-maligned piston fighter was about to begin. But when Milch reviewed the performance figures, he saw that this latest version was no better than its forerunners. He estimated that even if improvements could be made, the Me-209 would not become operational for at least another year. He told Göring the 209 should be scrapped, and the Me-262 sent full speed ahead.

The Reichsmarschal wasn't so sure, and certainly not about to cancel an order by Hitler. Nevertheless, he'd heard glowing reports of the

Me-262 from some of the Luftwaffe's best pilots, including General Adolf Galland. He decided to see the Me-262 for himself, and requested a demonstration. On 2 November 1943, one was conducted for him at Lechfeld. Professor Messerschmitt was present, ready to answer any questions he might have.

The Reichsmarschal's grasp of technical matters was limited, to say the least. He referred to the modern avionics used in radio navigation as "gadgets." He also mistrusted the reflector gunsight, and looked with disdain on enclosed cockpits. But he understood speed, and appreciated its value in combat. When Göring saw Gerd Lindner fly the V6 over the field at 900 kph, its jet engines emitting an eerie howl, he couldn't believe it. Never before had he seen an airplane fly so fast.

The Reichsmarschal asked about the production schedule. Messerschmitt said he hoped the first in the series would be coming off the line in January.

What about armament? Willy replied that the nose bay would carry four cannons, per specifications approved by the Air Ministry.

And could the aircraft carry bombs? Knowing how touchy the subject was, Messerschmitt hesitated. There were plans for a fighter-bomber version in the design center, though that project had been pushed aside in favor of the pure fighter. But finally he said yes, the jet could carry either two 500 kg bombs or one 1000 kg bomb in racks under the fuselage.

Göring was satisfied. He said the Führer was scheduled to review some of the Luftwaffe's newest aircraft later in the month, and the Me-262 should be demonstrated for him at that time.

That was good news to Messerschmitt, because he knew the importance of such an event—it would be the first time Hitler would see the aircraft fly. He assured Göring the jet would be ready.

The demonstration took place on 26 November at the Insterburg military airfield in East Prussia. It was a chilly, windswept day, and the sky was overcast. Test pilots Karl Baur and Gerd Lindner flew two prototype Me-262s from Lechfeld, the V4 and the V6, to give the command performance.

Willy Messerschmitt and his team of engineers and mechanics were there early, making preparations. Other manufacturers were on hand as well, and a number of new airplanes were lined up on the tarmac. Firefighting apparatus and an ambulance were standing by, along with emergency repair equipment and tow trucks.

Messerschmitt noticed that a Heinkel He-219 was attracting attention from Luftwaffe officers. The big twin-engine airplane was already considered an excelled night fighter. On its first combat mission, pilot Lt. Werner Steib had shot down five enemy bombers. The designer of the He-219 was Robert Lusser, who was explaining the aircraft's features to onlookers. After leaving his employment with Messerschmitt in 1938, Lusser had, among other things, worked on Heinkel's flying bomb project.

Heinkel himself was not present. As punishment for his public tirades against the Nazi government, he had been forced to sell his shares in the company, which were acquired by none other than Hermann Göring. The transaction was typical of the corrupt practices that went on in the Nazi hierarchy.

The only other jet on hand today was an Arado Ar-234 bomber. It was on static display, and would not be flown. Walter Blume, head of Arado and its chief designer, was talking with some Luftwaffe pilots.

Thus far the Ar-234 had been a disappointment. On 2 October, the V-2 prototype had crashed because of engine failure, killing the test pilot. The problem was the result of Arado's inability to secure the best turbojets, which went to Messerschmitt for the Me-262 program. Blume was bitterly resentful.

It was past noon by the time Hitler, Göring, Speer, Milch and a retinue of high-ranking Luftwaffe officers arrived from Berlin in a Ju-52. The Führer greeted the builders cordially, and remarked to Messerschmitt that it was good to see him again. Although it was apparent to Willy that Göring had built up Hitler's expectations, the Me-262 was not the first to fly. Instead, demonstrations of the various aircraft went on for several hours, while Messerschmitt waited impatiently. It wasn't until late in the day that a Luftwaffe captain informed the crowd that the Me-262 would be next.

Karl Baur was to fly the V4. Gerd Lindner would act as a backup in the V6, and would fly it only if there was a problem with the V4. The Me-262s did not yet have self-starters, and mechanics used a portable benzine motor to start the engines of both aircraft. As the turbojets warmed up, Hitler and the others stood watching from a reviewing stand. Willy Messerschmitt joined them, no doubt feeling more than a little anxious.

Baur was cleared for takeoff. He carefully opened the throttles, and the gray-painted aircraft began rolling down the runway. As always it moved very slowly at first, and gradually picked up speed. But just as the V4 lifted off, the left engine flamed out. The wing dipped and Baur corrected before it could hit the concrete. He then cut the power to the right engine and brought the aircraft down safely.

It was an inauspicious beginning. Baur climbed out of the cockpit, and the V4 was towed back to the ramp.

Now the demonstration was up to Lindner. He took off, and the V6 climbed without incident. The engines ran perfectly. When he reached an altitude of 3,000 meters, Lindner put the jet into a dive and quickly recovered. He conducted sweeping turns, and performed a series of slow rolls. The Schwalbe seemed as sure and as graceful as its namesake. Lindner then made a high-speed pass. He flew past the onlookers, turned, and came back to make another. Everyone watched the swift gray aircraft intently.

Lindner's next maneuver was a bold gamble. As the audience stared openmouthed, he brought the jet down to no more than 10 meters above the ground and steered straight toward the reviewing stand. Everyone, including the Führer, flinched and crouched low. Just before reaching the stand, Lindner pulled back the stick and sent the Me-262 streaking upward. The ground shook and the air was filled with the acrid stink of burnt fuel.

The men glanced at Hitler nervously, and to their surprise, he was quite calm. After Lindner landed, Hitler called him to the reviewing stand and asked how fast the aircraft had flown.

Lindner stood at rigid attention. "Mein Führer, on the second pass it was indicating just over nine hundred kilometers per hour."

Hitler dismissed him and turned to Messerschmitt. "Can the aircraft carry bombs?"

The Professor gave him the same answer he'd given Göring. "Jawohl. Either two 500 kg, or one of 1,000 kg."

Hitler glared at the assembled officers. His voice rose. "You fools! Here at last stands the blitz bomber! For years I've been waiting for this aircraft. Here it is, and nobody has recognized it. With this aircraft I will break the enemy terror flyers!"

He then asked Milch the status of the Me-262 program. The Air Minister replied that the aircraft was being built as a fighter, and that delivery was some weeks away.

Hitler's cheeks flushed in anger. "A fighter? I order it to be put into production at once as a *bomber*!"

There was no response from the others, let alone an argument. Nor did anyone point out that Hitler himself had ordered a cutback of the Me-262 program the previous August.

As for Messerschmitt, it's doubtful that he fully understood the implications of Hitler's directive. As far as producing the Me-262 as a bomber was concerned, it had long been talked about, but no one, including Messerschmitt, had taken the idea seriously. And no one would now. The only thing that mattered was that the Me-262 program would be given a hard push.

It was a gross misperception. Hitler not only meant exactly what he'd said, but he would take steps to see that his order was carried out. And that resolve would have a significant impact on Germany's fortunes in the war.

52.

Despite the renewed pressure to put the Me-262 into series production, delays in the program continued. More testing was required before volume manufacturing could begin, and in late December 1943, only four prototypes were flying.

One bright note was the delivery of the new Jumo 004 B-1 turbojets. Built of stronger alloys, they were much more reliable than their predecessors. Messerschmitt engineers mounted them in the Me-262V7, and on 20 December the aircraft made the first of several successful flights.

One of the important aspects the engineers were also anxious to test was weaponry. The design approved by the RLM called for four Mk-108 cannons to be carried in the nose bay. Obviously, firing four 30mm cannons simultaneously could produce considerable shock to the airframe, but it might also have an adverse effect on the aircraft's stability in the air. The engineers debated whether armament that powerful was necessary. The combat experience of Luftwaffe fighter pilots had shown that an enemy bomber could be brought down by a few well-placed 30mm rounds. Were four cannons actually needed?

The subject of firepower in various aircraft had often risen before this. Adolf Hitler, a micromanager as always, had argued about it with General Galland. At one point Hitler had insisted an Me-410 destroyer be equipped with a cannon that was built for use in an armored car. This was the 50mm KWK-5, which weighed 2,000 pounds. The idea was ludicrous, of course. Yet, following orders, engineers bolted the gun to the underside of the airplane's fuselage. When the Me-410 took off, the extra weight slowed it down and made it hard to control.

Galland spoke with contempt of "that monster sticking three meters out in front." But the general did concede that Hitler was right in principle; it was the weapon that was wrong. The concept was abandoned.

There was a good reason, however, to arm the Me-262 with four cannons. The jet was so fast that pilots would have much less time to aim and shoot than they would in a piston fighter. Therefore, as much firepower as possible was necessary.

Certainly it was hard to fault the weapon itself. The Rheinmetall-Borsig Mk-108 was a marvel of compactness and efficiency. It was electrically operated, and after each shot the breech was reloaded by compressed air from metal bottles that were stored on either side of the Me-262's nose. The cannons were fired by pressing buttons on the control stick. The engineers came up with a unique safety device, which when flipped up became the firing button for the top two cannons. Beneath it was a second button that fired the bottom two. On a later version the top button would fire all four cannons at once. Spent cartridges were expelled from chutes on the underside of the nose section, just forward of the compressed air bottles. A combat movie camera, activated by triggering the cannons, was fitted to the tip of the nose.

As for striking power, the rate of fire of an Mk-108 was 11 rounds per second, and the shells exploded on contact. The engineers concluded that an Me-262 pilot should be able to destroy an enemy in an *augenblick*—the blink of an eye.

The team also strengthened the jet's forward bulkhead to withstand the effects of the cannons' recoil. Testing then commenced, first on the ground, and later in the air. The results were excellent. A high degree of accuracy was achieved, and no problems in the aircraft's performance were caused by firing what pilots called the *presslufthammer*—the jackhammer.

After that, series production of the Me-262 was finally begun in the Messerschmitt factory at Lepheim. There were delays, however, due to a scarcity of experienced machinists, tool operators, and metal fabricators. So to fill the jobs, women were often recruited. Most had been members of the *Bund Deutcher Madel*, the girls' side of the Hitler Youth. They were especially adept at tasks requiring not only mechanical aptitude, but steady hands and a calm temperament.

Unskilled laborers were needed as well, and Messerschmitt AG employed thousands of them in its various plants. Some were prisoners of war, and others had been rounded up by the SS in occupied territories, including France, Poland, and Czechoslovakia. While many employers forced these people to live in squalid conditions and work until they died from exhaustion or disease, Willy Messerschmitt treated them relatively well. He saw to it that they slept in heated barracks and had adequate amounts of food.

Nevertheless, there were never enough workers, skilled or unskilled. And though Armaments Minister Albert Speer directed the manufacturing for all three branches of the German armed forces, he sometimes favored the makers of equipment for the army and the navy. When Professor Messerschmitt requested more workers for the Me-262 program, he was unable to get them.

The reason for this was hard for Erhard Milch to understand. He remained convinced that above all else, air power was vital if Germany was to survive, let alone have any chance to win the war. He wrote in his diary how troubled he was when at night, in his hunting lodge north of Berlin, he'd hear the distant roar of bombers en route to blast the capital once again. Couldn't Speer understand the need for more aircraft, especially fighters?

Or was it because the Armaments Minister resented Milch's independence, and considered him a rival who had to be held in check? Finally Milch decided that the only practical way to break the roadblock was to concede absolute authority over the Air Ministry to Speer. So he announced that from then on, the RLM would take its orders directly from the Armaments Minister.

Immediately a significant change occurred. Speer began giving aircraft companies the same support he gave the builders of tanks and submarines. And none of them benefitted more from this than Messerschmitt AG. With more workers and a larger flow of materials, new life was injected into the Me-262 program.

Milch was gratified by the turnabout. But he had other fears. Was it already too late? What would happen when the Allies were able to produce long-range fighters to escort their bombers? At the moment, fighter escorts over Germany were a rarity. The P-47s could fly only part way on a mission, even with drop tanks. Running low on fuel, they had to turn back before the bomber formation reached the target.

The twin engine Lockheed P-38 Lightning, on the other hand, could stay in the air much longer; it was also fast and remarkably maneuverable. Because of its pair of booms, German pilots called it *der Gabelschwantz Teufel*—the forktail devil. However, there were few P-38s in Europe. In fact, only two USAAF fighter squadrons were equipped with them. Many more served in the Pacific theater, and it was there that P-38s carried out their most renowned combat feat.

U.S. intelligence analysts had decrypted Japanese radio messages that said that on 18 April 1943, a bomber would fly Admiral Isoroku Yamamoto from Rabaul to Bougainville. Yamamoto was Japan's top naval commander, and knowing what his loss would mean to the enemy, U.S. Navy Admiral Chester Nimitz ordered an attack.

Sixteen P-38s were sent from Guadalcanal to intercept the flight of six Zero fighters and two Nakajima Betty bombers. When they met, four of the Zeros were shot down. An American pilot, 1st Lt. Raymond Hine, was also killed. Then 1st Lt. Rex Barber dove on one of the bombers and riddled it with a burst from his 20mm cannon and four .50-caliber machine guns. Trailing smoke, the aircraft crashed in the jungle. Later, Yamamoto's body was found beside the wreckage of the bomber, his Samurai sword clutched in his hand.

P-38s also took part in many other momentous actions in the Pacific. Major Richard Bong became the leading American ace of the war, achieving 40 victories while flying Lightnings.

But in the ETO, the P-38 was not the fighter of choice; most pilots preferred the P-47. And neither General Spaatz nor General Eaker were enthusiastic about the Lightning, because they knew there was a basic flaw in the aircraft's design.

The fault showed up in high-speed dives, when air flow over the cockpit and wing center section produced violent buffeting of the tailplane. On occasion that resulted in complete loss of control. Although Lockheed engineers attempted to correct the weakness, they never fully succeeded.

Another problem was that the P-38 was difficult to maintain. The

Allison engines did not function well in the extremely cold European winters, and for the less skilled pilot, a P-38 was a handful when an engine failed. Still another defect was the inability of the gear to withstand rough treatment. That was partly due to the airplane's weight of 21,600 pounds, which was more than that of a fully loaded Blenheim bomber with a crew of three.

Finally there was the issue of cost. A P-38 was twice as expensive to build as a P-47 Thunderbolt, and to the U.S. War Department, that was a serious drawback.

For all those reasons, there were limited numbers of P-38s in Europe. And because of its shorter range, the P-47 was not suitable as a long-range fighter escort, either. Therefore, the bombers had to go it alone when they approached their targets, and the losses increased with every raid.

General Eaker knew his 8th Air Force could not go on taking that kind of punishment. He begged the American aircraft industry to give him a tough, dependable fighter that could fly all the way to the target, engage the enemy in combat, and return to England. General Spaatz made the same urgent request, and so did the Air Force Chief of Staff, General Arnold.

At the end of 1943, the commanders of the USAAF finally got the answer to their pleas. The fighter was the North American P-51, the Mustang.

53.

The project began in April 1940, when the British Purchasing Commission, headed by Sir Henry Self, proposed that North American Aviation Co. construct Curtiss-designed P-40 Warhawks under contract for the RAF. James H. "Dutch" Kindelberger, an aeronautical engineer who was CEO of the company, told Self he had a better idea.

Kindelberger said a North American designer, Edgar Schmued, had drawn plans for a new fighter that would use the same Allison V-1710 engine as the P-40, but would outperform it. The British were willing to make a deal, if North American would create a prototype in 120 days. If it tested well, North American would receive an order to build 300 of the fighters.

The prototype was designated NA-73. It was produced in only 104 days, but without an engine because of delays at the Allison factory. Eventually the liquid-cooled V-12 was installed, and the NA-73 was flown for the first time on 26 October 1940 by test pilot Vance Breese. Its performance was even better than what Kindelberger had promised.

Like Willy Messerschmitt, Schmued believed a fighter should be light, fast, and simple to build. And like the Bf-109, the new North American fighter was a tail dragger with stressed metal skin. It had nearly symmetrical laminar flow wings that produced less drag at high speed, and all surfaces were butt-jointed and flush riveted.

But unlike the Bf-109, the wings had a main spar and an equally strong second one to which the ailerons and flaps were attached. Also unlike the Bf-109, the retractable wheels were twelve feet apart, making the airplane easier to land. The retractable tail wheel was linked to the rudder, which made it steerable and added to stability on the ground. The fighter's Allison V-1710 engine provided 1,100 hp and weighed only 1,595 pounds. But a major drawback was that it did not have a turbo-supercharger, and for that reason didn't perform well at high altitudes.

In October 1941 the first production aircraft, designated the P-51 and called the Mustang, reached England. In compliance with British specifications it was armed with four .50-caliber machine guns and four .30-calibers. Its top speed was 370 mph at 15,000 feet, and rate of climb was 1980 feet per minute.

The British were pleased with the airplane and ordered 300 of them. Although because of the Mustangs' poor performance at upper altitudes, the RAF was reluctant to have them engage enemy fighters in combat. Instead, they were assigned to fifteen RAF squadrons, and used mostly to photograph enemy installations and to strafe trains and other ground targets in France.

Early in 1942 Ronald Harker, a Rolls Royce test pilot, flew a Mustang and was impressed with its speed and maneuverability. He then posed an interesting question. If the airplane's lack of power at higher altitudes was a handicap, why not mount a Merlin engine in one and see whether that made a difference? Rolls Royce engineers undertook the conversion, and on 30 April Harker made another test flight.

The results were startling. Not only was the Merlin-powered Mustang much faster at every altitude, it was even 30 mph faster than a Spitfire Mk V. What's more, the Mustang had twice the range of the

British fighter. Two self-sealing tanks in the wings held a total of 190 gallons of fuel, vs. 100 in a Spitfire.

The Packard Motor Car Co. was then licensed to build Merlin engines in the U.S. North American Aviation undertook conversion of the aircraft at its plants in Inglewood, California and Dallas, Texas. The Packard Merlins were bench-tested and ran perfectly. They could be taken to 61 inches of manifold pressure for takeoff, and could be boosted to 67 inches for emergency power in combat.

The first of the Inglewood-produced Mustangs, designated the P-51B, rolled off the assembly line in May 1943. The first built in Dallas, the P-51C, was produced in August. Again flight tests showed a leap in performance. A Mustang reached 445 mph in level flight, which was 100 mph faster than the Allison-powered version. The rate of climb was now 3,320 feet per minute.

But it was the range that was truly awesome. With two 150-gallon drop tanks, the P-51 could fly 2,200 miles, staying in the air for almost nine hours!

Late that fall Mustangs from both the Inglewood and Dallas plants were rushed to England. They were assigned to 15 fighter groups of the 8th and 9th Air Forces in England, and the 12th in Italy. Tooey Spaatz and Ira Eaker had their bomber escorts, and American pilots were armed with a potent new weapon.

It would not be long before the Luftwaffe realized what it was up against, and what effect the Mustang would have on the war in the air.

54.

In early 1944 the U.S. 8th Air Force increased its efforts to destroy the enemy's aircraft industry. A mission was planned for 11 January, calling for 663 bombers to attack the factories at Magdeburg, Halberstadt, Brunswick, and Oschersleben.

The raiders took off shortly after dawn, loaded with thousands of tons of HE and incendiaries. Although they'd been promised fighter escorts all the way to targets deep inside Germany, there was a problem. The weather was so bad that the mission should have been scrubbed from the outset, but as it was, two of the three divisions turned back because the sky over England was laced with icy rain. Only the First Division refused to quit.

There were 180 B-17s in the First. They broke through the heavy overcast and formed up, and as they headed for their target at Oschersleben, they were joined by 50 Mustangs of the 354th Fighter Group. On seeing the P-51s, the bomber crews cheered.

The Mustangs moved in close, staying just above the bomber stream. Most of the fighter pilots had been in combat before this mission, including Major George Bickell, who was flying his "Peg O My Heart." So had Lt. William Nacy, whose Mustang was "Marionette," and Lt. Harry Fisk, flying "Duration Plus." Lt. Donald Nee, in "Cisco," had earlier been a member of the RAF. But none of them had seen as much combat as their leader, Major James H. Howard. Painted on the nose of his P-51 was "Ding Hao!"—Chinese for "Very good!"

Howard had been born in China, the son of an American eye surgeon working in Peking. He graduated from Pomona College, trained as a pilot in the U.S. Navy, and served aboard the carrier USS Enterprise. In 1941 he resigned his commission and went to Burma, where he flew with Gen. Claire Chennault's Flying Tigers. He became a squadron leader, flew 53 missions in a P-40 Tomahawk, and shot down six Japanese aircraft. After Pearl Harbor he returned to the States and joined the USAAF.

As he led the P-51s on today's mission, Howard was chafing under the rules he'd been given. The Mustangs were to stay with the B-17s at all times—only if the bombers were attacked could they give chase. The major knew that was wrongheaded. Experience had taught him that fighters should be encouraged to attack the enemy without restraint, and not be kept on a short leash. At the briefing today he'd protested, but to no avail.

German radar tracked the B-17s from the time they crossed the Dutch coast. The operators plotted the bombers' course and alerted squadrons of the Luftwaffe's 3rd Air Fleet. The images on the radar screens indicated that more than two hundred bombers would be taking part in the raid, but what the radar operators did not realize was that some of the blips represented fighter escorts.

Consequently, when the German pilots caught sight of the approaching bombers, they were startled to see Mustangs flying above the formation. How was this possible? How could fighters have such range? With no time to waste, the Germans climbed for altitude, and roared in to attack. A few went after the Mustangs, but most charged the bombers. Following orders, the American pilots held their position until the Germans reached the box formations of B-17s. Only then did the P-51s engage, and the result was a wild melee. Some Luftwaffe pilots attacked B-17s head-on, while others made swooping, angled passes from above. Some dove and then zoomed up from underneath, firing at the bombers' bellies.

Howard's fighters made a valiant effort to defend the B-17s. As they did, the major saw that bombers in the leading box had split away from the rest and were being pummeled by the enemy. He peeled off and went to give aid and as he did, he caught a Bf-110 and shot it down with a quick burst.

Next, Howard saw a Fw-190 beneath him. When the German fighter pulled up into the sun, Howard fired at it until the pilot jettisoned the canopy and bailed out. The tumbling canopy almost hit Howard's airplane. A moment later he found himself alone in the midst of 30 German fighters, both Bf-109s and Fw-190s. Ignoring the odds, he took them on.

For a full 30 minutes, Howard fought an incredible battle. It was witnessed by the pilot of a B-17 in the 91st Bomb Group, Lt. Col. T.R. Milton, who said it was the greatest example of combat flying he ever saw in his two tours in the 8th Air Force.

Howard put on a classic display of scissoring, horizontal and vertical. He dove his Mustang, half-rolled it, and stood it on its tail. He made turns so tight G forces crushed his gut. During that exhausting half hour he shot down two Bf-109s and an Fw-190. Another enemy fighter was a probable, and two others were so badly damaged they broke off and limped away. When he had no more ammunition, Howard foiled attacks on the bombers by diving at the Germans and throwing off their aim.

Then at last the sky was clear of enemy aircraft, and the B-17s still flying had finished their bomb runs. Howard and the other pilots moved into position above the bombers and accompanied them home. When the major landed his fighter, there was only one bullet hole in it. None of the B-17s he defended had been lost.

So grateful were the crew members of the 401st Bombardment Group that they sent a recommendation to Washington that Major Howard be awarded the Congressional Medal of Honor. A few weeks later it was approved, and General Spaatz pinned the medal on

Howard's chest. He was the only fighter pilot in the European theater to win the decoration.

But not all the American aircraft that flew the mission that day came back. A total of 15 bombers had been shot down, along with five escorts. The Americans claimed 40 kills, though the numbers were probably inflated.

That same month, Allied forces made an amphibious landing at Anzio, a bay on Italy's west coast, 30 miles south of Rome. Code-named Shingle, the operation was ill-conceived from the outset. Thousands of American and British troops were put ashore from 250 ships, while more than 2,600 aircraft provided cover for the landings, attacking enemy airfields and other installations. At first opposition was light, but soon German forces under General Albert Kesselring put up stiff resistance. The result was a stalemate, with casualties steadily mounting on both sides.

By the beginning of February, deliveries of the new Mustangs to England were in full swing. The constant influx of new fighters enabled the 8th Air Force to expand its missions, even though the commanders stubbornly clung to their rules of engagement. The Luftwaffe's General Adolf Galland was quick to spot the error in the Americans' tactics. "They made the same mistake we did in our first attacks on England," Galland said. "The fighters were all flying in tight formation close to the bombers, instead of free-ranging. It cut down their effectiveness."

The Americans were not alone in making mistakes. Reichsmarschal Göring insisted that Luftwaffe pilots attack the bombers, instead of shooting down as many fighters as possible. It was a foolish directive, inasmuch as elimination of the escorts would have greatly increased the bombers' vulnerability. Galland argued with Göring over this, but was unable to dissuade him. It was not until many other Luftwaffe pilots protested that the Reichsmarschal admitted they might be right. Even then it was a struggle to get him to change his orders.

By then the Allies were ready to launch "Big Week." As before, the objective was to have the Americans pound the German aircraft industry by day while the RAF hit targets at night.

In five days beginning 20 February, B-17s and B-24s dumped 10,000 tons of bombs on the manufacturing plants. Augsburg was hit again, and so were Regensburg and Wiener-Neustadt. The factory at

Leipzig was leveled. A total of 700 Bf-109s were destroyed, including an invaluable crop of night fighters. Bad weather finally brought about a pause in the raids. The Allied forces had lost a total of 320 bombers and 48 fighters, but both Eaker and Harris considered the week a success.

Hermann Göring responded in his usual way, blistering the Luftwaffe fighter pilots in a fiery speech. When he finished he went on leave for three weeks to one of his estates, a castle in Veldenstein. It was easy to see why the pilots despised him.

In Berlin, Feldmarschal Milch concluded that the German aircraft industry could not endure more destruction by enemy bombers. Accordingly, he decided to increase the workweek to 72 hours in the plants producing fighters. Already heavily burdened, the exhausted workers were now required to do more. As an incentive, each was given an extra bit of food and clothing.

Another decision was to accelerate the flying bomb program. Additional workers and materials were allotted to the Volkswagen factory at Wolfsburg, where the V-1s were being built. Milch relished the idea that when the V-1 attacks began, a bomb would fall on some part of London every half hour. The British people would never know where the next one would land. He believed it would drive them crazy with fear.

A third decision was more sweeping, and far more important to Germany's survival. Milch laid out a plan for a new organization called Fighter Staff, which would oversee the dispersal of the aviation industry, a plan that was approved by Speer and by Hitler. Over the following months, virtually all aircraft production was shifted from the shattered factories to various hidden locations. These ranged from forests and caves to hastily built plants disguised as farm buildings and storage sheds. They were very difficult to detect from the air. As a result, the Allied air forces were no longer able to obliterate an entire aircraft plant and kill its workers in a single raid. With the new system, the production of fighters rapidly increased.

Hitler then ordered Armaments Minister Albert Speer to oversee the construction of two huge underground aircraft factories. To make them bombproof, they were to be constructed of thick layers of reinforced concrete. Each factory would be solely devoted to producing the aircraft the Führer referred to as his blitz bomber, the Me-262.

55.

Before construction of the underground factories could get underway, Messerschmitt had plenty of other problems. The bombings of "Big Week" had devastated the plants at Augsburg and Regensburg. Hundreds of workers had been killed, and many of the buildings destroyed. Yet miraculously, most of the Me-262 prototypes at Augsburg escaped damage once again. And the facility at Oberammergau was not targeted, as the Allies did not even know it existed.

Professor Messerschmitt agreed that dispersing the manufacture of aircraft was a sound idea. In accordance with the plan, he had the Me-262 test department moved to Lager Lechfeld. A team of engineers headed by Fritz Kaiser went to the airfield to continue tests.

The program was bedeviled by accidents. On 9 March 1944, test pilot Kurt Schmitt put the Me-262V6 into a steep dive. When he attempted to pull out he was too low, and the aircraft went into a high-speed stall. Schmitt was killed in the crash.

Then on 18 March, the Me-262V8 was delivered to Lager Lechfeld and used for further testing of the MK-108 cannons. At an altitude of 2,000 meters, a Bf-110 towed a sleeve of white canvas while the Me-262 made firing passes. With Gerd Lindner at the controls, the jet scored a number of hits. The test was spoiled, however, when an old problem reemerged. Just as the V8 touched down on the runway its nose gear collapsed. The aircraft was severely damaged, and repairs would take weeks.

As the test program went on, Fighter Staff was showing impressive results. In March, more than 1,500 new fighters were built by the now widely dispersed aircraft plants. And that same month, the first series Me-262 at last came off the production line at Leipheim.

While these propitious events were taking place, the Luftwaffe was gaining the upper hand in its battles with the RAF. On 30 March, 750 British bombers attacked Nuremberg. It was a cold night, and their contrails could easily be seen and plotted. As a result, chaff dropped by the aircraft failed to disguise the direction in which the bombers were flying. The German radar screens were foiled, but observers' eyes were not. The Luftwaffe was alerted to put up a *Schwerpunkt* defense.

Accordingly, fighters from a dozen bases were assembled over the target as the bombers approached. The sky was wreathed in a high thin cloud layer, perfect for the *Wilde Sau* techniques pioneered by Major Hajo Hermann. Searchlights bounced their beams off the clouds, and flak batteries fired hundreds of star shells. Also, the German aircraft were carrying the SN2 radar, as well as the Naxos X, which read the bombers' own radar emissions. It was a simple matter for the Luftwaffe pilots to pick out their adversaries and close in.

The night-fighters were Bf-110s, He-219s, and Ju-88s. They were armed with rockets and *Schrag Musik* cannons, and the men flying them were combat veterans. The result was a slaughter, with 95 Lancasters shot down. When the battered survivors returned to England, another twelve crashed and burned. Altogether, nearly a thousand British airmen were killed or wounded in the raid. The loss ratio was one of the highest the RAF suffered in the war.

To Erhard Milch, all this was highly gratifying. The Luftwaffe had knocked the enemy back on its heels, and the German aircraft industry was building fighters at a furious rate. Milch began to believe the war might be winnable after all, or at least, the Reich homeland could be successfully defended against the RAF.

The American bombing campaign was a different story. The 8th Air Force not only continued its daily attacks, but the number of bombers taking part steadily increased. The Americans occasionally succeeded in locating the hidden aircraft manufacturing sites and destroying them, but to the German commanders, that was not surprising. Karl-Otto Saur, Speer's chief assistant, pointed out that there were six million foreign workers in Germany's factories, and they frequently slipped vital information to the enemy. Communists in the Nazi government passed on intelligence as well.

Next, the Americans began conducting high-volume raids on Berlin in broad daylight, escorted by ever-greater numbers of fighters. On a sunny afternoon in April, German citizens heard the wail of the sirens and hurried into the shelters. As they did, more than 500 B-17s roared overhead in precise formation. With them were 300 Mustangs.

The Luftwaffe scrambled to intercept, and two hundred Bf-109s and Fw-190s waded into the intruders. A savage battle ensued, as the enemy dropped 1,600 tons of bombs on the German capital. But the Americans paid a price, losing 68 bombers and 11 of the escorts. German losses were 32 fighters.

A few days later the 8th Air Force returned, dropping roughly the same amount of explosives and losing almost as many aircraft. The damage the bombs did to the city was terrible, but the blow to the citizens' morale was worse. Once more Göring ranted and raved, though Luftwaffe pilots were now accustomed to his outbursts. They did their best to ignore "Meyer."

By this time the Reichsmarschal had begun to worry about his position. He had good reason to worry, as his enemies were anxious to replace him as Hitler's closest confidant and adviser. One such rival was Joseph Goebbels. Another was Heinrich Himmler, the head of the Gestapo. And still another was Martin Bormann, a fanatical anti-Semite who was in charge of domestic legislation. All of them detested Göring. But there was only one rival he actually feared. That was Albert Speer.

Over time, the Armaments Minister had impressed Hitler so favorably that the Führer had begun speaking of him as a possible successor. When Göring got wind of this, he seethed with resentment. For years he'd been promised the top job when Hitler stepped down, and now this young upstart just might beat him out of it.

Obviously, Speer had to be put in his place. Or better still, be made the subject of Hitler's wrath. An opportunity arose when Speer claimed exhaustion from overwork and went on leave, spending several weeks at the village of Merano in the Italian Alps. As he rested and enjoyed spring skiing, he was unaware of the skulduggery going on in Berlin.

With Speer away, Göring introduced Xaver Dorsch to the Führer. Dorsch was head of the Todt Organization, which was responsible for construction projects in the occupied territories. Göring told Hitler that Dorsch was a far better organizer and builder than Speer, and unlike Speer, he was completely loyal. He would never fail to carry out an order from the Führer.

Speer, Göring said, had been directed to construct two large underground factories where Me-262 aircraft would be built, but he'd made no progress, and the highly qualified Dorsch was prepared to take his place. Hitler was angry to hear that his orders had been taken lightly, but he hesitated when it came to punishing Speer. The Armaments Minister had served him too well to be tossed aside. And Hitler was aware of Göring's talents as a manipulator, so for the moment, he left Speer in place.

Another who saw Speer's absence as an opportunity was Feldmarschal Milch. The Air Minister was resentful that Speer had blocked his attempts to use an Autobahn tunnel as a hidden site for building Me-262s. Instead, Speer ordered ball bearings to be manufactured there. Milch also wanted to construct an extension to the underground factory at Nordhausen, where A4 rockets were being built. The extension would be used to produce 1,000 Me-262s per month. With Speer on leave, Milch requested a go-ahead from Hitler, and the Führer gave it.

As always, Milch's intentions were influenced by his hatred of Willy Messerschmitt. He told Göring that the new plant would be used to build both the Me-262 and the Junkers turbojet engines. Messerschmitt, however, would not be in charge of the program; instead, it would be run by Junkers. Göring refused to go along with Milch's plan, and made sure Messerschmitt learned about it.

At this point Hitler was confronted with major problems. The war in the east was going badly, with the Soviets driving the German army back and inflicting heavy losses. The Soviets had a virtually inexhaustible supply of fresh troops, and were also receiving a large supply of weapons and supplies from the U.S., transported to the port of Murmansk by American merchant ships. And in Italy there was more bad news. The Americans and the British under the command of Field Marshal Alexander were steadily moving up the boot. Soon they would take Rome.

But most troubling of all, Hitler knew the Allies were preparing to invade France. Once on the mainland, they could launch a drive into Germany. The invasion must be stopped, and the Führer was confident he knew exactly how to do it.

56.

Hitler's plan comprised three parts. The first involved reinforcing the so-called Atlantic Wall, which ran all along the coasts of Holland, Belgium and France. He ordered Feldmarschal Erwin Rommel to strengthen the fortifications.

The Desert Fox directed the construction of many more concrete bunkers and pillboxes that housed antitank guns, machine guns, and cannons. He also put in great numbers of antitank obstacles, and had more than six million mines laid on the beaches and in the water just offshore.

The second part of Hitler's plan involved beefing up homeland defenses. By now the Führer fully realized the threat posed by the Allied bombings. He cared little for the plight of German civilians, but was concerned about damage to the nation's industries. As Milch and Speer had warned, if the ability to produce war materiels were destroyed, it would be impossible to fight on, and the war would be lost.

Therefore, Hitler ordered an increase in the production of fighters, to provide what he called an umbrella over Germany. Ironically, this was what Milch had been urging for more than a year. During that time the Führer had ignored his pleas.

The third part of Hitler's plan called for defeating the Allies' invasion forces on the beaches. He believed they would be unable to penetrate Rommel's fortifications, and as they were being torn apart by shellfire and exploding mines, bombs dropped by highspeed Me-262 bombers would finish them off.

Because the Me-262 was to play such a key role, Hitler was still angry that Speer had ignored his order to build underground factories for production of the jets. Seeing an opening, Göring again reminded him that Xaver Dorsch was much better qualified than Speer to do the work. Hitler took Göring's advice, and turned over construction of the new Me-262 factories to Dorsch.

When Speer returned from leave and learned what Hitler had done, he was shocked, as this was the first time he'd been out of favor with the Führer. Göring, of course, was delighted. He believed Speer had been defanged, and thus eliminated as a rival. Milch, on the other hand, was not pleased by Hitler's decision. He'd get the new factories, but Speer had often been helpful to him in the political skirmishes. Göring remained a devious enemy, and Milch felt that with these new developments his own position would be threatened as well.

Therefore Milch went to the Führer, who was at Klessheim castle being shown a display of new armor, and spoke to him on Speer's behalf. Milch said Speer was an extraordinarily gifted administrator who was staunchly loyal to the Führer. It would be very unfortunate if his abilities were no longer utilized.

Hitler listened, and finally said that Milch could tell Speer he was "very fond of him." Relieved, Milch reported Hitler's remark to Speer, thinking Speer would now be back in charge of building the Me-262 factories.

Milch was wrong. It was Xaver Dorsch who was ordered to construct the underground factories after all.

But Speer was a clever infighter. He retained his authority as Armaments Minister and became stronger than ever. And he agreed with Milch that as many fighters as possible should be produced, which would be in accord with Hitler's wishes as well. The expansion of the fighter program also would mean a reduction in the building of bombers. From 600 bombers a month, production would be cut to 250. General Korten saw this as the end of the bomber force, and objected strenuously. Milch explained to him that bombers were no longer important, because their function would be superseded by the flying bombs that would soon be launched against London.

These conflicting views came into focus on 23 May 1944 when Göring called a conference to discuss the future needs of the Luftwaffe. When told by Milch of the decision to reduce the building of bombers, the Reichsmarschal would have none of it. He said Hitler wanted more bombers, not fewer. In fact, Göring went on, he and the Führer were in agreement on the Luftwaffe growing to a force of 14,000 aircraft, with 5,000 more being produced each month. At least 900 of the new airplanes should be long-range four-engine bombers capable of carrying great loads of explosives. They should be similar in type to the Allies' Lancaster and the Flying Fortress.

It was true, Göring said, that mistakes had been made in the past. Aircraft such as the Ju-88 and the He-177 had been designed to serve as both conventional bombers and dive bombers, and that was a bad idea. It was all Udet's fault, but there was no point in agonizing over that now. Instead, it was important to plan for the future.

Accordingly, the Air Ministry should order the production of the new bombers at once. Fighter-bombers such as the Me-262 and the Arado 234 were fine for their purpose, but the heavies were better suited for taking the fight to the enemy.

Listening to this, Milch was confounded. What had happened to the Führer's concept of an umbrella of fighters over Germany? Why was German air power once again to be used offensively, a strategy that had already proved to be a failure? And now the Me-262 was being loftily dismissed as merely a fighter-bomber?

It was possible, of course, that no such agreement between Göring and Hitler had been reached. But before Milch could argue about it,

Göring said that the Führer wished to review the aircraft program later that day.

The meeting was held at the Berghof, Hitler's magnificent home at Berchtesgaden, in the southernmost part of Germany. The huge house in the Bavarian Alps was sumptuously furnished with antiques and art stolen from vanquished countries, and its broad terraces gave views of the Führer's native Austria. A dozen servants kept the place running smoothly. Eva Braun spent much of her time there, and was on hand today. So was Blondi, Hitler's prized Alsatian dog.

In the great room Oberst Edgar Petersen presented a report to Hitler on aircraft production. Present were Göring, Milch, Speer, and Saur. General Galland was also there, along with several Luftwaffe staff officers. The Führer showed little interest in the facts and figures, until Petersen referred to the Me-262. Hitler stopped him and asked how many of the jet bombers had been built.

Milch answered. "None, mein Führer. The Me-262 is being manufactured exclusively as a fighter aircraft."

Hitler was thunderstruck. He was expecting the Allies to attempt an invasion of France at any time now, and here he was being told that one of the weapons he was counting on to repel the enemy did not exist!

Milch hastily explained that extensive design changes would have to be made to convert the Me-262 to a bomber. And even if that were done, he said, the jet would be capable of carrying only one thousand kg of explosives.

Hitler cut him off. Eyes bulging, his face red, the Führer shouted, "Who pays the slightest attention to the orders I give? I gave an unqualified order, and left nobody in any doubt that the aircraft was to be equipped as a fighter-*bomber*!"

There was a moment of tense silence, and then Hitler demanded to know the weight of the aircraft's armor, guns and ammunition. He was told they added up to well over 1,000 kg.

"You don't need any guns," he roared. "The plane is so fast it doesn't need any armor plate, either. You can take it all out!"

It was General Galland's turn to be startled. He began to say that doing so would be unwise, but Hitler cut him off as well.

Milch then tried again to explain. He said only a few words before the Führer went into a tantrum, calling the Air Minister a stubborn fool and a blockhead. The tirade went on for several minutes, spittle flying from Hitler's mouth as he spouted invective.

At that point Milch could restrain himself no longer. Without thinking he yelled, "Mein Führer, the smallest infant can see that this aircraft is a fighter, and not a bomber!"

Again there was silence in the room. His face still red, Hitler made no reply, but simply stared at Milch. It was clear to those present that Milch had just committed career suicide.

57.

It was not a matter of sudden death. Milch's political demise was a dragged-out affair that took place over several weeks. It began with his being kept out of meetings, and gradually came down to the elimination of his duties as Air Minister. Ironically, the man he'd considered his benefactor and political ally made no effort to save him. In fact, Albert Speer did the opposite, consolidating his position as ruler of all arms manufacture in the Reich, including the production of aircraft.

Other enemies used Milch's vulnerability to justify their own actions, making him a scapegoat for their own mistakes. Göring blamed him for not developing the Me-262 as a fighter-bomber, and for attempting to emasculate the bomber arm of the Luftwaffe. Göring also tried to undermine Speer by turning over responsibility for all armament to Karl Saur. But Speer was too shrewd an opponent, and made sure that his grip as Armament Minster remained firm. In discussions with Hitler, Speer also emphasized the Luftwaffe's failures, ascribing them to Göring.

The Reichsmarschal was not unaware of his own liability. There were further attacks on Ploesti, and on the synthetic fuel plants at Leuna-Merseburg and Politz. The raids greatly weakened German industry, as well as the armed forces, by reducing the amount of oil and benzine available to them.

For Willy Messerschmitt, the turbulence within the Air Ministry was highly disruptive to his work. He received orders from Göring to suspend all production of the Me-262 as a fighter and to produce the aircraft as a fighter-bomber as rapidly as possible. Messerschmitt did not dispute Göring's claim that past errors regarding the role of the jet had been caused by Milch.

By then the impending invasion of France loomed like a specter over

Germany's leaders. Yet there was still a shortage of front-line aircraft, and Me-262 series production had been brought to a halt. Messerschmitt knew it would be impossible to reverse course and turn out meaningful numbers of the jet as fighter-bombers in time to make a difference.

On 6 June 1944, the inevitable took place. Shortly after midnight, British and American paratroops were dropped into Normandy, and airborne soldiers were flown in on gliders. There were brief exchanges of gunfire, but German defenders thought this action was a feint.

The Germans expected the actual invasion to take place at Pas de Calais, because a large Allied force was poised directly across the Channel from it. But in fact, what they saw was a ghost army, consisting of wooden mockups of tanks and airplanes. The U.S. 9th Air Force also played an important part in the ruse. Its medium bombers carried out repeated attacks on German installations at Pas de Calais, further convincing the German High Command that this was where the Allies would invade.

Instead, when Wehrmacht soldiers looked out of their bunkers on the Normandy coast at dawn on 6 June, they beheld the largest invasion armada ever assembled. Some 6,939 vessels were approaching, including 4,126 transports and landing craft, six battleships, 26 cruisers, 181 destroyers and destroyer escorts, 540 minesweepers and tugboats, and hundreds of merchant ships.

Above them in the gray sky were 11,268 aircraft.

The invasion was code-named Operation Overlord, and was directed by Supreme Commander Dwight Eisenhower. It began with a furious bombardment, as warships lofted thousands of shells onto the bunkers and pillboxes and the network of trenches. At the same time American and British aircraft bombed and strafed the emplacements. The Germans returned fire, pouring a stream of projectiles from their heavy artillery as the landing craft began moving toward the beaches.

The defenders consisted of only four combat divisions, because the bulk of the German forces were gathered at Pas de Calais. But the division facing the Americans at Omaha was one of the Wehrmacht's best. This was the 352nd Infantry, and its men were veterans who'd fought in Russia. The Germans put up a fierce defense. Many of the landing craft never made it as far as the beach, and instead were blown out of the water by cannon fire, or destroyed by mines, or became hung up on underwater obstacles. The ocean was red with the Americans' blood.

But the Germans could not stop the attack. U.S. infantrymen swarmed onto the beach, and though many were cut down, they prevailed. Army Rangers climbed the cliffs to the German positions, killing most of the enemy soldiers there. Tanks and self-propelled guns, as well as tons of ammunition and supplies, were put ashore by LSTs. Before the morning was over, the Americans had suffered more than 3,000 casualties, but they had established a beachhead and pushed the Germans back.

The troops of the U.S. 4th Infantry Division who went ashore on Utah Beach found the resistance the lightest of the invasion. Of the 23,000 men who landed there, only 197 became casualties. The 4th pressed on to link up with the 101st Airborne.

On Sword Beach, British commandos went in ahead of the regular infantry, led by Private Bill Millin, a 21-year-old Scotsman. Wearing a kilt his father had worn in the First World War, Millin strode up the beach playing bagpipes. Shells exploded overhead and machine-gun fire kicked up sand all around the commandos, but they seized their objectives. The infantry penetrated five miles by nightfall.

The Canadians had a rough time of it on Juno. Eleven German batteries of 155mm guns and nine others of 75mm guns blasted away at them, joined by withering fire from machine guns. But their tanks helped clear a path, and the Canadian infantrymen fought their way inland. They took casualties of 50 percent.

On Gold Beach the casualties were also heavy because the British tanks were not put ashore on time. Another problem was that the Germans were dug in at a small village, and though it took hours to dislodge them, the British troops managed to get to Bayeux before dark.

The Germans were hampered by damage to their communication system wrought by French Resistance fighters. The French cut telephone and telegraph wires, destroyed roads and bridges, and sent fake signals that confused the defenders. Additionally, the German commanders were not as alert as they might have been. They were headed by Feldmarschal Gerd von Rundstedt, and the commander of Army Group B was Feldmarschal Rommel. At the time the invasion began, Rommel was at home in Herrlingen, celebrating his wife Lucie's birthday with her and their son.

When Feldmarschal Wilhelm von Keitel heard that Allied troops were landing on the beaches, he telephoned von Rundstedt from Hitler's headquarters and asked, "What shall we do?"

Von Rundstedt replied, "Make peace, you fools!"

His advice was ignored, of course. But Hitler neither forgot von Rundstedt's words nor forgave him for saying them. Not long afterward, the Führer replaced him as Commander in Chief West with Feldmarschal Günther von Kluge.

When the news of the invasion reached Rommel, he rushed to his Mercedes and his driver took him at breakneck speed across Germany and into France. Late that afternoon he reached Rheims, where he telephoned Rundstedt's headquarters and ordered the 21st Panzer Division to counterattack at once.

Under General Edgar Feuchtinger, the 21st punched through the British forces and reached the coast at Luc-sur-Mer. At that point Allied aircraft flew over and dropped thousands of parachutes behind the Panzers. The parachutes were only a supply drop that happened to land in the wrong place, but Feuchtinger thought they were paratroopers. He panicked and pulled his forces back. It was the only counterattack of the day, and ultimately became an ignominious failure.

By that evening 155,000 troops had landed and established bridgeheads of 80 square miles. They had sustained more than 10,000 casualties, but Rommel was the first to admit that the invasion had been a success. Now the job would be to try to halt the Allied advance across France.

Of all the mistakes the Germans made that day, two rankled Rommel most. One was the absence of the Navy. Except for an attack by a torpedo boat that damaged an enemy destroyer, there had been no sign of Admiral Raeder's warships.

The second mistake also involved absent forces. From the beginning the Allies had established complete air superiority, and to Rommel, this was infuriating. Where was the Luftwaffe?

The answer was supplied by General Galland. Whereas the Allies attacked Normandy with more than 11,000 heavy and medium bombers, fighters and fighter-bombers, the Germans had only 319 aircraft in place to meet the enemy on the day of the invasion. Here again the German High Command had been outmaneuvered by the Allies. The RAF and the 8th Air Force had continued their bombing of German cities and industrial sites without letup, and most Luftwaffe fighter units were kept in the Reich to defend against them. In France, only the Third Air Fleet was on hand, and it too was badly handicapped because the U.S. 9th Air Force had bombed its airfields until many were unusable.

Of the German aircraft that attempted to stop the aerial onslaught at Normandy, 42 were shot down. In contrast, the USAAF lost four B-24s, six B-26s, five A-20s, two P-38s, and seven P-47s. Considering the odds, it was a wonder the Luftwaffe's losses weren't even worse than they were.

As for the Me-262s, not a single one took part in the battle.

58.

Six days after the invasion of Normandy, Germany was ready to fire the first V-1 flying bombs at London. British Intelligence had known about the new weapons as early as 1942, and Churchill had authorized Operation Crossbow in an effort to disrupt their development. The RAF had then raided the factories where the V-1s were being built, as well as the launch sites in France. But the raids did little damage.

On 12 June 1944, ten of the missiles were launched from ramps on the French coast at Pas de Calais. None reached the target—instead, they either fell into the sea or crashed in open country. The designer, Robert Lusser, and the engineers were not discouraged, and the next day they tried again with a single V-1. This time the missile worked perfectly, rapidly crossing over the Channel and exploding in the outskirts of London.

During the following week, dozens of the flying bombs struck the British capital, killing 42 civilians and injuring hundreds more. Just as the Germans had envisioned, people in London were terrified, never knowing when the next bomb would fall from the sky, or where it would land.

Hitler and his commanders were delighted by the success of the new weapon, and so was Joseph Goebbels, who had named it. The "V" stood for *Verveltung*, meaning retaliation.

Professor Messerschmitt was also pleased. He'd been sure the flying bomb would be effective, and was intrigued by its design. The V-1 was 7.90 meters long and had a wingspan of 5.3 meters. Its warhead was packed with Amatol, which was an 80-20 mixture of ammonium nitrate and TNT (ironically, Amatol had been developed by the British). The V-

1's guidance system and the engine were what particularly fascinated the Professor. Once a V-1 was launched from its ramp, an autopilot regulated height and speed. Feedback from a magnetic compass controlled the rudder and elevator to maintain direction.

The engine was a pulse jet, the simplest type of jet engine. Fuel was injected into the combustion chamber as air was forced through shutters that acted as a one-way valve. When the fuel-air mixture was fired, the shutters closed and the expanding gas was blown out the tailpipe, providing thrust.

The process was repeated at a rate of 100 times per second. When sufficient time had expired for the bomb to have reached its target, a device cut the elevator control cable. The spring-loaded elevator then snapped downward and sent the craft into a steep dive. On impact two fuses, one in the nose and the other in the belly, exploded the Amatol.

People in London called the weapon the buzz-bomb, because of the sound made by the engine. It was also called the doodle-bug, after a noisy Australian insect. As the V-1 went into its dive, the engine was starved of fuel and cut out. For a few seconds there was an eerie silence, followed by a violent explosion.

As the V-1s continued to rain down on London, there was no letup in the bombing of the German aircraft industry. On two occasions, French workers escaped from Messerschmitt factories with drawings and information on the Me-262. When the data was studied by the Allies, they were able to increase their own efforts to produce jet fighters. The Americans had several in the works, including the Bell P-59A and the Lockheed P-80A. Meanwhile, the British ordered the production of 120 Gloster Meteors.

During this time American fighter strength in Europe increased rapidly. More Mustangs were shipped to England, and more pilots clamored to fly them. Not only were the P-51s great combat airplanes, but their extraordinary range meant they could go wherever the action was.

General Spaatz and the other U.S. air commanders decided that each fighter type should play the role for which it was best suited. The P-47 Thunderbolt was probably the nearest to indestructible of any fighter in the war, but even with drop tanks it could stay in the air no more than four hours. That was less than half the endurance of the Mustang. Therefore, P-51s began doing most of the bomber escort work, while many P-47s were relegated to ground support and strafing duties. In the summer of 1944, the Jugs destroyed hundreds of German locomotives, and countless tanks, trucks and other vehicles. With heavy armor, and eight .50-caliber machine guns putting out 7,200 rounds per minute, they were fearsome machines.

In July, P-47s also did some of the shorter-range escorting of bombers, and they got into their share of dogfights as well. A number of American pilots became aces flying them, the most successful being the members of the famed 56th Fighter Group, commanded by Col. Hubert Zemke.

The pilots in the 56th were known as Zemke's Wolf Pack. Among them were such colorful characters as Capt. Francis "Gabby" Gabreski, whose score would reach 28 kills. Another was Major Robert Johnson with 27, and Capt. David Schilling with 22. Zemke himself would have 17 confirmed before he crashed behind enemy lines and was taken prisoner. Everyone who flew the P-47 praised the big fighter for its incredible stamina. After a battle with Fw-190s, Major Johnson described the damage his airplane had sustained:

> There are twenty-one gaping holes and jagged tears in the metal from exploding 20mm cannon shells, and my count of bullet holes reaches past a hundred. The propeller has five holes in it. Three cannon shells burst against the armor plate, a scant inch away from my head. Two others blasted away the lower half of my rudder. One shell exploded in the cockpit and ripped away the flap handle. Behind the cockpit, the metal is twisted and curled. That jammed the canopy, trapping me inside. The airplane had done her best. Needless to say, she would never fly again.

Eventually many of the fighter groups equipped with the P-47 would have their aircraft replaced by Mustangs; even fewer P-38 Lightnings would be sent to the ETO.

In Germany at this time there was general confusion among the engineers working on the Me-262. With Milch out of the picture, no one dared challenge Hitler's insistence that the aircraft was to be built strictly as a fighter-bomber. But to Willy Messerschmitt and the design team, that was nonsense.

Nevertheless, an official order from the RLM specified the aircraft was to be redesigned to carry as heavy a bomb load as possible, and then rushed into production. What's more, it was not to be referred to as a fighter, but only as a fighter-bomber.

Its name changed as well. No longer was an Me-262 a *schwalbe*. Apparently calling it a swallow was considered too tame, so instead, a new name appeared. From then on, the Me-262 was officially to be known as *Der Sturmvogel*—the Stormbird. The new name was much to Hitler's liking, and to Göring's as well. Stormbird had a Wagnerian ring to it, fitting for the new blitz bomber. The name most likely was conceived by Goebbels, inasmuch as it first appeared in *Spiral*, the magazine put out by the Propaganda Ministry.

Predictably, the engineers considered the name just so much claptrap. But as time went on, some of them accepted it, and applied it to both the fighter-bomber version and the pure fighter; at least the name sounded dramatic. Although others continued to call the fighter the *schwalbe*, most pilots, as well as most engineers, referred to any version of the aircraft simply as the 262, or the turbo.

To Willy Messerschmitt, the new name was irrelevant. He was more concerned with the foolishness of being ordered to turn his creation into something other than what he'd envisioned for the past five years. He oversaw the work of converting the aircraft to a fighter-bomber, but with little enthusiasm.

Meanwhile, the Luftwaffe was eager to get its hands on quantities of the jet. A special unit had been formed, designated Erprobungskommando 262. It was to be equipped with the new aircraft as soon as they were available. The pilots in Ekdo 262 had been drawn from III Gruppe Zerstörergeschwader 26, where they had flown Bf-110s. All had combat experience. Their commander was Hauptmann Werner Thierfelder, who would train them in tactics suited to the jet.

The first 16 airplanes delivered to Ekdo 262 were soon followed by seven more, but they were all the A-1a fighter version, and putting them into service would conflict with orders from the Führer and Reichsmarschal Göring. Therefore a second order was issued, permitting the fighters to be used only for training purposes, which at least gave Thierfelder's pilots an opportunity to fly them.

Becoming accustomed to the jet could be tricky. The main difficulty for most pilots was learning to handle the throttles properly. The dilemma was the same as always—if the throttles were advanced or closed too quickly the engines would flame out, or even catch fire. Should that happen at low altitude the aircraft would stall and very likely crash. The pilots also learned that the Me-262 was a totally different airplane from anything they'd flown before. It wasn't hard to fly, but it demanded gentle treatment. Rough, rapid maneuvering could produce engine failure as well.

Another problem was the short life of the turbines. After running only ten hours, the engines had to be completely overhauled. And that, of course, cut down on the time pilots could spend learning to fly the airplane.

Adding to the confusion was the establishment in June of another unit. This one was formed for the express purpose of employing the Me-262 as a fighter-bomber. Its commander was Major Wolfgang Schenk, and its pilots were members of bomber wing KG51. Like those in Ekdo 262, they had experience with instrument flying and with multi-engine aircraft, which would make it easier for them to transition to the jets. The unit was designated Erprobungskommando Schenk.

As a result of the new orders, Messerschmitt AG began turning out the Me-262 A-2a. The aircraft was supposedly a fighter-bomber, but in fact it was a fighter with bomb racks. It had more armor, and extra fuel tanks. One additional tank containing 50 gallons was installed beneath the pilot's seat, and another of 130 gallons was positioned to the rear of the original.

Two bombs would be carried under the forward section of the fuselage. In flight it would be necessary to empty the rear fuel tank first, in order to maintain balance after the bombs were let go. And to save weight, two of the four cannons were removed. Nevertheless, at takeoff the aircraft had become heavier by 325 kg, which made getting it off the ground a problem once again. To solve it, a pair of Borsig RI 502 takeoff assistance rockets were added.

Twenty-eight of the fighter-bombers were produced and delivered to Major Schenk's unit at Lager Lechfeld. They arrived early in July, and Schenk's pilots began training to fly them as bombers. Early experience with the aircraft was not encouraging.

For one thing, the A-2a was too fast for accurate level bombing, and also proved unsatisfactory as a dive bomber. The Revi 16B optical gunsight, though effective for air-to-air combat, was of no use against ground targets. And a rapid pullout after a dive could cause engine failure. Consequently, hitting an objective with precision turned out to be next to impossible.

While Schenk's pilots were struggling with bomber training, an event took place that would seriously impair Germany's conduct of the war. On 17 July, four RAF Spitfires were flying over Normandy when the pilots spotted a German staff car racing along a road. Escorted by two motorcycles, the open car was headed toward the front lines. There was a lone occupant in the rear seat, obviously a high-ranking officer.

One of the pilots swung around and dove on the car from behind. He opened fire, his tracers tearing holes in the pavement and then slamming into the car. The vehicle flipped over and landed upside down in a ditch beside the road. The pilot flew on, not knowing he'd come within a millimeter of killing one of the ablest Wehrmacht leaders, Feldmarschal Erwin Rommel.

By then Rommel had concluded the war was lost. He'd expressed that opinion to Hitler, but it only made the Führer angry. Now when Rommel was needed most he was in a hospital with multiple skull fractures, and doctors were afraid he might not recover.

The following day brought another stroke of bad luck. The Ekdo 262 units' commander, Werner Thierfelder, was flying his Me-262 over Landsberg when both engines failed. The aircraft crashed and Thierfelder was killed. Hauptmann Horst Geyer, a veteran fighter pilot, then took over command of Ekdo 262, and the men rallied around him.

But a day later there was a further setback, when American bombers attacked the Messerschmitt factory at Leipheim. Seven Me-262s were destroyed, and three others were damaged. A dozen workers lost their lives. Professor Messerschmitt was troubled by this chain of events. Attempts to use the Me-262 as a fighter-bomber were turning out poorly, just as he'd predicted, and the enemy's bombing of the Lepheim plant would disrupt the production schedule.

Yet those things paled in comparison with what happened next. One day after the raid on Lepheim, Messerschmitt was shocked to learn than an attempt had been made to kill Adolf Hitler.

59.

Reports of the incident were fragmented and unclear, and rumors abounded. Messerschmitt tried to find out what had happened by telephoning friends in the German military leadership, but they too were confused, and it was hard for him to sort out the facts. Days passed before he was finally able to put together the truth about the event, and what had led up to it.

What the Professor learned was that on 20 July, a young Wehrmacht officer had gone to a meeting in Hitler's command center, carrying a bomb in his briefcase. He was Oberst Claus Schenk Graf von Stauffenberg. Tall and lean, with black hair and an erect bearing, Stauffenberg was the paradigm of a professional German officer. During Operation Barbarossa, he'd served as a major in the 6th Panzer Division. Though he fought bravely, he was disgusted by atrocities committed by the SS.

In 1942 he was badly wounded when his staff car was blown up by a land mine. As he staggered from the wreck, a Soviet airplane strafed him, resulting in the loss of his right forearm, two fingers of his left hand, and his left eye. Following a long hospital stay, Stauffenberg was assigned to army headquarters in Berlin and promoted to oberst. It was then that he joined a group led by Major General Hermann von Tresckow, whose purpose was to eliminate Hitler. Members of the secret organization included Wilhelm Canaris, Ulrich von Hassel, Peter von Wartenburg, Ludwig Beck, Julius Leber, Carl Goerdeler, Hans Oster, Fabin Schlabrendorff, and Erwin von Witzleben.

In late 1943 and early 1944, Stauffenberg, Tresckow, Olbricht and the others made plans, a number of times, to kill Hitler, but he was always out of reach. Fearful of Allied air raids, the Führer was spending little time in Berlin. Usually he was at Wolfschanze, his command center at Rastenburg in East Prussia, or at the Berghof, his Alpine home in Berchtesgaden. The conspirators resolved that no matter what the cost, the assassination must be carried out.

Their plan was code-named Operation Valkyrie. General Friedrich Fromm knew about the plot but stayed more or less neutral, waiting to see how matters panned out. If the assassination succeeded, he and Generals Ludwig Beck and Erwin von Witzleben would be in charge of the German Army.

On the morning of 20 July 1944, Stauffenberg and his aide, Hauptmann Werner von Haeften, were flown to Rastenburg in a Heinkel He-111. At noon Stauffenberg entered Hitler's Wolfschanze. He stepped into the conference room, carrying his briefcase. Twenty men were present, discussing the battles in France with Hitler. Maps were laid out on a heavy table built of oak. Stauffenburg took a seat, and placed his case under the table.

The bomb was attached to a timer that Stauffenburg had activated earlier. He checked his watch, and waited as patiently as he could. At 1210 he excused himself to make a telephone call, and left the room.

At 1240, the bomb exploded. Four men in the room were killed, one of them the Luftwaffe's General Korten. But a leg of the table shielded Hitler from the blast. Hitler's right arm was badly injured and he suffered burns and bruises. He was also rendered temporarily deaf, but was otherwise intact.

Stauffenberg was standing outside the building when the explosion occurred. He and others nearby were rocked by the concussion, and when he saw the smoke and flames, he assumed Hitler was dead. Stauffenberg and his aide rushed to the airfield and climbed into the Heinkel. The pilot flew them back to Berlin where they went to Fromm's office. Not long after that they learned that the attempt had failed.

At 1900 Hitler made a radio address to the nation. He described the explosion of the bomb, and identified Colonel von Stauffenberg as the one who had planted it near him. He then assured his listeners that except for a few minor skin abrasions, he was alive and well. He said the plotters were "A very small clique of ambitious, unscrupulous, criminal and stupid officers who formed a conspiracy to do away with me, and at the same time wipe out virtually the entire staff of the German High Command."

His voice rising, he declared that, "The circle which these usurpers represent has nothing to do with the German armed forces, and above all nothing to do with the German army!" He added that any person who was associated with the conspirators would be shot. And to restore order, he said he had appointed Heinrich Himmler to be "Commander of the Home Forces."

He wound up the speech with these words: "Once again I take this opportunity, my old comrades in arms, to greet you, joyful that I have once again been spared a fate which, while it held no terror for me personally, would have had terrible consequences for the German people. I interpret this as a sign from Providence that I must continue my work, and therefore I shall continue it."

Minutes after the conclusion of Hitler's speech, General Fromm received a call from the Gestapo wanting to know whether Stauffenberg had returned. Fromm realized at once that the plot had been traced back to his office, and that he was in danger. In an effort to save himself, he tried to have Stauffenburg arrested.

Fighting then broke out between officers loyal to the Nazi government and those supporting the uprising. Stauffenburg was wounded, and Fromm's forces regained control. Fromm quickly conducted a court martial with himself as the sole judge, during which he condemned Stauffenburg, Olbricht, Haeften, and another conspirator, Albrecht Merz von Quirnheim, to death.

At ten minutes past midnight on 21 July, guards took the four men out into the courtyard. As they stood there Stauffenberg shouted, "Long live free Germany!" The four were then shot.

Fromm was ready to have a number of other officers shot as well, probably to prevent them from revealing his knowledge of the conspiracy. But at that point an SS unit arrived and stopped any further executions from taking place. The officer leading the storm troopers was Otto Skorzeny.

Still worried about his own standing, Fromm hurried to speak with Joseph Goebbels. He proclaimed his loyalty to Hitler and tried to take credit for preventing the coup. Smelling a rat, Goebbels had him arrested. Fromm later committed suicide.

Many others took their own lives as well. Tresckow walked into a field, carrying a hand grenade. He pulled the pin and the grenade exploded, blowing his head off.

In the following weeks Himmler's Gestapo seized anyone who might have had any connection to the plot, however remote. As many as 5,000 people were arrested. Savagely vindictive, Hitler ordered more than two hundred of them tortured and executed. The Führer's favorite means of disposition was to have the condemned men hung while being filmed by motion picture cameras. Often Hitler would invite others to join him in viewing the films, chuckling as he watched his enemies die in agony.

Like most other citizens, Messerschmitt was deeply affected by what had happened. There was growing anger about the war and Hitler's leadership, and yet it was as if the attack had been against the nation itself.

A few days later, an event took place that gave him, as well as the men in the Luftwaffe, a mighty lift. On 26 July 1944, the Me-262 at long last met the enemy in combat.

PART V

THE STORMBIRD GOES TO WAR

60.

On 26 July Leutnant Alfred Schreiber took off from Lechfeld in Me-262 A-1a WNr. 130 017. It was a warm, sunny day, and there had been no reports of an impending attack by American bombers. This would be a routine training flight, though the magazines of the aircraft's four Mk-108 cannons were fully loaded. Schreiber enjoyed flying the jet and was proud of having been selected to join Ekdo 262. Because he'd logged many hours in Bf-110s, he found the transition to the new type relatively easy.

Takeoffs in the turbo could be a bit worrisome, and so could landings, due to the fragile nose gear. Also, the big powerplants hanging beneath the wings demanded great care in the way they were managed. But once aloft, this was a wonderful airplane. It was light on the controls, and presented no torque problem, or vibration. And instead of the roar of piston engines, the sound it made, as it sped through the air, was a hissing noise. Its drawback, however, was that its endurance was limited. The aircraft could stay up for an hour at most, and to be on the safe side, pilots were required to land after 50 minutes.

On a day like this, Schreiber regretted having to make so brief a flight. Except for scattered cumulus, the sky was clear, and the view of the snow-capped Alps was breathtaking. He glanced at the panel, noticing that the altimeter was reading 7,000 meters. His engines were running perfectly. Putting the airplane into a gentle bank, he flew toward Munich. He'd planned to circle over the city, and then return to Lager Lechfeld.

A moment later, he noticed flak bursting in black puffs a few kilometers ahead. That was odd. There was no enemy raid today, so what
could the gunners be shooting at? He scanned the sky, squinting against
the glare of the sun, and saw a speck off to his left and about a thousand meters higher. It was an aircraft, and it was headed west.

Mosquito! No other RAF airplane could fly that fast, and only the
pilot of such a plane could be so brazen. He concluded that the enemy
must be on a reconnaissance mission.

And the *Engländer* was about to get another surprise—the kind of
situation Schreiber and his mates in Ekdo 262 had been dreaming of. He
eased in a bit more throttle and began a sweeping left-hand climb.
Schreiber decided that the Tommy was probably oblivious to his presence. He'd be smug and arrogant, the way Mosquito pilots always were,
flying wherever they pleased over Germany. Their attitude toward the
Luftwaffe was one of superiority.

Well, today this one would be taught a lesson. With 30mm cannon
shells.

When he reached the same altitude as the Mosquito, Schreiber leveled off and swung around behind it. The Me-262 was much faster than
the other aircraft, and he began rapidly closing the distance between
them. It was thrilling to see the enemy grow larger in his gunsight.

Suddenly the Mosquito picked up speed, and Schreiber realized the
Tommy must have caught sight of him. Now the enemy pilot would be
wondering what sort of strange machine was chasing him, but it didn't
matter. The turbo kept right on gaining.

Schreiber flipped up the safety at the top of the control stick with
his right thumb. He had a choice of firing all four guns or only the top
two. He decided on all four. But just as he was about to open up on the
enemy aircraft, it went into a steep dive. Schreiber swore between
clenched teeth. He gently put the stick forward and followed, and as the
Me-262 plunged downward, Schreiber glanced at his airspeed indicator.
He was already passing through 900 kph. Easy now. Even if he were to
lose his quarry, it would be better that than lose the turbo. He backed
off a bit, flattening the angle of descent.

Seconds later, the enemy aircraft pulled out of its dive. As it rose, it
came up in line with the Me-262 and once again, Schreiber would get a
chance. He waited as patiently as possible, the turbo rapidly overtaking
the Mosquito. At about 500 meters he opened fire, his tracers streaking

across the sky toward the British airplane. Abruptly it broke left.

The Me-262 flashed past, and as it did Schreiber looked over and got a brief glimpse of the enemy's cockpit. The navigator in the right-hand seat was looking back at him.

Schreiber wheeled the turbo around, taking care not to make the maneuver too sudden. When he completed the turn he began lining up for another shot. To his surprise, instead of trying to run away the Mosquito was turning toward him.

It was now obvious that the enemy pilot was an old hand. At least he knew fighter tactics, and would now be trying to shoot Schreiber before Schreiber shot him. But the turbo could out-gun him.

At that point the two aircraft were closing at a combined speed of at least 1500 kph, and again Schreiber pressed the firing button. So effective was the recoil mechanism that the Me-262 hardly shuddered as the cannons spit out shells. But he wasn't lined up quite properly, and the tracers missed once more. In an instant the aircraft had passed one another. They were so close that the turbo was rocked slightly by the enemy's slipstream as it went by.

Scheiss! Come around again, as quickly as possible!

Schreiber made a 15-degree bank to the right, wheeling about to get into position for another shot. He knew what the problem was: the Me-262 still had a tendency to yaw slightly, and correcting lateral instability while shooting was difficult, especially at high speed.

Strangely, the Mosquito hadn't fired at him. Was the aircraft unarmed? That was possible, especially if it was set up purely for purposes of reconnaissance.

Armed or not, the enemy was doing the same thing as before, hurtling toward him. Schreiber pressed the firing button, but the Mosquito pilot was jinking his airplane just enough to dodge the turbo's cannon shells. Again and again the two repeated the high-speed, head-on passes, and each time with the same result. By now Schreiber was frustrated and angry. If this kept up he'd run out of ammunition and fuel, which could mean the end of his airplane.

On the next one, he came around in as tight a turn as he dared make, and put the turbo into a dive. When he pulled out of it and brought his nose up, the Mosquito's belly appeared in his gunsight. He fired, and to his satisfaction saw a large chunk of the enemy aircraft break off.

The Mosquito then fell away, obviously out of control. It was finished, there could be no doubt of that. He watched until it disappeared into a cloud on its way down.

Schreiber was thrilled. His machine had performed beautifully, even if its great speed had reduced maneuverability and the yaw had interfered with his marksmanship. The important thing was that he'd just made the first kill ever achieved by an Me-262. Now it was time to get home, before his tanks ran dry. When he landed and reported to Haupmann Geyer, the CO was delighted to have the news, and as Schreiber had expected, so were the other pilots. In the mess at dinner there were toasts, and also ribbing about his having made so many misses.

The footage from the nose camera was processed and reviewed. Because of the sun's glare the images weren't entirely clear, but they showed the Mosquito taking hits, and a piece of it coming off, and then the crippled aircraft going down. No one doubted that Schreiber had scored a victory.

Telephone calls were made to Reichsmarschal Göring, to General Galland, and to the RLM. And also to Messerschmitt, who passed on the welcome news to his engineers. The Me-262 had at last been blooded, and in its first battle had lived up to expectations. The Luftwaffe had its powerful new weapon.

What none of them knew was that the Mosquito had not been hit. Schreiber had seen a part coming off the aircraft, and the film had recorded it, but the part was the outer door of the belly hatch that broke away because of extreme stress in a turn. The pilot, RAF Flight Lt. Wall, had then nursed the airplane over the Austrian Alps and landed safely in Fermo, Italy. At the Fermo airbase, Wall wrote up the incident in RAF combat report No. 2256.

The Germans remained oblivious of the actual outcome of Schreiber's encounter. And thus, for everyone involved with building and flying the Me-262, and for the Luftwaffe in general, the battle had given new wings to their spirit.

61.

Schreiber's victory was a cause for celebration, though it did nothing to dampen Adolf Hitler's conviction that his Sturmvogel should be deployed as a fighter-bomber. He insisted that the Me-262 A-2a begin operations at once. Accordingly, Göring ordered Wolfgang Schenk's 3/KG(J)51 sent to France.

On 27 July, the unit arrived at the Luftwaffe base at Châteaudun. Schenk was ordered to lead nine of the fighter-bombers in an attack on the Allied bridgehead in Normandy. They were forbidden to descend below 4,000 meters, so as to prevent the enemy from learning that the jets had become operational.

Schenk's Me-262s had no bombsights. Instead, the pilots were told to release their bombs as soon as the target passed from view under the wings. Considering the altitude and the speed of the aircraft, the instructions were absurd. Nevertheless, the pilots flew over the bridgehead and dropped their bombs as ordered. They inflicted no meaningful damage. And the enemy did not suspect that the attacking aircraft were jets.

Following the invasion, the Allied forces were commanded by Field Marshal Montgomery. Throughout June and much of July, they had advanced more slowly than planned and were now only a few miles inland, and nowhere near their scheduled objectives. In the open country to the east, the British and Canadian Armies were held up by veteran German mechanized forces, including the 9th, 10th, and 12th Waffen SS Divisions, plus tank battalions. In the west, the American 1st Army struggled to get through the thick, almost impenetrable hedges of the bocage terrain. Most of the Germans facing them were infantry units, along with the Panzer Lehr, the 2nd Panzer, and the 17th SS Panzer Divisions.

The Germans inflicted more than 20,000 casualties while their own forces sustained even greater numbers of dead and wounded. A major problem for them was the failure of the Luftwaffe to contest the enemy's air superiority. With little opposition, the Allied fighters and bombers roamed almost at will, making it impossible for the Germans to bring up replacements and supplies on the roads in daylight. Any convoys that made the attempt were mauled by fierce strafing and bombing attacks. As a result, moving troops and supplies had to be done at night. The flow was reduced to a trickle.

Despite the lack of air support, the Germans put up stubborn resistance. The Americans blamed Montgomery for dragging his heels, and Supreme Commander Eisenhower ordered General Omar Bradley to devise a new plan of attack. Bradley's plan was Operation Cobra, and began with massive bombing of the enemy. Then the U.S. 2nd and 3rd Armored Divisions, together with the 1st, 4th, 9th, and 30th Infantry Divisions, punched a hole in the German lines at Saint-Lo.

With Rommel wounded and out of action, the Wehrmacht forces were poorly led as well as short of supplies and replacements. On 30 July Feldmarschal Günther von Kluge sent a message to Hitler's headquarters at Rastenburg that said, "The whole western front has been ripped open. The left flank has collapsed."

The maneuver was led by General George S. Patton's 3rd Army. His fast-moving armor had swung around and attacked the Germans from the rear, resulting in a defeat that was one of the worst suffered by Germany in the war. More than 400,000 men were lost, as well as 1,500 tanks and self-propelled guns. Afterward, General Eisenhower visited the battlefield and said, "You could walk for miles stepping on nothing but German corpses."

On the eastern front the situation was equally grim. Soviet forces had smashed through the German Army Group Center and crossed what had been the Polish border back in 1939. They were now driving toward Prussia.

Hitler ordered all reserves rushed to the defense of the Fatherland, which left the beleaguered forces in the field with no hope of replacements. Most Luftwaffe units were pulled back to Germany as well, and what little aerial support they'd provided now disappeared.

Kommando Schenk, on the other hand, remained where he was. The Me-262 fighter-bombers flew frequent sorties, though with no more success than when they first arrived. They flashed high over the Allied positions and dropped bombs, but it was impossible to determine whether they'd done any damage.

Thanks to the combat report by Mosquito pilot A.E. Wall, the RAF was aware that the Me-262 had become operational. Spies informed the British that several Luftwaffe units were finishing up their training, and RAF pilots were ordered to be on the lookout for German jets.

Not all British airmen heeded the alert, and on 2 August, Leutnant Schreiber found another opportunity. Flying his Me-262 over Munich at 6,000 meters, he came across a lone Spitfire that apparently was also on a reconnaissance mission. This time the British pilot seemed completely unaware he was being stalked. Approaching rapidly from behind,

Schreiber closed to within 400 meters before he opened fire with all four cannons. Several of his explosive shells struck home, and the enemy aircraft blew up.

Schreiber flew through smoke and debris, and when he came about he saw that no trace of the Spitfire remained. He returned to Lechfeld and again landed with his fuel tanks almost dry. Once more his fellow pilots joined him in a celebration.

Although Willy Messerschmitt was glad to have the news, at this point the Professor was dealing with many difficulties. Chief among them was producing aircraft despite relentless attacks by American bombers on his company's factories. Nevertheless, the various plants continued to manufacture large quantities of the Bf-109, the Bf-110, and the Me-410. In its belated but frantic efforts to bolster homeland aerial defenses, the RLM had ordered all Me-410s to be converted to destroyers. As a result they now carried two MG-151 cannons in the bomb bay, and were used primarily to attack the USAAF's Flying Fortresses and Liberators.

The assignment was ill-advised. The 410s were no match for the Mustangs that now escorted the bombers, and P-51 pilots easily outmaneuvered the slower twin-engine aircraft and shot them down. In frustration, one Me-410 pilot, Feldwebel Wolfgang Martin, ordered his gunner to bail out. He then rammed a B-17.

At Messerschmitt AG, Willy wrangled constantly with Fritz Seiler over what he considered mismanagement of the company. Deeply stressed, the Professor suffered from bouts of what was described as asthma. He also underwent a hernia operation, recovering at Dr. L. Saathoff's Sanitarium in the Allgäuer Alps. After his discharge Lilly insisted that he rest, but he was impatient to get back to work. When he returned to Oberammergau he resumed his Juno cigarette habit.

During this time Messerschmitt was continually bedeviled by asinine orders from the RLM. While maximum efforts were supposedly being made for the defense of Germany by the Luftwaffe, he was directed to go on producing the fastest fighter in the world as a fighter-bomber, a quantity of which were to be built as reconnaissance aircraft.

As much as Willy loathed Erhard Milch, and as intense as their mutual enmity had been before Milch was sacked, the Air Ministry had never needed his organizational ability more than it did now. The Professor understood that the orders affecting the Me-262 were made in compliance with Hitler's demands, but that did not justify them, particularly since the fighter had begun proving its mettle in combat.

On 8 August, Leutnant Joachim Weber of Ekdo 262 encountered another Mosquito flying over Munich. The aircraft belonged to the RAF's 802nd Reconnaissance Group, and the crew was shooting photographs. Weber closed in on the intruder. By this time British airmen were taking the threat of jet attacks seriously. When the pilot caught sight of the shark-like aircraft, faster than anything he'd ever seen in the air, he immediately flicked the Mosquito into a tight left turn, and the Me-262 whipped past him. But then he made the mistake of trying to outrun it, and with his throttles wide open, the RAF pilot headed south for the Alps. He got as far as Lake Ammersee before Weber caught up with him. It took only a few well-placed rounds of 30mm cannon fire to blow the Mosquito out of the sky.

There was no question now, in the minds of Luftwaffe pilots, what the correct use of the Me-262 should be. The Sturmvogel was living up to its name—not as a bomber, but as the fastest, most fearsome fighter in the air.

And soon the RAF would have further proof of that as well.

62.

The first encounters with jets convinced the RAF that they should be put out of action as soon as possible. The British knew at least some of the machines were based at Leipheim, and that the site had been severely damaged in a raid by American B-17s. Now they wanted to learn whether the base was still operating. If so, Allied bombers would pay it another visit.

On 15 August, a Mosquito of the 60th Squadron of the Royal South African Air Force was sent from San Severo in Italy to take photographs. The pilot was Capt. Saloman Plienaar, and his navigator was Lt. Archie Lockhart-Ross. They flew up the Adriatic Coast, crossed the Alps, and went on to Leipheim.

The base was heavily camouflaged, but Lockhart-Ross had no trouble picking it out. He squinted through the bombsight used for focusing the camera, and began shooting photos. He'd made about a dozen exposures when he saw an aircraft take off from the disguised runway. It seemed to climb slowly at first, but then picked up speed.

Lockhart-Ross told Plienaar they'd been spotted. The captain had no desire to wait around for a jet fighter to take a shot at them. They had their photos; it was time to leave.

The Me-262 pilot thought otherwise. When he reached their altitude he swung into position and quickly approached from the rear. Just as he fired, Plienaar broke right, which must have surprised the German, inasmuch as Mosquitos and most British fighters usually broke left when attacked. The unexpected turn undoubtedly saved the lives of the crew. A fusillade of 30mm cannon shells could bring down a Lancaster or a B-17, let alone a Mosquito. As it was, one shell struck the aircraft's left wing. The shell tore away the aileron, but fortunately for the two British airmen it did not explode.

As Plienaar leveled off, the jet came around for another try. With only one aileron, the Mosquito could not make the quick turns a dogfight demanded. His controls sluggish, Plienaar tried to confuse his pursuer by breaking left, but the Me-262 pilot was not fooled. He fired again, and one of the shells clipped the Mosquito. Plienaar's throttle linkage became either jammed or severed, and when he attempted to make another turn, the Mosquito plunged into a lefthand spin with the throttles wide open.

The violent, twisting dive pinned Lockhart-Ross in the nose of the airplane. He tried to rise but G-forces held his body fast and pulled the oxygen mask off his face. Without oxygen, he began losing consciousness due to cerebral hypoxia.

At the moment, Plienaar had his own worries. The Mosquito was spinning down at a speed that threatened to tear it apart, and the controls were not responding. He realized the aircraft would soon drill a large hole in the Bavarian landscape.

But as the airplane lost altitude, the engines' superchargers cut out. Plienaar then found he could back off the starboard throttle but not the port. He brought the stick neutral and applied opposite rudder, which stopped the spin. By bracing both feet and hauling back on the stick, he pulled the Mosquito out of the dive.

It was a miracle that the aircraft was still flying. It was barely airworthy, however, with the port engine continuing to roar at full throttle and no aileron on that side. He was able to steer by crabbing the airplane with the rudder and adjusting the starboard throttle. Lockhart-Ross managed to get hold of his oxygen mask and stick it back onto his face. After a moment he crawled back up into the cockpit and got into his seat.

The German was not about to abandon the chase. As Plienaar struggled to stabilize the airplane, the Me-262 made another pass. Lockhart-Ross saw him coming and called out a warning. Plienaar broke left once more, and as the jet flashed by, Lockhart-Ross could see it clearly. The strange aircraft had large engine pods under the wings.

The Me-262 gained altitude and again came about. Plienaar then drew the same conclusion Wall had reached in July. If he was to survive, he'd have to meet the enemy's attack head-on. With his engines completely out of phase and with only one aileron, that would be no small trick—but it was do it or be shot to pieces. He advanced the starboard throttle, put in right rudder and shoved the stick over. The Mosquito made the 180-degree turn.

Avoiding the jet's cannon fire turned out to be easier than Plienaar expected. As he tried to focus on the aircraft that was hurtling toward him, the Mosquito was jinking by itself because of its damaged controls. He saw the enemy's tracers, and saw them miss. And the jet flashed past.

Plienaar and the enemy pilot then repeated the maneuvers, with the same result. Apparently because of his blinding speed, the German was unable to line up for a clean shot. His shells went awry, and before he could correct he was past his target.

As the two aircraft continued their macabre dance, Plienaar decided escape was impossible; sooner or later the jet would finish them off. Turning once more toward the enemy aircraft he yelled, "I'm going to try to ram the bugger. If we have to go we might as well take him with us."

But now it was Plienaar who missed. The jet flashed over their heads, so close the exhaust from its engines shook the Mosquito. Plienaar then saw some cloud below them, and dove into it. When the Mosquito came out, it was at a very low altitude. The Me-262 broke off and flew away.

The airmen were alive, but exhausted. And they now had another problem to deal with: getting home.

The Mosquito was in rough shape. If it didn't crash, it might run out of petrol before they could make it back. One alternative would be to land in Switzerland, but that would mean internment for the rest of the war. Instead, Plienaar decided to try for the base at San Severo. He began climbing, and Lockhart-Ross gave him a heading of 135 degrees. When the Mosquito flew over the Alps its belly nearly brushed the snow-capped peaks.

That brought them to still another hazard. Udine in northeastern Italy was ringed with German flak batteries. The battered airplane would make a nice fat target.

Plienaar thought they might be able to surprise the enemy gunners. He took the Mosquito back down to the level of the rooftops and advanced the throttle of the starboard engine. With both engines howling and the airplane flying erratically, they zoomed over the city. The Germans must have been too astonished to act, because not a single shell was fired at them.

Plienaar backed off the starboard throttle, and they flew on. Minutes later the two men saw the Adriatic, dead ahead. Lockhart-Ross called out a correction of a few degrees to the south, when suddenly four fighters appeared out of the sun and dove on them. Again the navigator shouted a warning, and when Plienaar looked up, he thought that now they'd had it for sure. But to the immense relief of both men, the fighters turned out to be Spitfires.

San Severo was on the spur of the Italian boot, just above Foggia. The Spitfires escorted them most of the way before the pilots waved and flew off. As Plienaar glanced at the fuel gauges, he saw that both needles were touching empty.

The runway was east-west, and the wind almost always came off the sea. Plienaar made another of his gingerly turns, coming around to line up for touchdown. On final, he shut off the fuel cocks and the magnetos to kill the engines, and lowered his flaps. Then he pulled the gear handle.

It didn't work. He tugged again, and nothing happened. There was a manual override, but that didn't work, either. He had no hope of getting the wheels down, and in a belly landing the Mosquito would probably disintegrate. The aircraft hit the runway and skidded, the bent props and the bottom of the fuselage throwing up showers of sparks. And in the last miracle of the day, the wreck more or less held together. As it came to a halt, an ambulance and a fire truck raced toward it.

The two men climbed out, finding it hard to believe that the aircraft hadn't caught fire, and that they'd suffered nothing worse than a few bruises. The Mosquito looked like a pile of splintered plywood. Later, a live 30mm projectile was found buried in the main spar of the port wing.

The mission proved extremely valuable to RAF Intelligence. Lockhart-Ross had taken photos not only of the base at Liepheim, but also of the enemy aircraft that attacked the Mosquito. These were the first clear pictures of an Me-262 seen by the Allies. The photos, along with the navigator's personal observations, also revealed that the jet was rather slow getting off the ground. So until it gained altitude and the turbines enabled it to reach combat speed, an Me-262 would be at its most vulnerable.

The RAF analysts understood something else as well. For any fighter they or the Americans might put up, outrunning one of the German jets would not be possible. On the other hand, the jet's speed also prevented it from making turns as tight as those performed by a Spitfire or a Mustang. Therefore, the only way to contend with an Me-262 in a dogfight would be to do what Wall and now Plienaar had learned to do the hard way. You had to turn inside it, and line up and shoot as quickly as possible. Before it lined up on you.

63.

After the Normandy breakout, the strategy of the Allied armies was to mount a three-pronged advance. The 12th Army Group under Omar Bradley was to smash its way across France and Belgium, while the 21st Army Group under Bernard Montgomery would go through Holland. The 6th Army Group, led by Jacob Dever, would invade Southern France. The objective of all three was to take the war into the German homeland as rapidly as possible.

A popular impression of France during the occupation by the Germans depicts brave resistance fighters struggling against their oppressors. For the most part, the opposite was true. While a few French men and women were saboteurs or spies, the majority readily cooperated with the Germans. The Vichy government sent thousands of Jews to concentration camps, and thousands of Frenchmen to Germany, where they worked as slave laborers.

For German soldiers stationed in Paris, it was the best duty they could ask for. And for troops on leave, there was no more desirable destination than the city of lights. Bars, restaurants, movie and burlesque theaters, dance halls and brothels all did a thriving business, and virtually anything could be purchased on the black market.

General Eisenhower considered Paris to be of little military value, and intended to bypass it. Now that the German front in Normandy had collapsed, the American forces were moving much more rapidly than expected. The fastest was Patton's Third Army, which had gone through Belgium and crossed the German border at Aachen. Taking Paris, in Eisenhower's view, was not worth a battle. However, General Charles De Gaulle, leader of the Free French Army, insisted on capturing the city. Finally Eisenhower acceded, and allowed French troops go in first. Paris was then secured by the U.S. 4th and 28th Infantry Divisions.

Meanwhile the invasion of Southern France had been launched as Operation Dragoon. The name was chosen by Churchill, who complained that the Americans had dragooned him into approving the invasion. Defending the area against General Jacob Devers' 12th Army Group was German General Johannes Blaskowitz.

On 15 August the U.S. Navy battleships Texas, Nevada and Arkansas, together with the British battleship Ramillies and the French battleship Lorraine, pounded the German positions along the coast east of Marseilles. More than 50 cruisers and destroyers also took part. Next, three American divisions of the VI Corps and a French armored division were landed and led the assault. They were joined by glider combat teams and French commandos. On the first day of the operation, more than 94,000 Allied troops and 11,000 vehicles were put ashore.

Air cover was provided by US Navy Grumman F6F Hellcats of VF-74 Squadron, flying from escort carriers. During eleven days of the operation, the Navy fighters flew 432 sorties. They destroyed more than 500 German vehicles and 50 trains, bombed roads and bridges and strafed enemy troops. The only Luftwaffe fighters the Hellcats encountered were four Bf-109s over the tiny island of Port-Cros, a short distance from the French coast. When the German pilots saw a large number of enemy aircraft bearing down on them, they turned away and flew off. The Hellcats were not as fast, and the Bf-109s disappeared into the Mediterranean mist.

Two days later U.S. Navy Lt. Ed Castenedo attacked a Ju-88 bomber of 1/KG26 near Valence and shot it down. And a day after that

Castenado and Ens. Hulland destroyed a Dornier-217 of KG100 flown by Feldwebel Krug. These were the first aerial victories scored by the U.S. Navy in the European Theater. In all, four American pilots were killed in the operation.

The invasion forces quickly seized the ports of Marseilles and Toulon, establishing a bridgehead. A fleet of U.S. merchant ships delivered vast quantities of supplies, including high-octane aviation gasoline. The Allied Divisions then began moving north.

Operation Dragoon was a great success. At a cost of 4,500 American casualties and a little more than 5,000 French and British, the Allies gained two major ports. By sending troops and supplies through them, they forced the Wehrmacht to fight on yet another front. German casualties were approximately 125,000.

One part of the Allied strategy that did not bring about a satisfactory result was the thrust into Holland, code-named Operation Market-Garden. Directed by British Field Marshal Bernard Montgomery, it was badly conceived and poorly executed. While preparations for the Normandy invasion had taken more than a year, Market-Garden was slapped together under Montgomery's orders in a few weeks. His objective was to race through Holland and drive into the Ruhr, which he claimed would bring an end to the war. Apparently the British commander was eager to pull off a brilliant stroke after his sluggishness in the Normandy sector.

The Market part of the operation called for the largest airborne assault in the history of warfare, for which three Allied divisions would take part. The US 101st Airborne would be dropped at Veghel and cross the canals, and the U.S. 82nd Airborne would land and cross the bridges over the Maas and the Waal Rivers, 60 miles behind the German lines. The British 1st Airborne Division and the Polish 1st Airborne Brigade would descend on the bridge over the Rhine at Arnhem. Next, British armored units under General Brian Horrocks were to race up the road and cross each bridge, finally relieving the 1st Airborne troops at Arnem. That was to be the Garden phase.

The operation was launched the morning of 17 September. On paper, it might have seemed feasible, but when executed, it was a disaster. For one thing, the Germans were much better prepared than the Allies believed them to be. Two Panzer Divisions were near the landing objectives, something the Allies were completely unaware of. For another thing, many of the airborne troops landed in the wrong places.

And in still another miscalculation, the terrain made it impossible for the plan to succeed. The road over which the British armor would travel was narrow, with deep ditches on either side. When the Germans bombed and shelled the road, not only were tanks, equipment and personnel lost, but a horrific traffic jam stopped the advance cold.

The mistakes put the British 1st Airborne troops in a bind. They were to be relieved by XXX Corps within four days, but on the ninth day the armor still had not reached them. They were fighting off a Panzer division, and were low on ammunition. The Polish brigade had been almost completely destroyed.

Finally Montgomery concluded the situation was hopeless, and ordered the 1st Airborne to withdraw. Of the 10,000 men who'd been dropped onto Arnhem, only 2,600 came out, many of them wounded; the rest were either dead or prisoners of war. But perhaps the people who suffered most in the fiasco were the Dutch civilians. Great numbers of them had been injured by the shelling and many more had lost their homes. Over the winter they would face starvation in the bitter cold.

Once again, the Luftwaffe had played no more than a minor role. Fw-190s equipped as fighter-bombers had struck at XXX Corps when the British armor was moving toward the bridges, but they were driven off by Spitfires and P-47s. The greater damage was done by German artillery that had fixed the ranges long before Market-Garden began.

Me-262s of KG(J)51 took part in the battle. They attempted to bomb the Nigmegen bridge, but were unsuccessful. British antiaircraft gunners claimed to have shot down several of the jets, though their accounts might have been merely wishful, since KG(J)51 records show no losses in attacks on the bridge. At that time the squadron was commanded by Major Kurt Unrau, based at the Volkel and Eindhoven Airfields. It was joined there by III Gruppe, and in addition to attacking the enemy during Operation Market-Garden, its pilots flew sorties against the Allies near Antwerp, and Louvain.

Defending Antwerp was particularly important to the Germans, because they knew the enemy needed the port to send in supplies to its ground forces. The Me-262s attempted to bomb the Allied positions in the area, but again they were ineffective. The jets' speed, combined with their altitude restrictions and the absence of bombsights, prevented them from hitting ground targets with any consistency. The bombs they dropped usually missed altogether.

By now the Luftwaffe had been severely weakened. Although in September the aircraft factories had produced the largest number of German fighters of the war, a total of 3,175, fewer experienced pilots were available to fly them. Added to this was the reality of fuel shortages.

Germany's ground forces were also locked in desperate struggles. The Red Army was battering its way through the Balkans and into East Prussia, while the American, British, Canadian, and French Armies attacked from the west and south. The British who had invaded Southern France were pushing north into the Rhône Valley. Rumania had capitulated, and the Allies would soon capture the Ploesti oil fields.

In General Patton, the Americans at last had a field commander with all the dash and verve of Rommel. A brilliant tactician, Patton used the principles of blitzkrieg as skillfully as any German general. His 3rd Army had taken Verdun and would soon link up with the British forces. It was as if a giant fist were closing around the Fatherland.

Incredibly, Hitler continued to brush aside his generals' assessment of the situation. In a conference in his bunker at Rastenburg, he insisted the war could be won if only the Wehrmacht commanders would stiffen the resolve of their troops and fight on. Present were Feldmarschal Gerd von Rundstedt, who had been reinstated and was now Commander In Chief West, and also Generals Hans Speidel and Heinz Guderian. Speidel said it was like listening to the ravings of a madman.

Whipping himself into a frenzy, the Führer proclaimed, "We will continue this battle until, as Frederick the Great said, our damned enemies get too tired to fight any more!"

He pointed to himself as a perfect example of the warrior who refused to be defeated. Victory, he shouted, depended on iron will. And now he would crush the enemy's forces by unleashing his miracle weapons!

One of the few such weapons actually in existence was Werner von Braun's V-2, which the Germans had just begun to launch against London. A wingless rocket, the V-2 was a considerable step up from the V-1. It was much larger, at 14 meters in length, and much deadlier. The Amatol warhead weighed 1,000 kg.

Unlike the Fieseler buzz bomb, the V-2 was silent. It was propelled by burning a mixture of alcohol and liquid oxygen that was forced into the combustion chamber by a steam turbine. The system generated 24,947 kg of thrust for liftoff. The V-2's flight path then described a high arc, as thrust increased to 72,574 kg. When the V-2 reached maximum velocity, its speed was 5,760 kph, or 3,110 mph. The motor burned for only 60 seconds, sending the rocket to an altitude of 96,000 meters, or 314,880 feet. From launch to target took only about five minutes. When the V-2 reached London it plunged down and exploded. Each strike was enough to wipe out a city block.

The V-2 was also different from its predecessor in a way that made it even more terrifying. While the V-1 could sometimes be shot down by antiaircraft guns or by well-trained Spitfire pilots, there was no defense against the V-2. Its enormous speed and its high, arcing flight path made it invulnerable. And because it was silent before it landed, there was no warning—there would simply be a terrific blast. Homes and buildings would be wrecked, people would be dead, and no one knew where or when the next one might hit.

But Hitler's boast that he would crush the enemy with this miracle weapon was hollow, inasmuch as the V-2 was only effective when used against a widespread and heavily populated city such as London. Its gyro-pilot guidance system, which was similar to that of the V-1 and also aided by radio beams, could direct it no closer than the general vicinity of a target. So for tactical military purposes, it was practically useless.

Another miracle weapon Hitler had ordered developed was the Volksjaeger, or people's fighter. This was a lightweight, single-seat jet that could be produced cheaply. It was built by Heinkel, and designated the He-162.

Göring, of course, hailed the project as another example of the Führer's brilliance. The He-162 would be turned out by the thousands, he proclaimed, and even by the tens of thousands. If one were damaged it would simply be discarded, because it was so cheap to build, and a new one would take its place. What's more, the jet was so simple to fly that it could be piloted by young boys. Teenagers would be trained quickly on gliders and then given a brief period of instruction in the Volksjaeger; after that, they would be ready to attack the terror bombers. Apparently Göring considered such pilots as expendable as the jets.

To Adolf Galland, the concept of the aircraft and its youthful pilots was ridiculous, and with his usual lack of tact, he said so. Göring was furious with him, and refused to consider his objections. Though Heinkel was to go full speed ahead with the project, few of the so-called people's fighters were ever built, and they never became a factor in the war.

Still another miracle weapon Hitler had in mind was the Me-262. But thanks to his years of waffling and his demands that the Sturmvogel be produced as a fighter-bomber, the program had been badly compromised. By this time only a relatively small number of the jets had been delivered. And of those, fewer still were pure fighters.

Nevertheless, the Me-262A1a fighter was proving to be everything Willy Messerschmitt had hoped. It could outfight anything the Allies put up against it. Within just a few weeks, pilots flying the jet shot down four Mosquitos and five Spitfires.

Significantly, pilot Helmut Lennartz then destroyed a B-17 over Stuttgart. Lennartz approached the bomber from behind, and one burst from his cannons shot the port wing off the Flying Fortress. Lennartz watched the wreck spiral down and crash.

But as effective as the jets were, there simply were not enough of them. In late September at least six were lost in accidents. Only one was destroyed in combat, and that one had been about to land when it was attacked by a flight of P-47s. The pilot, Oberfeldwebel Ron Lauer, crash-landed and ran from the wreck to avoid being strafed by the Americans.

Now the pilots of Ekdo 262 were facing the possibility that no replacement jet fighters would be coming to their unit. Due to Hitler's orders, only the ineffective fighter-bombers were being built. The pilots' anxiety was understandable. They knew that in the Me-262 they had the best fighter of any nation, and yet the Führer refused to recognize it.

64.

In the German homeland, punishment by Allied bombers steadily increased. While the USAAF sent fleets of B-17s and B-24s on missions whose purpose was to destroy key German manufacturing facilities, the RAF continued to hit population centers.

Air Marshal Harris insisted on calling it strategic bombing. He had Lancasters and Halifaxes drop their multi-ton loads on many towns and cities, irrespective of their importance to the production of war materials. He argued that the attacks were justified, because most locations were also industrial sites. If RAF bombs were to hit a factory, all well and good. But Harris's other objective remained the same: he wanted to kill as many civilians as possible. During the autumn of 1944 more than 130,000 houses were destroyed, and at least 80,000 Germans died in the raids.

Some of the most effective RAF attacks were the nightly bombings of cities in the Ruhr. By striking targets such as Duisburg, Scholven, Wesseling, and Bottrop, the raiders all but paralyzed German synthetic petrol production. Of 91 plants producing the vitally needed fuel, only three were undamaged.

The Allied attacks were also making it difficult for the Germans to transport materials of any kind. Trucks were bombed and strafed, and so were trains. Barges on the rivers and waterways were destroyed as well.

This was deeply worrisome to Albert Speer, who realized what it portended. Although the mines in Saar and Upper Silesia were still held by the Germans, moving the coal to the factories while under aerial attack was a precarious undertaking. And without coal as a source of energy, the factories would be unable to produce weapons, effectively ending the war. Consequently, Speer saw to it that eighty-five percent of aircraft production was devoted to building fighters.

Although fuel shortages remained a problem, the dispersal of the aircraft plants worked astonishingly well. The industry had once been concentrated in a total of 27 large factories, but airplanes were now being produced in 729 medium and small facilities around the country. All were masterfully camouflaged, and as a result, aircraft production was up. Yet there were fewer pilots to fly the planes, and the paucity was becoming critical. Reichsmarschal Göring's response was to order the training of more pilots, and in less time.

The training period had already been shortened twice before, which had led to greater numbers of pilots being turned out by the schools and at a faster rate, but at the expense of quality. Now the B schools, for advanced training, were eliminated, and trainees were sent from the A, or primary, schools, directly into front-line service.

That meant that pilot candidates were learning to fly in simple biplane trainers like the Bücker-131, and then were taking off in fighters with 2,000 hp engines. After logging as few as 40 hours of total flight time, and with little training in fighter tactics, they were assigned to active units. Some of the teenaged boys who were going up in Bf-109s and Fw-190s to attack Allied air fleets were barely able to fly the airplanes, let alone handle them in combat. Meanwhile, the average RAF or USAAF pilot had logged at least 300 hours before seeing action.

Inadequate training time wasn't the only problem. The quality of the Luftwaffe fighter forces was diminished further by pulling experienced instructors out of the schools and sending them to the Geschwaders as replacements. An example was what happened to a fähnrich named Heinz Suhrbeer.

As early as primary school, the tall, strongly built cadet was recognized as a natural-born pilot. He soloed after only eight hours, and finished primary with the highest marks. After achieving similar success in advanced training, he was taught to fly multi-engine aircraft and learned aerial navigation. So good was he that, to his disappointment, he was made an instructor at the Prenzlau training base.

Despite his disappointment, the duty had its advantages. He lived well, and was often granted weekend leave. He also met a beautiful young woman named Charlotte Krueger, who was the manager of the Duckforschriftenstelle, the library at the base. They spent as much time together as possible.

By 1943 Suhrbeer had logged more than 3,000 hours in a wide range of aircraft, and had taught hundreds of young men to fly. When the pilot shortage had become acute, he was abruptly transferred to JGIII, the unit known by the honorific name, "Udet's Boys." He flew a Bf-109, and because of his outstanding skills, his staffelkapitän, Oberleutnant Fritz Stehle, made him his wingman. The instructor who replaced Suhrbeer at Prenzlau was nowhere near as capable, and the student pilots suffered for it.

In the fall of 1944, a new program was instituted. It called for a number of airmen who'd logged many hours in multi-engine aircraft to be transferred to Lager Lechfeld, where they would fly newly assembled Me-262s as test pilots. Suhrbeer was one of them. Certainly he was well qualified. During his seven years in the Luftwaffe, he'd flown almost every type of aircraft built in Germany, as well as many captured French and British machines. He thought the new assignment wouldn't be all that difficult.

There were two stages in the testing procedure. First he was required to make a thorough ground inspection of a newly assembled Me-262, joined by either a master mechanic or an engineer. Together they checked every centimeter of the aircraft, from the nose to the tail. Any problem had to be corrected before the jet could be flown.

The engines, which had already been tested by Junkers, would be started and run up. When everything was found to be satisfactory, the aircraft would be ready for Suhrbeer to conduct the flight test.

That seemed simple as well. He had to take off and put the jet through a series of maneuvers, then return to the base and land. He would do it three times, and if the aircraft passed the test, it would be certified for operations and sent into combat. If not, it would be grounded and its problems resolved.

Suhrbeer flew at least six new machines a day. And as flawless as the aircraft might have appeared on the ground, glitches frequently showed up once they were in the air. Sometimes control cables jammed. Or a new airplane would begin vibrating, threatening to break up. There were leaks, and bolts came loose. Electrical fires broke out. Engine failures were not uncommon, and Suhrbeer made more dead-stick landings than he could remember. A number of his fellow test pilots were killed.

Sometimes surprises cropped up later on, after an Me-262 was cleared for service and sent to a unit. One such incident involved a young Leutnant named Hans Busch. He'd been flying Bf-110s before being assigned to jet duty in KG51, and had excellent skills. Exceptionally tall, with blond hair and blue eyes, he was by nature calm and deliberate. On a day with unlimited visibility, he was scheduled to make a cross-country flight from his base at Neuburg in an Me-262 A2a, Werk #170049.

After startup and a careful check of the systems, he eased in full power and began rolling down the concrete runway. His speed slowly increased, the needle of the indicator moving past 160 kph, then 170, 180. Everything normal, all in good order.

To sense the point at which the jet was ready for liftoff, he put in a little back pressure. The aircraft felt lighter, and he gently pulled the stick back farther. And the starboard engine failed.

By that time he was moving fast. The jet began swinging right, and he tried to correct by applying the left brake. That didn't work, and left rudder had no effect, either. There was a farmhouse just off the runway, and he was rushing toward it.

Now what? Chop the throttles and abort the takeoff? Or try to take off with one engine? If he tried to stop, he'd never make it. Instead, he'd plow into the farmhouse and bring the aircraft and himself to a very dramatic and fiery end.

So go for the takeoff! He pulled back the stick and in what seemed a miracle, the jet lifted off the runway. It soared over the farmhouse, nearly clipping the chimney. Busch quickly pulled the lever to retract the gear.

Now there was a road ahead of him, and beyond it a line of trees. Holding his breath, he kept the aircraft in a climbing altitude as the trees loomed closer. The engine pods brushed the treetops, yet he cleared them as well. *Gott sei dank*!

But it was no good. The Me-262 suddenly rolled to the right, and would not respond to the controls. A plowed field was below and it seemed to rise up to meet him, and the starboard wingtip hit the earth and the jet began a series of violent cartwheels, disintegrating as it did.

Busch was flung about in the cockpit, his body straining against his belt. He had no idea how many times the wreck flipped over, but finally it came to a stop, sitting upright on the field. Then, one of the 900-gallon fuel tanks exploded, and he was enveloped in a ball of fire.

The flames seared his face and hands. He unbuckled his belt and tumbled over the side and onto the ground. He was dimly aware that the section containing the cockpit had been completely separated from the rest of the wreckage, and that burning pieces of the jet were scattered over a wide area. He also realized there would very likely be another explosion. Barely able to see, and in terrible pain, he staggered away and fell to the ground. Not long after that he heard the wail of a siren and then the murmur of voices as he sank into unconsciousness.

When he opened his eyes he was in a hospital, and a medic was swathing him in bandages. A doctor told him he was lucky not to have lost his sight, and even luckier to be alive. He was one of the few ever to survive such a crash.

He didn't know it, but Messerschmitt had saved him by building extra strength into the cockpit of the Me-262. The Professor had done so because at some point the jet might be pressurized. After a few weeks Busch was back in action.

That fall the pilots in the fighter geschwaders were a mixture of youngsters and a few old hands. The boys who didn't learn fast enough died, while those who did learn became more proficient. On 28 September, they shot down 64 B-17s and B-24s, and another 41 on 7 October. Some of the kills were scored by Bf-109s, but many bombers were brought down by Fw-190s, which were much easier for the younger pilots to fly.

As the American losses mounted, U.S. General Doolittle complained to ETO Commander General Spaatz that the bombers still lacked sufficient fighter protection. Doolittle said the ratio of one fighter to every two bombers was inadequate and asked for more. Already nine American Mustangs and P-47s were in the air for every German fighter, but Spaatz relayed the request to Washington, and production was stepped up further.

On the German side, General Galland risked invoking Hitler's wrath by saying the Me-262 should be employed as a fighter and not as a fighter-bomber. He backed his argument by recounting the aircraft's failure in bombing missions, and by comparing that with its prowess as a pure fighter. In the past, such assertions would have sent the Führer into one of his famous rages. But to Galland's surprise, Hitler acceded. At the end of September he ordered an increase in production of the fighter version of the jet.

Galland was gratified, of course. But not until much later would he learn the truth about why Hitler had changed his mind. If he had known what lay behind the reversal of orders, the general would have been appalled.

65.

Willy Messerschmitt was reinvigorated by the change in orders from the Air Ministry. He had high hopes that the Me-262 might yet be the salvation of Germany, and he welcomed the directive to build greater numbers of the jet as pure fighters.

At this point, components of the aircraft were being constructed in many secret places. The wings were built in an autobahn tunnel near Stuttgart, while the fuselages were turned out by the Oberzell works near Passau, and by a plant in the forest at Hagelstadt. From Günzburg came the nose section, and from Lauingen, the engine cowlings. The rudders and landing flaps were produced in Wasserburg.

Assembly of the parts took place in different locations as well. Among them were concealed revetments near the Messerschmitt factory at Regensburg, and an underground plant at Augsburg. Another assembly point was Kuno 1, an outdoor facility in the forest near the Leipheim Air Base. At Kuno 1 a heated tent covered the assembly line, and there was also a firing range and engine test-run stations. Workers slept in wooden barracks. The entire facility was hidden under camouflage nets strung from trees.

Once assembled, the Me-262s were trucked to Lager Lechfeld. After test flights by experienced pilots like Heinz Suhrbeer, they were flown to their assigned Luftwaffe airfields.

Messerschmitt was proud of his firm's ability to produce the fighters despite seemingly insurmountable handicaps. Although Regensburg and Augsburg, in particular, were pounded repeatedly by Allied bombers, the number of Me-262s that were put into service steadily increased.

However, during that autumn his spirits were dampened by several events. One was the death of Feldmarschal Erwin Rommel. Messerschmitt had considered the Desert Fox a man of integrity as well as an outstanding military leader. Feldmarschal Walther Model made the announcement. "The nation," he said, "mourns the loss of one of its greatest commanders." Model explained that Rommel had died in the hospital at Ulm on 14 October as a result of wounds sustained on 17 July, when his car was strafed by an enemy aircraft.

The truth, of course, was quite different. Long before the invasion of Normandy, Rommel had concluded that Hitler should be removed from power. While he was recovering from the fractures of his skull and cheekbones, and the injury to his left eye, he was visited by his former chief of staff, General Hans Speidel. They discussed Hitler's conduct of the war, during which Rommel expressed his opinion of the Führer.

"That pathological liar," Rommel said, "has now gone completely mad. He is venting his sadism on the conspirators of 20 July, and this won't be the end of it."

Rommel was right. The following day Speidel was arrested by the Gestapo. He never revealed that Rommel had supported the plot against Hitler, but Himmler claimed his operatives had discovered evidence of the feldmarschal's complicity.

Rommel was at home on 14 October when Generals Wilhelm

Burgdorf and Ernst Maisel drove to his house. They gave him a choice. He could either stand trial and be convicted of crimes against the Führer, or he could take his own life.

They had brought with them a capsule of cyanide, which they said would kill him in three seconds. He would then be given a state funeral, and his family would be spared the usual steps that would otherwise be taken against them. Rommel bade farewell to his wife and son, and got into the car. He was driven to a remote spot, where he swallowed the capsule.

Afterward, Hitler wired condolences to Frau Rommel, expressing "sincerest sympathy." Professor Messerschmitt attended the funeral, along with many other German leaders, both civilian and military. The oration was delivered by Rommel's old friend Feldmarschal von Rundstedt, while the Führer stood at attention near the swastika-draped casket.

The same month another event brought Messerschmitt further sorrow. Dr. Langbehn, the lawyer who had helped him and Lilly with the purchase of Hochried, was also arrested by the Gestapo. Like many others, Langbehn was charged with involvement in the 20 July plot. He was tried in the Volksgericht, the so-called peoples' court that was presided over by the sadistic Judge Roland Freisler.

Messerschmitt then made a bold and dangerous move. He sent a letter directly to Hitler, pleading for Langbehn to be spared. In the letter he said the lawyer had been his friend and consultant for many years, and could not have been disloyal. Hitler did not reply. Instead, a military adjutant wrote to Messerschmitt two weeks later, informing him that the accused had already been executed.

The third sorrowful event was another death, this time of a man who had been close to Willy from the earliest days of his career. Theo Croneiss, whose relationship with the Professor had begun in 1925, died of heart failure on 7 November 1944. At the time of his death, Croneiss had been chairman of the board of directors of Messerschmitt AG, and chairman of the advisory board of all the subsidiary factories. As Willy said when he gave the funeral oration, "In Theo Croneiss I have lost my most faithful friend. He will not be forgotten."

That fall there was good news as well. More Me-262 fighters were going into combat, and they continued to perform ably, posting a number of victories.

In the beginning, many of the jet fighters' victims were photo-reconnaissance aircraft. The Americans lost nine of them, including five F-5s, which were the beefed-up version of the Lockheed P-38. The F-5s were faster than their predecessors, but they had no hope of outrunning the jets.

The RAF also sustained losses to the new German fighters. Among them were four Mosquitos and a Spitfire that made the mistake of trying to fight it out. Another Mosquito was badly damaged and crash-landed at Dubendorf, in Switzerland.

An Me-262's speed often enabled it to attack before the pilot of the enemy airplane knew he was being targeted. One such encounter involved Lt. Robert Hillborn of the RAF's 7th Reconnaissance Group.

On a cool September morning, Hillborn took off in his camera-equipped Spitfire XI and flew to Stuttgart. His mission was to photograph the Daimler-Benz works. Despite the mauling by both British and American bombers, the plant continued to produce engines as well as tanks and other military vehicles. When Hillborn reached the city he put the Spitfire into a shallow bank and began taking photos. Some flak came up, but he was well above the black bursts. The first clue that he was not alone came when he heard loud bangs, and the Spitfire was jolted by the impact of 30mm cannon shells. The engine seized, and an instant later an enemy aircraft flashed over him from behind.

Hillborn was astonished by how quickly it had happened, but he knew he had to get out of his fighter. He yanked his ejection lever and was catapulted from the cockpit. He was severely jolted when he hit the air, and again when his parachute opened.

As he floated downward, he glimpsed a twin-engine airplane rapidly disappearing in the distance. Only then did he realize that he'd been attacked by a jet.

The pilot who shot Hillborn down was Lt. Schreiber of Ekdo 262. When Schreiber returned to Lechfeld, his combat film showed tracers from his cannons ripping into the Spitfire. It was Schreiber's third victory in an Me-262.

The following day Squadron Leader Fleming of 540 Recon Squadron also fell victim to a jet. Fleming was flying a Mosquito and, like Hillborn, was oblivious to the danger, when cannon fire suddenly destroyed his airplane. The victorious Me-262 was flown by Oberfeldwebel Gobel, another Ekdo 262 pilot.

Two jets were lost, however, when RAF pilots flying Tempests spotted the Me-262s as they were taking off from Rheine. The action confirmed that the jets' greatest weakness was their vulnerability during takeoffs and landings. From then on, Allied fighter pilots looked for Me-262s that were just lifting off from the runway or going in to touch down. When the jets were low and slow, they were virtually defenseless.

Willy Messerschmitt was heartened by the reports of Me-262 victories, but there were also other battles he was hoping to hear about. When would the jets engage more enemy bombers? That would be the most important test of all.

The pilots knew that as well, and were eager to engage the huge fleets that were devastating Germany.

66.

Oberfeldwebel Helmut Baudach was a typical member of the original Ekdo 262. When the unit was moved from the Netherlands to Lager Lechfeld in Germany, he was happy to be back in home territory. Even with all the travails of wartime, there was an air of *gemütlichkeit* in Bavaria. Baudach was proud to be flying a jet fighter—a brand new Me-262 had been assigned to him directly after it had been tested on the same field. Like his fellow pilots, he was anxious to fly the fighter in combat, especially against British and American bombers.

Before joining Ekdo 262, Baudach had already been a successful jagdflieger. He'd achieved 20 victories, most of them while flying an Fw-190, and that made him an *experte* twice over. He'd also logged time in a Bf-110, and the multi-engine experience, plus his record, had helped get him assigned to jets.

On a pleasantly warm autumn day, Baudach enjoyed a leisurely lunch with the other pilots in his unit. One of the many advantages of life in the Luftwaffe was that there was usually plenty of good food. Today the fare at mittagessen was schweinbraten mit knödel, and steins of excellent Bavarian beer.

Although not a commissioned officer, Baudach wasn't treated much differently from those who were. Among combat pilots there was an easygoing camaraderie that was unlike the rigid hierarchy of the Wehrmacht. That was another advantage of serving in the Luftwaffe, particularly in a fighter staffel.

Over coffee and cigarettes after lunch, Baudach and the others carried on the usual banter. Many of the jokes centered on Reichsmarschal Göring, for whom the pilots openly expressed contempt. Der Dicke, they agreed, should have been put out to pasture long ago.

Their talk was interrupted by an insistent buzzing from the loudspeakers, followed by orders to scramble. Instantly the mood changed to one of charged excitement. The pilots raced out to the aircraft lined up on the camouflaged tarmac, and Baudach climbed into the cockpit of his Me-262. A buxom blond member of the Women's Auxiliary stood on the wing root and helped him strap in, which was another thing he liked about this branch of service. He made a bawdy remark to her, and she laughed and wished him luck before stepping down.

Me-262s were now equipped with a self-starter system. A two-cycle Riedel engine was mounted in the intake section of each turbine and connected to the turbine shaft by a claw clutch. Baudach started the Riedels, and when they reached 1,000 rpm he turned on the aircraft's fuel pump and ignition, which in turn started the turbojets.

Warmup took only a few minutes. With the engines running at 8,000 rpm, the internal gas temperature quickly reached 700 degrees Centigrade. He ran down the checklist from memory, noting intake pressure vis-a-vis exhaust, the fuel injection pressure, oil pressure, electrical systems, and hydraulics. Next he switched on the radio and closed the canopy. Slowly advancing the throttles, he taxied to the end of the runway. Two other aircraft were ahead of him.

The gauges now showed rpms at 8800, temperature 800 degrees Celsius. Pressures okay. Flaps at 20 degrees down. The jets ahead of him took off, and then it was his turn.

As always, he was amazed by how quiet the airplane was. Even as he turned into the wind and accelerated along the runway, the sound was mostly rushing air and the hiss of the turbines. What a difference between this and a fighter with a 2,000 hp engine thrashing a prop.

After liftoff he retracted gear and flaps, taking care not to hurry. That was the trick to flying an Me-262; every move had to be made gently. Once you got the hang of it, handling one was a simple matter.

Climb-out was another exhilarating experience. While the jet moved slowly at first, it soon picked up speed and began streaking upward. At seven thousand meters he leveled off and moved into position behind and to the right of the leader. Another jet was on the leader's left.

The pilots had found that rather than flying in the four-aircraft schwarm of piston fighters, the jets were better suited to formations of three. The unit was putting up six aircraft, so there would be three more Me-262s behind Baudach. The metallic voice in Baudach's headphones gave him a course of 003 degrees. The controller then said a large flight of enemy bombers escorted by fighters was flying on a straight line into East-central Germany. That meant they were Americans; the RAF attacked only at night.

It was easy to guess the bombers' target. These days the Amis rarely bothered changing course in a series of feints as they had at one time. Now they flew directly to their objective, which most likely was Leipzig. The city was an important center for the manufacture of precision instruments.

From the radio chatter, Baudach learned the enemy had already been intercepted by fighters, and a running battle was taking place. He was sure the Luftwaffe pilots were making the raiders pay dearly. With the strengthening of the homeland defenses, there were now more fighters ready to give the Americans bloody noses. He felt tension mount as he pictured the clash up ahead.

The airspeed indicator read 885 kph. Even at this speed it seemed to be taking too long to get to the action. As he impatiently scanned the sky, all he saw were wisps of cirrus.

And suddenly, there they were. Over Bad Dürrenberg, the air was filled with whirling aircraft. He could see flashes in the wings as they fired their guns.

Those were fighters. Germans and Americans were mixing it up above a great fleet of heavies flying due east, so many that the bombers' rear-most combat boxes were not visible. The stream of enemy aircraft seemed to stretch to infinity.

Keeping pace with the leader, Baudach climbed another thousand meters. Then all three jets dove into the melee and each pilot tried to zero in on one of the enemy. Baudach flipped up the safety on his stick as he picked out a Mustang and closed on it. The enemy fighter was banking left, and Baudach adjusted his turn to line up for a shot. Too late! The Mustang dove, and the jet whipped past.

Pulling up, Baudach looked for another opportunity. As he did, he was startled to see two airplanes collide in a fiery crash only a few meters ahead of him. He couldn't tell whether they were American or

German; there was only a ball of fire and then oily smoke and an instant later he was past that as well.

Again he climbed, and turned to fly over the oncoming formation of bombers. They were B-17s, and they were being harassed by Fw-190s. The bombers were sending streams of machine-gun fire at their attackers, but some of the Focke-Wulfs were getting strikes. As he watched, a B-17 fell out of its combat box and spun downward.

Baudach dove on another of the bombers, firing as he went. The viermot seemed to stagger as his shells punched into it, but whether it was fatally damaged he couldn't tell. He continued his dive, and leveled off beneath the formation. As he did, a Mustang crossed in front of him at a slight angle.

This time he'd make sure. He pulled into position behind the enemy aircraft, not wanting to risk a deflection shot. Considering the jet's speed, it was better to line up astern before firing. He pressed the trigger and his tracers were a cluster of yellow balls that burst from the Me-262's cannons and raced toward the Mustang. He was getting hits! He could see strikes on its tail and fuselage.

Abruptly the American fighter blew up. Baudach flew through a cloud of debris and just as suddenly he was again in clear air. He banked gently and looked for another target.

Two more Mustangs were attacking a Focke-Wulf some distance below him, and smoke was trailing from the German aircraft. He closed on one of the enemy fighters, and in his excitement made the mistake of firing too soon. The Mustang broke left and Baudach's shells missed altogether.

He was about to come for another try when a glance at the fuel gauges told him to forget it. To his disgust, it was time to go home. That was the trouble with the turbos. They gulped fuel with an insatiable thirst, and it seemed that no sooner were you in action than you had to leave. Reluctantly he turned south and throttled back, setting the RPMs for slow cruise. When he landed at Lechfeld the gauges were showing empty.

Baudach's films confirmed the hits on the B-17, and the victory over the Mustang. That kill was his first in a jet, and his 21st over all. He didn't know it, but the Mustang was from the 364th Fighter Group of the 8th Air Force, and the bombers he and his comrades had attacked were B-17s of the 100th Bomb Group, known as the Bloody

Hundredth because of its many losses.

The Americans claimed 15 German fighters shot down that day, and the Luftwaffe also claimed 15 enemy fighters destroyed. Eleven bombers had been downed. None of the turbos were lost.

For the Me-262 pilots, there was much to celebrate. Baudach drank shots of schnapps and joined in singing "Deutsche Piloten" and "Flieger und Sieger," and other Luftwaffe songs. He'd have a headache in the morning, but he didn't care.

67.

As Me-262 pilots gained more experience in flying the Me-262 in combat, all were in agreement that special measures should be taken to protect them at the beginning and end of their flights. For one thing, there was a need for the airfields to be more effectively disguised. The pilots concurred that the huge nets over the hangars and other installations were fairly effective, but they felt that overall, the camouflage could be improved.

The runways were the worst problem. They were easy to spot from the air, and scorch marks left on the pavement by jet engine exhausts were a sure tipoff to enemy airmen flying reconnaissance. As much as possible, the pilots said, runways should be hidden when not in use.

For another thing, it would help to have piston fighters fly top cover when Me-262s were taking off and landing. It was obvious that the enemy had quickly become aware of the jets' vulnerability at those critical times, and that was when they did their hunting. More 88mm flak batteries would be a good idea as well.

Admittedly, only a handful of Me-262s had been lost in combat so far, and some of those were destroyed by AA fire. One such incident had occurred when Lt. Rolf Weidemann was hit over Diest while on a bombing mission. Another was when German flak gunners in Holland mistook Unteroffizier Herbert Schauder's aircraft for an Allied bomber and shot it down. But the others had been lost while the jets were just getting off the ground, or when they were on final approach.

The talk then turned to tactics. Once aloft, speed was a boon, of course—but it could also be a hindrance, especially if the pilot didn't know the best way to use it. In a dogfight, the standard practice of scissoring was fine for a Bf-109 or an Fw-190, but not for an Me-262. An astute enemy flier would realize he could outmaneuver an attacking jet by turning inside it, which had been done a number of times. The pilots were aware that making abrupt turns was to be avoided. Bank too sharply in an Me-262 and you ran the risk of engine flameout. It had led to fatal accidents even in practice flights, and if you lost power in combat the game was up.

Therefore, whenever possible, an Me-262 should rely on a fast-closing attack from astern—that was when the jet was at its best. Baudach could attest to that, and so could many of the others. You wanted to line up on the enemy and give him a good squirt with the cannons before he knew you were there. Deflection shots were far more difficult, again because of the jet's speed. And the Revi gunsight wasn't much help, either. Any angle greater than 30 degrees usually insured a miss, thanks to the enemy's ability to break quickly.

Attacks on bombers presented special problems, which were different from engaging a fighter. It was true that Feldwebel Lennartz had easily shot down a B-17 over Stuttgart back in August, but that was because the Fortress had been alone. That in itself was unusual, inasmuch as the bombers almost always flew in large fleets. Their standard battle formations comprised tight combat boxes, which enabled them to protect one another with massed machine-gun fire. An enemy squadron of twelve aircraft formed such a box, with four elements of three aircraft each. A group would have three squadrons, or 36 planes. A wing consisted of three groups, for a total of 108 bombers. On some raids the Allies would fly five or six wings, or even more. And now with hundreds of Mustangs escorting the bombers, the Me-262 pilots were heavily outnumbered.

Although they'd encountered heavies several times since Lennartz's victory, the jets had claimed only a few kills. The pilots agreed that having to deal with large numbers of fighter escorts was the main obstacle, especially now that the Mustangs were ranging freely out in front of the enemy formations. And even when an Me-262 penetrated the fighter screen and reached the bombers, the jets' speed was again a factor. Typically the bombers would be flying at about 350 kph, and an Me-262 attacking at more than twice that rate would have little time for a firing pass. If you weren't a good shot, you had almost no chance to make a hit.

Some pilots felt it would be best to use the boom-and-zoom type of attack, diving on the enemy from above and firing, then pulling up and away. The angle of the dive would present the largest silhouette of the bomber, resulting in more of a target to shoot at. Others said it would be better to continue the dive after firing rather than risk a rapid pull-up. Or maybe boom-and-zoom would be all right if the dive were kept very shallow. The so-called roller coaster attack might also work, though it wouldn't allow the pilot much time to fire with accuracy.

But what the pilots couldn't dispute was that no matter how they did it, attacking a Fortress in an Me-262 was a lot better than in an Fw-190 or a Bf-109. Many of the pilots were veterans of such battles, and closing on the tail of an enemy bomber through a hail of .50-caliber bullets was not a pleasant task.

Most of all, the pilots wanted more aircraft. They realized the Messerschmitt plants were doing their best to produce them, but the supply was a trickle. With more Me-262s, they were sure they could blow enough of the Allies out of the sky to make a real difference.

And one other point. Supposedly they were at Lechfeld to form a special jet squadron, which was to be fully staffed with qualified pilots. Ideally, it would be led by a commander who knew his business, yet so far that person hadn't appeared. When would he?

General Galland answered that question on 26 September, when he ordered Major Walter Nowotny to take charge of the unit. Nowotny had all the ability the Me-262 pilots could hope for, and all the credentials to prove it. Fine-featured and slim, with black hair and a cocky attitude, Nowotny was one of the Luftwaffe's top aces. Only 23, he'd already posted 255 victories.

Most of the major's record had been achieved on the eastern front, where his exploits were legendary. On several occasions he'd made multiple kills, knocking down five or six of the enemy in a single battle. And on one memorable day over Leningrad, he shot down ten Soviet aircraft.

He'd also displayed great personal courage. In a dogfight with Soviet I-53s off Riga Bay, his Bf-109 was riddled with machine-gun bullets. The battered fighter crashed into the frigid waters, and Nowotny climbed out just as it sank. Cold and wet and bleeding from wounds, he spent three days and nights in a rubber dinghy before reaching shore.

On another sortie, near Novgorod, he destroyed four Ratas while refusing to bail out of his smoking Bf-109. Afterward he crash-landed, and leaped from the flaming wreck as it skidded along the ground. When he recovered from his wounds, he flew an Fw-190 and continued to run up his score.

In recognition of his heroism, Nowotny was awarded Germany's highest decoration, the Knight's Cross with Oak Leaves, Swords and Diamonds. The Luftwaffe then assigned him to administrative duties, rather than risk losing him, but he hated being grounded and agitated constantly to get back into the air. He got his wish when he was sent to Pau for training in an Me-262. The aircraft was made for him. He loved the speed, and the sense that only the best of the best could fly this entirely new and superior type of fighter.

After he took command, the unit was officially dubbed Kommando Nowotny and moved to two airfields in northern Germany. One was at Achmer, the other at nearby Hesepe. Nowotny immediately set about expanding his outfit into a complete fighter gruppe. When at full strength, the gruppe would have three staffeln of 16 aircraft each. There would also be a Stabschwarm, or headquarters flight, consisting of four more. Thus Kommando Nowotny would eventually comprise 52 jet fighters.

Like a good commander, the major listened carefully as his pilots expressed their views. They said that because Me-262s needed a long takeoff run, the runways at Achmer and Hesepe were barely acceptable. Nowotny had them lengthened. Next, the pilots complained about inadequate camouflage. The major saw to it that new, better designed nets holding clumps of brush were made up. He had the nets arranged so that they could be positioned quickly over the airfields, including the runways when they were not in use. Then there was the problem of vulnerability when taking off and landing. Nowotny petitioned General Galland to send piston fighters, so there would be top cover for the jets over both fields. Galland transferred a gruppe of Fw-190s to Achmer. This was III/JG54, commanded by Hauptmann Robert Weiss.

There were four staffeln under Weiss. They were led by Hauptmann Karl Bottlander and Oberleutnants Willy Heilmann, Peter Crump, and Hans Dortenmann. All had extensive combat experience.

Their Focke-Wulf fighter was the D model. Pilots called it the Longnose Dora because it mounted a liquid-cooled 2100 hp Jumo 213A V-12 engine, rather than the air-cooled radial BMW. Armament was two 13mm MG131 machine guns and two 20mm MG151/20E cannons.

Finally, there was the need for more flak batteries. Nowotny applied pressure, and they were installed. The batteries were the latest type, which had been expanded from four 88mm cannons to eight. Each gun would fire 120 rounds per minute, lofting 10 kg shells as high as 10,600 meters, where they would explode in a burst of steel splinters.

The major drilled his pilots hard. He had them fly several times a day, practicing combat maneuvers. The sessions were not without misfortune, however. On 4 October, the Kapitan of 2 Staffel, Hauptmann Alfred Teumer, was on final approach when both his engines failed. The Me-262 slammed to earth, killing him. Nowotny replaced him with Oberleutnant Franz Schall, who had scored 117 kills while serving with I/JG52 in Russia.

The Kommando was still nowhere near full strength, when on 7 October, Nowotny led 11 of his charges to intercept American bombers attacking Magdeburg. The target was an aircraft production plant. When the Me-262s arrived, Nowotny saw that the oncoming bombers were B-24 Liberators. He estimated there were 300 of them, and probably more. They were flying at 6,500 meters, and escorted by P-47s that were apparently equipped with extra fuel tanks to increase their range.

The jets were the first on the scene, though the major knew from radio transmissions that controllers were sending squadrons of piston fighters as well. He could hear the excitement in the pilots' voices. As he gained altitude in readiness to lead an attack, his flight was seen by the Thunderbolts. The American fighters came up to do battle, but were unable to climb as fast as the jets. Nowotny picked out a P-47, rolled over and dove on it.

The enemy pilot's wingman must have warned him, because the P-47 broke left in a tight turn and Nowotny was unable to line up for a shot. As he flashed through the swirl of enemy aircraft, he was careful not to handle his Me-262 as roughly as he would an Fw-190, instead recovering gracefully and climbing once more. At that point, a flight of Bf-109s showed up, and the fighting immediately became a series of dogfights. Nowotny and the others in his Kommando tried to break through the P-47s, so as to get at the bombers.

Oberleutnant Franz Schall succeeded. He attacked a Liberator, making the type of shallow dive his fellow airmen felt would be most effective. When he fired his cannons he was only about two hundred meters above the B-24, and the shells hit the cockpit. Apparently the strikes killed the pilot and copilot, because the bomber flipped over and went into an inverted spin, out of control. Schall knew better than to watch it go down. Instead, he pursued another B-24, but had to break off because of machine-gun fire from the bomber and from others in the box.

As the enemy began their bomb runs, Oberfähnrich Heinz Russel ignored warnings about attacking too closely from the rear. He slipped in behind a B-24 and concentrated his fire on the tail. Because of his speed there was time to fire only a few shells, but they silenced the tail gunner and did enough damage to the aircraft to send that one down as well. Unfortunately for Russel, a P-47 caught him just as he was pulling up after firing at the bomber. Pieces of the jet were torn off by the Thunderbolt's machine guns, and both its engines quit. Russel jettisoned his canopy and bailed out. The crippled 262 had slowed down, but it was still moving so fast that when Russel jumped, it was as if he'd run into a brick wall. Nearly senseless, he opened his parachute by instinct alone. When he landed he was bruised, but thankful to be alive.

Before fuel shortages forced the jets to withdraw, Feldwebel Lennartz again scored. The bomber he attacked had still not dropped its bombs, and when his cannon shells struck the B-24, it exploded.

Oberleutnant Paul Bley also lost his aircraft that day, but not to enemy gunfire. Instead he made too hasty a turn, which caused his engines to fail, and he was unable to restart them. He too bailed out, and like Russel, lived to rejoin the unit and fight again another day.

The P-47 that shot down Russel was flown by Col. Hubert Zemke, commander of the 56th Fighter Group known as Zemke's Wolf Pack. In the confusion typical of those huge air battles, Zemke thought he had destroyed a Bf-109. It was only when his combat film was viewed that he learned that he'd scored one of the first aerial victories over an Me-262.

As for Nowotny, the major was more than satisfied by the way his pilots had acquitted themselves. They'd made a few mistakes, but by and large they were operating just as he'd hoped. And he was sure the best was yet to come.

68.

On the same day as the Magdeburg raid, another battle took place near

Achmer. It began when 8th Air Force Lieutenant Urban Drew of the 362st Fighter Group approached the area in his Mustang. Drew was the leader of the 375th Fighter Squadron, and he and his pilots were returning to base after escorting B-17s in attacks on targets in Czechoslovakia.

There had been reports of Me-262s operating in the vicinity, and Drew was keeping a sharp eye out for them. As he looked down, he was startled to see two twin-engine aircraft taxi onto a runway and take off. Drew realized at once what they were. He ordered his Deputy Squadron Leader, Captain Bruce Rowlett, to cover him.

Drew's combat report described what happened next:

"Waited until both jets were airborne, then rolled over from 15,000 feet and caught up with one Me-262 when he was 1,000 feet off ground. I was indicating 450 mph. Me-262 couldn't have been going more than 200 mph. I started firing from approximately 400 yards, 30 degrees deflection, and as I closed, I saw hits all over the wings and fuselage. Just as I passed him I saw a sheet of flame come out from near the right wing root, and as I glanced back I saw gigantic explosions and a sheet of red flame over an area of 1,000 feet. The other Me-262 was 500 yards ahead, and had started a fast climbing turn to the left. I was still indicating 440 mph, and had to haul back to stay with him. I started shooting from about 40 degrees deflection, and hit his tail section. I kept horsing back, and hits crept up his fuselage to his cockpit. Just after that I saw his canopy fly off in two sections, his plane roll over and go into a flat spin. He hit the ground on his back at 60 degrees angle and exploded violently. I did not see the pilot bail out. Two huge columns of smoke came up from the Me-262s burning on the ground."

The first aircraft Drew destroyed had been flown by Leutnant Gerhard Kobert. The pilot of the second was Oberfeldwebel Heinz Arnold. The action was witnessed from the ground by Hauptmann Georg-Peter Eder, who had intended to lead the flight but was prevented from taking off because of an engine flameout.

For unexplained reasons, Hauptmann Robert Weiss's Fw-190s were not in the air providing cover when Drew attacked. Also, the crews of the flak batteries were slow in reacting; it wasn't until the two jets were piles of blazing wreckage that the gunners opened up.

When the 88mm shells began bursting, Drew ordered his wingman, Lieutenant Robert McCandliss, to join him in making evasive maneuvers at treetop level. Instead, McCandliss, who was on his sixteenth mission and had not yet achieved a victory, disobeyed and attacked the flak batteries. That proved to be a mistake. The gunners were only too happy to have a shot at the American pilot who dared strafe them. There were so many batteries in the area that all the crews had to do, was put up a barrage, and the Mustang flew straight into it. The last Urban Drew saw of McCandliss's Mustang, it was afire from nose to tail and going down. There was nothing to be done for him; the squadron leader flew on.

Drew was not aware of it, but McCandliss had just enough altitude to bail out. He jumped clear, pulled his ripcord, and the chute blossomed. The hard landing sprained his ankles, but otherwise he was not seriously hurt. German troops quickly surrounded him and took him prisoner, and he spent the rest of the war in a Stalag Luft in eastern Germany.

When Drew returned to base, he was anxious to see his combat films, but to his irritation, the gun camera had malfunctioned and he could not verify his claims. The others in his flight had not seen the Me-262s destroyed, so they couldn't back him up.

In the weeks following the attack at Achmer, the many small plants that were constructing components of the Me-262 increased their efficiency. As a result, the pace of assembly also improved, and the aircraft were turned out in greater numbers. Though most of these were the pure fighter, a few of the fighter-bombers were still being built, even though their performance in combat continued to be less than satisfactory. Not only were they unable to bomb with accuracy, they were also 100 kph slower than the fighters, which made it easier for enemy pilots to shoot them down.

Nevertheless, the Air Ministry was not willing to give up on the idea of the Sturmvogel as Hitler's high-speed bomber. When Messerschmitt was ordered to come up with a new version, his team designed the Me-262 A/2a/U2. In this aircraft the entire forward section was removed, including the cannons, and a new nose made of glazed wood was fitted in its place. A bombardier lay inside the nose and focused on the target with a Lotfe 7H bombsight. Examples of the jet were sent to Lager Lechfeld for testing.

Flown by Gerd Lindner and Karl Baur, the Me-262 A/2a/U2 achieved good results. According to the test pilots' reports, bombs dropped from altitudes as high as 5,000 meters landed with acceptable accuracy. But there were problems with the aircrafts' aerodynamics, and the project stalled. Another version of the Me-262 the team designed was a trainer with two seats in tandem. This would enable instructors to fly with pilots being introduced to the aircraft. Not many of the two-seaters were built; most pilots new to the jet received only ground instruction, and learned by flying it.

As more Me-262s went into service, American fighter pilots kept them busy in dogfights, which prevented many of the jets from attacking the bombers. As a result, most of their victories, as well as their losses, occurred in combat with Mustangs and Thunderbolts. Leutnant Schreiber also had success in engagements with Lightning F-5s, shooting down two of them in one battle on 29 October.

For Schreiber, the day was memorable for another reason as well. The Lightnings belonged to the RAF 7th Photo Recon Group, and were accompanied by Spitfires. After Schreiber got his second kill he pulled up in a climbing right turn, and his Me-262e collided with a Spitfire. Both aircraft burst into flames. The British pilot, Flight Lieutenant Wilkins of RAF 4 Squadron, was killed. Although singed and only half-conscious, Schreiber jumped from the burning wreckage and popped his chute. He landed intact, and a day later was back in the air.

Also on 29 October, Feldwebel Büttner and Oberfeldwebel Göbel of Kommando Nowotny ran across a flight of P-47s that were shooting up a train. The low-flying Thunderbolts made perfect targets. Each pilot chose one and dove on it, taking care not to pick up too much speed. One quick burst of cannon fire from the cannons was all that was needed. As the two P-47s spun in, the others quickly rose to give chase, but all they saw were wisps of exhaust smoke as the jets pulled away and disappeared.

With additional Me-262s becoming available, General Galland was eager to establish more units with them. In the first of these, KG54 was given the new designation KG(J)54, and received its jets at the beginning of November. I Group of this unit was established at Giebelstadt, and a second part of it, designated IIKG(J)54, was sent to Neuburg. A training unit was also formed, and stationed at Lechfeld, with Hauptmann Eder appointed commander. The pilots assigned to the unit were all veterans, so instruction simply covered the characteristics of the aircraft. Eder would lead them in combat when he thought they were ready.

A major problem was the growing shortage of J2 jet fuel. Pilots were limited to one hour of flying circuits of the field, two hours of aerobatics, one hour of cross-country, one hour of flying at high altitude, and two hours of practicing formation flight. Many accidents occurred, most of them fatal.

By then American pilots were encountering Me-262s with increasing frequency. On 1 November, three wings of 8th Air Force bombers were en route to bomb Gelsenkirchen, a city on the Rhine, when they were attacked by four jets of Kommando Nowotny. The B-17s and B-24s were escorted by Mustangs of the 20th and 352nd Fighter Groups, as well as Thunderbolts of the 56th Group.

The bombers were flying at 8,500 meters, a higher altitude than usual. But the Me-262s were still higher, and despite the enormous disparity in numbers, the jets dove in with cannons blazing. Oberfeldwebel Willy Banzhaff sent his shells into a Mustang of the 77th Fighter Squadron, killing the pilot, Lt. Dennis Allison. Other Mustangs gave chase, but they had no hope of catching the Me-262. Banzhaff could have escaped altogether, but he committed a tactical error. Instead of continuing his dive, he pulled up. A P-47 pilot, W.L. Groce, shouted into his mike: "Spread out, and we'll get him if he turns!"

Banzhaff did, climbing and swinging left. Groce and Lieutenant W.T. Gerb of the 352nd poured machine gun and cannon fire into the jet, and its port engine became wreathed in flames. The aircraft went into a spin, and Banzhaff bailed out.

Groce then followed an order that had recently been issued by the USAAF High Command. He came about and fired at the German who was hanging defenseless in his parachute harness. This was a practice Luftwaffe pilots could not believe was happening, but it was. Many Americans as well could hardly believe the order, and refused to carry it out. Fortunately for Banzhaff, Groce missed.

But Banzhaff's good luck was not to last much longer. On 3 November, he and another member of Kommando Nowotny were flying near Hesepe when they were spotted by the pilot of a Hawker Tempest Mk. V. One of the most powerful piston-engine fighters of the war, the Tempest mounted a 2,400 hp Napier Sabre engine and was armed with four 20mm Hispano cannons. RAF Wing Commander J.B. Wray was at the controls, and reported:

"I was flying at about 18,000 feet when I sighted two Me-262s. They were camouflaged blue-grey and were flying in a southwesterly direction. They saw me and turned in a wide arc to port. I had already launched an attack, opening to full throttle and diving. My speed was in the region of 500 mph. I closed to about three hundred yards on the starboard aircraft and opened fire with a four-second burst, hitting the tailplane. The Me-262 continued on course and started to pull away, but before he got out of range I fired again. Suddenly a large piece flew off the aircraft and he flicked over onto his back and disappeared downwards into cloud in an inverted position. I followed, but the thickness of the cloud made it impossible for me to maintain contact."

Wing Commander Wray did not learn until after the war that the jet had sustained fatal damage. It crashed at Hitfeld, and its pilot, Willy Banzhaff, was killed.

On 5 November, Me-262s of Kommando Nowotny attacked another fleet of 8th Air Force bombers. Feldwebel Büttner shot down a Mustang and a Thunderbolt, and Oberfeldwebel Baudach also destroyed a Thunderbolt. Nevertheless, they were unable to penetrate the fighter screen and get at the heavies.

By then a few more American fliers were learning the best way to engage the jets. Among them was a pilot who in later years would become one of the world's most famous airmen. He was Charles E. Yeager.

69.

Chuck Yeager had grown up poor on a hardscrabble farm alongside the Mud River in Myra, West Virginia. As a kid he butchered hogs, picked beans, and shot squirrels to help put food on the family table. In high school he was a fine athlete, playing on both the football and baseball teams. He was also a good student, particularly in mathematics. His hobby was tinkering with old cars.

In 1941, Yeager joined the US Army Air Corps as a private, serving at the Victorville, California airfield where he showed special aptitude as a mechanic. After two years he was promoted to sergeant and chosen for pilot training at Luke Field, Arizona, where Yeager's instructors said he was a natural. They taught him to fly in a Stearman biplane, and soon he was wringing it out in aerobatics. He won his wings and a promotion to Flight Officer on 10 March 1943.

Assigned to the 363rd Squadron of the 357th Fighter Group, Yeager moved up to flying P-39s at the Air Corps base at Tonopah, Nevada. Training there was rigorous. Some of his squadron mates washed out, and others were killed in accidents. Yeager's reactions to these misfortunes was a shrug. Anybody who bought the farm was "a dumb bastard," which was a fighter pilot's way of handling the possibility of his own death. One of Yeager's fellow pilots was Bud Anderson, who flew with him throughout the war and became a life-long friend. Together they and the other young studs often visited the bars and whorehouses in Tonopah, and sometimes raised enough hell to be chased by the sheriff.

The group was then sent to California for training to fly as escorts for bombers. While there Yeager met his future wife, Glennis Faye Dickhouse. "She was pretty as a movie star," he said, "and making more money than I was."

Next, the group moved to Casper, Wyoming for still more training. On 23 October 1943, Yeager very nearly lost his life when his P-39's engine caught fire and he had to bail out. He made a rough landing, fracturing several vertebrae. For a while it was questionable whether he would ever fly again, but he refused to give up, and after a long hospital stay convinced doctors that he'd fully recuperated. He rejoined his squadron just in time, for at the end of December, the 357th Fighter Group was shipped overseas to England.

Early in 1944 the unit became the first in the 8th Air Force to be equipped with Mustangs. The pilots received the rugged new fighters with great enthusiasm. Yeager thought the P-51 was the best aircraft he'd ever flown, and named his "Glamorous Glennis," after his girlfriend.

On his seventh mission, escorting bombers to Berlin on 4 March, he posted his first victory, shooting down a Bf-109. The following day he flew escort duty again, and over France he was bounced by three Fw-190s. The German pilots were old hands; while two of them attacked him from behind, the third dove on him and shot up his Mustang. The engine seized, and he bailed out. He landed in a forest, bleeding from numerous injuries, and hid there for two days.

During that time he had nothing to eat but a chocolate bar, and at night would sleep huddled under his parachute. On the third day he was discovered by a farmer, who put him in touch with members of the French Resistance.

On 30 March, with the help of the Maquis, Yeager escaped to Spain. It was a miserable trip, climbing over the Pyrenees in the freezing cold and sleeping in caves, while the Germans searched the mountains from the air in a Fieseler Storch. But he eventually made it to Madrid, where he stayed until the U.S. consulate arranged for his return to England on 15 May.

His troubles were not over, however. He was told a regulation prevented anyone who had evaded capture from going back into combat. The theory was that if he were shot down again he might reveal information concerning the Resistance to the Germans. Yeager appealed directly to General Eisenhower, who cleared him to rejoin his group.

With his extraordinary flying skills, his 20/10 eyesight and his aggressiveness, Yeager established an excellent record. He once downed five German fighters in a single battle. And on 6 November 1944, he saw an Me-262 for the first time.

That day Yeager's group, led by Major Robert Foy, was returning from a mission to Germany. The fighters were escorting B-24s that had bombed factories near Minden, 70 kilometers east of Osnabrük. With the 357th was another fighter group, the 361st, also flying Mustangs.

Once the bombers reached a safe area, the two fighter groups left them and split up. The pilots of the 357th swung west, heading back to base, and a few minutes later were attacked by five Me-262s of Kommando Nowotny. Yeager turned to meet them. He'd heard about the new type of aircraft, but actually witnessing their speed was a surprise. One of them fired at him and missed, and as it hurtled by, he opened his throttle and put his Mustang into a vertical bank. When he came about he fired his .50-caliber machine guns and got a few strikes on the jet. Moments later the enemy aircraft vanished into cloud.

In chasing the Me-262, Yeager had become separated from his wingman and the other Mustangs in his group. Now he was alone. He eased back on his power settings, and again turned for home.

As he flew over Achmer, he noticed what he thought was a well-disguised airfield with an extremely long runway. He decided to have a closer look, and descended toward it. His combat report described what happened next.

"I spotted a lone 262 approaching the field from the south at 500 feet. He was going very slow, about 200 mph. I split-essed on him, and was going around 500 mph. Flak started coming up very thick and accurate. I fired a single short burst from around 400 yards, and got hits on his wings. I had to break straight up, and looking back saw the enemy aircraft crash-land about 400 yards short of the field. A wing flew off outside the right jet unit. The plane did not burn."

This was Yeager's only encounter with an Me-262. By war's end he'd posted eleven and one-half victories, most of them over Bf-109s.

70.

The day after Yeager destroyed the Me-262 at Achmer, General Adolf Galland arrived at the base to make an inspection. He was greeted warmly by Major Nowotny and the other pilots, many of whom he knew personally. Galland asked about recent action, and was informed of the previous day's loss. It was another instance, Nowotny said, when an Me-262 had been shot down while landing. There had been no top cover because the Fw-190s were engaged elsewhere, and the jet had made a prime target for the attacking Mustang. Although flak was heavy, the enemy fighter was not hit.

As a veteran fighter pilot himself, Galland had much respect for Nowotny. The major not only had an outstanding combat record, but was also a natural leader and an inspiration to his men. Those were the main reasons Galland had chosen him to command the unit. Galland was also a great believer in the jets, despite their vulnerability at the beginning and end of a flight. From the first time he'd flown one, he was convinced they could make a decisive difference in the war. Given enough of them, he believed Germany could dominate the enemy's air forces.

Over mugs of ersatz coffee in Nowotny's office, the two men continued their discussion. One of the general's concerns was that the Allies seemed to be making a special effort to wipe out the Me-262s, especially now that they'd located their bases. Nowotny said he wasn't worried— the turbos could more than hold their own. And the previous day's loss had probably been due to a random encounter; otherwise more than one Mustang would have been involved.

The major then asked about the shortage of jet fuel, which was growing worse by the day. Could anything be done about it? Galland replied it was unlikely. Although J2 was less complicated to manufacture than synthetic benzine, the attacks on plants in the Ruhr had made a serious dent in Germany's ability to produce it. And Arms Minister Speer was warning that soon, even less might be available.

On a more optimistic note, the general spoke of Fighter Command's renewed strength. In spite of the relentless bombing, there was a marked upswing in aircraft production, thanks to the RLM's dispersal of the manufacturing facilities. This had made it possible to develop a new plan for mounting the largest attack on Allied bombers since the beginning of the war.

The plan had been designated by the Luftwaffe as the "Great Blow." It called for a concentrated assault on a bomber fleet as it flew toward a target in Germany. A total of eighteen Jagdgeschwaders with 3,700 aircraft and pilots would take part.

First, 2,000 fighters of the 1st Fighter Corps would attack the bombers. Next, 150 fighters of Luftwaffe Command West would hit the surviving enemy aircraft as they attempted to return home, then another 500 fighters of 1st Corps would hit them again. At the same time, 100 night fighters would screen the borders of Sweden and Switzerland and shoot down any stragglers or damaged bombers that tried to land in those places.

Luftwaffe planners were confident that the entire enemy fleet would be destroyed. The cost to Germany was estimated to be about 400 fighters and up to 150 pilots. Galland believed the Great Blow would be so effective that the enemy air forces would cancel their bombing program.

Nowotny agreed that the Allies would never accept such losses. And the prospect of making so devastating an assault was exciting to contemplate. He looked forward to taking part with his unit—the Me-262s would have a field day.

The major was worried, however, about the unreliability of the turbojet engines. When they were running properly, the speed of the Me-262s gave the aircraft a great advantage over enemy fighters. But too often the engines failed, and at the worst possible times. Galland replied that Professor Messerschmitt had made the same complaints, and was constantly urging the engine manufacturers to come up with more reliable power plants. Supposedly BMW had such an engine in the works, but there was no word on when it might become available.

Later, Galland and Nowotny joined the unit's pilots for a dinner of rindfleisch, kartoffeln and bottles of good French Burgundy. As usual, the mood in the mess was jovial and upbeat. Afterward, the general and the gruppe leader went on talking for hours, drinking Cognac and smoking cigars.

In the morning the sky was overcast, but by mid-afternoon it had mostly cleared. Galland and Nowotny were watching ground crews service the Me-262s when suddenly the work was interrupted by the howl of air raid sirens. Looking toward the north, they saw a formation of B-17s appear in the distance. The bombers were escorted by Mustangs and Thunderbolts, and apparently were attacking the nearby town of Rheine.

The long-nose Fw-190Ds of 3/JG54 were quickly scrambled. Some of them stayed over the field to provide top cover for the jets, while others flew toward the enemy force. The American fighters turned to meet them, and soon a number of fierce dogfights were underway.

The Kommando's pilots ran to their Me-262s, eager to join the battle. Galland went into the operations shack, where he could follow the action by monitoring radio transmissions.

Nowotny jumped into his own fighter, and prepared for takeoff. But no sooner had he warmed up the turbojets than one of his engines failed, and he was unable to restart it—the exact situation he'd been complaining about. Frustrated, Nowotny watched as Oberleutnant Günther Wegmann taxied out and smoothly left the runway. A moment later, Leutnant Franz Schall also took off. As the two Me-262s rose in the cool November air, a pair of Thunderbolt pilots saw them and rushed to attack, but Fw-190s held them off.

Wegmann and Schall were keenly aware of the Thunderbolt pilots' intentions. The Americans were now busy contending with the Focke-Wulfs at about 3,000 meters, and when the two Me-262s reached that altitude they went right on climbing. They leveled off above the fight, and then Wegmann and Schall dove on the Thunderbolts, firing as they went.

Shells from Wegmann's cannons struck a P-47's fuel tank, and the big fighter exploded. Oily smoke filled the air where it had been, and bits of debris rained downward. Schall missed his target on the first pass, causing the American pilot to decide that the Fw-190s and an Me-262 were more than he could deal with. He turned away, which was what Schall had been hoping he'd do. Tracking the Thunderbolt from behind, Schall rapidly caught up with it and fired a well-aimed burst. The P-47 lost one of its wings and spun wildly as it plummeted to earth.

The pilot did not get out before it crashed.

By that time the enemy bombers attacking Rheine had dropped their bomb loads and were leaving the area. German fighters were still sniping at them, and Schall saw one of the B-17s slowly roll over and go down with its engines on fire.

Schall and Wegmann then returned to Achmer under the watchful eyes of Fw-190 pilots who were circling over the field. The pair landed and taxied to the tarmac, and when they climbed out of their cockpits, Nowotny and Galland offered congratulations on their victories. Mechanics began refueling the Me-262s and restocking their magazines.

Not long afterward the sirens sounded again, and the pilots quickly returned to their aircraft. This time it was Wegmann's fighter that developed engine trouble. He and his ground crew were unable to get the turbos started, and Wegmann finally gave up in disgust.

Nowotny's engines, on the other hand, had been attended to by the mechanics, and now they were running well. He took off, with Schall and Oberfeldwebel Baudach right behind him. Controllers reported the bombers were attacking Merseberg, a town just west of Leipzig.

Three more Me-262s got into the air from Hesepe, and once again the Fw-190s of III/J54 were also scrambled. Nowotny, Schall and Baudach reached the battle in a few minutes, just as the enemy aircraft were finishing their bomb runs.

The bombers were B-17s, though in the heat of the moment Nowotny misidentified them as Liberators. He estimated there were about four wings, escorted by a large number of fighters. Bf-109s were jousting with the escorts, and plumes of smoke trailed from several aircraft that were going down in flames. At least two of the burning wrecks were bombers. Parachutes were also visible, the yellow ones German, the white American. As Nowotny and the others entered the conflict, some of the enemy fighters fired at them from long range. None scored hits. Moments later Schall slipped behind a Mustang and brought it down with a quick burst.

Schall was then attacked by another P-51. The fight didn't last long; the enemy pilot made too wide a turn and Schall sent cannon shells into that airplane as well. The Mustang broke apart in the air.

Meanwhile, Nowotny chose a bomber that was leading an element, and approached its right rear from a slight angle. He could see the tail gunner swing his guns around and begin shooting, the tracers whizzing toward the Me-262. Nowotny opened up with his cannons, sending 30mm shells into the bomber's fuselage. The B-17 lurched like a wounded animal, and then slowly slid out of the formation. As Nowotny came around and looked back, he saw it go nose down and begin to spin. Two parachutes appeared, but that was all.

Schall had still more work to do. He caught sight of a Thunderbolt a few hundred meters below and to his left, and put his aircraft into a shallow dive. As he closed on the P-47 it pulled up, giving him an even better target, but only one of his cannon shells hit the enemy fighter.

The Thunderbolt was flown by Lieutenant Charles C. McKelvy of the 359th Fighter Group. Although badly damaged, it somehow held together. As McKelvy eased the battered airplane down to a lower altitude, he was attacked again, this time by an Fw-190D flown by Oberleutnant Hans Dortenmann of 3/JG54. Dortenmann blasted the limping P-47, and McKelvy crash-landed what was left of it. Only slightly wounded, he climbed out of the wreckage and was taken prisoner.

Next, Schall spotted a box of B-17s over Quakenbrück. They were some distance from the main formation and not protected by escorts. He banked toward them, and as he did, he himself was spotted by a pair of Mustang pilots of the 357th Fighter Group. They were Lieutenants Warren Corwin and James Kenny.

The Americans attacked, and Kenny got several hits on Schall's jet. As the three aircraft maneuvered, Corwin made an ill-timed split-S that put him squarely in the Me-262's gunsight. Schall fired, and one of his shells ripped into Corwin's Mustang. Two other pilots of the 357th, Lieutenants John Sublett and John England, heard Corwin mutter into his mike, "Son of a bitching jet job got me." They asked his condition, and he said he'd been wounded and his aircraft had lost its port wing. There were no more transmissions after that, and the wreckage of Corwin's Mustang was never found.

Kenny was unaware that Corwin had been downed. He again saw the Me-262, and chased it below a bank of cloud. Firing another burst, he got several additional hits, whereupon the jet began flying erratically and the pilot bailed out. Kenny switched off his guns and buzzed the German with his camera running. When viewed later, the film clearly showed the pilot dangling beneath the yellow canopy. Schall was severely wounded, but he would live.

By now Nowotny was low on fuel. He pulled away from the formation of enemy bombers and flew toward the base at Hesepe. As he approached the field, he was attacked by several Mustangs. His aircraft was hit, but he swung around and caught one of the enemy with cannon fire. The P-51 spun out and crashed.

At that point the flak batteries began firing, and the bursting shells discouraged the other Mustangs. As they left the area, one aircraft stayed behind, flown by Lieutenant R.W. Stevens of the 364th Fighter Group. Stevens made one last run at Nowotny's Me-262.

General Galland was still in the operations shack, following the action by radio. As he recalled, "Nowotny reported that one of his engines was damaged. He was flying on the right engine alone, which made him vulnerable. I stepped outside to watch his approach to the field, when an enemy fighter fired at him and pulled away not far from us."

Nowotny then made his final transmission. He shouted, "My god, I'm burning!"

Galland: "I heard the sound of his jet engine, and we saw the 262 come through the light clouds at low altitude, rolling slightly and then hitting the ground. There was an explosion, and a column of black smoke rose from behind the trees. We took off in a car and reached the site, and it was Nowotny's plane. After sifting through the wreckage, the only things we found were his left hand and pieces of his Diamonds decoration."

Ever the stoic warrior, Galland revealed none of his grief to the surviving pilots of the Kommando. Major Walther Nowotny had been a personal friend as well as a Luftwaffe hero, but now he was gone, and nothing would bring him back. Galland promoted Hauptmann Georg-Peter Eder to become commander of the unit.

71.

Hauptmann Eder was an accomplished combat pilot, and one of the best at flying the turbo. The husky blond Prussian had achieved his first victory in an Me-262 by downing a Lockheed Lightning F-5 of the 7th Photo Reconnaissance Group on 6 October 1944. That kill was added to the 78 he'd scored in piston fighters, 22 of them U.S. bombers.

The day after Galland promoted him, Eder engaged a flight of

Mustangs in his Me-262 and shot down two of them. But he was well aware that defeating enemy fighters was not nearly as important as downing bombers. The heavies were the weapons that were crippling German industry and killing civilians, and destroying them had to be the number one objective. As the new commander of the jet unit, he urged his pilots to concentrate as much as possible on attacking the viermots.

On 11 November, Eder led five Me-262s to the area just west of Frankfurt, where Luftwaffe fighters were in combat with a large fleet of B-17s and their P-51 escorts. As the jets approached the battle, some of the Mustangs tried to cut them off, but Eder avoided the enemy fighters by climbing steeply until he was about eight hundred meters above them. He then flew over the B-17s to the tail end of the bomber stream. Coming about, he dove toward one of the combat boxes of four-engine aircraft.

At that point his indicated airspeed was 950 kph, which was about the limit at which an Me-262 could be maneuvered without risking loss of control, and even then he was taking a chance. At any moment the jet might whip into a spin. Nonetheless, he stayed in the dive and closed on the B-17 that was leading the box. When he was only two hundred meters from the target he fired his cannons. Eder was a good marksman. In the second or two before his turbo flashed by, the explosive 30mm shells slammed into the Fortress between the number three engine and the starboard wing root.

As Eder pulled out, G-forces shoved him deep into his seat. Taking care not to turn too abruptly, he swept upward and looked back. His strikes had torn the wing off the B-17, and the wreck was spinning toward the earth. Again he flew back toward the rear of the formation. As he did, he saw that a few of the German piston fighters had gotten past the Mustangs and were attacking the bombers. Tracers laced the sky, pouring from the guns of the fighters and the B-17s.

Wheeling around once more, Eder picked out another Fortress and eased the stick forward, his finger on the firing button. As the bomber loomed larger in his gunsight, he fired a short burst into the enemy aircraft's fuselage. This time he hit the bomb load, and the target exploded. Half-blinded by the flash, he was shaken by violent jolts as the Me-262 flew through the shock waves and the detritus, and went on down below the stream of aircraft.

As far as he could tell, the jet had suffered no serious damage, but a glance at his fuel gauges told him he had little time left. Maybe he could get one more. As he began to pull up, he caught sight of a Mustang chasing a Bf-109. Continuing to haul back on the stick, he brought the jet up under the P-51 and fired. At least two of the projectiles punched into the belly of the enemy fighter, and the Mustang rolled away in flames. The pilot did not bail out.

Now Eder had no choice but to break off and return to base. In fact, he'd be lucky to make it. He knew an Me-262 could stay in the air for only an hour, and if pushed at combat speeds as he'd pushed this one today, 50 minutes would be tops. Using the lowest possible power settings, he got back to Lechfeld and landed without further incident. He joked with his ground crew that the engines had been running on fumes. There were also dents in the nose and wings of his aircraft, put there by debris from the exploding B-17.

Eder's technique in attacking bombers had served him well. He'd become the first jet fighter pilot to kill two heavies in one sortie. As if to prove it hadn't been a fluke, a week later he again posted multiple victories in a single battle.

On that occasion another large fleet was conducting a raid on Mannheim. As before, Eder climbed high over the stream of enemy aircraft and picked out a B-17. He then made a shallow dive on the targeted bomber from the rear, and destroyed it with his extraordinarily accurate cannon fire. Several Mustangs tried to catch him as he pulled out of the dive, and began regaining altitude, but the jet was too fast for them. Twice more he dove on Fortresses and shot them down with quick bursts. Finally he was forced to return to base, his fuel tanks once again almost dry.

Adolf Galland carefully read the combat reports that detailed Eder's exploits and those of his pilots. During the few weeks they were in action, they'd accounted for 22 enemy airplanes. More than half were heavy bombers. But the jets had sustained losses as well. Twenty-six Me-262s had been destroyed, though only eight had been shot down. All the others were lost through various mishaps; among those, three crashed on landing and two on takeoff because of engine failure. Two were wrecked when their landing gear collapsed, and another collided in mid-air with an enemy aircraft. Five came back with battle damage, and crash-landed.

Galland realized the unit was badly in need of rest. On 14 November, he had it withdrawn from Achmer and sent to Lechfeld, where the airmen would be able to relax as the jets were being overhauled. On the whole, the general was highly encouraged. While at Lechfeld the unit was reformed as III/JG7, and became the Luftwaffe's first fully staffed jet jagdgeschwader to go into regular service. This was what Nowotny had wanted, but never lived to see.

In late November, Galland waited impatiently for the order that would launch the Great Blow. The fighter wings were poised and ready, and all that was needed was a day of perfect flying weather—it was then that the Allied bombers would be given a reception beyond anything they could imagine.

At last Galland was called to Berlin for the much-anticipated meeting with Göring. He flew his Bf-109 to the Luftwaffe airfield at Strausberg, and from there a staff car drove him to the capital. By this time the city was a shambles. Many of its once-splendid buildings were hulks, and many others had been completely destroyed. In a number of places crews were fighting smoldering fires, while in others civilian workers struggled to clear streets littered with rubble from the incessant bombings. A pall of smoke hung in the air, infusing it with an acrid stink. Military personnel were everywhere.

As he approached the massive Luftwaffe Headquarters building at the corner of Wilhelm Strasse and Leipzig Strasse, Galland saw that it had been severely damaged in the air raids. He casually returned the guards' salutes and went inside, where he waited in the first-floor conference room until Hermann Göring entered. With the Reichsmarschal were his adjutant and a half-dozen officers of lesser rank who, in Galland's opinion, were nothing but toadies.

As usual, Göring was splendidly attired, though the fancy blue uniform could not hide his enormous gut. Nor did his imperious manner fool Galland. Ever since the debacle of the Normandy landings, Göring had been pushed aside by such connivers as Heinrich Himmler and Martin Bormann. Nevertheless, he was asserting his authority as arrogantly as ever.

The group took seats at the table, and the adjutant handed Göring a stack of fitness reports on the various Luftwaffe units. The Reichsmarschal said the reports indicated the bomber and reconnaissance forces, as well as the fighter groups, were all in good shape. He'd also confirmed their readiness by making a number of personal inspections.

Galland agreed that the fighters and their pilots were primed and ready; all that was needed now was the order to launch the Great Blow. However, instead of issuing it, the Reichsmarschal announced that there were new orders. Most of the Luftwaffe's forces were to be moved to the western front, with only the 300th and the 301st Fighter Wings to remain behind. The transfer had to be completed within the coming two weeks.

Galland was astonished. He said flatly that this was totally opposite to what he and the fighter commanders had been preparing for over the past months. The whole idea of the Great Blow was to defend the homeland—leaving only two fighter geschwaders in the Reich would be suicidal.

Göring reddened. This was a direct order, he said, and Galland was not to challenge it.

But Galland did. He said the fighters had been organized to make a massive attack on enemy bombers. Each geschwader now had 70 aircraft. The airfields at the front could not accommodate forces of that size. Think of the maintenance equipment, and the fuel supplies, and the support personnel.

Adjustments must be made, Göring bellowed. And the move must be carried out as ordered!

Galland tried to argue further, pointing out that even the question of which units would go to which fields would require study. The logistics of such transfers would present tremendous problems, with nearly four thousand fighters affected. Couldn't the Reichsmarschal see that?

By now Göring was furious. He pounded the table with his fist and shouted that he wished to hear no more insolent comments. He told Galland to initiate the transfers at once, and to keep him closely informed of progress.

As he left the building, Galland tried to figure out what was going on. He could think of no reasonable explanation, and it was obvious that he was being deliberately kept in the dark.

72.

Willy Messerschmitt was also feeling frustrated, believing that a large force of Me-262s could have halted the enemy's bombing campaign on the homeland. But wrong-headed decisions by Hitler and his sycophants had compromised the program. The irony was that now at last, the High Command seemed to recognize how desperately Germany needed an effective interceptor. Yet on orders from the Air Ministry, more of the fighter-bombers than the pure fighters were still being built. At least production of both versions had been stepped up, and BMW was developing new turbojets. The engineers assured Messerschmitt that these would not fail the way the Jumos often did, but he'd heard such claims many times in the past.

Meanwhile, experiments were underway in which a rocket engine would be employed along with the turbos. That would enable the Me-262 to take off more rapidly, so it would be less vulnerable to attack by enemy fighters. The project was being handled by the engineers Degel and Althoff. The aircraft they were working on was dubbed Interceptor I, and would be powered by two BMW jet engines, and one Walter HWK R II-211 rocket engine mounted at the rear of the belly. The rocket fuel would last just long enough to boost the aircraft to combat altitude. Special heat-shielding metal would used to protect the underside of the fuselage.

At the same time, BMW was developing turbojets that would integrate the rocket boosters. Whenever those became available, Degel and Althoff planned to use them in Interceptor II. The rockets would be the BMW type 109-718, and would add 1,250 kg of takeoff thrust to the 800 kg of the engines.

While most of the flight tests were conducted at Lechfeld, other testing went on at the Augsburg factory. Some of it was done by Eberhard Stromeyer de Raulino, the Baroness's son. He'd joined the Luftwaffe hoping to fly in combat, but the RLM insisted that he was too valuable as an engineer.

Early in December, the Air Ministry challenged the Me-262's performance in combat. Only a few pilots had managed to shoot down bombers. Why was this?

General Galland explained that it was due to a shortage of the Me-262s. On some days, six or eight would be in action against as many as four hundred enemy fighters. The most jets put up at one time had been twelve, making it difficult for the Me-262s to get close enough to the bombers to destroy them. But it was not for lack of trying, no matter what Reichsmarschal Göring might have said on the subject.

Another deterrent was the bombers' defenses. Their formations of tight combat boxes enabled them to concentrate a great amount of machine-gun fire on any attacking fighter. Yet the basic problem was that there simply were not enough of the jets in service. "I would rather have one Me-262," the general said, "than five Bf-109s!"

Messerschmitt agreed with Galland's assessment. He urged the RLM and Armaments Minister Speer to give him more materials and more laborers. Speer replied that tanks and other war materiel were also badly needed, not just aircraft. Efforts would be made to get him what he wanted, but for the moment, Messerschmitt was ordered to try equipping the Me-262 with more powerful armament.

The Professor was not convinced. He believed the firepower of the Me-262's four cannons was more than sufficient to bring down a bomber. Nevertheless, he instructed the engineers to equip a test aircraft with six of the 30mm MK-108s.

Much of the development and testing was conducted at the Tarnewitz Luftwaffe station. The aircraft in which the heavier armament was installed was the Me-262 A-1a/U5. As Messerschmitt had expected, the results were not encouraging. The problem wasn't the number of guns so much as it was a pilot's ability to bring them to bear on the enemy.

Officials at the Air Ministry then ordered Messerschmitt to try using a larger caliber weapon. It was an idea that had already been disproved, but he set the engineers to work on it. They equipped an Me-262 with a 50mm Mauser MK214A tank cannon, and dubbed it the *Pulkzerstorer*, or formation destroyer. It would be months before it was ready for flight-testing, and in the end the concept would again be a failure.

A new gunsight was also tested, as a possible replacement for the Revi 16b reflector type. This was the EZ42, which used a simple onboard computer to calculate the proper lead before a pilot fired at a target. Though there were glitches in the device, the engineers continued to work on that as well.

Still another idea that appealed to the RLM involved equipping an Me-262 with unguided air-to-air rockets. These projectiles offered several advantages: they were of simple design, had a long range, and carried enormous explosive power. This was one approach Messerschmitt thought might produce the desired results. The rockets first tested were the type Wgr-21, and the type R100BS. Both had been designed for ground assault, and it quickly became evident that they were unsuitable for aircraft. The potential was too great, however, for the project to be abandoned. The search for a dependable rocket continued.

The RLM then urged Messerschmitt to produce a night fighter version of the Me-262. The Luftwaffe already had the He-219, the Ju-88, and the Bf-110, and all were equipped with radar and the multi-gun batteries pilots called Schrage Muzik. Bf-109s and Fw-190s in the Wilde Sau unit were also in action.

Nevertheless, large fleets of RAF bombers continued to carry out devastating attacks on German cities, and with its great speed, an Me-262 theoretically would be more effective than any other aircraft. Moreover, an Me-262 night fighter would become an efficient Mosquito killer. For years the RAF's fast wooden aircraft had flown over Germany with impunity, and only when they were attacked by a jet had they met their match. Properly equipped, Me-262s would swat the night-prowling Mosquitos.

For such a variant, a two-seat configuration would be required. One airman would pilot the plane, while the other operated the radar and navigational equipment, and also served as gunner. Messerschmitt had already built a two-seat trainer, but conversion to a night fighter would be more complicated, because of the extra mechanisms that had to be accommodated. So that too would take months. The aircraft to be modified for the purpose was designated the Me-262 B-1a/U1.

In the interim, a Luftwaffe night fighter unit was established. This was 10 Staffel of NJG11, stationed at Burg Airfield, near Berlin. The commander was Major Gerhard Stamp, a veteran who had flown more than 500 missions. The new unit's aircraft were all single-seat Me-262 fighters, with no special night-fighting equipment. It would not be until the following March that the two-seaters would reach 10/NJG11. But that did not deter the pilots from entering combat with the single-seaters soon after the unit became operational.

On the night of 12 December 1944, the RAF conducted another massive raid on Berlin. The bomber stream comprised six hundred Lancasters and stretched for miles. As usual, chaff was dropped to confuse the German radar operators, and Mosquitos dropped pathfinder flares to guide the bombers to the target. The capital was still the most heavily defended city in Germany. It was ringed with hundreds of flak batteries, and several squadrons of He-219s and other piston-engine night fighters were based in the area. Powerful searchlights probed the sky and countless 88mm shells exploded as the Lancasters made their bomb runs.

At Burg, Oberleutnant Kurt Welter ran to his Me-262. The base had been alerted some minutes before the bombers approached the target, and mechanics had already warmed up the aircraft's engines. Welter took off with two other jets and made a climbing turn toward the city, where night fighters were engaging the enemy.

Welter was another combat veteran. He'd been a Wilde Sau pilot before being assigned to 10/NJG11, and earlier had achieved 30 victories flying an Fw-190. Tonight he was determined to put his new jet to good use.

The sky over Berlin was filled with roaring aircraft, and streaked with tracers from their guns. A number of planes, mostly bombers but some fighters as well, were falling in flames. Welter selected a Lancaster and squinted through his gunsight as he raced toward it. He pressed the firing button, and saw his tracers reach out for the target. And then suddenly he was past it. As he pulled up, he realized the reason he'd missed his target. In his eagerness, he was handling the jet as he would a slower fighter. With an Me-262 you had to start firing sooner, and try to get in some hits before you flashed by. He came about, and looked for another opportunity.

The Lancaster he picked next was banking left, turning away from the city for the trip home. He put the jet into position about six hundred meters behind it, and when he began firing again his cannon shells apparently hit one of the bomber's fuel tanks. The big aircraft burst into flames and flipped over, spinning as it went down. It was the first night victory scored by an Me-262.

That same night, a number of high-ranking officers were called to a conference with Hitler. General Galland was not invited to attend. When he learned what had been discussed, he realized at last why he had been ordered by Reichsmarschal Göring to move all Luftwaffe fighter units to the western front, leaving only two wings to defend the homeland.

The order had been bad enough. But now that he knew the reason behind it, Galland was convinced Germany had embarked on a path of sheer madness.

73.

On the night of the meeting, Feldmarschal Gerd von Rundstedt and a dozen of the top German field commanders on the western front were driven by bus to Ziegenberg. There they entered a large underground concrete bunker.

This was another of Adolf Hitler's secret command centers. The walls were covered with maps, and radio operators were busy with their wireless apparatus. The Führer was surrounded by a group of staff officers that included Feldmarschal Heinz Guderian and Feldmarschal Walther Model. Also present were Generals Hasso Manteuffel and Sepp Dietrich.

Hitler's appearance was shocking. He was thin and haggard and his face was pale. When he walked he dragged his right leg, apparently the result of wounds he'd suffered in the 20 July assassination attempt. There was also a twitch in his left hand that he tried to hide. But there was no change in his eyes, which burned with the same intensity as ever. And when he spoke, it was in the harsh tones that had become so familiar to everyone in Germany. It was obvious that in spite of his physical infirmities, his fervor had not diminished.

The Führer told the group of officers that he'd formulated a new plan, code-named Operation Greif. Until then, the plan had been known only to a few trusted members of the High Command. Four days from now, Hitler said, the Wehrmacht was to launch a massive attack against the Western Allies. It would be the largest German offensive since the invasion of Normandy, and would catch the enemy completely by surprise.

He'd been making preparations for months, and had pulled together 2,500 tanks and heavy artillery pieces. Twenty-eight divisions were poised to strike, with another six in reserve. Göring had four thousand fighter planes ready to take part.

The first objective of the attack was to drive through the Ardennes and smash the U.S. 1st and 3rd Armies, then the German divisions would go all the way to Antwerp. Recapturing that port would prevent the Americans from bringing in supplies and ammunition. Next, the Germans would roll up the British and Canadian armies that were on the borders of Belgium and Holland.

The crushing defeat would wreck the Allied forces, Hitler claimed.

He would then be free to mount a similarly powerful counterattack against the Soviets, who had been stalled in Poland and East Prussia since October. Execution of his plan would be a masterstroke that could well bring the war to an end in Germany's favor.

Rundstedt was amazed. He'd had no idea that such a plan was being formulated. And as soon as he heard it, he knew the operation was doomed to fail. The German forces were not nearly large enough for the plan to succeed. Rundstedt learned later that Feldmarschal Guderian, the Chief of The General Staff, had tried to dissuade Hitler from undertaking the offensive. Guderian was in charge of the eastern front, and pointed out that since most of the forces making the attack would be pulled from that sector, it would leave only the thinnest defenses to contend with the Soviets. Also, the German Army was not half as powerful as the one that had slashed through the Ardennes in 1940.

The Führer reacted as he usually did when opposed, becoming fiercely angry. He shouted that he'd been in command of the army for five years and knew more about conducting an offensive than Guderian or anyone else on the General Staff. The operation would go forward as planned.

At the conclusion of the meeting, many of the officers had the same opinion as Rundstedt and Guderian—that Hitler's plan was nothing more than a wild gamble. Yet in the long tradition of the German soldier, they would do their best to make it succeed.

The following day, General Galland was informed by Göring of the planned offensive. When he heard the plan, Galland realized he'd been betrayed. Now he knew why his fighters had been moved to the western front; instead of striking the Great Blow, they would be sent into a fight that Germany had no chance of winning. But he was also aware that once the Führer had decided on a course of action, nothing could shake his resolve.

On the night of 15 December, a thick mist hung in the frosty air of the Ardennes Forest. Two Panzer armies, one led by General von Manteuffel and the other by SS General Dietrich, quietly moved into place along a seventy mile front between Manschau and Trier.

The two generals were markedly different in almost every way. Manteuffel was a tiny man of aristocratic background who'd been a professional military officer most of his life. He'd fought with distinction in the First World War, and in the Second was one of Rommel's commanders in the African desert. Later he was a highly effective field commander on the eastern front.

In contrast, Dietrich was tall and bear-like. He'd been an army sergeant in the 1914–18 war, and during Hitler's rise to power was one of his bodyguards. Dietrich had eventually become an SS general, and as a commander in Russia was noted for his savagery. His troops had committed countless atrocities.

The fog that now obscured the movement of the German armies had been predicted by meteorologists to last at least five more days, which meant Allied aircraft would be grounded. The enemy forces were enjoying a lull before Christmas, and would be caught napping.

Shortly before dawn on 16 December, the stillness was shattered by the roar of a German artillery barrage. For two hours, HE shells rained down on the Americans and the British. When the barrage ended, Tiger tanks and masses of German infantry appeared like ghosts out of the fog. Fire erupted from their cannons and machine guns as they rolled over the enemy positions. They achieved breakthroughs in a dozen places.

The German advance quickly transformed the shape of the front lines, creating an elliptical curve; the Allies called the German offensive the Battle of the Bulge. In the sudden, unexpected attack, thousands of American soldiers were killed, and thousands more were taken prisoner. The heaviest snowstorm in years then fell on the region. The roads were covered in knee-deep drifts that caused traffic jams in many places. It also forced the Panzers to use more of their limited supply of fuel.

In the northern part of the sector, Dietrich's army was unexpectedly held up by the fierce resistance of the U.S. 2nd and 99th Infantry Divisions at Losheim and the Elsenborn Ridge. In the center, Manteuffel made better progress, pushing toward Bastogne. To the south a lesser force, led by General Erich Brandenberger, protected the German flank.

By the second night, Manteuffel's armored units had penetrated as far as Stavelot, a town only a short distance from a huge supply dump that contained three million gallons of gasoline. By seizing it, the Germans could immediately replenish their fuel stocks, instead of having to wait for more to be brought up. That would enable them to move faster.

But the Americans realized what was at stake, and stiffened resistance. The Panzers changed course and entered a narrow salient between Monschau and Bastogne. At the same time, another scheme in the German offensive began causing pandemonium among U.S. forces. It was the work of SS Panzer Brigade 150. Leader of the brigade was one of Hitler's favorites, Colonel Otto Skorzeny.

As bold and resourceful as ever, Skorzeny had assembled a group of English-speaking German soldiers and outfitted them with U.S. Army uniforms and dog tags taken from the dead. Driving captured tanks, jeeps and trucks, they slipped through the lines and fired on the confounded Americans. Others wore helmets and armbands identifying them as Military Police, and created much confusion at crossroads by sending U.S. forces in the wrong direction.

One of the brigade's most effective ploys was initiated when a fake MP allowed himself to be captured. He told American interrogators that several of the imposters were on their way to the Paris headquarters of General Eisenhower, with a mission to kill the Supreme Allied Commander. The story was not true, but it served its purpose. The Americans were forced to waste time and effort checking personnel who might be Germans disguised as U.S. troops. In the end, most of the men in Panzer Brigade 150 were rounded up and shot. Although in typical fashion, Skorzeny escaped.

Meanwhile, Manteuffel's 5th Panzer Army continued toward Bastogne. Capturing the town was vital to the Germans, because it was at a road juncture close to the Meuse River—they needed to punch through and cross the bridge over the Meuse in order to go on. But if the Americans could hold, they would block the main roads and stop the German advance.

At the time, the U.S. forces in Bastogne were only a headquarters staff, and they were hastily preparing to leave. To shore up the defenses, the 101st Airborne Division, which was refitting at Reims, was ordered to rush to the town. Its troops drove all night in trucks with their headlights on, and arrived at dawn on 18 December, just ahead of the Germans.

When Manteuffel's armored units got there, they found Bastogne occupied by seasoned soldiers who were determined to stay and fight. The Germans surrounded the town, and repeatedly assaulted the defensive positions, but for four days, the Americans held. They sustained 40 percent casualties, with many of their platoon leaders and company commanders either wounded or killed. By the fifth day they were almost out of medical supplies, ammunition and food.

On 22 December, General Heinrich von Luettwitz, commander of the German XLVIIth Armored Corps, sent a note to General A.C. McAuliffe of the 101st, demanding that the Americans surrender. McAuliffe sent back a one-word answer: "Nuts!"

At that point the U.S. 2nd Armored Division was moving toward the area from the north to launch a counterattack, and units of Patton's 3rd Army were racing up from the south. The German commanders realized time was running out. At 0300 hours on 23 December, the Germans began a series of desperate attacks on the beleaguered Americans. They moved Tiger tanks close to the enemy positions and fired their 88mm cannons at point-blank range. But still the Americans held.

And then at last the weather cleared. Immediately great numbers of American and British aircraft took off and began attacking the German armies and their supply lines. Thunderbolts, Typhoons and Marauders bombed and strafed German armor and troops on the narrow mountain roads, while Spitfires and Mustangs battled Luftwaffe fighters in the air. The reinforcements and the gasoline the Germans had been promised never appeared.

As Manteuffel said later, "On the evening of the 24th it was clear that the high water mark of our operation had been reached. We now knew that we would never reach our objective." Nevertheless, the Germans made one last attempt to capture Bastogne. For hours on Christmas day they assaulted the Americans with tanks and infantry, and yet McAuliffe's stubborn defenders still would not yield. The next day an armored column of Patton's Third Army arrived, and their Sherman tanks hit Manteuffel's forces from the rear. After a fierce firefight, the Americans broke through and relieved the 101st Airborne troops.

The Germans withdrew in disarray, leaving the battlefield strewn with their dead. They also left behind most of their tanks. Many had been destroyed in battle, but others had simply run out of gasoline.

Just as General Galland had feared, the German fighter squadrons had been poorly prepared for the offensive. The bases on the Western front were not equipped to handle them, and the hastily transferred pilots and support personnel had not had time to become properly organized. Some of those airfields did not have sufficient supplies of fuel for the squadrons assigned to them, and at others there was a shortage of ground crews. And there was a rash of accidents, including midair collisions.

Once the weather improved, more than two thousand American and British fighters and fighter-bombers attacked the German aircraft. In addition to engaging the Germans in the air, the Allies destroyed many of their planes on the ground by strafing and bombing the airfields. Often Luftwaffe fighter pilots attempting to land found the runways rent with bomb craters, and the hangars and supply sheds and barracks in flames.

But where were the jets? Where were the Me-262s when they were so badly needed?

74.

As it turned out, a number of Me-262s took part in the Ardennes offensive, but only a few were pure fighters. Most were fighter-bombers, and they were poorly suited to supporting the ground forces.

The jets had no air brakes, so if a pilot tried to dive on a target to achieve greater accuracy, his airspeed would quickly exceed limits and he'd lose control. He had no proper bombsight, either, so if he tried to bomb from a higher altitude, he was almost sure to miss. As General Galland put it, the only objective a pilot could hit under those circumstances had to be no smaller than a town. As a result, the Me-262s flew dozens of sorties, but did little damage to the enemy. And because most of them were flown by bomber pilots and not by experienced fighter pilots, they were highly vulnerable in air-to-air combat.

On 25 December, RAF Flight Lieutenant Jack Boyle was sitting down to Christmas dinner at Heers when an Me-262 flashed over the airfield. He and other members of 411 Squadron ran to their Spitfires and took off, but by then the jet had disappeared. A few minutes later Boyle's wingman reported engine trouble, and reluctantly the pair headed back to base.

Boyle was annoyed, having looked forward to another encounter with the enemy. As he neared Heers, he impetuously put his Spitfire IX into a steep dive, his airspeed reaching 500 mph. Suddenly he saw an Me-262 below and ahead of him.

For a split second Boyle thought it was a trick of his imagination. But the jet was real; he could see the black crosses on its wings. He leveled off close behind the enemy aircraft, flicked off his safety catch, and began shooting. His report stated,

"My first burst of cannon fire hit his port engine pod and it began streaming dense smoke. He immediately dove for the deck as an evasive tactic, but with only one engine he couldn't outrun me. I scored several more hits before he clipped some tall tree tops and then hit the ground at an almost flat angle. His aircraft disintegrated in stages from nose to tail as it ripped up the turf for several hundred yards until only the tailplane assembly was left and it went cartwheeling along just below me at about my speed. Fire and smoke marked his trail. As I circled, farmers emerged from their barns and waved up at me."

Boyle had become the first Spitfire pilot to shoot down an Me-262 unaided. The airplane he destroyed was flown by Oberleutnant Hans-Georg Lamle of I/KG(J)51, who was killed in the crash.

Later that same day, four Spitfires of the Royal Canadian Air Force's 403 Squadron were patrolling in search of enemy fighters when one of the pilots spotted three of the jets. The Me-262s were 2,000 feet above the Spitfires, and appeared to be flying at a relatively low cruising speed. Squadron Leader J.E. Collier realized the Spitfires hadn't been seen because they were in the jets' blind spot. He and his pilots climbed rapidly and, still undetected, opened fire on the enemy aircraft. Collier described the action:

"I fired my first burst from about 70 yards at the leader of the V formation they were flying and obtained a hit on the starboard engine, which burst into flames. His two wingmen broke away in opposite directions, pursued by the other three of our flight who were hampered by the tremendous acceleration of the 262. I followed my target down until I saw him bail out."

The three jets in this action were also members of I/KG(J)51. The aircraft shot down by Collier carried the markings 9K+MK. Its pilot was Feldwebel Hans Meyer, who was killed when his parachute failed to open. On 29 December, another fighter-bomber of I/KG(J)51 was lost, this time to antiaircraft fire. Splinters from a shell pierced the Me-262, and it spun down out of control, killing Leutnant Wolfgang Oswald.

As far as General Galland was concerned, these events all resulted from the stupid misuse of jet aircraft. Instead of turning loose a large number of Me-262 fighters on the enemy, the Luftwaffe had sent a mere handful of jets, and most were carrying bombs. Only a few of the pure fighters were involved in the offensive.

In those battles, the Me-262 fighters were members of 3/JG7. One of the pilots was Oberfeldwebel Erich Büttner, who had downed a Mustang and a Thunderbolt the previous month while flying with Kommando Nowotny. On 23 December he'd shot down another Mustang, and later the same day, destroyed a Lightning.

On 29 December Büttner was again patrolling over the Ardennes when he saw a Mosquito circling high above the battlefield. Büttner gave chase, and the British pilot, Flight Lieutenant Olson of 544 Squadron, resorted to the usual tactics, opening his throttles to outrun his pursuer.

That mistake cost Olson his life. Büttner rapidly closed on the Mosquito, and from a distance of 200 meters fired his cannons. The explosive shells shattered the wooden fuselage of the enemy aircraft and set it on fire. Ablaze and trailing black smoke, the wreck tumbled down into the thick forest.

Another Mosquito fell to the guns of an Me-262 fighter on the last day of 1944. This time the German pilot was Feldwebel Helmut Baudach of 3/JG7, who had already scored four victories earlier while flying with Ekdo 262 and Kommando Nowotny.

Baudach's encounter was similar to that of Büttner. The pilot of the Mosquito, Warrant Officer Bradley of 464 Squadron, tried to pull away from his attacker. In a matter of seconds Baudach caught up to the enemy aircraft. His cannon fire hit one of Bradley's fuel tanks, and the Mosquito instantly blossomed flames and fell out of the sky.

Galland once again complained to Göring that more Me-262 fighters were what was needed, and not the fighter-bombers—though he knew it would do little good. Galland also argued that since the offensive had failed, all fighter squadrons should be returned to Germany to defend the homeland.

Göring's response was to turn a deaf ear and order a counterattack. Code-named Operation Bodenplatte, its objective was to destroy the enemy's airplanes on their fields in Belgium, Holland, and the north of France. Every German aircraft on the western front was to take part.

At first light on the morning of 1 January 1945, Luftwaffe fighters, night fighters, and bombers took off. They flew at low levels and caught the enemy by surprise, bombing and strafing their bases. Hundreds of

Allied aircraft were destroyed on the ground. The assault was a shock to the American and British commanders, who had no idea that the Luftwaffe still had so many aircraft, or that they were capable of carrying out an operation of that size. On dozens of bases, Allied airplanes were left wrecked and burning.

But for the Germans, it was as if they'd stepped on a tiger's tail. Fighters from Allied fields were hurriedly put up, and the two forces were soon joined in a battle that took place over an area of more than a hundred square kilometers. In the swirling fight British and American aircraft outnumbered the Germans by more than two-to-one. And in addition, the pilots of the Spitfires, Tempests, Mustangs and Thunderbolts were more experienced than most of their opponents.

Me-262s of I/KG(J)51 also participated in Operation Bodenplatte. Twenty-one of them strafed airfields at Eindhoven and Hertogenbosch in Holland. The bases were heavily defended by antiaircraft batteries, which sent up a storm of flak. One jet was shot down, and another was damaged.

For the Germans flying piston aircraft, the tally was far worse. Great numbers of their airplanes were destroyed, and the countryside was dotted with their smoking remains. When the battle ended, the Luftwaffe had lost over 300 fighter pilots. Even more disastrous, the dead included 59 leaders. Those men had years of experience, and were irreplaceable.

Adolf Galland had never felt so bitter. He believed that if the 28 Panzer and infantry divisions, plus the 4,000 aircraft that were engaged in the offensive had been sent to the east, instead of being squandered in the Ardennes, the Soviets could have been halted. That would have given Germany a chance to work out an armistice with the Western Allies.

He was wrong, of course. First, in the agreement reached in the Casablanca conference, and later confirmed in the one at Yalta, the Allies would accept nothing less than total surrender. Stalin remained intent on grabbing as much European territory for the Soviet Union as possible.

Second, Hitler would never capitulate—an armistice would be unthinkable. As always, he was interested only in punishing his enemies. For him, exacting vengeance was not merely an objective, it was a compulsion. Therefore, instead of withdrawing from the Ardennes as the members of his High Command advised, Hitler ordered a new assault. To command it, he appointed SS General Heinrich Himmler, a man other generals considered totally unqualified.

Under Himmler's direction, eight divisions attacked in the Saar on 2 January, and the following day nine divisions made an all-out assault on Bastogne. These forces were Hitler's last reserves, and both desperate attempts failed.

By that time, a British-American counterattack had begun from the north, and in mid-January what remained of the German divisions had no other option but to pull back to where they had been at the beginning of the offensive some weeks before. Now totally exhausted, with their ranks thinned and equipment destroyed, they would be unable to stop the ineluctable might that was aligned against them.

Nonetheless, the Führer continued to rave about carrying the fight to the enemy. He howled that he would crush their will by sending more V-1 and V-2 rockets into London, and then he would fire rockets against the Soviets. He would smite his opponents with jet aircraft and with secret weapons he had not yet revealed. To the members of his staff it sounded like the babbling of a madman, which is what it was. Hitler had become delusional, and his failure to grasp reality had cost his nation dearly.

In the Battle of the Bulge, Germany lost 120,000 men killed and wounded. Six hundred tanks and 6,000 vehicles were destroyed. The Americans had suffered heavy losses as well: 8,000 killed, 48,000 wounded, 21,000 captured or missing, 733 tanks destroyed. The British and Canadians lost 1,400 dead. But there was a critical difference: the Allies, particularly the Americans, could restore their ranks with fresh troops and replenish their supplies and equipment, while the Germans could not. As a result, this was to be Hitler's last major offensive of World War II.

As for General Galland, Reichsmarschal Göring blamed him for the failure of the Luftwaffe in the air battles. Galland was summoned to a meeting at Luftwaffe headquarters in Berlin, and informed by Göring that he was being relieved as General of Fighters. The Luftwaffe's best commander was summarily fired.

PART VI

ARMAGEDDON

75.

Throughout the grim winter, air raids by the Allies on targets deep inside Germany continued without letup. And as before, the commanders of the RAF and the USAAF held markedly different views as to what the objectives should be.

Air Marshall Harris never wavered in his belief that Germany would be brought to her knees by area bombing of her population centers. Almost every night, Lancasters and Halifaxes dropped thousands of tons of high explosives on cities that had already been reduced to smoking ruins. Berlin, Frankfurt, Hamburg, Munich, Cologne, Düsseldorf, and many other places were subjected to the same devastating attacks, again and again. It was true that factories in those areas also sustained extensive damage or were destroyed. Nearly every city in Germany had industries whose output in one way or another contributed to the war effort.

But for German citizens, the bombing had an intensely personal impact. To them it was like living in hell. Since the attacks might occur at any time during the night, sleep was next to impossible; people never knew whether they would live to see the morning.

When the great fleets of bombers arrived, the alarms would fill the air with their mournful wail, and people would be forced to go down into the underground shelters. If they did not, they chanced being killed by the explosions, or crushed by falling buildings, or incinerated by the raging fires. So they huddled in the cold, damp concrete vaults, bleary-eyed and shivering, while the earth trembled from the violent shocks.

In the daytime, conditions were no better. Daytime was when the Flying Fortresses, Liberators, and Marauders showed up. Again the sirens would send people scurrying to the shelters, and the Americans would add to the misery by dumping their own vast loads of explosives. In addition to the hazards imposed by the bombing, there were shortages of food and medicine. In the winter many families had little to eat, and no coal to heat their homes. Weakened by malnutrition and exhaustion, people died from pneumonia, influenza, and other diseases.

And yet, except when curtailed by bad weather, the aerial attacks never abated. Night after night the bombers came, raining death and destruction while flak batteries sent streams of shells up into the sky. Dawn brought a brief respite, while firefighters grappled with the blazing wreckage, and medics did what they could to treat the wounded. Then at midday, more bombers added to the horror. No wonder people readily adopted Goebbels' term, referring to the enemy airmen as *terrorfliegers*.

Unlike the RAF, the USAAF continued to advocate pinpoint bombing, maintaining it would cripple key German industries, thereby bringing the war to an end. The Americans claimed the Norden bombsight enabled them to drop two-thousand pounders straight down the factories' smokestacks. But in fact, the Norden was not nearly as accurate as the air commanders said it was. Bombardiers found it difficult to make calculations while flak was bursting around them, or when their aircraft were being fired upon by enemy fighters. Sometimes they were wounded, or the bombers were thrown off course by exploding 88mm shells. As a result, the bombs frequently missed their targets altogether, sometimes by miles. And just as often the misdirected explosives fell on German civilians.

For all that, it was the bombing by the Americans that had the desired effect. Although only an estimated 25 percent of U.S. bombs struck the targeted factories, that was enough to deal German manufacturers a severe blow. Production was drastically slowed, and in many instances brought to a halt.

An exception was the German aircraft industry. With airplanes being assembled in subterranean factories, and in forests, caves and mountain tunnels, the output held steady, and in some cases actually increased. Bf-109s and Fw-190s in particular were produced in near-record numbers.

The problem now was that there were fewer pilots to fly the planes, and less fuel to run their engines. It was by reducing the availability of fuel, that the American 8th and 15th Air Forces were able to hammer the last nails into the Luftwaffe's coffin. By the end of January, the German refineries were producing less than one fourth the amount of high-octane petrol they'd been turning out a year earlier. Therefore, many fighter units had rows of new airplanes hidden beneath camouflage nets, but the nearby fuel storage tanks were empty.

Thus, the Luftwaffe could put up only small numbers of fighters against the enormous fleets of Allied bombers and their escorts. The ratio was often fifteen to one, and in many raids the German defenses consisted of flak alone.

When the Luftwaffe aircraft did go up, they found it increasingly difficult to penetrate the enemy fighter screen. In defending against a daylight raid by the Americans, forty or fifty German fighters would be pursued by hundreds of Mustangs and Thunderbolts whose pilots were eager to claim victories.

As General Galland pointed out, the jagdwaffe had lost 300 pilots in the Ardennes offensive alone. And in the preceding year more than a thousand others had been killed, including many staffelkapitäns and geschwader commanders. Now, many of the German airmen had only limited experience, and often they were easy pickings for the American and British fighter pilots.

Among the German night fighters, the problems were even more severe; aircraft like the He-219, the Ju-88 and the Bf-110 required great skill to fly in combat at night. Teaching aerial navigation and radar approaches took time, and time was a luxury the Germans did not have. On the ground there were growing difficulties as well. The offensives in the west and in the east caused a critical shortage of soldiers, and to replace those killed and wounded, the army pulled men from Luftwaffe ground crews and sent them to combat units as riflemen.

In their place, more women were pressed into service. On every Luftwaffe base they worked as mechanics, armorers and radio technicians. Many were young and attractive, showing off their charms in tight-fitting black coveralls. That was fine with the pilots, and the women were happy to keep the airmen's morale up. At night they shared the pilots' bountiful supplies of champagne and brandy, and often their beds as well. The pilots called them blitz girls.

But the women were a rare bright note. The men had plenty of problems to gripe about, such as abuse from the Reichsmarschal, the lack of fuel, and flying with inadequately trained replacement pilots. The youngsters coming from the flight schools lasted an average of three missions before being killed.

Confusion at the Air Ministry did not help. How to fight back against the bombers was an unending debate, for which there was never a shortage of hare-brained ideas.

One proposal called for Ju-88s to fly above the enemy bombers and release heavy lengths of chain down onto them. In theory the chains would foul the bombers' propellers, causing them to crash. This never went beyond the discussion stage.

Another idea called for German aircraft to drop bombs on the bombers. It was actually tried, but the bomb carriers were shot down before they could get into position.

Still another brainstorm called for Ju-88s to be equipped with howitzers. One of the huge guns would be mounted in the fuselage with the barrel pointed downward, and in this scheme the cannoneers would fly above the bombers. One shot, it was argued, would be enough to destroy any B-17 or B-24. Like many others, the idea never got off the ground.

A concept that did fly was the Natter Viper. A stubby, rocket-powered, single-seat interceptor with 2,000 kg of thrust, it was armed with either 24 spin-stabilized 73mm Fohn rockets or 33 R4M 55mm rockets. The Viper also bore an explosive charge that could be set off by ramming an enemy aircraft. The project got as far as the construction of several prototypes, but only one of them was flown, and only once. It crashed shortly after takeoff and the pilot was killed.

In the face of all this, Reichsmarschal Göring remained as intransigent as ever. Germany had the best fighter in the world, but he refused to use it. Instead, he kept large numbers of Me-262s in reserve, to be used as bombers.

At the same time, more pilots from bomber squadrons were transferred to newly formed Me-262 units. Two of the units, I/(ERG)KG(J) at Pilsen and II/(ERG)KG(J) at Neuberg, were used for training. Five others were to be operational. Those were KG(J)6 at Prague, KG(J)27 at Marchtrenk, KG(J)30 at Smirschitz, KG(J)at Giebelstadt, and KG(J)55 at Landau. All were part of the Reichsmarschal's bomber reserve.

To the fighter pilots, this was idiotic. It was bad enough that Göring berated them publicly, accusing them of cowardice while he praised those in the bomber command. But for him to deny them the one weapon they were sure would enable them outfight the enemy, was unconscionable.

When they could stand it no longer, five of the Luftwaffe's top pilots decided to take action. They formed a group and petitioned Göring to be heard, so that they could tell Der Dicke to his face what they thought of his orders.

76.

All five of the pilots had been decorated by the Führer. The ringleader was Oberst Günther "Franzl" Lützow, who had shot down 108 enemy aircraft beginning with the war in Spain. One of the others was Oberst Johannes "Macky" Steinhoff, who had taken command of JG7, having achieved 170 victories thus far. Another was Oberst Hannes Trautloft, who like Lützow had fought with the Condor Legion in Spain. His record now stood at 560 combat missions and 58 victories. Then there was Oberst Eduard Neumann, who had also flown in Spain, and later in North Africa; at the present time "Edu" was Commander of Fighters in Northern Italy. The fifth pilot was Oberst Gustav Rödel, who had been Adolf Galland's wingman in the Battle of Britain. He'd flown hundreds of missions in defense of the homeland, and had a record, at this point, of 98 victories.

On 19 January, a cold, slushy day, the five went to Haus Der Flieger, the Luftwaffe headquarters building in Berlin. They were shown into a conference room, where they waited for an hour before Göring would see them. When at last the Reichsmarschal arrived, he was accompanied by his adjutant and General Koller, and by two general staff officers and two stenographers. The five pilots leaped to their feet and saluted.

They were struck by the changes in Göring's appearance. His body was as obese as ever, but the face was not the one they had seen in the past. In Steinhoff's description, "It was a weary face, bloated and with folds like an old woman's falling from the mouth to the double chin, which in turn folded over the pale blue uniform collar encircling the massive neck. His flaccid skin showed traces of pink powder."

Lützow was the spokesman. He distributed copies of a memorandum that laid out the points the pilots wanted to make. Then he launched into his speech.

He began politely enough, but his words soon became heated. In a loud voice he said the pilots of the Jagdwaffe were tired of being unfairly accused of lacking courage. He said they still had the means of putting an end to the reign of terror by the Allied bombers, if only the Reichsmarschal would release all the Me-262s for service as fighters. What's more, Lützow went on, the Jadgwaffe should always be led by men of long experience and great ability. Therefore, it had been a very serious mistake to dismiss General Galland from his position as General of Fighters.

Even though he must have suspected this was coming, Göring's jaw dropped. Never before had an officer shown the audacity to speak to him in this fashion. He slammed a meaty hand down on the table and began to interrupt.

But Lützow refused to let him. In an even louder voice, the colonel said that the Jagdwaffe would no longer stand for fully manned bomber units, such as the IXth Corps, being held in reserve and fitted out with jet aircraft while what was left of the Jagdwaffe bled to death. The pilots in the reserve bomber units should be placed under experienced Jagdwaffe officers at once.

For Göring, this was too much. "You fighter pilots," he said, "there's no system to the way you fight. You haven't trained your pilots to go right up to the bombers and give them no quarter. When I think back to the war in Flanders . . ."

Lützow would not back down. He said the Reichsmarshal seemed to forget that the fighter pilots had been flying missions for more than five years. During that time they'd been shoved around like Gypsies, going from one theater to another while their ranks grew ever thinner. The important thing was for the bomber groups to be transferred to Fighter Command. That was vital for the nation's air defense, if it wasn't already too late.

By now Göring was nearly apoplectic. "Transfer them? That's exactly what I'm not going to do! I'd be a fool not to keep this powerful, magnificent reserve for the moment when I decide to strike the decisive blow. You want the Me-262, but you're not going to get it because I'm giving it to the people who know what to do with it, namely my bomber pilots."

Lützow shot back: "And you, sir, have simply ignored the existence of the enemies' four-engine bombers completely. You've given us no new aircraft, no new weapons!"

"How dare you?" Göring shouted. He glared at the pilots. "Instead of sitting on your asses hatching plots you should be with your units, leading them against the enemy!"

He picked up a copy of the memorandum. "What is this preposterous rubbish, funny little bits of paper with so-called points of discussion written on them. What you're presenting me with is mutiny!" He tossed the memorandum aside. "It's absolutely monstrous," he went on, "that you should conspire behind my back to pursue devious paths that represent a grave infringement of your duty as soldiers and your obligation of loyalty to me. I shall take appropriate action!"

Struggling for breath, the Reichsmarschal got to his feet. He pointed a pudgy finger. "You, Lützow! I'll have you shot!"

With that he stormed out of the room.

77.

Over the next few days the mutineers waited nervously for the Reichsmarschal to carry out his threats. And one by one, the pilots were dealt their punishment.

Neumann was curtly informed that he was no longer Commander of Fighter Pilots in northern Italy. In fact, he now had no job at all.

Lützow was not shot. Instead he was sent to Italy, to take over Neumann's former command. He was also forbidden to contact General Galland or any of his fellow conspirators.

Oberst Steinhoff was summarily removed from his command of JG7. His replacement was Major Theodor Weissenberger, who came over from JG5.

Both Rödel and Trautloft were relieved of their duties and not reassigned. Thus the abilities of five of the most experienced pilots in the Luftwaffe were to be wasted.

The Reichsmarschal's paranoia did not stop there. Suspecting that the mutiny had been secretly planned by Adolf Galland, Göring had him exiled from Berlin. Galland was replaced, as General of Fighters, by Oberst Gordon Gollob. All fighter units were informed by teleprinter of Galland's dismissal, and that, as far as the Reichsmarschal was concerned, was the end of the uprising.

Meanwhile, Allied bombers continued to hit their targets, meeting only slight resistance from the Jagdwaffe. The German fighters were badly handicapped by an ever-diminishing supply of fuel. The only oil fields still in German hands were those in Hungary, and with Silesia lost and the Ruhr in ruins, coal production was one-fifth of what it had been a year earlier.

Only the Me-262s had adequate supplies of fuel, because their turbojets ran on J2, instead of the high-octane petrol required by piston engines. J2 was produced from torbanite, shale and bituminous coal, of which larger amounts were available. Thus the Me-262s could fly more frequently.

In combat, however, misuse of the jets went on as before. The pilots of KG(J)51 and KG(J)54 had all come from bomber units, where they had flown Ju-88s and He-111s. They knew multi-engine and instrument flying, but next to nothing about fighter tactics. Many were lost.

The action on 9 February was typical. A fleet of 1,100 B-17s and B-24s, escorted by 700 P-51s, flew a mission to bomb Zwickau. The target was the site of factories that once had produced the Horch and Audi automobiles, and were now building tanks. KG(J)51 scrambled ten Me-262s to intercept the raiders.

At 8,000 meters above Fulda, American fighter pilots saw the jets and swung toward them. But Oberstleutnant Volprecht Freiherr zu Eisenach circled around behind a Fortress in the lead group, and rapidly overtook the heavy aircraft. He fired a burst from his cannons, and as the B-17 fell, six crewmen bailed out, their parachutes white dots in the gray sky.

Eisenach's satisfaction did not last long. He made the mistake of executing a wide, sweeping turn away from the bombers, and one of the Mustangs turned inside him. Captain Donald Bochkay of the 357th Fighter Group led the jet perfectly, and caught it with a stream of .50 caliber bullets. Eisenach was killed, and his burning aircraft crashed near Limburg.

Several other German pilots committed the same type of error, and paid for it the same way. USAAF Lieutenant John Carter, also of the 357th, shot down two more of the jets, and Lieutenant S.C. Ananian of the 359th Fighter Group destroyed another. A minute later Major Robert Foy of the 357th scored hits on an Me-262 flown by Gruppen-kommandeur Major Ottfried Sehrt. Carter then closed in for the kill.

Sehrt tried to outrun Carter's Mustang, but his aircraft had lost one engine and the other was smoking. The jet shuddered from the impact of additional hits, and Sehrt blew off his canopy and bailed out. Dazed from being slammed by the wall of air, he pulled his ripcord and drifted to earth near Frankfurt. Three more jets joined the scuffle, and Oberleutnant Günther Kahler and Oberleutnant Walter Draht were also killed. Major Sehrt was one of the few survivors that day. For KG(J)51, the battle was a disaster.

The pilots of KG(J)54 fared no better. They lost many of their aircraft, because they too came from bomber squadrons and were not trained to fly fighters in combat. They engaged vastly superior numbers of Mustangs, and many were killed. In marked contrast, JG7 under Major Weissenberger was now fully operational, and staffed by experienced fighter pilots. The Jagdgeschwader had three gruppe of aircraft, plus fuel, ammunition, spare parts and support personnel.

On the same day as the calamitous battle at Fulda, Weissenberger's staffel of 12 aircraft attacked a flight of 850 Fortresses that were escorted by 500 fighters. Despite the odds, the jets waded into the Mustangs, determined to get past them and on to the bombers.

By now the American fighter pilots had developed tactics of their own for engaging Me-262s. One of the most effective was for several Mustangs to cut off a jet, forcing it to turn and giving others a shot at it. As always, they were aided by their ability to turn more tightly than the faster enemy aircraft. Another maneuver the Americans used to good advantage was the split-S. From a greater height they would roll the Mustang over onto its back and dive at high speed on the jet. With luck they would then be in position to open fire on it.

On this day the Mustangs did a good job of preventing the Me-262s from getting at the bombers. The Me-262s' limited range meant they had enough fuel for no more than a few minutes of combat; consequently, the longer the escorts could keep the enemy away from the B-17s, the better.

One Mustang pilot, however, failed to see a jet closing on him from behind. The pilot was Captain Browning of the 357th Fighter Group. His wingman yelled a warning, but it was too late. Leutnant Karl Schnörrer fired his cannons from 250 meters, and Browning's aircraft blew up.

Meantime, a few of the jets did manage to penetrate the fighter screen. One was flown by Leutnant Rudolf Rademacher, who earlier in the war had recorded 81 victories in Bf-109s. He had also been a member of Kommando Nowotny before joining JG7. Rademacher had a different view of how to mount an attack. While it was generally agreed that the best way to approach a Fortress was from the rear, many pilots backed off the throttles when doing so, fearing that if they didn't their speed would carry them past the objective before they could get strikes. As a result, they gave away much of their speed advantage and became easier targets for both the bomber's machine guns and the vengeful Mustangs.

Rademacher, however, followed Eder's example and attacked from the rear at full speed. He picked out a B-17 in one of the lead boxes, and as it loomed larger in his gun sight he fired all four of the Borsigs. The tracers punched into the bomber's tail, and it began to burn. Rademacher then pulled back the stick and zoomed upward. Some of the Mustangs attempted to follow him, but he was quickly out of range, approaching the jet's ceiling of 11,450 meters. Next he dove and made the same type of pass on another B-17. The big bomber fell out of the formation, its number one and number two engines pouring black smoke.

Rademacher's fuel gauges told him he was finished for the day, and he headed back to base. The other pilots of the Staffel were not through, however. Hauptmann Eder and Oberleutnant Günther Wegmann each shot down a B-17. Then they too were forced to break off contact with the enemy because they were running low on fuel.

In all, it had been a successful operation for JG7. But the irony was that they had downed a mere four Fortresses out of the hundreds that took part in the raid on Berlin.

78.

At this point General Eisenhower had 85 superbly equipped divisions under his command. They were rapidly closing on the Rhine, and a steady flow of replacement troops, tanks, ammunition, and supplies made them virtually unstoppable.

The German commander, Feldmarschal von Rundstedt, wanted to pull his battered forces back across the wide river. The Rhine would provide a natural defensive line, and there would be time for his troops to reorganize and be refitted.

Hitler refused to allow it. Obsessed as always with the idea that only offensive action was acceptable, he ordered Rundstedt to stand and fight. It was as if the Germans were caught in an enormous meat grinder. By the end of February the Wehrmacht had lost another 350,000 men, including 293,000 taken prisoner.

The situation in the east was equally bleak. Field marshal Zhukov's forces had captured Warsaw and then thrust deep into Prussia, and were now only 80 kilometers from Berlin. Firing thousands of Katyusha rockets and blasting the Germans with heavy artillery and the cannons of their T-34 tanks, the red troops drove the defenders back. They burned, pillaged and raped as they cut a swath of destruction through the Fatherland.

Among some British and American politicians, there was reluctance to go on punishing German civilians by bombing them. The end of the war was clearly in sight, and it made little sense to kill innocent people, but others disagreed. Proponents of bombing claimed that now was the time to strike the deathblow against the Nazis—if German civilians died in the attacks, so be it. Civilian deaths would only prompt their leaders to capitulate sooner.

Joseph Stalin was adamantly in favor of this strategy. At a conference with Churchill and Roosevelt in the Black Sea port of Yalta, the Soviet dictator demanded that the bombing be not only continued, but intensified. Moreover, he wanted Dresden added to the target list, reasoning that it would make it impossible for the Germans to circumvent the other centers by rerouting the troop trains.

In reality, the only trains passing through Dresden were those transporting evacuees away from the eastern battle zones. Even though Allied Intelligence had determined that the ancient city had no significant military value, Churchill and Roosevelt went along, and ordered an attack on Dresden by the combined air forces.

RAF Air Marshal "Bomber" Harris was eager to oblige. He planned a heavy assault on the city, and RAF briefing notes said the attack would "show the Russians what Bomber Command can do."

The first raid was carried out by the RAF early in the evening of 13 February 1945, when 796 Lancasters and nine Mosquitos dropped 1,478 tons of high explosive, and 1,183 tons of incendiary bombs on the city. A second attack took place three hours later, when 529 Lancasters dropped 1,800 additional tons. Nine Lancasters were lost in the two raids.

The following day, it was the Americans' turn. Three hundred B-17s dropped 771 tons of high explosives on the city, using the railroad yards as the aiming point. A few Bf-109s from a Luftwaffe base near Dessau put up a spirited defense, but six of them were shot down by American fighters, and the others were forced to break off when they ran low on fuel. The 8th Air Force lost three bombers in the attack, and no fighters. And according to RAF records, some of the Mustangs were ordered to strafe traffic on the roads around the city.

By this time in the war, the Allies had refined their bombing techniques to achieve total destruction systematically. The methods had been learned earlier in raids on such places as Hamburg and Cologne, and now in Dresden they were followed to the letter. First, the high-explosive bombs blew the roofs off buildings. Next, the incendiaries were dropped into the interiors, setting them afire. Then the whole process was repeated, in order to destroy the fire-fighting crews and their apparatus.

On 15 February the American bombers returned, and repeated the same type of attack. The raids were hideously effective, creating a vast firestorm with temperatures reaching 1,500 degrees Centigrade. The mass of superheated air rose rapidly, and as it did, cooler air from outside the city rushed in and sucked people into the fire.

One survivor, a woman named Margaret Freyer, remembered:

> The firestorm is incredible, there are calls for help and screams from somewhere but all around is one single inferno. To my left I suddenly see a woman. I can see her to this day and shall never forget it. She carries a bundle in her arms. It is a baby. She runs, she falls, and the child flies in an arc into the fire. Suddenly, I see people again, right in front of me. They scream and gesticulate with their hands, and then to my utter horror and amazement I see how one after the other they simply seem to let themselves drop to the ground. Today I know that these unfortunate people were the victims of lack of oxygen. They fainted and then were burnt to cinders. Insane fear grips me and from then on I repeat one simple sentence to myself continuously: I don't want

to burn to death. I do not know how many people I fell over. I know only one thing, that I must not burn.

Another survivor, Lothar Metzger, also had a vivid recollection:

We saw the burning street, the falling ruins and the terrible firestorm. My mother covered us with wet blankets and coats she found in a water tub. We saw terrible things: cremated adults shrunk to the size of small children, pieces of arms and legs, whole families burnt to death, burnt coaches filled with civilian refugees, dead rescuers and soldiers. Women were calling and looking for their children. Fire was everywhere, and the hot wind of the firestorm threw people back into the burning houses they were trying to escape from.

Still another survivor was Otto Sailer-Jackson, a keeper at the Dresden Zoo. He too recalled the horror:

The elephants gave spine-chilling screams. The baby cow elephant was lying in the narrow barrier-moat on her back, her legs up in the sky. She had suffered severe stomach injuries and could not move. A 90 cwt. cow elephant had been flung clear across the barrier moat and the fence by some terrific blast wave, and stood there trembling. I had no choice but to leave these animals to their fate. I had known for one hour now that the most difficult task fate could ever bring was facing me. 'Lehmann, we must get to the carnivores,' I called. We did what we had to do, but it broke my heart.

Many RAF crew members were appalled as well. Roy Akehurst, a radio operator in a Lancaster, remembered:

It struck me at the time, the thought of the women and children down there. We seemed to fly for hours over a sheet of fire, a terrific red glow with thin haze over it. I found myself making comments to the crew: 'Oh God, those poor people.' It was completely uncalled for. You can't justify it.

In all, the bombing virtually wiped out the city. More than 78,000 dwellings were destroyed, along with thousands of buildings, including hotels, banks, churches, factories, theaters, shops, administrative buildings, warehouses, schools, and post offices. Nineteen hospitals ceased to exist.

But the worst losses were human. No one knows how many people were killed or wounded. The best estimate puts the dead at about 35,000, with perhaps 300,000 others injured. Among the casualties were thousands of Allied prisoners of war, including many Americans.

Yet the raids did not end. On 2 March, 406 B-17s dropped another 940 tons of high explosives and 141 tons of incendiaries on the ruined city. And it still wasn't over. On 17 April, with the end of the war only three weeks away, B-17s struck once more. In that attack, 580 B-17s dropped 1554 tons of HE and 165 tons of incendiaries on still-smoldering Dresden.

In Berlin, Josef Goebbels made the most of the city's destruction, describing it as the most barbaric in history. His Propaganda Ministry claimed that the total number of deaths exceeded 300,000. Photos of the horribly burned dead were circulated, including many showing the corpses of children. Air Marshall Harris was described as the author of the atrocity, and the man most responsible for the campaign of terror bombing. As reports of the attacks and their effects reached Allied political leaders, many expressed outrage. And many who had endorsed the scorched-earth strategy now backed away; Sir Winston Churchill was one of them.

Hitler's reaction revealed his deteriorating mental condition. He stumbled about in a blind rage, shouting that he would take revenge by using every possible means to destroy Germany's foes, including his miracle weapons.

Few such weapons existed. By now the V-1s and the V-2s were no longer a threat; the U.S. Army had destroyed most of the launching sites as it drove through France and Belgium. Another miracle weapon, the Me-163 Komet, had turned out to be largely ineffective. Though the Komet carried five tons of fuel, the fuel was quickly exhausted, burning it 17 times faster than a turbojet. Allied fighter pilots soon caught on to the Komets' vulnerability, and chased them down and destroyed them.

In casting about for other weapons, the Führer asked about the Me-

262s. Reichsmarschal Göring brought him up to date on their exploits in attacking enemy bombers, and Hitler then wanted to know what part Adolf Galland had played. Göring had no choice but to tell him Galland had been dismissed from his position as General of Fighters, and that at the present had no assignment.

That induced another fit of fury. "Stop this nonsense at once!" Hitler roared. "Give Galland a unit!"

79.

Hermann Göring owned a number of sumptuous residences, including the Veldenstein castle in Bavaria and the Mautemdorf castle in Austria. But his family home was Karinhalle, the hunting lodge he'd built on a vast tract of heavily forested land near Friedrichwalde, 80 kilometers north of the capital. The estate was named after Karin von Kantzow, his first wife, who died in 1931 at age 42. Göring lived there with his second wife, Emmy, and their daughter Edda.

The term hunting lodge was a misnomer. Although the architecture was traditional German, with thick walls faced in stucco and a steep roof of dark gray slate, it would be more accurate to call the place a palace. The huge structure was furnished with priceless antiques, tapestries, and paintings looted from all over Europe, and it contained so much booty that many of its treasures had to be stored in a separate wing. Karin was entombed in a stone mortuary in the garden.

When Adolf Galland reported there on a cold wet day near winter's end, he already knew why Göring had summoned him. One of Hitler's adjutants had confided to him that on orders from the Führer, he was to be reactivated. It would be interesting to see how the Reichsmarschal handled the situation.

Karinhalle was heavily staffed with Luftwaffe enlisted personnel who worked as Göring's servants. One of them saluted Galland and took his coat and cap, and led him into a room furnished with leather sofas and chairs. Persian rugs covered the floor, and logs were blazing in a great stone fireplace. Galland took in the array of mounted animal heads that hung on the walls, and the glass eyes of deer, stag, bears, lions, leopards, as well as a cape buffalo, that stared back at him. He dropped the stub of his cigar into an ashtray.

The Reichsmarschal appeared a few minutes later and greeted

Galland with a perfunctory Heil Hitler. Galland noted that the fat man did not look well; his face was bloated and there were dark shadows under his eyes. Göring's attire, however, was cheerful. It was one of his informal getups: a white silk blouse with puffy sleeves, an embroidered vest, olive-green knee britches and shiny black boots. His belly seemed more protuberant than ever.

Göring poured Cognac for both of them, his manner casual and friendly. He raised his snifter. "Prost!"

"Prost!" Galland responded. He swallowed some of the fiery liquid, and found it very good. But he would have been amazed if it weren't.

Göring then opened a humidor, and offered it to his visitor. Inside were fine Canary Island cigars. Galland chose one and lighted it. He blew out a stream of fragrant smoke and waited once more.

Göring announced that he had made a decision. After giving careful consideration to Galland's record, not only as a great fighter pilot but also as an outstanding commander, he had resolved to take no further action against him. In fact, he had rescinded the grounding order. He was sure the general had learned his lesson, and thereafter would be loyal to the Luftwaffe and its leader. It was obvious to Galland that Göring was pretending to be the stern but generous judge. Galland replied that he had always tried to serve the air force and the Fatherland to the best of his ability.

Next, Göring said he recalled Galland's belief in the fighting value of the Me-262. Therefore he'd decided that the general should form a new unit, which would be equipped with the jet fighters. The unit would be completely independent, and Gordon Gollob, the new General of Fighters, would have no jurisdiction over it. In fact, the unit would be under no jurisdiction of division, corps, or fleet. Galland could choose his own pilots.

Now Galland was genuinely surprised. He'd expected to be given a new command, but this was considerably more than that. He said he would begin putting the unit together at once.

Göring wasn't finished. He suggested the rebellious pilots who were now unassigned could join Galland's new command. Lützow, for example, and Steinhoff. "You can have those two right away," Göring said. "And anyone else you want."

Galland said that was an excellent idea. Lützow and Macky Steinhoff were among the best who'd ever flown for the Luftwaffe.

Neumann, Rödel, and Trautloft were outstanding as well. Leading pilots like that against the enemy in an independent unit, equipped with jets, would be the fulfillment of a dream.

But Galland had no illusions as to Göring's true motivation. The Reichsmarschal had devised a clever scheme that would enable him to follow Hitler's order, and at the same time rid himself of a group of troublemakers.

Put Galland and the others into Me-262s and send them into combat? That was a good way, Der Dicke must have figured, to get them all killed.

Galland raised his snifter and drained the contents. It really was excellent Cognac.

80.

The pilots assigned to JV44 were delighted to join a new unit led by General Galland. Especially pleased was Macky Steinhoff, who believed the assignment would bring his career back to life. But the rest were not the men Göring had generously promised Galland, possibly due to administrative mistakes, or a mixup in orders. Whatever the reason, the so-called conspirators failed to arrive, and instead, Galland was supplied with pilots who were young and inexperienced. Some had suffered wounds in combat, and left hospital beds determined to fly with Galland. Only a few, like Major Karl-Heinz Schnell, whose record stood at 72 kills, were veterans.

For Galland, pilot staffing was only one hurdle. Assembling aircraft, equipment, and ground personnel was difficult as well. Capable technicians, tools, and parts were hard to come by, and strafing by enemy aircraft made it all but impossible to move materiel on the roads, except at night.

The squadron was based near Brandenburg, a town 40 kilometers west of Berlin. JG7 was on the same field, which was large and well camouflaged. Galland pulled strings to get as many Me-262s delivered to him as possible, but he didn't have nearly enough, even though the hidden factories were rapidly turning them out. Too many, in the general's opinion, were still being sent to the bomber wings, KG(J)51, and KG(J)54.

Galland relied heavily on Steinhoff. An outstanding pilot, Macky had also commanded a geschwader. Together they went about whipping the outfit into shape, with Galland as the CO and Steinhoff in charge of training pilots.

Despite the problems, morale was excellent. The atmosphere was even more relaxed than in most units of the Luftwaffe, and the pilots paid little attention to military discipline. They were also smartly dressed. Thanks to Galland's connections, everyone was issued brand-new uniforms. The pilots wore gray leather jackets with velvet collars, leather-trimmed breeches, and fur-lined boots. Yellow silk scarves were knotted around their necks, and their black pistol belts and holsters carried pristine Walther P-38s.

But living conditions were very different from those in the past. The airmen bunked in ramshackle barracks, and the senior officers were quartered in small houses nearby. Galland and Steinhoff, whose rank had once entitled them to occupy luxurious flats, each had one room. Though the food was also drab, consisting mostly of potatoes, cabbage and canned meats, there was plenty of beer, wine and brandy. At night the pilots were happy to share their beverages with the young women who worked on the base.

For Steinhoff, training the pilots was often exasperating, and on one occasion, it nearly cost him his life.

The flight was supposed to be routine. The man who was to fly with him was a Leutnant Blomert, who had come from a bomber squadron equipped with Ju-88s. He was eager to learn fighter tactics, but hadn't flown even rudimentary aerobatics since flight school. They took off and climbed to 3,000 meters, with Blomert in position as Steinhoff's wingman. Thin white layers of cirrostratus were far above them, and visibility was six-to-eight km in haze. Steinhoff turned to the east and flew over the capital.

Berlin was in ruins. Most of the buildings were shattered hulks with no roofs and blown-out walls. Smoke was rising from still-smoldering fires that had been set the night before when Mosquitos again dropped bombs.

Macky flew on, and minutes later saw the front lines, marked by pinpoints of light from artillery fire. It was hard to believe that the Soviet forces were now so near to Berlin. Steinhoff had known for a long time that the war could not be won, and yet the sight filled him with anger. He descended to get a better look at the action on the ground.

Suddenly from the left, a Yak fighter flashed across his bow, so close he almost rammed it. Startled, he turned and followed the enemy aircraft, trying to line up for a shot, but he had too much speed and went past it before he could draw a bead. He pulled back the stick and climbed steeply, and as he did another fighter swung behind him and fired its cannons. Tracers streaked over the jet's cockpit, missing his head by centimeters.

Damn it, where was Blomert? His would-be wingman had left him exposed, and if the Russian had aimed a hair lower Steinhoff would be dead by now. But he held the climb, and the jet's superior speed quickly took him out of range.

After that he circled over the lines, and far below he saw black shapes he recognized as Soviet fighter-bombers. They were Sturmoviks, and were bombing and strafing German army vehicles that were crawling along a shell-pocked road. Soldiers were leaping from their machines and diving into ditches to escape the murderous fire.

Steinhoff put the jet into a shallow descent and closed on one of the enemy aircraft. As the Sturmovik loomed larger, he placed the luminous spot in his gunsight on its fuselage and pressed the trigger. The Borsigs spit out a stream of shells that hit the Sturmovik squarely and tore it into flaming pieces.

Macky then began to look for another one, until Blomert's voice came through his headphones. His errant wingman said he was running low on fuel, and Steinhoff's own gauges told the same story. He turned to the west.

When he landed at Brandenburg and climbed out of the cockpit his uniform was soaked with sweat. Blomert was already on the ground, looking a bit sheepish. Steinhoff shook his head. JV44 had a long way to go before it would be ready for the important work of attacking American bombers. Its pilots needed a good deal more training, and as for today's little dustup, he had been lucky. He could only hope he would continue to be.

81.

Over at JG7, there were operational difficulties as well. The unreliability and short life of the turbojet engines made it hard for mechanics to keep the Me-262s flying. Three dozen aircraft were the most JG7 was able to put up at one time. As good as they were, 36 jets against a fleet of more than a thousand enemy bombers and fighters was hardly an equitable match, especially when American and British pilots were rapidly improving their tactics for fighting Me-262s. Also, many of the Allied wings were now based in France, and the shorter distance to Germany meant their aircraft could spend more time in combat.

On 22 February 1945, JG7 was severely tested. That day the Allies flew huge numbers of aircraft in support of its advancing armies, as well as B-17s that were assigned to bomb Berlin. In response, the Luftwaffe put up the jets of JG7, along with Bf-109s and Fw-190s from its dwindling fighter forces.

Thirty-four Me-262s took off, and following vectors provided by the ground controllers, the pilots flew a course of 181 degrees to intercept the heavies. At 4,000 meters over Stendal they sighted several hundred B-17s and their escorts; the bombers were then only about 80 km from Berlin. Among the jet pilots were two of JG7's boldest, Oberfähnrich Heinz Russel and Oberfeldwebel Hermann Buchner. With Buchner leading, they moved in to attack. As they did, P-51s of the 352nd, 363rd, and 364th Fighter Groups cut them off.

The first of the American fighters to reach the jets were 61 Mustangs of the 364th Group. Buchner opened his throttles and flashed through the mass of Mustangs, then climbed and turned back to line up on one of them. The fighter he picked out belonged to Lieutenant Cliff Hogan's section, and was flown by Lieutenant Francis Radley. Hogan saw Buchner's jet appear out of the sun, and called to his pilots to break. They did, but for Radley it was too late. Buchner's cannon shells hit his fuel tank, and the aircraft instantly became a mass of flames. It spun down through the clouds, and Radley was unable to get out.

Meanwhile Unteroffizier Hermann Notter took aim at a B-17 that was in the rearmost box. Ignoring the stream of machine-gun fire from the Fortress and others nearby, he waited until he was only a short distance from the enemy's tail. Then his cannon shells punched into the B-17 and set it on fire. Notter pulled up, hurtling over the stricken bomber and missing it by no more than a few meters. Wreathed in flames, the B-17 rolled over and fell out of the formation.

Notter didn't wait to see whether parachutes appeared. Instead, he quickly sighted in on another Fortress that was farther ahead in the formation. Again he fired, and again he got strikes. Fire erupted in that

B-17 as well, and it began spiraling downward, trailing a long column of black smoke.

Notter was not the only jet pilot to achieve multiple kills that day. Leutnant Hans Waldmann shot down a Mustang, and with the warning light on his fuel gauge glowing, he destroyed another. He then headed back to base.

But despite the resolve of the German pilots, only three B-17s were shot down, a ratio the USAAF High Command would always find acceptable. The bombers' escorts, on the other hand, took a much worse beating. Twenty-two P-51s were lost.

One of JG7's pilots was Oberfeldwebel Helmut Baudach, the young Bavarian who'd been a member of the original Ekdo unit. Baudach's record while flying a jet was five kills, all enemy fighters. Today he hoped to add a Fortress.

At 5,000 meters over Schonwalde-Niederbayern, Baudach's Me-262 was boxed in by Mustangs of the 352nd Group. He turned away, intending to go after the bombers, and as he did one of the P-51s hosed his airplane with .50-caliber machine-gun bullets. Damage to the jet was fatal, and Baudach rolled the crippled aircraft onto its back and popped the canopy. He unfastened his safety belt and dropped out of the cockpit. The Me-262 was still moving fast, and the vertical stabilizer struck his head. He fell dazed and bleeding for more than a thousand meters before pulling his ripcord. His chute opened and he landed in a field, where soldiers found him and took him to a hospital. He died a few hours later.

The day was not a good one for the fighter-bombers, either. One encounter involved a pair of Me-262s of 2/KG(J)51. The leader was Leutnant Kurt Piehl, who sighted an American armored column on the Pier-Düren highway near Aachen. The jets throttled back to bleed off speed, and swooped low to strafe the tanks and armored vehicles. Several of the targets blew up as the 30mm explosive projectiles found their mark.

At that point the Me-262s were themselves attacked. P-47 Thunderbolts of the 9th Air Force's 365th Fighter Group spotted the strafing jets far below, and the leader of White Flight, Lieutenant Oliver Cowan, dove to pounce on the enemy fighters. Cowen knew his adversaries were much faster than his P-47, so he opened his throttle wide and used water injection to push his speed to 530 mph. His machine-gun fire tore into

Leutnant Piehl's Me-262, and it crashed and burned. Piehl was killed, but the second jet escaped.

Three days later, P-51s of the 4th Fighter Group strafed antiaircraft batteries near Leipzig. The 88mm guns were mounted atop stone flak towers, and had been giving Allied aircraft hell. The Mustang pilots hoped to put the guns out of action. They'd been at it for a few minutes when one of the P-51 pilots, Lieutenant Carl Payne of 334th Squadron, caught sight of an Me-262 slightly above him at his one o'clock. Pushing the Mustang hard, Payne got close enough to let off a burst, and the jet became completely enshrouded in flames. It crashed near Debendorf, killing the pilot, Oberleutnant Josef Bohm of III/EJG2.

For KG(J)54, the day's disasters had not ended. Equipped with new jets, Gruppen I and II were ordered to bomb American armored units that were advancing toward the Rhine. The pilots were willing enough, but hardly any of them had been in combat—nor had they logged much time in Me-262s. Sixteen of the aircraft took off from their base at Giebelstadt, led by Leutnant Josef Lackner of 5 Staffel. After assembling, they began to climb through the clouds.

The pilots were in for a stunning surprise. A large flight of Mustangs of the 55th Fighter Group was directly overhead. As the jets began emerging from the cloud tops, the P-51 pilots could hardly believe what they were seeing. Their leader, Captain Donald Penn, shouted, "Drop tanks and engage!"

The Mustangs fell on the Me-262s like eagles after their prey. The inexperienced German airmen were bewildered to find themselves surrounded by more P-51s than they'd ever seen. They attempted to maneuver, but each was attacked by several Mustangs. Several of the jets were hit, though none fatally. Leutnant Lackner decided the best way to save his charges was to get them back into the clouds. He quickly dove, the others descending with him. They went through the cloud layer, and seconds later were once again below it in clear air.

But the Mustang pilots were not about to let them off the hook. They followed the Me-262s down, and Captain Penn saw that the pilot of one of them was trying to get his badly damaged aircraft to an airfield a short distance away. Penn knew that when jets were landing they were unable to accelerate rapidly, because their engines needed time to spool up. The Me-262 lowered its gear and made a left-hand turn toward the runway. Penn dove on the jet, and walked a stream of .50-

caliber tracers from its tail to its cockpit. The aircraft rolled onto its back and dove into the ground. The pilot who died in the fiery crash was Josef Lackner.

Other Mustang pilots were also scoring. Captain Donald Cummings attacked another jet whose pilot was attempting to land and caught it with a burst. The aircraft crashed on the runway, killing Feldwebel Klaus Heinz Clausner of 5 Staffel. Still another damaged jet tried to land and Captain Penn got that one as well. Lieutenant Donald Menegy claimed one damaged, and Lieutenant Billy Clemmons claimed another.

The same day a new Kommandeur, Major Hans-Georg Baetcher, arrived to take over III/JG(J)54, and found that there were only twenty aircraft left in the entire geschwader. His shattered unit was transferred to Prague-Ruzyne airfield in Czechoslovakia, and was never again a factor in the war.

Just as General Galland had warned, the Me-262 had once again proved to be totally ineffective as a bomber. In his view, the misuse of this magnificent machine was criminal, but he suspected that matters would soon grow worse.

82.

In the year 1945, spring arrived early in Germany. And with the mild weather came the mud. Worsening road conditions further hindered delivery of fuel and equipment to the various Luftwaffe fighter bases, but did little to hinder the advancing Allied armies. And it had no effect on the bombing campaign—the RAF and the U.S. 8th and 9th Air Forces attacked targets throughout Germany.

Yet, to General Galland's disgust, Göring continued to send most newly constructed Me-262s to KG(J)51 and 54 for service as bombers. Galland protested strongly, arguing that his unit could not fight without aircraft, but his objections were swept aside. Only one-fourth of all new jets were put into operation as fighters. A mere handful reached Galland's JV44.

By the first week in March, the American and British armies had totally crushed Rundstedt's forces, pushing to within a few kilometers of the Rhine. General Hodges, commander of the U.S. 1st Army, hoped to cross the river at Remagen. Only two bridges remained, the Germans having destroyed all the others. Spearheading Hodges' attack was the 9th Armored Division.

General George S. Patton was also moving rapidly. His Third Army had trapped the remains of eleven German divisions and taken thousand of prisoners. Now he too was driving hard toward the Rhine. Patton intended to have his engineers construct a pontoon bridge at Oppenheim, which was about 140 kilometers south of Remagen.

Hitler was furious over these developments. In a conference with Chief of Staff Guderian and other military advisers, he heaped scorn upon Feldmarschal Rundstedt, saying the commander's leadership in recent battles had been shamefully inept. The Führer announced that Rundstedt would be replaced by Feldmarschal Kesselring, who had put up such stubborn resistance in Sicily and in Italy.

The enemy must not cross the Rhine, Hitler thundered. No bridge is to remain standing! Any commander who fails to hold his position will be shot. And when enemy forces approach, they must be smashed by jet bombers!

When that last order was relayed to Göring, the Reichsmarschal readily complied, assigning KG(J)51 the job of attacking the advancing Allies. And for good measure, the Me-262s were to be joined by Arado jets of III/KG76. Long delayed by turbojet problems, the Arado Ar234B had only recently become operational—very few were flying, because the Junkers Jumo 004B engines were as unreliable as ever. Nevertheless, Major Hans-Georg Batcher, Kommandeur of III Gruppe, promised that his bombers would be ready.

On 7 March, tanks of the U.S. 9th Armored Division reached the banks of the Rhine at Remagen. The crews were surprised to find that the old Ludendorff railroad bridge, spanning the river, was undamaged. It was, however, wired for demolition. As American combat engineers rushed to sever the wires, a powerful charge went off, and then another. The explosions shook the old structure and blew pieces out of the piers, yet the bridge held together. Nevertheless, the 32-ton Sherman tanks would not be able to cross until the bridge was reinforced.

On the German side, none of the tanks and cannons Hitler had ordered to defend the bridge were anywhere near it, and neither were any German aircraft. There were, however, machine-gun emplacements and riflemen on the bank, and a storm of fire erupted from them. A number of American soldiers were hit, while others returned the fire with M-1s and BARs.

The firefight went on for hours, and the Americans were unable to advance. Then, as darkness was falling, they brought up bazookas. The rockets knocked out most of the German machine-gun crews, and as the smoke cleared, the Americans charged. A fierce hand-to-hand struggle took place, fought with rifles, pistols and trench knives. More than half the defenders were killed or wounded, and most of the survivors surrendered. A few disappeared into the forest.

Within the first 24 hours, 8,000 American troops crossed the bridge. The engineers worked feverishly to reinforce the piers, and soon the tanks crossed as well.

When the news reached Hitler, his response was to let fly with his usual howls of anger. And as usual, he blamed someone else for the debacle. This time it was Guderian, who later wrote a description of the Führer's reaction.

"His fists raised, his cheeks flushed with rage, his whole body trembling, he was beside himself with fury and had lost all self-control. His eyes seemed to pop out of his head and the veins stood out in his temples."

It wasn't the first time Guderian had seen Hitler in such a state, nor would it be the last. He stood at attention as the supreme commander raved on. "Why didn't you have the tanks and the cannons in place?" the Führer shouted. "And where were my jet bombers? Why is the bridge still standing? Have it destroyed at once! And court martial those officers who were supposed to blow it up! I want them executed!"

The next day, Major Hans Scheller, Major Herbert Strobel, Major August Kraft, and Leutnant Karl Heinz Peters were convicted of dereliction of duty and shot. And the jets were ordered to finish the job of destroying the bridge.

Thirty Me-262s of I/KG(J)51 and eight Ar234B bombers carried out the attack. By then the Americans had installed antiaircraft guns near the river, and they put up enough flak to disrupt the jets' efforts. The aircraft dropped bombs from an altitude of 3,000 meters, and not a single one landed close enough to do any damage.

Fifty Tempests of RAF 274 Squadron then reached the site. The big British fighters dove out of the sun at speeds approaching 500 mph, firing their 20mm Hispano cannons. Some of the Me-262s and Arados were damaged, and the pilots decided not to try dogfighting the fast,

heavily armed Tempests; instead, they opened their throttles and headed back to their bases.

To General Galland, and to JG7's Kommandeur, Major Weissenberger, the jets' bungling at Remagen once again showed the fallacy of
using them as bombers. Both men agreed that the Luftwaffe needed
more Me-262 fighters, along with a way to make them more efficient as
killers of viermots.

As it was, too many of the jets were being lost in combat against the
Fortresses and Liberators, and too many others were being destroyed on
the ground by bombs and strafing. Still others were being lost in accidents. Pilots were dying, and the old hands were impossible to replace.
Something had to be done about the problems. But what?

83.

General Gollob and other high-ranked Luftwaffe commanders said
losing Me-262s in combat was unfortunate, but losses were to be
expected. Especially when the jets were outnumbered in most battles by
a factor of at least fifty-to-one, and sometimes by one hundred-to-one.

Losses due to accidents, however, were another matter entirely. To
the consternation of the commanders, the accident rate among Me-262s
was extraordinarily high. Many of the mishaps could be traced to
engine failure, and some to structural faults, such as jamming of the tail-
adjustment mechanism. Others were due to mistakes made by the pilot.
But whatever the cause, the accidents were usually fatal.

The instructors tried hard to reduce pilot errors. Training was improved, with greater emphasis placed on the need to handle the controls
gently. An overly abrupt turn, it was explained, could starve a turbojet
of air, causing it to fail. Attempts to stretch an Me-262's range was
another mistake to be avoided. Some pilots crashed because, in the
frenzy of combat, they'd run the tanks dry. This led instructors to urge
closer monitoring of the aircraft's fuel supply. Pilots were also taught to
use the jet's speed to their advantage, rather than trying to fly the
machine as they would a piston fighter. Go fast, shoot, and get away.
Those were the keys to successful combat tactics in an Me-262.
Engaging in dogfights was discouraged.

Landings could also be hazardous. The glide ratio of a jet was much
shorter than that of a piston aircraft; therefore, closing the throttles

completely on final approach was forbidden. The engines had to provide just enough thrust to get the heavy machine onto the runway, which contributed to another difficulty: an Me-262 landed hot. The jet came over the threshold at 250 kph, much faster than a Bf-109 or an Fw-190. And instead of touching down on the mains and holding the nose up as long as possible on rollout, pilots sometimes committed the same old blunder of landing hard on all three wheels. That could collapse the nose gear, and often did.

But by far the major cause of accidents was engine failure. By the spring of 1945, Junkers had improved reliability somewhat, though the problem was never completely overcome. A turbojet would quit for no discernable reason, and often the failure would occur at the worst possible moment—when the jet was taking off, and its throttles were wide open. The engines would seem to be running perfectly, and then without warning one or both would either stop or flame out. The aircraft would crash, in most cases killing the pilot.

The engineers went on struggling to overcome the problem. Though they knew they were greatly handicapped by the lack of suitable metals, they also knew it was something they could do nothing about.

Meanwhile, Willy Messerschmitt was busy with designs for new aircraft. One was the Bf-109H, a beefed-up version of the venerable Gustav. The Air Ministry had tried to kill the project, but Messerschmitt stubbornly kept on with it. Other designs he was working on were jets that would be successors to the Me-262. They were designated the P-1101, P-1110, and P-1111. The first of them had already reached the stage of prototype construction, and a finished aircraft was scheduled for delivery to the Luftwaffe by the spring of 1946.

During this time the pressure on Messerschmitt was intense. He knew the war was lost, though refused to admit it. He was also aware of Hitler's deteriorating mental condition. In every respect the situation was hopeless, yet he tried to carry on as usual.

Stress continued to take a toll on him physically. He ignored his doctor's warnings, and smoked incessantly. And if not for the Baroness, he would have neglected to eat. Lilly saw to it that despite the shortages he had meals of meat and vegetables as well as fruit. And thanks to her, Hochried was a place of tranquility and comfort. With its elegant furnishings and its splendid views of the Alps, the villa was a different world from the hectic Messerschmitt complex at Oberammergau.

Shifting his headquarters to the small former army base had been a wise decision. In fact, the Allies never fully understood what went on there until after the war. Willy commuted to his office in his Mercedes, its tank filled with aviation gas. The trip took only about fifteen minutes, and on the way he thought about the challenges facing him.

One of the most important was the question of how to make the Me-262 more effective in combat against the enemy bombers. As always, he listened carefully to what pilots told him about their experiences in flying his airplanes. The greatest difficulty, they said, was getting the Me-262 close enough to a viermot to shoot it down without being shot down themselves.

Now in the middle of March, Messerschmitt was hoping that ballistics engineers might soon solve the problem. The weapon they were developing was a new air-to-air rocket, and unlike the missiles previously tested, this one showed promise. Its technical designation was the R4M. But the name given it by the engineers was the Orkan. If it worked as Messerschmitt hoped, the name would be appropriate. In German, Orkan meant hurricane.

84.

As with many innovations in aerial warfare, the R4M rocket was born of necessity. The Luftwaffe had determined that the Me-262's original armament of 20mm cannons was inadequate, inasmuch it took an average of 23 hits to down a B-17. That led to equipping the jet with 30mm Borsig MK 108s—it would take only three well-placed 30mm rounds to knock down a bomber.

The trouble was, many pilots had to reduce speed in order to aim accurately. The Borsigs had a relatively low muzzle velocity, which meant they had to be fired at close range, exposing pilots to the blizzard of machine-gun fire put out by bombers flying in a combat box. Larger cannons were tried, 50mm MK 103s, though they weren't suitable, either. The 103s had a higher muzzle velocity, but their weight and bulk reduced the aircraft's performance. So the Air Ministry ordered the ballistics experts at the Deutsche Waffen und Munitions Fabrik to push development of the R4M. The project was directed by Dr. Kurt Heber.

The first efforts were disappointing. The rockets were wildly inaccurate, as well as unstable. But knowing what was at stake, Heber and his group redoubled their efforts. The design they eventually settled on featured a simple steel tube that was a little less than one meter in length, with a solid-fuel rocket engine at one end and an impact-fused warhead at the other. It weighed 3.2 kg. Directional control was improved by fitting it with eight slender fins that popped out of the tail when it was fired.

Even then the Orkan was not truly accurate, but the theory was that if enough of them were fired at once into a formation of bombers, at least one was bound to strike a target. The 55mm warhead contained a powerful charge of Hexogen, and a single hit could destroy a heavy aircraft. Moreover, the rocket was effective up to 1,000 meters, which meant it could be fired a safe distance from the enemy's machine guns.

Willy Messerschmitt quickly saw the Orkan's potential. He supervised the installation of wooden racks that would enable an Me-262 to carry twelve of the missiles under each wing. That armament was in addition to the jet's four 30mm cannons. The pilot would have a choice of firing the rockets in salvos of six, or all 12 in each rack at the same time.

Tests were then conducted in the air. They showed that for the rockets to achieve the proper trajectory, the Me-262's nose should be raised slightly before firing. The best distance to the target was about 800 meters, which still would be outside the range of the enemy's machine guns. In all, the tests were highly encouraging, though the R4M had yet to see actual combat.

On 18 March 1945, the U.S. 8th Air Force sent three bomb divisions to attack Berlin. The fleet comprised 1,327 bombers escorted by 750 fighters. JG7 put up 37 Me-262s to intercept, led by the geschwader's commander, Major Weissenberger. None of the jets were armed with rockets.

Ten Me-262s made the first pass. Whipping through the screen of Mustangs, Weissenberger shot down a First Air Division Fortress with his cannons. Then he attacked another and downed that one as well. Leutnants Rademacher and Sturm, and Oberfeldwebel Lübking each destroyed a B-17, and Leutnant Schall picked off a Mustang.

The bombers' Initial Point was 20 kilometers west of Berlin, and as they approached it, four more jets attacked. One Fortress, flown by Lieutenant John Schwikert of the 457th Bomb Group, was shot down. Another was badly damaged, but Lieutenant Craig Greason brought it home on three engines and with part of his port wing gone. Four American gunners claimed to have damaged the attacking jets.

Then the R4M Orkan went into action for the first time. Six Me-262s armed with the rockets were scrambled from their base at Parchim, and directed by controllers to the enemy bombers. Members of JG7's 9 Staffel were led by Oberleutnant Günther Wegmann. The other pilots were Oberleutnant Karl-Heinz Seeler, Leutnant Karl Schnörrer, Oberfähnriche Walter Windisch, Oberfähnriche Günther Ulrich, and Fähnrich Friedrich Ehrig.

When the jets reached the bomber stream, they approached to the rear of the Third Division, which was over Rathenow and escorted by P-51s of the 359th Fighter Group. Günther Wegmann was the first to line up behind the formation of heavies. With mounting excitement, he punched the buttons that would send electric signals to the rockets and ignite them.

He was too anxious. Not waiting to aim with the Revi gunsight, and forgetting to raise his aircraft's nose, he fired salvo after salvo, emptying his racks. The Orkans were like fiery comets, emitting flames and black smoke as they streaked toward the viermots, yet because of Wegmann's haste, most of them missed.

One, however, struck home. The rocket drove into a B-17, exploding its cargo of bombs. A bright flash lit the air and other aircraft were rocked by the concussion. Wegmann was thrilled by his victory. Out of rockets, he pressed closer to the enemy and fired his cannons. He got strikes on the starboard wing of a Fortress, but as he flew past, .50-caliber bullets from other bombers sliced into his fighter. One shattered his cockpit canopy, and another smashed his instrument panel. A third bullet mangled his right knee.

Despite the pain, he retained control and descended below the stream of bombers. Enemy fighters pursued his damaged jet, intent on finishing him off, but he used his speed to pull away from them. He leveled off at 4,000 meters and turned northwest, heading back toward Parchim. Moments later his starboard engine burst into flame. In agony from his wounded knee and scorched by the rapidly spreading fire, he closed the throttles and bailed out. He counted to ten and pulled his ripcord.

He landed hard, in a field near Wittenberge. A farmer found his battered, unconscious body, and summoned a Red Cross nurse. She

stanched the bleeding and got him to a hospital, where a surgeon ampu-
tated his leg. He lived, but never flew again.

The other rocket-equipped jets also made successful attacks that
day. Ehrig, Ulrich and Schnörrer were more circumspect than Wegmann, firing their missiles from a distance of about 600 meters. Each of
them scored a victory over a B-17. Seeler, on the other hand, made the
same old mistake of getting too close. One of his rockets destroyed a
Fortress, and he then flew directly into a field of fire from four other
bombers. His aircraft was blown to pieces, and his body was never
found.

In all, JG7's pilots claimed twelve bombers and three Mustangs,
losing only three Me-262s. But to the Americans, results of the day's
combat were much more distressing. In addition to the bombers that
were shot down by the jets, twelve more B-17s and a B-24 were lost to
German fighter units and to flak. Many other bombers sustained damage, including 15 that were so badly shot up they were scrapped after
returning to base. Ten others crash-landed on the Soviet side of the front
lines. Twenty-one fighters did not return.

The great news for the Luftwaffe was the success of the rockets. The
Me-262 pilots had proved they could get kills without exposing themselves to the murderous machine-gun fire of the bombers. It was as if
they'd been handed a priceless gift. At JG7, it was time for celebration.
In the mess that night Luftwaffe songs were sung, and quantities of
cognac and champagne were drunk. Their best days, the pilots said,
were just ahead.

As soon as he heard reports of the battle, Professor Messerschmitt
contacted the Air Ministry and urged that the jet units be supplied with
large quantities of the rockets. The response was an order to the
Deutsche Waffen und Munitions Fabrik to build them in quantities of
25,000 per month.

Messerschmitt was exultant. Now at last the world's best fighter
would have armament worthy of it!

85.

Armed with rockets, Me-262s had become awesome war machines.
They still were far too few in number to suit Galland and other leaders,
but those that did fly and fight had at last realized their deadly poten-

tial. They created havoc among the fleets of Allied bombers. Flying at more than twice the bombers' speed, Me-262s now had a weapon so powerful that one hit would blow a four-engine aircraft out of the sky. And yet the fighters could fire their rockets from a safe distance, invulnerable to the bomber's machine guns.

The American commanders, on the other hand, at first considered the rocket-armed Me-262s to be only a minor hindrance. They took note that no matter how lethal, there were never more than a handful of the newly armed jets in action. In fact, the commanders believed that the Luftwaffe had been virtually eliminated as a defensive force. For proof, they pointed out that often a raid would take place with not a single Bf-109 or Fw-190 challenging the bombers. So to them, an occasional attack by Me-262s was of little significance.

By then the USAAF had devastated most of Germany's factories. Considering this, Generals Arnold and Doolittle decided to switch tactics and conduct area bombing. Population centers were selected, and fleets of more than a thousand bombers, escorted by hundreds of fighters, were sent to obliterate them. The only real hazard, the commanders believed, was flak.

In late March, however, that changed dramatically. On the 19th, B-17s of the 3rd Air Division attacked Chemnitz, an old city of 300,000 people in eastern Germany. The weather was poor, rain clouds impeded visibility, and the Mustang escorts lost contact with the bombers. As the B-17s approached the target, the crews were startled to see 28 jet fighters appear from out of the clouds. The gunners trained their weapons and waited. But instead of making the usual firing passes, the Me-262s flew past and moved far to the rear of the formation. Then they turned, and from a range of about 700 meters, sent a fusillade of fiery, smoke-trailing rockets into the combat boxes.

The result was chaos. Four B-17s, one from the 96th Bomb Group, another from the 385th, and two from the 452nd, were struck and exploded. Four others were so badly damaged it was unlikely they would make it back. The air seemed filled with dead and dying bombers.

The Me-262s were led by Leutnant Karl Schnörrer of JG7, who had replaced the wounded Günther Wegmann. Schnörrer had shot down one of the Fortresses, and the other victories were attributed to Oberleutnant Franz Schall and Oberfeldwebels Helmut Lennartz and Heinz Arnold. Another had fallen to Oberfeldwebel Gerhard Reinhold.

Then it was the jet pilots' turn to be surprised. The Mustangs had picked up radio chatter from the B-17s, and used it to locate the embattled bombers. When the Americans arrived, they dove on the unwary Me-262s with guns blazing. Captain R.S. Fifield shot down the jet flown by Oberfeldwebel Heinz Mattuschka of 10/JG7, and Major Robert Foy destroyed that of Leutnant Harry Myer of 11/JG7. Both German pilots were killed when their airplanes crashed near Eilenburg.

But the remaining Me-262 pilots quickly recovered their wits. Leutnant Rademacher pulled up beneath a Mustang and blew it apart with cannon fire. Oberstleutnant Heinz Bär of III/EJG2, also shot one down. After that, Unteroffizier Harald Konig destroyed a B-17 of the 384th Bomb Group with the last of his rockets, and Gefreiter Hans Heim sent another down in flames. Two more Fortresses were damaged beyond repair.

Back at USAAF headquarters, the commanders were jolted by reports of the battle, and correctly perceived the rocket attacks as a potential for disaster. Now the Germans not only had a fighter that was far superior to anything else in the air, but a weapon to go with it. It seemed incredible that at this late date the Luftwaffe might rise again, Phoenix-like, to strike a fatal blow against the Allied bombing campaign.

Something had to be done quickly, and General Doolittle wasted no time in issuing orders. The Me-262s, their bases, and the factories that were building them, were to be destroyed in all-out assaults.

Accordingly, the 2nd Air Division attacked the training base at Neuburg with 125 B-24s. Escorted by 110 Mustangs, the big bombers swept over the field at low altitude and dropped tons of high explosives on the aircraft parked there. A total of 80 machines were on the tarmac, 70 of them jets. The others were Ju-52s and a scattering of Bf-110s. The bombs destroyed many of the airplanes, and the remainder were badly damaged.

A large number of personnel were either killed or wounded in the attack. Among them were mechanics and instructors, as well as pilots being taught the techniques of flying an Me-262. Damage to the field and the buildings was extensive, and the runways were pitted with bomb craters.

Similar raids were conducted on Luftwaffe bases at Parchim and Brandenburg, and because reconnaissance had revealed jet activity at

Riem, that airfield, too, was mauled. A nearby factory at Bäumenheim, mistakenly believed by U.S. Intelligence to be building jets, was also bombed by B-24s of the 2nd Division. But the Me-262 plants hidden away in tunnels, caves, and forests remained undiscovered and unscathed.

However fierce the American raids, they had only a limited effect on Me-262 combat operations. Ground workers, many of them borrowed from the ranks of the Volksturm, labored through the night to clean up the mess and patch the holes in the runways. A day later, on 20 March, the jets were flying again.

That afternoon, 22 Me-262s of JG7 were directed to Hamburg, where B-17s were again bombing the ravaged city. The Fortresses were of the First Division, and were escorted by Mustangs of the 355th Fighter Group. Strategically the raid was of little value, inasmuch as Hamburg had already been blasted to rubble in earlier attacks. But the fact was that the Allies were running out of targets.

As the jets approached from the east, the American fighters met them head-on in an attempt to prevent them from reaching the bombers. Outnumbered as usual, this time by about thirty-to-one, the Me-262s split up, with half engaging the Mustangs while the others raced toward the B-17s.

Feldwebel Otto Pritzl was the first to fire his rockets. One Fortress of the 303rd Bomb Group was struck and exploded, and as the other jets began launching their R4Ms, Pritzl came about and shot down a second bomber. Next, Fähnrich Ernst Pfeiffer, Fähnrich Hans Christer, Oberfeldwebel Helmut Heiser, Oberleutnant Sturm, and Oberfeldwebel Buchner all fired salvos. A total of nine B-17s were hit by the deadly Orkans and went down in flames. Only a few crew members were able to take to their parachutes.

The German pilots paid for the victories, however. Four of the jets that tangled with Mustangs were shot down. Lieutenant Vernon Barto of the 339th Fighter Group destroyed one of them, and Lieutenant Robert Irion, also of the 339th, downed another. Obergefreiter Fritz Gehlker died when his burning Me-262 crashed at Bad Segeburg, and Oberfeldwebel Erich Büttner, though wounded, bailed out and landed safely near Kiel. Both were members of 10 Staffel.

Over the following days it became increasingly clear to the Allies that their worst fears concerning the jets were being realized. The rocket-firing Me-262s were running up victories at an increasing rate, and most of the vanquished aircraft were not fighter escorts, but bombers.

On 21 March, pilots of JG7 shot down 12 Fortresses and a Liberator, and added a Mustang and a Thunderbolt to the kills.Later, Oberstleutnant Bär destroyed another Liberator, and that night Feldwebel Karl-Heinz Becker of 10/NJG11 downed a Mosquito. The following day was even worse from an Allied standpoint; 13 Fortresses, two Mustangs and another Mosquito were shot down. And the day after that the jets destroyed 14 Fortresses and Liberators, plus a Mustang and two Mosquitos.

On the 24th, Me-262s of JG7 were again in action, with Oberleutnant Fritz Stehle leading his staffel against a fleet of B-17s over northern Germany. Stehle had pulled strings to have his old wingman, Heinz Suhrbeer, returned from test-piloting duty. As the jets moved in to attack, they were confronted by a large number of P-51s that were escorting the bombers.

Suhrbeer was in position off his leader's starboard quarter. As Stehle drew a bead on a Mustang, Suhrbeer moved closer to protect the Oberleutnant's tail. He could see telltale cherry-red tracers flashing toward them from both the bombers' machine guns and those of other Mustangs. And as always in large air battles, the noise of roaring engines and massed gunfire was horrendous.

Suddenly, Suhrbeer's left engine failed. At the same time, his right turbo was running hot and might also flame out. He radioed, *"Meine links pferd ist lame!"*

Stehle knew what a lame horse meant in a battle like this one. He radioed back, *"Raus, Heinz—schnell!"*

Suhrbeer bailed out, but with the sky full of Mustangs, he didn't dare pull his ripcord. Too many German pilots had been shot while in their parachutes for him to take that chance. Instead, he went into freefall. Never before had he felt anything like the eerie sense of flying with only his outstretched arms as wings, sailing down through the clouds, the earth slowly spinning beneath him.

Numb from the bitter cold, he dropped more than 5,000 meters before he opened his chute, landing on a muddy patch that was soft enough to lessen the shock. As he got to his feet, he found himself not far from Schwerin, the town where he'd grown up. Carrying his chute, he walked to a road and hitched a ride in an army truck that took him to his family's home.

Heinz Suhrbeer had married Charlotte Krueger on 20 January. Not long afterward, the Luftwaffe flight school where she managed the library was shut down because of bomb damage. The school had then been moved from Prenzlau to Schwerin, where Charlotte was staying with her husband's family.

When she caught sight of Heinz in his mud-spattered flying gear, Charlotte's eyes widened. "What are you doing here?"

He grinned and said, "I came down to see you."

That night the Suhrbeers had a family celebration. They knew Heinz was lucky to have survived, and that it would take a great deal more luck for him to live through the war. In the morning he left and made his way back to JG7. The following day he was once again at the controls of a jet, flying wingman to Stehle.

By now the Allies were baffled as to how the Germans had beaten them to the punch by sending Me-262s into operations. Their own efforts to build jet fighters were still confined to test-flying prototypes. They knew the German aircraft had been designed by Messerschmitt, because they had drawings and specifications that had been smuggled out of Germany by spies and Communist sympathizers. But the only times they'd seen the actual machines were when their aircraft were in combat with them, or when they recovered wrecks.

And then they got a break. On a misty morning, test pilot Hans Fay took off from Schwäbisch Hall in an Me-262-2a, Werke Nummer 111711. He knew the war would soon end, and he wanted to avoid capture by the Russians. He landed at Rhein-Main and turned the jet over to the Americans. After interrogation Fay was sent to a P.O.W. camp. He survived the war.

Now for the first time, the Allies had an undamaged Me-262. USAAF and RAF aeronautical engineers and ballistics experts swarmed over it, and later the aircraft was repainted and flown by Allied test pilots. The consensus was that the Me-262 had not only reached operations sooner than their own aircraft, but in many respects was much more advanced.

The RAF's Air Marshal Harris decided that the German night defenses had become too proficient, and ordered a switch to daytime operations. One of the first targets would be the Blohm und Voss engineering works on the island of Kuhwerder, just off Hamburg. Blohm und Voss was a major shipbuilder, and also produced torpedo bombers and flying boats.

On 31 March, Mosquito Pathfinders led a fleet of 428 RCAF Lancasters and Halifaxes to the island. The Canadian bomber crews were not used to flying in the tight formations favored for daylight raids. Instead they flew as they had at night, in a long, loose stream, and as a result, they had few of the crossfire defenses that American combat boxes employed. Another mistake lay in a failure to hook up with the RAF Mustangs that had been assigned to meet them over Holland and escort them to the target. As they approached Hamburg, the bombers were spread out over a great distance. And they had no fighter protection.

I/JG7 scrambled 38 jets from Parchim, led by Oberleutnant Franz Schall. Shortly afterward, the geschwader put up 20 more. Ten of these were led by Oberleutnant Fritz Stehle and his wingman Heinz Suhrbeer, and ten by Oberleutnant Hans Grünberg.

"*Fliegen 180,*" the controller radioed. "*Dicke autos, pauke-pauke.*" Calling the bombers fat cars was controller slang, as was pauke-pauke, which literally meant kettle drum, and was the order to attack.

Minutes later the German pilots caught sight of the enemy, and were surprised that they were not Americans, but Tommys, and were flying in a ragged formation that made them ideal targets. The jets began firing their rockets. As the R4Ms streaked toward them, the Canadian pilots maneuvered the heavy aircraft in abrupt turns, jinking and twisting to throw off the Germans' aim, but it was impossible to avoid the fiery flock of Orcans.

A total of 17 RCAF bombers were destroyed. Oberleutnant Schall accounted for two, Oberleutnant Stehle three, Oberleutnants Sturm and Grünberg two each, Leutnant Schall two, and Oberfeldwebel Buchner and Fähnrich Ehrig one apiece. The other four were downed by flak. Many of the remaining bombers were badly damaged, with dead and wounded among their crews. Eventually the Mustangs arrived and succeeded in driving off the jets, but by then the Germans had fired all their rockets and were running low on fuel. Four Me-262s had been lost in the battle. The others returned to base.

The action seemed to confirm the Allies' fears. The RAF and USAAF commanders did not know how many Me-262s the Luftwaffe had, nor did they know at what rate the jets were being built. Nevertheless, General Doolittle was determined to wipe them out. Thirty-four German airfields were bombed to oblivion, including some that were not used by jet aircraft at all. Suspected construction sites were repeatedly hit as well.

The most important blow to the jet forces, however, was not the bombings, but the steady attrition of pilots—very few of the old hands were still alive.

86.

The Allies were keenly aware of the need to eliminate as many Luftwaffe pilots as possible, which was why American fighter groups had been ordered to machine-gun enemy airmen after they bailed out. Some U.S. commanders tried to rationalize the order. It was only logical, they told the fighter jocks—if a German pilot was allowed to land, he'd no doubt be back in the air the next day, trying to shoot you down. It was therefore better to kill him while he was still in his parachute.

Though most American pilots refused to obey the decree, not all of them did. A few picked out the yellow parachute that identified the man dangling beneath it as German, and shot him with their .50-caliber guns. One such jet pilot was Leutnant Hans-Dieter Weiss. In a battle with 3rd Division B-17s over Berlin, Weiss expended his rockets and then attacked one of the Fortresses with his cannons at close range. American gunners set his Me-262 afire and he bailed out. His body was found on a street in the capital, riddled with bullets. A number of others met the same fate.

Many German pilots found the practice hard to believe, and others refused to believe it. They suspected the reports were more of Josef Goebbels' lies, until they witnessed what they regarded as an appalling violation of the air warriors' unwritten code. The German High Command, however, was also ruthless, and far more barbaric. Adolf Hitler, by now forced to face the inevitable defeat of the Third Reich, called for total abandonment of the rules of war. All captured Allied airmen, the Führer declared, must be shot.

At this point Hitler was a physical wreck, and rarely seemed sane. Adding to his infirmities were the large quantities of drugs prescribed by his quack physician, Dr. Theodor Morell. Members of the High Command realized this, and usually let his more bizarre orders slide.

His directive to shoot prisoners was not the worst of his directives.

The German people, Hitler shouted at Albert Speer, were not worthy of surviving the war. As for the German nation itself, that too should be destroyed. The Allies should find nothing of value left within its borders; the land should be rendered totally barren. Speer recognized this as madness, and at great personal risk he defied Hitler. Some government officials, however, agreed with the Führer, and many gauleiters resolved to defend their towns at all costs. They announced that they would fight as long as possible, and if that reduced their communities to smoking wreckage, so be it.

One of these fanatical crackpots was Gauleiter Wachtler, who presided in Messerschmitt's hometown of Bamberg. With its castle, its churches and its many other historic buildings, the ancient city was one of the most beautiful in Germany. The Professor was horrified by the thought of it being destroyed. He argued vigorously against Wachtler's plans, pointing out that the Volksturm, mostly older men, women, and young boys, could hardly mount a successful defense against American tanks and artillery. And because of his prominence and his political connections, Messerschmitt succeeded in getting the Gauleiter to back down. Bamberg was spared.

And yet, though he knew the war was lost, Messerschmitt never wavered in putting his energy and design skills into improving his warplanes and planning new ones. This, despite his contempt for the lunatic ideas that poured forth from Berlin.

Meanwhile, the Me-262s went on battling the huge fleets of Allied bombers and their escorts. Pilots of the jet fighters never flinched as they continued to attack the overwhelmingly superior enemy forces. But Reichsmarschal Göring ignored their efforts, and issued orders that sent into action a secret unit called Sonderkommando Elbe. It was one of the most diabolical schemes of the war.

87.

The idea originated with Oberst Hans-Joachim Hermann, the same Hajo Hermann who had organized and led the Wilde Sau night fighters. Hermann's thinking was coldly objective. He reasoned that the Third Reich could not survive, let alone win the war, unless the Allied bombing campaign was brought to a halt. If the bombing could be stopped even temporarily, that would allow the Germans time to build large numbers of Me-262s. The jets would destroy so many enemy aircraft that Germany would once again have the upper hand. Gaining control of the air could lead to victory.

So why not organize a suicide unit, whose pilots would ram Allied bombers? The pilots would all be volunteers, and the unit would inflict so many losses that the enemy would be forced to give up the bombing campaign. None of the pilots would be veterans, of course. Instead, they would be young men drawn from the Luftwaffe training programs. They would be taught to ram the bombers with older Bf-109s, and thus both pilots and aircraft would be expendable. The unit would be known as Sonderkommando Elbe, named for the River Elbe, the last natural barrier to the east of Berlin. Their mission would be code-named Operation Werewulf.

In early 1945, Hermann took the plan to Reichsmarschal Göring, who was intrigued. But Göring hesitated, as it might prove detrimental to his political fortunes, which at the time were at a very low ebb. Yet, a fanatical mission of this kind just might succeed, and if it worked, it could restore the Führer's faith in him. Finally, Göring authorized a presentation of the idea to Luftwaffe leaders.

The conference was held at Luftwaffe Headquarters in Berlin. Göring did not attend; instead, he delegated responsibility to General Dietrich Peltz, Chief of Air Defense. Adolf Galland was still with his job as General of Fighters, but was also in attendance. Though he'd heard a rumor about the plan, he dismissed it as merely another cockamamy idea. Now to his disgust, Peltz and the others were embracing it—something that Göring had obviously encouraged them to do.

Galland alone argued against the plan. He asked where Hermann would be when the pilots carried out the mission. Hermann replied that he would be on the ground, guiding them.

"I thought so," Galland said. "So I'll be in agreement when you're willing to lead them yourself."

But Galland was outnumbered. The other officers thought the idea was viable, and one of them said that their Japanese ally had just such a program. Their pilots were called Kamikaze, or Divine Wind, and they were inflicting great damage on ships of the U.S. Navy. The fact that most of Japan's own navy had been sunk by the Americans was conveniently not mentioned.

In the end, Hermann's plan was approved. He and General Peltz organized Sonderkommando Elbe in secret, asking for volunteers who would carry out a special mission that could help save the Fatherland. The pilots would have only a ten percent chance for survival, but they would become heroes in the great tradition of German warriors.

Hundreds came forward, including a number of front-line pilots who were rejected because they were too valuable to lose. Hermann had hoped to have at least a thousand aircraft for the operation, but he was given only 180. He blamed Peltz, and was angry at what he considered the general's perfidy. Nevertheless, Hermann was determined that the mission would be carried out. Assisting him was Major Otto Koehnke, a bomber pilot and holder of the Knight's Cross, who had lost his left foot in Russia.

Once the volunteers had been selected, they were transferred to the Luftwaffe base at Stendhal. All were teenagers, and none had ever flown a high-performance aircraft. Their experience for the most part had consisted of flying biplane trainers. They were given two weeks of lectures and a few hours of flight time in patched-up Bf-109Gs that had been retired from combat. Instructions called for them to fly toward the enemy bombers accompanied by Fw-190s and Me-262s. While the fighters engaged the enemy escorts, each Werewulf pilot would pick out a bomber and dive on it. He would ram his fighter into the bomber's tail, and if possible, bail out.

The speed of the Bf-109, the pilots were told, would enable them to carry out their attack without being shot down by the bomber's gunners. Once its tail surfaces were destroyed, the bomber could not stay in the air. The pilots were also told that since most of them would not survive, those who died would be honored for their sacrifice. A message from Reichsmarschal Göring promised that a tomb would be erected to contain their remains and serve as a monument. Photographs of the pilots would be displayed in the tomb.

On 7 April 1945, the USAAF's Mission 931 sent 1,260 bombers escorted by 780 fighters to attack Hannover. As the huge fleet crossed the Dutch coast, German radar operators alerted the Luftwaffe. Peltz ordered Hermann to stand by; Operation Werewulf was about to be launched.

Hermann replied that the Sonderkommando Elbe unit was not yet fully prepared. A number of its Bf-109s were not in flying condition, and some of the allotted fuel had not arrived at Stendhal. Peltz said the situation in the Reich was desperate, and the order was to be obeyed. Hermann was furious, but he also realized that he'd been backed into a corner.

At 1100 Peltz told him to launch. Only 120 of his charges took off, joined by 110 Fw-190s of JG300 and JG301, and 52 Me-262s of JG7. General Galland's own unit, JV44, was still short of equipment and supplies, and would not take part. That was just as well, because he' wanted nothing to do with the operation.

When the Luftwaffe fighters reached the enemy bombers, Fw-190s engaged the Mustangs and Thunderbolts. Meanwhile, the Me-262s made passes at both the American fighters and at some of the bomber elements. The Sonderkommando Elbe pilots climbed to 7,500 meters, well above the melee.

One of the pilots was 19-year-old Feldwebel Claus Hahnn. It was the first time he'd flown at such an altitude, and he was surprised to find that his Bf-109 didn't respond as quickly as it did when nearer to the ground. His second surprise came when contrary to what he'd been told, Mustangs climbed up to meet him. Hahnn tried to ignore the American fighters, and to concentrate on the bombers. They were flying in their usual formation of combat boxes at three different levels. He chose a bomber in the high level, and prepared to dive on it.

Just as he pushed his stick forward, his Bf-109 was jolted. Over the roar of his engine he heard the rattle of bullets striking metal, and then felt excruciating pain. His left arm had been shattered above the elbow and he was unable to move it, but he was determined to continue his attack. As he hurtled down toward the B-17 he eased the stick back to flatten the dive, as he'd been instructed. His flying jacket was red with blood; he was dizzy and his vision was blurred. Tracers were whizzing toward him as his Bf-109 smashed into the bomber's tail.

After that Hahnn found himself floating under his parachute. He was semi-conscious and had no idea how he'd extricated himself from the wreckage and pulled his ripcord—all he knew was that he was desperately cold and in severe pain. Eventually he drifted to earth near Steinhuder Lake. He was taken to a hospital where doctors were able to save his arm, but from then on he was unable to use it. He was one of the few Werewulf pilots to survive the battle.

Several of the others also made successful attacks. The most spec-

tacular occurred when Feldwebel Heinrich Rosner rammed the
Liberator flown by Colonel John Herboth of the 389th Bomb Group.
The collision tore away the after part of the B-24's fuselage. Herboth's
bomber then slammed into that of Lieutenant Colonel George Kunkel
and ripped off its port wing. Both aircraft spun down and crashed, and
their crews were killed. Feldwebel Rosner also managed to bail out, and
he too survived the war.

But for the other Werewulf pilots, and for the pilots of the Fw-190s,
the battle was catastrophic. Most efforts to ram a bomber failed completely as the inexperienced young men either missed the target or were
shot down before they could reach it. The Fw-190s were flown by pilots
who'd logged little air time and had limited knowledge of combat
tactics.

The Americans slaughtered them. The Mustangs and Thunderbolts
were all flown by veterans, and they made short work of their youthful
opponents. Still other German fighters were destroyed by the crossfire
put out by the bombers, and before long, the sky was streaked with oily
smoke from burning aircraft, most of them German. The rammings had
brought down five B-17s and two B-24s, but of the 230 Luftwaffe piston fighters in action that day, only 15 returned to base. The Me-262s
fared better; three were lost in combat with Mustangs, and one collided
with a B-24, destroying both airplanes. The pilots of III/JG7 knocked
down one Liberator and three American fighters.

Sonderkommando Elbe would fly one more mission a week later,
with fewer aircraft and an equally dismal outcome for the Germans. By
now it was obvious, even to zealots such as Hajo Hermann, that there
was no hope of victory. Like the pilots of Operation Werewulf, the
Third Reich was going down in flames.

88.

The day following the first Werewulf debacle, JG7 was again in action.
Fifteen of its Me-262s attacked 200 Lancasters that were raiding
Hamburg. RAF Mustangs put up a spirited defense, and only one
Lancaster was lost, hit by a rocket fired by Oberleutnant Stehle.
Another JG7 pilot, Leutnant Hadi Weihs, destroyed a Lightning in the
same area. But for once, the rocket attacks against the bombers were
largely ineffective.

Later, Feldwebel Heiner Geisthövel ran across four Mustangs near Cottbus. Geisthövel had only recently joined JG7 and had little combat experience, but in a single firing pass he shot down one of the P-51s, and then trained his cannons on a second Mustang and destroyed that one as well.

There were also Me-262 losses. Just before sundown, a jet was shot down near Nördlingen by Lieutenant J. Usiatynski of the 358th Fighter Group, 9th Air Force. Another was lost in a battle with Thunderbolts of the 50th Fighter Group over Crailsheim. Four others were reported damaged.

At this time General Adolf Galland's JV44 was based at Munich-Riem. Conditions there were crude, and the base was often under attack by American fighters. The airmen were billeted in private homes in the surrounding villages, and before sunrise each morning they rode bicycles and motorbikes to the airfield. There was one staff car, a Volkswagen with an engine that converted wood to combustible gas. The unit was still short of Me-262s and pilots, and Galland had to scrounge for both. On one occasion he and Macky Steinhoff paid a visit to the Luftwaffe Pilot's Rest Home, hoping to find recruits.

The home was a beautiful old inn on the shore of Lake Tegernsee, in the Bavarian Alps. There, battle-weary pilots could enjoy fine food, wines and brandies, much of the fare brought to the inn from nearby Switzerland. Plenty of good-looking young women were available as well. When Galland and Steinhoff walked into the bar, they found the usual party going full blast. Some of the airmen were offering mock toasts to the despised Göring, and others were loudly singing the old Luftwaffe song, "Wir Fliegen Gegen England." One pilot was standing on a tabletop while giving a drunken imitation of a speech by Goebbels. Still others were nuzzling girls.

When the pilots caught sight of Galland, the room instantly grew quiet. No one commanded more respect than the man who stood before them now, with a crushed cap tilted back on his head and a cigar clenched in his teeth. He smiled and waved to put them at ease, and the party went on. Among those on hand were a number of old comrades, including Major Walter "The Count" Krupinkski, Major Erich Hohagen, and Major Gerhard Barkhorn. All three men were experten, and all three eagerly accepted an invitation from Galland to join JV44.

A few days later Oberst Günther Lützow returned from his exile in

Italy, and he too became a member. Thus, along with the novices, JV44 had some of the Luftwaffe's best fighter pilots. In fact, one of the veterans, Oberstleutnant Heinz Bär, had already recorded nine kills while flying a jet with III/EJG2, and those were in addition to the 220 victories he'd achieved in piston aircraft. Despite that, most of the pilots in JV44 had little or no experience in flying fighters. Training them continued to vex Macky Steinhoff.

On the afternoon of 8 April, Steinhoff was alerted by ground control to intercept a fleet of enemy bombers that appeared to be headed for Munich. He took off with Leutnant Gottfried Fahrmann as his wingman. Fahrmann was one of the novices.

The controller said the bombers were nearing Regensburg, and Steinhoff was instructed to fly a course of 105 degrees. He turned to it, and climbed through a layer of stratus to an altitude of 7,000 meters. Then another course change, this time to 060 degrees; as he made it, Fahrmann pulled into position off his port quarter.

Moments later, Steinhoff spotted the enemy bombers. There were hundreds of them, B-24 Liberators that were leaving long vapor trails in the gray-blue sky. He had fuel enough for only about fifteen more minutes of flying time, but he reasoned that should be enough for him to make at least one firing pass before being forced to return to Riem. He climbed above the bombers, intending to line up for a rocket shot from the rear. And as he did, he suddenly found himself in the middle of a great swarm of Thunderbolts.

The Americans seemed as surprised as Steinhoff. They whipped their aircraft about in a series of wild maneuvers, but with his speed he had no trouble eluding them. He flew on, and with Fahrmann still following, banked around to attack the bombers, leaving the P-47s far behind.

The best chance for a hit, Steinhoff decided, would be from underneath. He slipped below the level of the enemy, telling himself to make sure he was about 800 meters away before firing his rockets. He had to be extremely careful here; an abrupt change in throttle settings could cause the engines to quit. He raised the jet's nose and flipped the rocket switch to red.

But when he pressed the release button, nothing happened.

He cursed his luck. To come this far and have the mechanism fail was infuriating, and yet he refused to let this opportunity go by. He flew straight at the bomber stream and fired his cannons at the nearest B-24 from a range of only 200 meters.

Getting that close to the bombers was insanely risky, but his blood was up. His cannon shells pierced the tail of the Liberator and the heavy aircraft exploded, the blast tossing Steinhoff's jet upward like a scrap of paper caught in the wind. As he fought to regain control, he had a split-second impression of tracers arcing toward him from other bombers. But an instant later, he was high above the stream and out of range of the enemy gunners.

Amazed that the Me-262's engines hadn't cut out, he looked back. All that remained of the Liberator he'd hit was a black smear that marked its descent toward the earth. The other bombers continued on, their P-47 escorts near them. Fahrmann was nowhere in sight.

Now Steinhoff was low on fuel, and as he turned for Riem, he heard Fahrmann's voice in his headphones, saying he'd lost an engine was being attacked by fighters.

He's had it, Steinhoff thought. I can't help him.

Steinhoff then went on south to Munich-Riem, where he landed with his engines burning the last bit of fuel in the tanks. Other jets were taking off, the pilots eager to engage the same fleet of bombers he'd been battling. When he jumped down from his cockpit, a mechanic asked anxiously about Fahrmann. Steinhoff replied that he wouldn't be coming back. The man winced and turned away.

But incredibly, Fahrmann did make it back. He showed up the following morning battered and bruised, arriving at the field in the sidecar of an army motorcycle. He said that after the Mustangs shot his aircraft to pieces he bailed out. When he landed he was surrounded by soldiers pointing their rifles and spitting curses at the *"Verdammt Amerikaner."*

"Nein, ihr idioten!" Fahrmann shouted at them, *"Ich bin Deutsch!"*

Chagrined, the soldiers apologized and took him to a nearby farmhouse, where he was given a large tumbler of schnapps and a bowl of soup, after which he lay down and slept till dawn. He was then awakened by an army officer, who wrote out a pass and arranged to have a motorcycle take him back to Riem. He'd lost his helmet when he bailed out, so the farmer's wife wrapped her bright-colored scarf around his head.

A feldwebel drove the motorcycle. Upon their arrival at the base an MP berated the feldwebel, calling him a fool for riding around with a whore in his sidecar. Fahrmann snatched off the scarf and identified himself, thereby ending his travail.

Though he didn't know it, the Thunderbolt pilot who shot him down was Lieutenant J. Usiatynski. All Fahrmann knew for certain was that he was fortunate to be alive.

89.

For the German defenses, nothing had worked. Not concentrated fire from thousands of flak batteries, not attacks by the Me-163s, not Operation Werewulf, not the anti-aircraft missiles, not mass attacks by Bf-109s and Fw-190s. And not even assaults by Me-262s firing rockets and cannons. The Allies continued to mount their bombing raids, and though many of the heavies were shot down, there were always increasing numbers to take their place.

By now the Luftwaffe had still fewer experienced pilots. On 10 April, the last of the fighter reserves were sent up to intercept American bombers of the 8th, 9th, and 15th Air Forces that were flying missions against a wide range of targets in Germany, Hungary and Austria.

It would be one of the great air battles of the war. More than 2,000 Fortresses and Liberators were in the air that day, escorted by 1,200 fighters. They covered the sky in what seemed an endless canopy. Opposing the raiders were 115 Bf-109s and Fw-190s, and 55 Me-262s. Most of the piston aircraft were flown by neophytes, though a few of their leaders were veterans. As for the jets, it was the largest number to be engaged in combat at one time.

The opening round took place as B-17s of the 1st Air Division attacked Oranienburg, north of Berlin. The target was the site of large supply dumps that were ringed by flak batteries. The guns put up a hellish cloud of exploding shells, and shrapnel ripped into the Fortresses. Two blew up before they reached the IP, and others were badly damaged and forced to turn back.

Jets from I/JG7 then went after the top level of the bomber stream. The Me-262s attacked from astern in pairs, sending dozens of rockets into the enemy formation. Their shooting took a heavy toll on the B-17s of the 379th and 384th Bomb Groups.

Among the attackers was Oberleutnant Walter Schuck, who performed one of the most remarkable combat feats of any German pilot.

He made four high-speed passes, destroying a Fortress on each one. The first two victories were achieved with rockets, and after his supply was expended he shot down two more bombers with his cannons at close range.

Too close, as it turned out. On the last pass, his airplane became riddled by .50-caliber bullets from the bombers' gunners. Although badly wounded, Schuck was able to bail out. He would live, but his war was over.

Schuck was not the only jet pilot to post multiple kills that day; Oberleutnant Hans Grünberg was credited with two. Oberleutnants Stehle and Bohatsch each downed a Fortress, and so did Oberfähnrich Neuhaus and Unteroffizier Gerhard Reiher.

But JG7 suffered more losses among its already dwindling ranks. Captain John Brown of the 20th Fighter Group, flying a P-51D, knocked down one jet by turning inside it and hitting with a deflection shot as it flew over Berlin. The Me-262 caught fire and crashed among the ruined buildings. Captain John Hollins, Lieutenants Walter Drozd and Albert North accounted for three more jets, and Lieutenant Jerome Rosenblum and Lieutenant John Cudd shared a kill. Three other jets were damaged beyond repair.

At least six jets were lost that day while trying to land. Two of them were hit by fire from the Mustangs flown by Lieutenants H. Tanenbaum and R.J. Guggemos of the 359th Fighter Group, as they were on final at Gardelegen.

In addition, Fortresses of the 352st, 401st, 457th, and 487th Bomb Groups of the 3rd Air Division flew missions intended to obliterate the airfields where Me-262s were known to operate. Struck and badly damaged were the bases at Parchim, Brandenburg, Magdeburg and Lärz. The attacks on their home fields stung the jet pilots, and those who were in the air put up a furious defense. Bomber after bomber was destroyed, most often by rocket fire.

For the crew of a B-17, being struck by an Orcan was horrifying. If the aircraft had not yet released its bomb load, the bursting rocket would set off the tons of HE in the racks, resulting in the crew and the bomber vanishing in a fiery explosion. But if the bombs had already been dropped, the result for the crew could be even worse. When a rocket slammed into the fuselage of the bomber and exploded, the men who were not killed would be hideously burned and wounded by flying chunks of shrapnel or pieces of metal torn loose by the blast. Damage to the aircraft would be severe. Fires would rage, control cables would be jammed or cut, followed by the mortally wounded bomber falling into its death spiral. In those situations, escape by parachute was rare.

There were also instances in which a bomber went down because shrapnel from an exploding rocket penetrated the cockpit and killed the pilot. Lieutenant Steven Thompson died that way, and his copilot was unable to regain control of the B-17. The aircraft whipped into a violent spin, and centrifugal force prevented any of the crew from bailing out. The heavy bomber hit the earth at high speed, leaving nothing but a large hole filled with smoldering cinders to mark the spot.

The Me-262 fighter-bombers were also in action that day, making low-level attacks on U.S. armor and infantry units at Burg. As was so often the case, they were easy pickings for the American fighters. Lieutenants K.K. McGinniss and K.A. Lashbrook of the 55th Fighter Group caught two of them. The Mustangs dove on the jets, and before the low-flying pilots realized they were under attack, their machines had been torn apart by gunfire. Both died in the resultant crashes.

Despite the relentless raids by Allied bombers on the hidden factories, the aircraft could be replaced. Even at this late date, more Me-262s than ever were being built in the forests, tunnels and caves, but there was no way to replace pilots who were among the Luftwaffe's best. Mustangs shot down and killed Oberleutnant Walter Wagner, the staffelkapitän of 1/JG7, near Stendal. And Staffelkapitän Franz Schall of 10/JG7 died while landing at Parchim. Schall had destroyed a P-51 but his jet had been damaged in the process, and it rolled into a bomb crater and blew up. He left behind a record of 17 victories flying the Me-262, and 137 achieved in piston fighters. Also lost that day was Oberleutnant Walter Wever, the staffelkapitän of 7/JG7, shot down by a Thunderbolt near Neuruppin. And Gefreiter Karl Heim and Feldwebel Christof Schwartz, both outstanding pilots of 3/JG7, were shot down and killed near Berlin.

So severe were the losses that JG7 would never recover. Many of its leaders were gone, along with more than half of its most experienced airmen. In an effort to spare the battered unit from the advancing Americans, it was split up and relocated to Plattling, Mühldorf, Landau and Prage-Ruzyne.

Despite the fact that the jet forces had been decimated, Adolf Hitler continued to howl for revenge attacks by his Sturmvogels. He threatened to unleash his other miracle weapons as well, though they existed only in his sick mind. That was but one example of how the Führer refused to accept reality. Another was his reaction to a piece of stunning news that reached him late one night.

90.

Josef Goebbels had spent the day at the headquarters of General Busse on the Oder Front. As he returned to the shrapnel-scarred Propaganda Ministry Building on Wilhelmplatz, he was met by a visibly excited secretary.

"Great news," the woman cried. "Roosevelt is dead!"

Goebbels could hardly believe it. He had been hoping for a miracle, some sort of divine occurrence that would save the Reich. And here it was!

He hurried to his office and telephoned the Führer, who was in the bunker twenty meters below the battered Chancellory. Hitler had been there in secret since the failed campaign in the Ardennes, surrounded by members of his staff.

"Mein Führer," Goebbels said, "I congratulate you! Roosevelt is dead! It is written in the stars that the second half of April will be the turning point for us. This is Friday, April the thirteenth. It is the turning point!"

Hitler too became jubilant. He assured the Propaganda Minister that the American president's death meant the Allies would lose the will to fight. It marked a great opportunity, he said, for Germany to reverse its fortunes.

Once again the Führer was refusing to admit the truth. He'd been informed that the Americans had already reached Magdeburg, less than a hundred kilometers from Berlin, and to the east the Soviet army was so close that the thunder of their artillery could be heard in the capital. Regardless of his conveyed optimism and his boasting about miracle weapons, the end was near, and he had to have known it. It was probably why he ordered SS troopers to bring his mistress, Eva Braun, to the bunker from the Berghof in Obersalzberg. Although he'd never permitted her to appear with him at official functions, he was prepared to marry her. The ceremony would take place before the final cataclysm.

To the members of what remained of the Luftwaffe, the news of Roosevelt's demise meant little. It came to them through a feverish announcement by Goebbels, but they were preoccupied with other matters. The pilots were suffering from acute shortages of supplies, fuel and ammunition, and those problems were far more important. Unlike Goebbels, the pilots had an unvarnished view of the military situation. And despite their awareness of how grim it was, they refused to give up the fight; each day they put up a handful of aircraft against the hordes of Allied bombers and their escorts.

And they went on losing pilots. On 14 April a lone Me-262, flown by Oberleutnant Erich Stahlberg of 9/JG7, attacked a flight of Mustangs over Lonnewitz Airfield. The P-51s belonged to the 354th Fighter Group of the 9th Air Force. Stahlberg got a cannon strike on one of the Mustangs, sending it down. As he made a sweeping turn in an attempt to line up on another enemy fighter, the remaining P-51s cut him off. Captain Clayton Gross raked the jet with a three-second burst, and Stahlberg was killed.

At that point Galland's JV44 had yet to see action as a unit. Due to a paucity of spare parts, the staffel still did not have enough serviceable aircraft, nor did it have ample stores of fuel and ammunition. But among its twenty pilots, many were holders of the Knight's Cross; they were the elite of the Luftwaffe who were still alive. On 16 April, Galland led the staffel into action for the first time.

The general had Major Gerhard Barkhorn, Oberst Günther Lützow, and Major Wilhelm Herget with him as he attacked B-26 Marauders of the 322nd Bomb Group, 9th Air Force. His wingman was Unteroffizier Eduard Schallmoser. Galland called the medium bombers *halbstarke*, or half-strong, because they had only half the number of engines that powered the heavies.

The Marauders were flying in a tight formation over Landsburg am Lech, 25 kilometers southwest of Munich. There were sixteen of them, escorted by two dozen Thunderbolts. The fighters were weaving back and forth above the bombers.

During his years of flying Bf-109s, Galland had always favored getting close before firing at an opponent, which was how he was able to score 104 victories. He liked to say that when the enemy aircraft completely filled his gunsight, that was the time to open up. It wasn't the best way to attack with an Me-262, however, nor was it necessary when the jet was armed with rockets. Yet as always, Galland did things his way. He closed fast on the bombers, and from a distance of only 400 meters fired a salvo of 24 rockets.

The projectiles sailed true, and exploded in the middle of the formation. One of the Marauders blew up, and another lost a wing and most of its tail, and plunged toward the earth. Schallmoser launched his rockets as well, but failed to score hits. He also failed to break off in time to avoid being caught by fire from the bombers' machine guns. His aircraft shuddered under the impact of dozens of strikes, and spun down trailing smoke and flames.

Lützow and the others were busy jousting with the P-47s, but Galland could not see whether they were having any success. By now some of the Thunderbolts were desperately trying to catch him, though with his speed he had no trouble evading them. Climbing, he looked down at the remaining Marauders. He still had his cannons—could he get a third kill?

Not with his fuel gauges showing that his tanks were close to empty. Reluctantly, he turned away. His comrades had the same problem; they broke off the fight and followed him back to base. As the Me-262s came in to land, scores of workers were still patching craters in the runway that had been created by raiding American bombers earlier in the day. Once the jets were safely down, ground crews hastily towed them off the field and covered them with camouflage netting.

The general stood by on the airstrip for a few minutes, chewing a cigar and looking toward Munich. He witnessed American bombers attacking the city in waves.

Suddenly someone shouted, *"Achtung! Bombenangriff!"*

Galland sprinted to a nearby slit trench and dived into it, landing on top of a feldwebel who was shaking with fear. An instant later a flight of B-17s roared over the field and dropped their deadly loads. The air was filled with the shriek of falling bombs, and explosions shook the earth. Flak gunners put up a storm of 88mm shells, but only one of the enemy aircraft was damaged enough to bring it down. The bomber crashed and burned only a few meters from the runway.

When at last the attack ended and the rest of the B-17s were gone, Galland was surprised that he and the feldwebel hadn't been struck by flying splinters. As he climbed out of the hole and dusted himself off, he saw that the field was strewn with dead bodies and flaming wreckage.

A further survey revealed that one of the hidden jets had been destroyed by the bombing; fuel tanks and storage sheds holding tools and spare parts had also been hit. The General was grateful that none of his pilots had been killed.

That evening an unexpected event brought a smile to the faces of staffel members. An armored car drove onto the base and Unteroffizier Schallmoser climbed out, carrying his parachute. Except for an injured leg, he was unhurt. The pilots extended a hearty welcome and toasted him with brandy.

The ground crews worked all through the night, and the next day the staffel was again ready for operations. Thanks to the tireless efforts of the mechanics, this time Galland had eight Me-262s with him as he took off to engage a large fleet of B-17s. The jets didn't have to go far; the Fortresses were conducting another raid on Munich.

As the Germans wheeled in to attack, bombs were bursting on the city and the flak batteries were firing a steady barrage. A Fortress of the 305th Bomb Group was hit by AA fire and its bomb load blew, producing an enormous yellow blossom of flame and debris. The violent explosion rocked other aircraft in the formation, and one of them was thrown out of its combat box. That put the bomber directly in the course of a fast-closing Me-262, flown by Unteroffizier Otto Heckmann, who was unable to avoid a collision. His wing sliced through the rear of the B-17's fuselage, ripping off the tail section. The jet's wing tore away as well, and the aircraft tumbled out of control. All the men in the bomber, flown by Lieutenant Brainard Harris, died in the ensuing crash.

The collision occurred directly in front of Oberst Steinhoff. Macky pulled up to avoid piling into the wreckage, missing it by mere centimeters. He then turned toward another bomber that had strayed out of the formation and pressed the firing button that would launch his rockets. The missiles failed to ignite. It was the second time this had happened, and he was furious. Adding to his frustration, he was unable to get a hit with his cannons.

Other pilots were more successful that day. Although fiercely challenged by swarms of Mustangs, the jets of JG7 sent eight bombers down in flames, and damaged several more. One of the victories was scored by Major Georg-Peter Eder. It was his 25th while flying an Me-262, and would be his last of the war.

When JG44's pilots returned to base, they found the field had been bombed once again. Though the workshops were on fire and the runway was pocked with fresh craters, most of the pilots managed to avoid the holes and land safely.

Not everyone, however, was so fortunate. Major Barkhorn tangled with American fighters, and his Me-262 was badly shot up. Both engines cut out, and he crash-landed on open ground. He was severely injured when his unlocked cockpit canopy slid forward and crushed his neck. He lived, but General Galland had lost yet another of his best pilots.

There was some good fortune as well. To the delight of the staffel members, Schallmoser again turned up with parachute in hand. Amazingly, he was unhurt. His jet had collided with a Fortress, and after the wreck had fallen more than 5,000 meters he'd bailed out. The pilots immediately dubbed him, "The jet rammer of JV44." He grinned sheepishly and accepted their ribbing. Steinhoff told him he hoped to have the same good luck himself.

But Macky would not. Every combat pilot's luck was said to run out if he flew long enough, and Steinhoff had been flying far longer than most.

91.

On the morning of 18 April, the pilots of JV44 sat around in camp chairs at the edge of the field, smoking and drinking coffee, waiting for word of an impending attack by enemy bombers. That it would come was as inevitable as sunrise, and when it did they would scramble their jets and engage.

Today Oberst Steinhoff was pensive. Across the way a group of young female soldiers were busily preparing a flak battery for action, and he couldn't help but think how pitiful the Wehrmacht had become. Girls shooting at bombers? Ridiculous.

For that matter, what good was any resistance at this point? Why were German soldiers still fighting and dying? The Reich would soon collapse completely, and the war would be over. He thought of his wife, Ursula, and their two children, who were sequestered in northern Germany. He hoped they were all right; he hadn't seen them in months.

The field telephone rang, and one of the pilots answered the call.

When he hung up he said a large fleet of enemy aircraft was over Stuttgart and heading for Regensburg. Identifying the bombers' target was easy. The Americans no longer bothered to impose radio discipline, instead chattering freely and openly as they flew. Regensburg was 220 kilometers east of Stuttgart, and was the site of a Messerschmitt works.

The Americans' mission, too, seemed oddly futile. Why bother to bomb an area that had been pounded so often it was mostly rubble? And with the end of the war in sight, why do it now? Suffice it to say that the Americans had their orders as well.

General Galland rose to his feet. "I'll lead the first flight. Macky, you take the second. Let's go."

Minutes later Steinhoff was in the cockpit of his Me-262. The engines were running smoothly, and the magazines of the 30mm cannons were full. The racks under the wings were loaded with 24 rockets. As he waited for the signal to take off, Steinhoff reminded himself to rev the engines to the maximum before releasing his brakes. He would then run the aircraft almost to the end of the runway before pulling back the stick, providing him with as much speed as possible when the heavily loaded jet lifted off.

It was chilly this morning, and he knew the air at 7,000 meters would be much colder. In fact, the temperature would be as low as minus 40 degrees Centigrade—not a pleasant environment if he were forced to bail out. He watched as General Galland's flight of three jets became airborne, and a moment later the controller's clearance crackled in his earphones. He stood on the brakes and eased the throttles forward, keeping an eye on the rev counters. The aircraft trembled as the needles crept over until they were showing more than 8,000 rpm.

Go! He raised the toes of his boots from the brake pedals and the Me-262 began moving slowly, then with steadily increasing speed. Krupinski was behind him, and Steinhoff radioed, "Stay close to me, Count. As soon as I've fired my rockets, you go in to attack."

Still faster now. The runway had been hastily patched after the last bombing, and was too rough for Steinhoff's liking. But at last the aircraft felt lighter as it bounced over the bumpy surface. Now for liftoff. With the embankment at the end of the runway rushing toward him, he put in back pressure.

Suddenly a tongue of flame shot out of the left turbine, turning the engine into a huge blowtorch. The jet veered violently to the left, and he tried to correct with the rudder, at the same time pulling back hard on the stick.

The aircraft refused to fly. And no matter what he tried, he could not straighten it out, nor was he able to stop it. The jet hit the embankment with a terrific impact and he was thrown against the shoulder straps as the machine tumbled end over end in a wild somersault.

It came to rest with another stunning jolt, and the fuel tanks exploded, instantly filling the cockpit with flames. The oxygen mask was wrenched from his face and he felt searing heat as fire enveloped him. His hands working feverishly, he released his harness and undid the parachute catch, and then popped the canopy. He saw a turbine that had been ripped off his machine lying nearby, saw puddles of fuel that had become sheets of orange flame. He took a deep breath, and sucked fire into his lungs.

The pain was horrible, as if his chest was being stabbed by a red-hot sword. Somehow he had to leave this burning coffin.

As he grasped the edges of the cockpit, he was aware that the exposed skin on his wrists between his gloves and his leather jacket was peeling off. He forced himself to heave with all his strength, and pulled himself up onto the burning parachute pack on his seat. And then the rockets under the wings began firing, the projectiles exploding and making a hellish racket.

He stepped onto the wing and hopped down, then tried to run from the flaming wreck until realizing his legs wouldn't support him. He fell to his knees, and found he could no longer see because his eyes had swollen shut.

A voice called out to him, and hands dragged him to his feet. The voice said he'd be taken to a hospital. After that he was vaguely aware of a doctor and nurses fussing over him. His clothing was cut away and a needle was thrust into his arm; he then sank into merciful unconsciousness.

Steinhoff's accident was similar to the one experienced by Leutnant Hans Busch, a fiery crash on takeoff caused by engine failure. But Busch had been luckier—Steinhoff's injuries were much worse, the flames having burned away his eyelids, his lips, and most of his nose. Whether he would live was questionable, because burn cases as severe as his often died from infection. And if he did survive, what would he look like? As it turned out, he did live, though his face was hideously scarred. After the war he would become military commander of NATO forces.

As Galland flew on, he was informed by Kupinski that Steinhoff had crashed on takeoff. Macky had been a good friend and an invaluable assistant to the General, but Galland could not afford to dwell on the loss. He led Oberstleutnant Heinz Bär and Leutnant Gottfried Fahrmann on course, with Kupinski and Leutnant Hein Wubke following.

They met the B-17s just as they'd finished their bomb runs and banked away from the target. The jets maneuvered to attack, but the bombers were escorted by large numbers of Mustangs and Thunderbolts, and the enemy pilots were some of the 9th Air Force's best. As the jets lined up to fire their rockets they were cut off by the defending fighters, and when they did shoot, the rockets missed the targets.

Five jets against more than 400 fighters was hardly an even contest, especially when the escorts were flown by highly experienced combat pilots. Only Heinz Bär had success against them; he shot down two Thunderbolts of the 36th Fighter Group before the battle ended. The Me-262s then returned to base, having lost but one pilot, Macky Steinhoff, on the operation.

A few days later JV44 suffered another critical loss, and Galland lost another friend. The action took place when the staffel attacked a formation of B-26 Marauders of the 17th Bomb Group that were conducting a raid on ammunition dumps at Schwabmünchen. The bombers were again escorted by veteran American fighter pilots, this time members of the 365th Fighter Group who were flying P-47s.

The Me-262s approached the bombers at high speed from the rear of the formation. Before the Thunderbolt pilots could react, the jets fired their rockets. It was like shooting big-bore shotguns into a flight of birds. Two of the Marauders were hit and went down, one flown by Lieutenant Fred Harms, the other by Lieutenant Leigh Slates. Both bombers were of the 34th Squadron, and only one crewman, a gunner in Harms' aircraft, survived. He was Sergeant Edward Truver, who was taken prisoner as he stumbled out of the wreckage.

When the jets came about to make another firing pass, the Thunderbolts dove on them with a vengeance. Captain Jerry Mast lined up on the tail of Lützow's aircraft and began shooting. Lützow executed a steep turn and the burst missed, but ahead of him was another P-47 with Lieutenant Billy Myers at the controls. Myers attacked the jet head-on, and bullets from his six machine guns punched into Lützow's fuselage and wings. The Me-262 flipped over and plunged to earth at a speed the American pilots estimated as better than 600 miles an hour. So violent was the explosion that nothing remained afterward but a black depression in the earth, filled with glowing cinders. No trace of Lützow's body was ever found.

No one knew better than Galland what such losses meant. Though the general did not harbor illusions as to Germany's plight, Galland was still a warrior. He called his pilots together and said, "Militarily speaking, the war is lost. Even our action here cannot change anything. But I shall continue to fight, because the Me-262 has got hold of me, and because I am proud to belong to the last fighter pilots of the German Luftwaffe. Only those who feel the same are to go on flying with me."

When he finished speaking, a roar went up from the men surrounding him. They shook their fists, and vowed to fight to the last man.

92.

General Galland and the pilots of JV44 were not the only ones who stubbornly refused to give up the fight. The members of JG7, battered as their geschwader was, also vowed to carry on. So did the remaining Luftwaffe units, as well as many soldiers in the front-line infantry divisions, the crews manning U-boats, and a few other combatants in the German armed services.

And so did Willy Messerschmitt. He worked as hard as ever, energized by his hopes for various projects in the works. Among them, the one that he was most enthusiastic about was the P-1101.

The aircraft would be a single-seat fighter with a V-tail and tricycle landing gear, powered by one He-S 001 jet engine mounted in the rear of the fuselage. The cockpit would be in the nose, with a bubble canopy to provide the pilot with maximum visibility. The wings would be borrowed from the Me-262, swept back at 40 degrees, with the angle reduced at midpoint to 26 degrees. Armament would consist of two Mk-108 30mm cannons. R4M rockets would be fitted under the wings, and the aircraft could also carry an SC-500 bomb. Lighter and simpler to build than the Me-262, yet stronger and with less drag, the P-1101 would be faster and more maneuverable. It would represent the next generation of jet fighters, and would be even more formidable in aerial combat than its predecessor.

Messerschmitt had reason to hurry its development. Acutely aware that the rapidly advancing enemy forces were threatening Germany with total collapse, he believed he could have the new fighters flying by June, 1945. Once the jets were in the air, no Allied fighter could hope to contend with them.

By late April the prototype was 80 percent complete, and facing construction delays because of the slow delivery of components. Meantime American armored units were smashing their way across Germany, often covering 30 kilometers a day. But production problems were not the Professor's only troubles. He received another peremptory order, this one from Kreisleiter Schiede, the Nazi party official and local District Leader in Garmisch-Partenkirchen. Schiede directed him to turn over 81 members of his Oberammergau Research Department to the Volksturm for training as riflemen.

To Messerschmitt, this was more idiocy. The notion that he would disrupt the vital work on aircraft development to satisfy the demands of a blockhead like Schiede was ridiculous. He wrote to the District Leader that he was sorry, but he could not spare any of his employees. He also pointed out that the Führer had issued an edict that skilled workers in key defense programs were not to be called up for service.

Messerschmitt's reply made Schiede furious. The Nazi official huffed and puffed, accusing the Professor and members of his staff of disloyalty to the Reich. He announced that if necessary he would take harsh action to force compliance with his order. Messerschmitt ignored him.

But he could not ignore the rumblings from Berlin. It was unsettling to hear how Hitler was rapidly breaking down, both mentally and physically. Adolf Galland was also aware of the Führer's degeneration, but true to his word, he was determined to go on leading JV44 against American bombers. The staffel was in action every day, as was JG7. Both units continued to achieve victories, and to lose pilots.

On 26 April radar operators alerted the General that an enemy formation was 120 kilometers northwest of Munich. The bombers were at 6,000 meters, and headed his way. Galland led a flight of six Me-262s to intercept. Visibility was poor due to clouds and haze, but the Germans spotted the American aircraft as they flew over Neuburg on the Danube. There were about sixteen B-26s, and appeared to have no fighter escorts.

The bombers' course was almost directly opposite to that of Galland's flight. That meant the attack would be head-on, and he knew how hard it was to succeed with such an approach. He also considered a B-26 harder to bring down than a Flying Fortress; the Marauder pilots tended to fly tighter formations, and the fire put out by their gunners was remarkably accurate. Galland had seen a number of German fighters shot down by them.

The jets were closing at the rate of 300 meters per second, which meant there would be only a brief moment to fire. The bombers' machine guns were already putting out a stream of tracers, and Galland knew that only the most skilled fighter pilots could get hits. He flicked off the safety for the cannons, took aim at the lead bomber, and pressed the release button for the rockets.

They failed to ignite. In his excitement he'd forgotten to lift the second safety catch. Angry with himself for being so careless, he fired all four of his cannons at close range. Shells from the Mk-108s struck the bomber and it exploded. Galland then raised the nose of his jet and hurtled over the enemy formation, startled to see Leutnant Schallmoser's aircraft whizz past him, just missing his port wingtip. It occurred to Galland that the jet rammer didn't seem to care who he rammed, friend or foe.

The general banked left as steeply as he dared, and as he leveled off and closed on the rear of the enemy he picked out another B-26 and lined up on it. This time he made sure all safeties were off before firing. His rockets flashed into the formation and the aircraft he'd targeted took a hit and staggered out of position, trailing black smoke. He again pulled up over the bombers and looked back to see whether the one he'd damaged would crash. Apparently it would; the Marauder was ablaze and spinning down out of control.

Watching it was his second error. A stream of bullets from a Mustang hammered his aircraft and the instrument panel shattered before his face. He then felt a sharp pain in his right knee. To his chagrin, he'd been caught napping—in his eagerness to attack the bombers he hadn't seen that they had escorts after all, and now he was paying for it. The sky was suddenly filled with Mustangs, and they were anxious to finish him off.

The jet was still flying, but it was badly shot up. His left engine had been hit, and so had the right. Blood was pouring from his wounded leg.

He wanted to bail out, but the enemy might shoot him as he hung in his parachute. His only other option was to outrun the American fighters, provided, that is, his turbines didn't fail. As carefully as he could, he turned south. The damaged jet wasn't as fast as it normally was, but it was still faster than the pursuing Mustangs, and he pulled away from them.

Minutes later Munich lay ahead of him, with Riem to his left. As he reached the airfield and descended to make his approach, he discovered a new problem: the throttle linkage had been severed, and he was unable to reduce power. At the same time, he saw that the base was under attack by P-47s, who were strafing and dropping bombs. Galland had run out of choices. All he could do now was land as quickly as possible, before the Thunderbolts caught him. He shut down both engines, lined up on the runway, and brought the jet in at 275 kph.

The heavy aircraft hit hard. As it slammed onto the rough surface the tires blew, but for some reason the gear did not collapse. Despite the agony in his knee, he pressed the brakes and gradually brought the machine to a stop. He got out of the cockpit and hobbled to a nearby shell hole and fell into it.

The ground was shaking from the bomb bursts, and machine gun fire from the attacking fighters was kicking up dirt near where he lay. Adding to the cacophony was the roar of the enemy's engines, which made his ears ring. He fully expected to be hit at any moment.

A few seconds later he heard a different sound, and recognized it as the hum of a diesel engine. Peering over the edge of the crater, he saw an armored tractor pick its way around the rubble and head for him. The machine was being driven by one of his mechanics, and when it reached him he dragged himself aboard. Dodging bullets and shell holes, the mechanic then steered the tractor to a grove of trees off the runway. Galland clapped the man on the shoulder in a gesture of thanks and admiration for his courage.

The general was taken to a hospital in Munich, where doctors removed shell splinters from his knee. The limb was then encased in a plaster cast, which meant it would be weeks before he could walk again. Though he was eventually able to walk, the injury to his joint left his gait with a stiffness that would remain for the rest of his life. And he would never again fly in combat.

The pilots of JG44 carried on without him. On the day of Galland's last battle, Oberstleutnant Heinz Bär took command of the staffel.

93.

Kreisleiter Schiede, the Nazi party official, did not give up. At the end of April he wrote to Messerschmitt again, pressing his demand that 81 members of the Professor's Research Department be turned over to the Volkssturm for training. It was vital, he claimed, because "every hour brings the enemy closer to the heartland of Germany." As before, Messerschmitt did not reply to the letter. He was well aware that advancing American armored units were only a short distance from Oberammergau. For that reason he had all documents and drawings pertaining to the P-1101 sealed in watertight containers and hidden in nearby mountain caves.

On 29 April, tanks and trucks bearing U.S. troops rolled onto the grounds of the Messerschmitt complex. The American soldiers at first thought the place was of little significance. There were many workers there, but most were civilians, and the few German troops on hand were guards who offered no resistance. No artillery or antiaircraft batteries were present.

It was obvious, however, that this was an aircraft design center. Drawings on drafting tables and an abundance of metalworking equipment, engines and airplane parts made that apparent. The soldiers weren't sure what to do with what they found, so they destroyed most of it with axes. When they came across the unfinished P-1101 prototype in the underground hangar, they hacked off pieces for souvenirs.

It finally dawned on them that they'd made an important discovery—they'd found the location where the renowned Willy Messerschmitt carried on his work, and the tall, thin man with the graying hair and the pale face was the Professor himself. The facility was suddenly of some consequence, and in Messerschmitt they'd captured a valuable prize. He was arrested and placed under guard. The news was sent by radio up the chain of command, and word came back that Messerschmitt was to be held for interrogation.

Agents working for the French learned where the documents and drawings of the P-1101 had been hidden, and retrieved them. The agents sent the papers to the French government in Paris, and when the Americans found out what had happened and asked for their return, the

French officials refused to hand them over.

Willy Messerschmitt was deeply humiliated. His beloved country had been overrun by its enemies, and his company had been completely destroyed. And now, after all the information he could supply had been wrung out of him, he might be tried as a war criminal!

During those fateful days in late April another career ended, and far more ignominiously. On the 28th, Italian dictator Benito Mussolini left Milan in an attempt to escape the approaching American forces. Il Duce was put aboard a truck that was part of a German convoy headed for the Alps. Following the convoy in a car was a party that included his mistress, Clara Petacci, and her brother Marcello. When the vehicles reached the village of Dongo, they were stopped and searched by Communist partisans. Mussolini was wearing a German Army overcoat and helmet to hide his identity, but the partisans were not deceived, nor did they fail to recognize Clara Petacci. Both Mussolini and his mistress were taken captive, and the following day they were put up against a wall and shot.

Their bodies, and those of five executed Fascist officials, were hung by their heels above an Esso gas station in the Piazzale Loreto in Milan. Fifteen other Fascists were also shot, and their corpses were left lying about on the ground nearby. A mob gathered, with people shaking their fists and shouting imprecations against their former leader.

When Hitler learned of Mussolini's death, he fell into depression. More bad news came to him when General Weidling reported that the Russians had reached Wilhelmstrasse near the Air Ministry. Weidling said the enemy would batter their way to the Chancellory by 1 May at the latest.

Hitler was now forced to confront the truth. He sent a message to General Keitel, Chief of Oberkommando der Wehrmacht, saying it was no longer possible to defend Berlin, and that he would kill himself rather than surrender. He claimed that Göring and Himmler had betrayed him, as had the generals of the army. The Luftwaffe had lost its air superiority because of mistakes made by Göring. And since the navy had fought courageously, he was appointing Admiral Dönitz his successor.

Hitler married Eva Braun in a brief ceremony shortly after midnight, during which his followers wished them well and toasted them with champagne. The couple then retired to Hitler's private quarters.

After that a weird party took place in the bunker, where recorded music was played loudly, copious amounts of alcohol were consumed, and men and women danced and engaged in a drunken sexual orgy.

By then the Führer had decided that it was time for him to bring his life and Eva's to an end. Subservient to him as always, she agreed. Hitler ordered his chauffeur, Erich Kempka, to deliver gasoline to the bunker in preparation for what the Führer planned as a Viking funeral. Kempka rounded up 180 liters, and carried the fuel to the bunker as instructed.

At 3:30 PM on 30 April, ten days after his 56th birthday, Hitler bade farewell to his closest collaborator, Dr. Goebbels, and to Generals Krebs and Burgdorf. He had his dog Blondi poisoned, and his other two dogs shot. Then he and his bride went into their bedroom, where they took cyanide. Eva died at once, and as Hitler bit down on his capsule, he fired a shot from a Walther PPK into his brain. The bodies were carried out of the bunker and deposited in a shell hole in the garden. While explosions from Russian artillery shook the ground, gasoline was poured into the hole and lighted. Goebbels, Bormann, and the others watched as the flames mounted, their arms raised in a Nazi salute.

The following day, 1 May, Goebbels and his wife Magda poisoned their six children. Afterward Goebbels ordered an SS trooper to shoot him and Magda. The trooper fired two bullets into the back of each of their heads, and their bodies were doused with gasoline and burned.

Before her death, Magda wrote a letter to her son Harald. The young man was her only child by her first husband, Günther Quandt, the rich industrialist who owned controlling interest in BMW and the Varta Battery firm, as well as a large block of stock in Daimler-Benz. In the letter Magda said she would die along with Goebbels and her children because she believed that life in Germany after the war could not be worth living.

Bormann and most of those still alive in the bunker attempted to escape by following a German tank through the lines, but the tank was struck by a Russian shell and Bormann was killed. Generals Krebs and Burgdorf made no effort to escape; instead, they stayed in the ruins of the Chancellory and shot themselves.

That same evening, the Hamburg radio played a recording of Bruckner's 7th Symphony. The broadcast was interrupted by the roll of drums, and an announcer intoned, "Our Führer, Adolf Hitler, fighting to the last breath against Bolshevism, fell this afternoon in his operational headquarters in the Reich Chancellory. On 30 April the Führer appointed Grand Admiral Dönitz his successor."

The description of Hitler's death was a lie, of course. The Führer had not fought to the last breath, but had died a coward's death. The date was a lie as well. The announcer continued: "The Grand Admiral and successor of the Führer now speaks to the German people."

Dönitz declared that his first task was to save Germany from destruction by the advancing Bolshevik enemy. The Führer had died a hero, Dönitz said, but it was imperative that Germans go on fighting. But that too was a lie—the admiral's true purpose was to stall. He hoped to surrender what remained of the German military to the British and the Americans, rather than to the Soviets, and for good reason. Russian soldiers were already looting and pillaging, with their commanders' blessing. More than a hundred thousand German women would be raped by Red Army troops.

Dönitz sent Admiral Hans von Friedeburg, the new Commander in Chief of the German Navy, to General Eisenhower's headquarters at Reims to negotiate a surrender, but Eisenhower would not bargain. He insisted that the surrender be unconditional, and the German High Command was forced to accept his terms.

The report of Hitler's death surprised many members of the German armed forces, including the pilots of the jet staffeln. Though they knew the end of the war was near, it had not been necessary for Dönitz to urge them to continue fighting. They were determined to do that anyway.

94.

There was not much left to fight with. The pilots of JV44 used the last of their fuel in a flight to Salzburg. They had hoped to replenish their stocks there, but were disappointed to find that no fuel was available. The next day they stood on the field and watched helplessly as Thunderbolts circled overhead, out of range of the flak batteries. It was obvious that the Americans planned to capture the Me-262s intact. The pilots reasoned that if they couldn't fly, they at least could prevent the enemy from seizing their aircraft. When American tanks rolled onto the field, the Germans set fire to the jets. The flames reduced each of JV44's Me-262s to a puddle of molten metal, the graves marked by columns of black smoke.

At Prague/Ruzyne the few remaining fighter-bombers of KG(J)51 did have fuel—it was only a little, but enough for the pilots to keep their vow to fight on. Seven of them, along with their leader, Hauptmann Rudolf Abrahamczik, provided close support to the pockets of German ground forces that were holding out against the Russians. The jets strafed and dropped bombs, but the sorties were only a defiant gesture. On 6 May, Thunderbolts of the 9th Air Force attacked the fighter-bombers, damaging two, and killing the pilot of another, Leutnant Horst Schimmel.

The following day Germany signed a formal document of unconditional surrender, although Abrahamczik and his pilots were unaware of it. Again they flew against the Russians, and again they were attacked by American fighters. Leutnant Erwin Strothmann and Feldwebel Franz Poling were killed. Rather than become prisoners of the Russians, Abrahamczik led Leutnants Batel, Haeffner, and Froelich in a flight to the west.

JG7, also at Prague/Ruzyne, made several sweeps on those last days of the war. The unit had only a handful of serviceable aircraft, and though the pilots were looking for action, they did not engage the enemy. On 8 May, mechanics began burning the jets there as well. Except for the snapping and hissing of the fires, an eerie quiet settled over the base—no longer was the air rent with the roar of engines and the constant hammering of guns. The war was officially over.

But not for Oberleutnant Fritz Stehle. With growing anger, he watched as the jets were burned, aware that now the pilots and ground personnel who were still at Prague/Ruzyne had nowhere to go, no way to escape the Soviet forces that would soon overrun the field. He and his comrades would be captured, and he held no illusions about the treatment they could expect in Russian prison camps. As the mechanics prepared to torch the last Me-262, Stehle stopped them. After checking the aircraft, he found that there was still fuel in its tanks, but the rocket racks were empty, and so were the Borsigs' magazines.

Stehle barked orders. Armorers looked at him curiously, but did as directed. Though there were no more rockets on hand, they did have 30mm cannon shells, which were loaded into the jet's magazines. When they finished, Stehle climbed into the cockpit and started the Riedel motor and then the turbines. He closed the canopy and set the flaps at 20 degrees down.

What was he thinking? The orders from the Luftwaffe High Command, signed by General von Greim, were explicit—there was to be no further resistance. And yet, this was his life, not theirs. He had never disobeyed a direct order, but what authority did the failed leadership have at this point? For six long years, Stehle had fought for the Fatherland through some of the fiercest air battles of the war. Having served as a staffelkapitän, he'd seen many of his closest friends die. His record stood at 26 kills in the Bf-109, and ten more in the Me-262. And now, after all this, he was to surrender to the enemy meekly, like a whipped dog? No, he would not do that. He eased the throttles forward and the jet began its takeoff roll. The runway was patched and uneven, and the aircraft bounced its way along, slowly picking up speed until at last it left the ground.

Once airborne, he tucked in his gear and flaps and climbed steadily to an altitude of 3,000 meters. As always, he took pleasure in the sense of eagerness he felt in the aircraft—an Me-262 seemed to have a special spirit of its own. He turned north, his eyes scanning the horizon. Visibility was not good, obstructed by haze and patchy clouds. He was alone in the sky.

Below him, masses of men and vehicles were clogging the roads. They would be Soviets, of course, a vast horde of them. The long lines stretched away into the distance, with no German troops in sight. He made a wide 360-degree turn, looking down at the invaders. He contemplated what would happen to Germany under the heel of the Russian boot, and felt a surge of bitterness.

As he came around, he noticed a speck five or six kilometers ahead of him and slightly higher. It was an airplane, flying in the same direction he was. He flew toward it and approached from the rear, watching it carefully. As he came closer he recognized the aircraft as a Soviet fighter, a Yak 9. Apparently the pilot was unaware of his presence.

Stehle hadn't engaged in combat with a fighter of this type, but because the Luftwaffe put out data on all enemy aircraft, he was familiar with its specs. The Yak 9 was not particularly fast, he recalled, with a maximum speed of about 670 kph. It was powered by a Klimov V-12 liquid-cooled engine, and armament was one 20mm cannon and two 12.7mm machine guns.

What was the Russian pilot up to? Was he just lollygagging, having himself a joyride over the defeated Germans? Probably. Reminding himself not to fire too soon, Stehle climbed to the other aircraft's altitude. The Me-262's speed enabled him to approach the Yak quickly, and he kept it squarely in his gunsight. When it grew larger in the sight, at a distance of about 400 meters, he released the cannons' safeties.

He waited another few seconds, and then pressed the triggers. The four Borsigs spit out a stream of tracers, and the shells smashed into the Soviet fighter. Flames erupted from its cowling, and then the fuel tank exploded in a brilliant flash. Stehle flew through black smoke and bits of wreckage, and turned back toward Prague. He was tired and spent, and had nothing more to give. For him, as for Germany, the war was now truly over.

It was over for Willy Messerschmitt's superb creation as well, as no Me-262 would ever fly in combat again. Because its appearance had been a matter of too little, too late, it had never fulfilled its potential.

But the Me-262 had led the way into a new age of aviation.

EPILOGUE

Following his arrest, Willy Messerschmitt was put aboard a C-47 transport and flown to London. Along with a number of other German aircraft designers, including Kurt Tank, he was held in a hotel and only loosely guarded.

For the next three years, Messerschmitt and his fellow engineers were rigorously interrogated by British and American aviation experts who were eager to learn all they could about German rocket and jet propulsion technology. The Russians had also rounded up as many German scientists as possible, and were pursuing their own secret interests in creating the next generation of warplanes.

In 1948 Messerschmitt was released and permitted to return to Germany. No charges were brought against him as a war criminal, but he was forbidden to work in the development of aircraft. In fact, no company in Germany was allowed to build airplanes. Other industries were also in dismal straits, and few Germans had jobs. The country's coal mines had been shut down by Allied decree, and much of the food that had been produced in the farmlands was expropriated by the Soviets and sent to Russia. Many people in Germany starved, and others died of disease.

Then in 1947 came the miracle of the Marshall Plan. The program provided countries with cash that would enable their industries to rebound. Although the UK, France and Italy all received more money, no nation responded as vigorously as Germany.

Willy Messerschmitt seized the opportunity. He restored the factory at Augsburg, and began manufacturing sewing machines and auto parts, as well as prefabricated houses to replace the millions of homes destroyed in the war. There was also a shortage of automobiles, so his company built the Kabinenroller, which was a three-wheeled motor scooter with an enclosed cabin. The driver sat in front, with a passenger in the rear. Top speed was 80 kph, and the machine traveled 75 km on a gallon of fuel.

In 1951 the Spanish government brought Messerschmitt to Seville to work as a consultant to Hispano-Aviación. He and his engineers produced an updated version of the Bf-109, and went on to design the HA-100, a jet trainer, and the HA-200, a jet fighter, for the Spanish Air Force. While in Spain, Willy and the Baroness bought a second home there, and in 1952, after having been together for more than 25 years, they were married. He was 54, she was 61. A year later the government of Egypt hired him to improve that country's air force, but he found the officials impossible to deal with and returned to Germany.

In 1955 restrictions on aircraft production in Germany were lifted, and Messerschmitt joined his old rival, Ernest Heinkel, in building the French Fouga Magister under license as a trainer for the newly reborn Luftwaffe. Next he built Lockheed F-104 and Fiat G31 fighters under licence. In 1969 he merged his firm into the Messerschmitt-Bölkow-Blohm Group and was appointed chairman of the supervisory board. He took part in the formation of the European Airbus project, and contributed ideas for the construction of the new transport.

That same year Willy was invited to attend the graduation ceremonies in America for Luftwaffe pilots who had been trained by the U.S. Air Force. The festivities were held at Luke Air Force Base in Arizona, and he was asked to speak. For the next hour he stood at the lectern, chain-smoking cigarettes and discussing his views of aviation and the aircraft he'd developed during his career. Messerschmitt said that if he'd had reliable turbojet engines, and the German government had not been so misguided, his Me-262 "could have been completed in time for the Battle of Britain, which we then would have won."

"Even after the war," Messerschmitt went on, "an American general told me that if we'd had 200 Me-262s in combat during the Normandy invasion, it would not have been possible to make the landing. But I don't think we would have won in the end, not after America came in. I don't think we could have beaten America and its huge industries." He also said that Hitler had vetoed his plans for a long-range jet reconnaissance aircraft that could have been converted into a commercial airliner. "If we'd won the war, I could have had a passenger jet flying nonstop 7,000 kilometers from Frankfurt to New York by 1947 or 1948, almost ten years before the Boeing 707."

On Christmas day, 1973, the Baroness died. After all she'd meant to Willy, her death was a crushing blow. Five years later, on 15 September 1978, Messerschmitt died after undergoing a major operation in a hospital in Munich.

Willy Messerschmitt and the Baroness now lie side by side in crypts in the Porticusgruft of the cemetery in Bamberg. Only a few commemorations have been held to honor the life of this aeronautical genius.

* * * * *

Messerschmitt's P-1101 project did not die. After the capture of Oberammergau by American troops in May 1945, the damaged prototype of the jet stood outside for two years and deteriorated from exposure to the weather. But when Robert J. Woods of the Bell Aircraft Corporation learned of the aircraft's existence, he immediately grasped its significance.

Woods contacted Messerschmitt's chief designer, Woldemar Voigt, and together they revived the project. The prototype was shipped by them to the Bell factory in Buffalo, New York, where much of its technology was incorporated in the Bell X-5, the forerunner of a number of highly successful U.S. Air Force swept-wing jet fighters.

ACKNOWLEDGEMENTS

Many people provided me with valuable information as I wrote this book. I much appreciate their help, and thank them for their generosity and their enthusiasm for the project.

I'm especially grateful to the members of the Messerschmitt family, and to a number of men on both sides who flew in World War II.

Eberhard Stromeyer, the stepson of Willy Messerschmitt, was a trove of insights and little-known facts. In the discussions I had with him, I became familiar with aspects of the Professor's personality I would never have known about otherwise. I also learned many details of Messerschmitt's work and experiences that were extremely valuable to me in my efforts to present a fair-minded picture of the man.

Another family member who was very helpful was Willy's niece, Lydia Pschorn. When my wife and I visited Professor Messerschmitt's hometown of Bamberg, we stayed in the house that had been his boyhood home, and which the family now runs as a hotel. Frau Pschorn was most gracious and forthcoming, and she too provided me with fascinating stories and anecdotes. Her memories of her uncle were still very clear, and it was apparent that she felt deep affection for him.

Frau Pschorn put me in touch with Professor Gero Madelung, a cousin who lives in Munich. He provided the photo of Messerschmitt and the Baroness that appears in this book, and I wish to thank him for it.

Heinz Surhrbeer, a former Luftwaffe pilot who flew the Me-262 in combat, told me a great deal about life in the German air force, and about his logging thousands of hours in many types of aircraft. A photo of him on the bow of an Me-262 is also in the book. My wife and I visited Heinz and his wife Charlotte at their home in northern Germany a number of times. Heinz died on 16 September 2009.

Another former Me-262 pilot who has been very helpful is Hans Busch, a retired executive of General Dynamics Corp. Hans has been an American citizen for many years, and lives in southern California. His autobiography "The Last Of The Few," is excellent.

Thanks also to Jim Long, a former Spitfire pilot I first met 40 years ago. Jim fought in the Battle of Britain, and recounted his experiences during that fateful time, and about other aspects of the RAF's war in the air.

And my thanks to the late John Phillips, a former First Lieutenant in the USAAF who flew P-47s in combat. John too had much to say about his engagements with the Luftwaffe. Later he became president of the Antique Aircraft Association of America, and through him I came to know Bud Gurney, who learned to fly with Charles Lindbergh and barnstormed with him. I had the pleasure of flying Bud's 1925 De Havilland Gypsy Moth, which he based at the Santa Paula, CA airport.

Thanks are due as well to three former U.S. Navy fighter pilots for their contributions on combat tactics. They are retired Lt. Commander Jack Horan, who flew Corsairs in WWII; Lt. Bob Hallabeck, who flew a Hellcat in the Battle of Okinawa; and retired Lt. John Fox, veteran of more than 150 carrier landings in various jet fighters.

Finally, I would like to pay a personal tribute to Professor Messerschmitt's genius as an aircraft designer. I've owned a number of airplanes over the years, and one of the most interesting was a Messerschmitt Bf-108. The type first flew in 1934, and was well ahead of its time. For example, I've also owned three modern Beechcraft Bonanzas, and many aspects of their design were similar to those in the Bf-108. The Bonanzas were fine aircraft, but the Taifun was faster than any of them.

SOURCE NOTES

PRELUDE
RAF mission of 26 July 1944: Flight Lt. A.E. Wall's combat report no. 2256, now in the Imperial War Museum archives in London. Author interview with former RAF pilot James Long. John Foreman and S.E. Harvey "Me-262 Combat Diary" p. 34. *History of the Bavarian Motor Works:* records of the BMW Museum in Munich. *Development of the De Havilland Mosquito:* "Combat Legend De Havilland Mosquito" by Robert Jackson, pp. 5–41. *De Havilland Aircraft Company:* "History of De Havilland" by C. Sharp, D.H. Martin.

CHAPTER I
Messerschmitt family's vacation at Lake Constance in 1909; visit to Friedrichshafen to see zeppelins: Frank Vann "Willy Messerschmitt" pp. 12–13. *Ferdinand von Zeppelin's pioneering construction of lighter-than-air dirigibles; specifications of the LZ6:* Alexander Vomel "Graf von Zeppelin Ein Mann der Tat." *Young Willy's proficiency in mathematics; Willy's interest in autos, motorcycles and airplanes:* author's interviews with Lydia Pschorn, Messerschmitt's niece, and with Messerschmitt's stepson, Eberhard Stromeyer. *Messerschmitt's military service; association with Harth and growing proficiency as designer:* Frank Vann "Willy Messerschmitt" pp. 14–19.

CHAPTER 2
Turmoil in Germany following World War I; rise of Hitler and Nazi party: William L. Shirer "The Rise and Fall of the Third Reich" pp. 3–80. *Messerschmitt's education; ongoing efforts in designing and building gliders; break with Harth:* Frank Vann "Willy Messerschmitt" pp. 20–24.

CHAPTER 3
Messerschmitt's room in the Weinhaus Messerschmitt; financial help from his older brother, Ferdinand: Interview with Messerschmitt's niece, Lydia Pschorn. *Messerschmitt's first company, Flugzuegbau Messerschmitt Bamberg; Rhön Competition of*

1924; meeting Theo Croneiss: Armand van Ishoven "Messerschmitt, Aircraft Designer" pp. 25–27. *Performance of S15 at Rhön:* "Flugsport" September 1924. *Douglas Engineering Co. engines:* Cyrus and Richmond Dave "Fifty Years of Motorcycles."

CHAPTER 4
Messerschmitt's design and construction for Theo Croneiss of the M17; later development of the M18 and the M19; success in various competitive events: Frank Vann "Willy Messerschmitt" pp. 31–34. *Conversion of Messerschmitt's firm to a privately held stock company and his growing interest in the Nazi party:* Ibid. *Loyalty to Hitler of Rudolf Hess and Hermann Göring:* William L. Shirer "The Rise and Fall of the Third Reich" pp. 117–231.

CHAPTER 5
Hitler's increasing political prominence following his release from prison, and his relationships with women: A. Bullock "Hitler, A Study in Tyranny" pp. 89–171. *Messerschmitt becomes chief designer of BFW:* Frank Vann "Willy Messerschmitt" pp. 34–38. *Business dealings with Erhard Milch:* Ibid pp. 41–42. *Baroness Lilly von Michel-Raulino Stromeyer and the Stromeyer-Raulino Financial Group:* Ibid p. 40. *Baroness's personal interest in Willy Messerschmitt:* Author interview with Lydia Pschorn.

CHAPTER 6
BFW's financial problems; help from Stromeyer-Raulino Financial Group: Frank Vann "Willy Messerschmitt" p. 40. *Death of Hackmack in crash of M20b; Milch reaction:* Ibid p. 41. *German government's interest in having Messerschmitt design military biplanes:* Ibid pp. 42–43. *Messerschmitt's personal relationship with the Baroness:* Author interview with members of Messerschmitt family.

CHAPTER 7
Effect on Germany of world economic depression: William L. Shirer "The Rise and Fall of the Third Reich" pp. 117–150. *Actions of Hermann Göring and Ernst Roehm in Nazi party:* Ibid p. 120. *Hitler's maneuvering to gain power:* Ibid pp. 150–188. *Appointment of Milch as State Secretary for Air:* David Irving "The Rise and Fall of the Luftwaffe" p. 28. *Messerschmitt joins the Nazi party:* Frank Vann "Willy Messerschmitt" p. 49.

CHAPTER 8
Hitler disposes of Ernst Roehm: William L. Shirer "The Rise and Fall of the Third Reich" pp. 219–222. *Milch orders BFW to build Dornier and Heinkel aircraft under license:* Armand van Ishoven "Messerschmitt, Aircraft Designer" pp. 73–4. *Messerschmitt builds the M35; Rudolf Hess wins Zugspitz Trophy of 1934 flying the aircraft:* Ibid p. 77. *Messerschmitt builds aircraft for Romanian airline, is forbidden by German government to build for other nations:* Ibid pp. 78–79. *Robert Lusser contributes to development of M37, which becomes Bf-108; Elly Einhorn*

calls her Bf-108 Taifun; success of Bf-108 leads to development of Bf-109: Ibid. *Messerschmitt's development of the Bf-110:* Anthony Pritchard "Messerschmitt," pp. 82–90.

CHAPTER 9
Events leading to war in Spain; involvement of Germany: Raymond L. Proctor "Hitler's Luftwaffe in the Spanish Civil War" pp. 11–50. *Creation of Condor Legion:* Ibid pp. 53–70. *Condor Legion in action:* Peter Elstob "Condor Legion" pp. 22–70.

CHAPTER 10
Bf-109s sent to Spain: Anthony Pritchard "Messerschmitt" pp. 30–31. *Various types of aircraft in Spain:* Peter Elstob "Condor Legion" pp. 42–43. *Adolf Galland exploits in Condor Legion:* Raymond L. Proctor "Hitler's Luftwaffe in the Spanish Civil War" pp. 164–165. *Fritz Seiler made trustee to thwart efforts by Milch and the RLM to seize control of BFW:* Armand van Ishoven "Messerschmitt, Aircraft Designer" p. 92.

CHAPTER 11
Günther Lützow's background and exploits as a fighter pilot in Spain: W. Brock-dorff "Der Landser Ritterkreuztrager NR 153 Oberst Günther Lützow." *Battle at Ochandiano, in which Hauptmann Lützow scored the first victory ever achieved in a Bf-109:* Raymond L. Proctor "Hitler's Luftwaffe in the Spanish Civil War" pp. 117–123. *Procedures for flying a Bf-109* were described to the author by former Luftwaffe pilot Heinz Suhrbeer, and by former U.S. Army Air Force pilot John Phillips.

CHAPTER 12
Improvements to the Bf-109: James Craig "Bf-109" pp. 12–26. *Werner Mölders' combat record:* Georges Blond "Born To Fly." *Bombing of Guernica:* Hugh Purcell "The Spanish Civil War." *Specially prepared Bf-109 sets new world speed record:* Armand van Ishoven "Messerschmitt, Aircraft Designer" pp. 101–102. *Charles Lindbergh's trip to Germany:* A. Scott Berg "Lindbergh" pp. 377–383. *Lindbergh's visit to the Messerschmitt plant:* Armand van Ishoven "Messerschmitt, Aircraft Designer" p. 111.

CHAPTER 13
Meeting in Augsburg at which representatives of BMW join Messerschmitt and his engineers and designers to discuss cooperation in the development of a jet aircraft: Willy Radinger and Walter Schick "Messerschmitt Me-262" p. 14. *Further details of the project:* BMW archives. Also Walter J. Boyne "Messerschmitt Me-262, Arrow to the Future" pp. 17–28.

CHAPTER 14
Hitler builds German military forces: William L. Shirer "The Rise and Fall of the

Third Reich" pp. 150–188. *Attempt by Georg Elser to assassinate Hitler:* Ibid pp. 654–656. *Conspiracy involving Generals Ludwig Beck and Kurt von Hammerstein:* Ibid p. 374–375. *German seizure of Czechoslovakia:* Ibid pp. 397–449. *Decision to change the name of the company from BFW to Messerschmitt AG:* Armand van Ishoven "Messerschmitt, Aircraft Designer" p. 108. *Development of the Me-264:* Ibid p. 115. *Development of the Me-209:* Anthony Pritchard "Messerschmitt" pp. 41–42.

CHAPTER 15
General Douhet's theories on the use of air power: Lt. Col. Richard H. Estes, "General Douhet: More on Target Than He Knew." *Göring's statement, "The Fuhrer does not ask me how big my bombers are, but how many there are":* David Irving "The Rise and Fall of the Luftwaffe" p. 55. *Condor Legion records:* Raymond L. Proctor "Hitler's Luftwaffe in the Spanish Civil War" pp. 253–254. *Troubles with the Me-210:* Frank Vann "Willy Messerschmitt" pp. 74–86. *Acceptance by the RLM of the Fieseler Storch:* Philip Makana "Himmelssturmer" p. 14. *German-Russian pact:* William L. Shirer "The Rise and Fall of the Third Reich" pp. 526–528. *Messerschmitt's view of the pact, reaction by the Baroness:* Author interview with Eberhard Stromeyer.

CHAPTER 16
Hans von Ohain's development of jet engines and work on the Heinkel He-178: "Journal of Engineering for Gas Turbines and Power," Volume 122 Issue 2, pp. 191–201. *Staging by General Reinhard Heydrich of an excuse for German forces to invade Poland:* William L. Shirer "The Rise and Fall of the Third Reich" pp. 518–520. *Invasion of Poland:* R.M. Kennedy "The German Campaign in Poland, 1939." *Tactics of the Wehrmacht in Poland:* Feldmarschal Erich von Manstein "Verlorene Siege" pp. 54–63. *Stuka bombing technique:* Bekker Cajus "The Luftwaffe War Diaries." *Polish pilots and aircraft:* Jan Koniarek, Don Greer, Tom Tullis "Polish Air Force 1939–1945."

CHAPTER 17
The phony war: "History of the Second World War Magazine Vol. 1 No. 4." *German invasions of Denmark and Norway:* Winston Churchill "The Gathering Storm" pp. 537–657. *Hitler setting a date for the invasions of Belgium, Holland and France:* David Irving "The Rise and Fall of the Luftwaffe" p. 86.

CHAPTER 18
Improvements to the Bf-109 in the Friderich version: Anthony Pritchard "Messerschmitt" pp. 58–77. *Alexander Lippisch's work:* Georg-Peter Diedrich "German Rocket Fighters of World War II" pp. 10–152. *Further development of the Me-262, including placement of the engines in underwing nacelles:* Willy Radinger and Walter Schick "Messerschmitt Me-262" p. 18.

CHAPTER 19
German invasion of France: Robert Wernick "World War II: Blitzkrieg" pp. 14–46.

French Air Force: Alistair Horne "How to Lose a Battle: France 1940" pp. 184–185. *General Maurice Gamelin:* Gerard Beaulieu "The Republic in Danger: General Maurice Gamelin and the Politics of French Defense 1933–1940." *Hitler's acceptance of General Manstein's plan:* Feldmarschal Erich von Manstein "Verlorene Siege" pp. 68–123. *Rommel's exploits:* David Irving "The Trail of the Fox" pp. 41–57. *Adolf Galland in France:* Adolf Galland "The First and the Last," pp. 1–9. *French surrender:* Francis Trevelyan Miller "History of World War II" pp. 214–223. *French-German air battles:* Major L.F. Ellis "The War in France and Flanders" pp. 98, 309, 312, 372–373.

CHAPTER 20

Messerschmitt invited to Berlin along with Ernst Heinkel and Ferdinand Porsche to be congratulated by Adolf Hitler: "Volkischer Beobachter" July 1940. *Hitler's Reich Chancellery:* "Die Kunst Im Dritten Reich," September 1939. *Hitler's relationship with Albert Speer:* Albert Speer "Inside the Third Reich." *Joseph Goebbels:* Speeches and Essays 1940. *Hermann Göring's massive thievery:* David Irving "The Rise and Fall of the Luftwaffe" pp. 148–149.

CHAPTER 21

Operation Sea Lion: William L. Shirer "Rise and Fall of the Third Reich" by pp. 760–768. *Invasion of Britain thwarted:* Ibid pp. 71–74. *A new Me-262 proposal:* Willy Radinger and Walter Schick "Messerschmitt Me-262" p. 18. *Issuance by the RLM of order for 20 trials aircraft:* Ibid p. 18. *New Managing Director Fritz W. Seiler:* Frank Vann "Willy Messerschmitt" p. 90. *Problems with the Me-210:* Ibid p. 90–91.

CHAPTER 22

Luftwaffe problems in Battle of Britain: Winston Churchill "Their Finest Hour" pp. 320–324. *Failure of Bf-110 in Battle of Britain:* Anthony Pritchard "Messerschmitt" pp. 92–96. *Bf-110 called dackelbauch by Luftwaffe pilots:* Ibid p. 92. *Luftwaffe plan:* Adolf Galland "The First and the Last" pp. 10–14. *Comparison of the Bf-109 vis-a-vis British fighters:* Ibid p. 17. *RAF viewpoint:* author's interview with former RAF Sgt. Pilot James Long. *RAF pilot Sailor Malan dogfight with Werner Mölders:* Graham Wallace "RAF Biggin Hill" pp. 47–48. *Failure of Ju-87 in Battle of Britain:* Adolf Galland "The First and the Last" p. 22. *Richthofen on fighter tactics:* Ibid p. 25.

CHAPTER 23

Luftwaffe bombing of London: William L. Shirer "The Rise and Fall of the Third Reich" pp. 777–778. *RAF response and Hitler's reaction:* Ibid pp. 778–780. *Messerschmitt Me-264 bomber:* Anthony Pritchard "Messerschmitt" pp. 118–124. *Indefinite postponement of Operation Sea Lion:* Winston Churchill "Their Finest Hour" p. 310. *British Royal Navy attack at Taranto:* Ibid pp. 543–544. *Luftwaffe use of radio-beam navigation in attack on Coventry:* William L. Shirer "The Rise and Fall of the Third Reich" p. 114.

CHAPTER 24

Continuing problems with Bf-109 undercarriage: Frank Vann "Willy Messerschmitt" pp. 65–67. *Article by Professor Messerschmitt on development of Bf-109 and Bf-110:* "Front und Heimat" February 1940. *Göring criticism of fighter pilots:* Adolf Galland "The First and the Last" pp. 28–29. *Luftwaffe raids on other cities in Great Britain:* Winston Churchill "Their Finest Hour" p. 377. *Heinkel jet fighter:* Anthony Pritchard "Messerschmitt" pp. 149–150. *Test of Me262V1 with jets plus piston engine:* Willy Radinger and Walter Schick "Messerschmitt Me-262" p. 23.

CHAPTER 25

Kurt Tank, aircraft designer: Eberhard Weber and Uwe Feist "Focke-Wulf 190, Wurger." *History of Focke-Wulf Aircraft Co:* Ibid. *Fw-190 engine:* David Irving "The Rise and Fall of the Luftwaffe p. 131. *Maneuvering by Ernst Udet to favor the Fw-190 over the Bf-109:* Ibid p. 137–138.

CHAPTER 26

Request by Rudolf Hess for Bf-110: Frank Vann "Willy Messerschmitt" pp. 74–77. *Hess flight to Scotland:* Joseph Hutton "Hess: The Man and His Mission." *Hess's mental condition:* David Moriarty "Rudolf Hess, Deputy Fuhrer."

CHAPTER 27

Willy Messerschmitt's compliance with request for Bf-110 by Rudolf Hess: Frank Vann "Willy Messerschmitt" pp. 75–76. *British reaction to Hess flight:* Winston Churchill "The Grand Alliance" pp. 48–55. *Hitler's reaction to Hess defection:* William L. Shirer "The Rise and Fall of the Third Reich" pp. 834–838. *Willy Messerschmitt's non-involvement in Hess plan for flight:* Frank Vann "Willy Messerschmitt" pp. 76–77. *Royal Navy pursuit and sinking of the Bismarck:* Winston Churchill "The Grand Alliance" pp. 305–319. *German attack on the Soviet Union:* Francis Trevelyan Miller "History of World War II" p. 364.

CHAPTER 28

Panzer drive into Russia: Erich von Manstein "Verloren Siege" pp. 175–203. *Luftwaffe in combat in Russia:* David Irving "The Rise and Fall of the Luftwaffe" p. 126. Also "U.S. Air Force Historical Study No. 153—The German Air Force versus Russia—1941." *Stuka in Russian campaign:* Hans Ulrich Rudel "Stuka Pilot." *Luftwaffe bombing in Russia:* Klaus Haberlen "A Luftwaffe Bomber Pilot Remembers." *Russian fighter pilot:* Alexander Pokryshkin "Sky Of War." *Decision by Hitler to attack Moscow:* William L. Shirer "The Rise and Fall of the Third Reich" p. 859.

CHAPTER 29

Wehrmacht struggles in Russian winter: James S. Lucas "War on the Eastern Front: The German Soldier in Russia 1941–45." *Werner Mölders, Adolf Galland et al:* Jon E. Lewis, editor "The Mammoth Book of Fighter Pilots." Messerschmitt's personal regard for Luftwaffe pilots including Mölders and Galland conveyed to author by Eberhard Stromeyer. *Order by RLM to build reconnaissance version of Me-262:* Willy Radinger and Walter Schick "Messerschmitt Me-262" p. 23. *RLM renewed interest in long-range bombers:* Anthony Pritchard "Messerschmitt" pp. 118–122. *Incompetence of Udet's department:* David Irving "The Rise and Fall of The Luftwaffe" pp. 123–124.

CHAPTER 30

Problems with Junkers engines because of metal shortages: Willy Radinger and Walter Schick "Messerschmitt Me-262" p. 23. *Development of the Me-163 rocket-powered Komet:* Anthony Pritchard "Messerschmitt" pp. 133–147. *Downfall of Ernst Udet ending in his suicide:* David Irving "The Rise and Fall of the Luftwaffe" pp. 127–139. *Death of Werner Mölders:* "Aces of the Luftwaffe."

CHAPTER 31

News of Japanese attack on Pearl Harbor: BBC broadcasts 7–8 December 1941. Articles in "Volkischer Beobachter" plus radio broadcasts in Germany same dates. *US declaration of war on Germany 8 December 1941:* Francis Trevelyan Miller "History of World War II" p. 948. *Germany and Italy declare war on United States:* Ibid. *German technical advisers in Japan:* Author interview with H. Winkler, German business executive who was in Japan before and during attack on Pearl Harbor. *General Billy Mitchell's efforts to alert US military to air power:* Burke Davis "The Billy Mitchell Affair." *Naval exercises at Pearl Harbor in 1932 directed by US Navy Admiral Harry Yarnell:* "Papers of Harry E. Yarnell," Operational Archives Branch, Naval Historical Center, Washington, DC. *Hitler speech on Pearl Harbor attack:* German archives, Munich. *Continuing problems with Me-210:* Frank Vann "Willy Messerschmitt" pp. 78–86. *Messerschmitt replaced by Theo Croneiss as managing director:* Ibid.

CHAPTER 32

Results of Me-210 production shutdown: Frank Vann "Willy Messerschmitt" p. 86. *Me-210 production resumed, aircraft now designated Me-410:* Ibid. *New turbojets arrive from BMW:* Willy Radinger and Walter Schick "Messerschmitt Me-262" p. 23. *Difficulties with BMW engines:* Ibid. *Flight test of Me-262V1 powered by both BMW turbojets and Jumo piston engine:* Ibid.

CHAPTER 33

Curtailment of flight tests by RLM: Ibid. *Otto Mader head of Junkers research laboratories:* Junkers Co. archives. *Göring visit to Augsburg:* author interview with Eberhard Stromeyer. *Data on Bf-109G, the Gustav:* Anthony Pritchard "Messerschmitt" pp. 71–77. *Doolittle raid on Tokyo:* US Naval Historical Center. *Ernst Udet's regard for Doolittle:* Hans Herlin "Der Teufels Flieger" p. 97. *German Propaganda Ministry reports on Battle of Midway:* Articles in "Volkischer Beobachter" April 1942. *Doubts among German commanders:* William L. Shirer "The Rise and Fall of the Third Reich" p. 915. *Death of Reinhard Heydrich:* Callum

MacDonald "The Killing of SS Obergruppenfuhrer Reinhard Heydrich." *RAF raid on Cologne:* David Irving "The Rise and Fall of The Luftwaffe" p. 164. *General Galland says Germany needs more fighters:* Adolf Galland "The First and the Last" p. 169. *Junkers 004A engines delivered to Augsburg:* Willy Radinger and Walter Schick "Messerschmitt Me-262" p. 25.

CHAPTER 34

Installation of Junkers Jumo 004A turbojet engines in Me-262V3 prototype: Ibid. *Shift of flight test from Augsburg to Leipheim:* Ibid. *Fritz Wendel flies the V3 in test:* Anthony Pritchard "Messerschmitt" p. 151. *Wendel's report:* Willy Radinger and Walter Schick "Messerschmitt Me-262" p. 25.

CHAPTER 35

RLM reaction to successful test of Me-262V3: Ibid p. 25. *Heinrich Beauvais crash at Rechlin Test Center:* Ibid. *Albert Speer appointed State Minister of Armament:* David Irving "The Rise and Fall of the Luftwaffe" pp. 147–148. *RLM orders construction of additional Me-262s:* Willy Radinger and Walter Schick "Messerschmitt Me-262" p. 30. *Tide turns against Afrika Korps:* William L. Shirer "The Rise and Fall of the Third Reich" pp. 919–925. *Record of Hans Joachim Marseilles:* Adolf Galland "The First and the Last" p. 115. *Marseilles' combat techniques:* Werner Schror "Fighters Over the Desert" p. 232.

CHAPTER 36

Battle of Stalingrad: Erich von Manstein "Verloren Siege" pp. 289–366. *Hitler's refusal to allow retreat:* William L. Shirer "The Rise and Fall of the Third Reich" p. 930. *German Losses:* Ibid p. 932 *German propaganda regarding the disaster and Hitler's order of a day of mourning:* "Volkischer Beobachter" January 1943. *Messerschmitt's reaction to Hitler's proclamation of a day of mourning:* Author interview with Eberhard Stromeyer.

CHAPTER 37

US 8th Air Force operations: Roger A. Freeman "Mighty Eighth." *Major General Ira A. Eacker:* Cover article "Life Magazine" November 29, 1943. *General Douhet's theories on the conduct of aerial warfare:* Guilio Douhet "Command of the Air." *Sir Arthur "Bomber" Harris:* Norman Longmate "The Bombers: The RAF Offensive Against Germany 1939–1945." *Eaker's successful argument for "round-the-clock bombing" to Winston Churchill at Casablanca:* Dewitt S. Copp "A Few Great Captains: The Men and Events That Shaped the Development of US Air Power."

CHAPTER 38

Eighth Air Force raid on Wilhelmshaven January 1943: 8th Air Force archives. *General Eaker's theories on bombing:* James Parton "Air Force Spoken Here: General Ira Eaker and the Command of the Air" pp. 25–76. *Republic P-47 Thunderbolt:* Charles W. Cain and Mike Gerram "Fighters of World War II." *Also*

Richard Ward and Ernest R. McDowell "Republic P-47 Thunderbolt." *P-47 in combat:* author interview with former Lt. John Phillips. *RAF use of radar and Window:* David Irving "The Rise and Fall of the Luftwaffe" pp. 212–214. *Battle of Kasserine Pass:* Francis Trevelyan Miller "History of World War II" pp. 565–573. *Germans begin withdrawal from Africa:* Ibid pp. 604–606. *Maiden flight of Gloster Meteor:* Anthony Pritchard "Messerschmitt" p. 155.

CHAPTER 39

New orders from RLM: Anthony Pritchard "Messerschmitt" p. 89. *Problems with Kammhuber line of fighter defense:* David Irving "The Rise and Fall of the Luftwaffe" pp. 224–225. *Hitler orders all fighters must be able to perform as fighter-bombers:* Willy Radinger and Walter Schick "Messerschmitt Me-262" p. 30. *Feldsmarschal Milch institutes Vulcan program:* Ibid. *Redesign of Me-262 as fighter-bomber:* Ibid. *He-280 dropped from development program by RLM in favor of Me-262:* Ibid p. 33. *Hauptmann Spate flies the Me-262:* Ibid. *Test pilot Willy Ostertag killed:* Ibid. *Adolf Galland flies Me-262, writes favorable report:* Ibid. *Milch orders series production of the Me-262:* Ibid.

CHAPTER 40

RAF attacks on the Ruhr: David Irving "The Rise and Fall of the Luftwaffe" pp. 222–225. *Milch comments on bombing attacks:* Ibid p. 224. *Major Hermann's views:* Ibid. *Major Hermann conceives Wilde Sau defense:* Ibid p. 226. *RAF raids on Ruhr dams:* BBC archives. Also article in "Guardian Unlimited" 6 May 2003. Also article in "Manchester Guardian" 18 May 1943.

CHAPTER 41

Wilde Sau in action: David Irving "The Rise and Fall of the Luftwaffe" p. 227. *RAF raid on Krefeld:* Ibid p. 225. *Employment of Bf-110 as night-fighter:* Anthony Pritchard "Messerschmitt" pp. 96–98. *Feldmarschal von Manstein's opinion of Hitler as military commander:* Erich von Manstein "Verloren Siege" p. 446. *Operation Zitadelle:* Ibid pp. 443–449. *Hitler calls off Operation Zitadelle and diverts forces to Italy:* Ibid pp. 448–449.

CHAPTER 42

Operation Husky: Vincent J. Esposito Ed.: "The West Point Atlas of Wars Vol. II." Also S.W.C. Pack "Operation Husky, the Allied Invasion of Sicily." *Patton characterization of Montgomery:* Rick Atkinson "The Day of Battle" p. 295. *Mussolini replaced by King Vittorio Emanuele III:* William L. Shirer "The Rise and Fall of the Third Reich" pp. 995–997. *Hitler's reaction to Mussolini's downfall:* Ibid p. 998.

CHAPTER 43

Operation Gomorrah planned by RAF Vice Air Marshall Harris: Gordon Musgrove "Operation Gomorrah—Hamburg Firestorm Raids." Also David Irving "The Rise and Fall of the Luftwaffe" pp. 229–231. Also Hans Erich Nossack "The End: Hamburg 1943."

CHAPTER 44
Eighth Air Force raid on Hamburg: Sir Charles Webster and Noble Frankland "Strategic Air Offensive Against Germany 1939–1945. Volume II Endeavor. Part 4." pp. 27–43. *Navigator who took part in raid:* Philip P. Dreiseszun "The Target for Today is Hamburg." *Reactions of Adolf Hitler, Albert Speer, Erhard Milch et al to Hamburg raid:* David Irving "The Rise and Fall of the Luftwaffe" pp. 229–232.

CHAPTER 45
Messerschmitt AG presents production plan for Me-262 to Air Ministry: Willy Radinger and Walter Schick "Messerschmitt Me-262" p. 35. *Test flight of Me-262V5 with makeshift gear and later with rocket assisted takeoff:* Ibid p. 33. *Messerschmitt demands more skilled labor:* David Irving "The Rise and Fall of the Luftwaffe" pp. 254.

CHAPTER 46
Development of the Fischer-Tropsch process: Anthony N. Stranger "Germany's Synthetic Fuel Industry 1927–1945." *Plan for raid on Ploesti oil fields:* John L. Frisbee "Into the Mouth of Hell, Air Force Magazine September 1988."

CHAPTER 47
Raid on Ploesti: James Dugan and Carroll Stewart "Ploesti, the Great Ground Air Battle of 1st August 1943." Also Robert Jackson "Bomber! Famous Bomber Missions of World War II."

CHAPTER 48
Milch and Speer agree on importance of aircraft production: David Irving, "The Rise and Fall of the Luftwaffe" p. 250. *Messerschmitt ordered to work on various versions of the Me-262:* Willy Radinger and Walter Schick "Messerschmitt Me-262" p. 35. *Collapse of the Italian government:* William L. Shirer "The Rise and Fall of the Third Reich" pp. 996–998. *Hitler schemes to rescue Mussolini:* Ibid pp. 999–1003. *Hitler chooses Skorzeny as rescuer:* Otto Skorzeny "Skorzeny's Special Missions."

CHAPTER 49
Problems with Me-262 nose gear, accident 4 August 1943: Willy Radinger and Walter Schick "Messerschmitt Me-262" p. 35. *Operation Pointblank:* Heywood S. Hansell Jr. "The Air Plan That Defeated Hitler." *Raids on Augsburg:* Archives of US 8th and 15th Air Forces. *Reaction of Hitler to raids:* David Irving "The Rise and Fall of the Luftwaffe" p. 235. *Hitler reacts to raid on Wiener-Neustadt, blames Jeschonnek:* Ibid. *Hitler orders Me-209 into production:* Armand van Ishoven "Messerschmitt, Aircraft Designer" p. 180. *Hitler orders a cutback of Me-262 program:* Anthony Pritchard "Messerschmitt" p. 153. *Raids on Regensburg and Schweinfurt:* William R. Emerson "Operation Pointblank: A Tale of Bombers and Fighters." Also Elmer Bendiner "The Fall of Fortresses." Also author interview with former Spitfire pilot James Long. *Jeschonnek suicide:* David Irving "The Rise and

Fall of the Luftwaffe" p. 235. *Raids on Berlin, reactions by Speer and Milch:* Ibid pp. 236–237.

CHAPTER 50

Maiden flight of the De Havilland Vampire jet: Willy Radinger and Walter Schick "Messerschmitt Me-262" p. 35. *Gerd Lindner test flight of Me-262V3:* Ibid. *Shift of Messerschmitt Ag to Oberammergau:* Frank Vann "Willy Messerschmitt" pp. 212. *Purchase of house in Murnau:* Ibid pp. 213–214. Messerschmitt hospitalized in Murnau: Ibid p. 215. *Operation Pointblank:* Heywood S. Hansell Jr. "The Air Plan that Defeated Hitler."

CHAPTER 51

Demonstration of the Me-262 for Reichsmarschal Göring: Willy Radinger and Walter Schick "Messerschmitt Me-262" p. 35. *Demonstration for Hitler at Insterburg airfield:* Armand van Ishoven "Messerschmitt, Aircraft Designer" pp. 185–186. Also David Irving "The Rise and Fall of the Luftwaffe" pp. 259–261.

CHAPTER 52

Delivery of Jumo 004 B-1 engines: Willy Radinger and Walter Schick "Messerschmitt Me-262" p. 35. *Tests of Borsig Mk-108 cannons:* Ibid. *Mk-108 cannons in Me-262:* Rheinmetall-Borsig AG archives. *General Galland's resistance to use of KWK-5 cannon:* Adolf Galland "The First and the Last" p. 170. *Women workers in German industry:* Armand van Ishoven "Messerschmitt, Aircraft Designer" p. 186. *Messerschmitt's treatment of workers in his factories:* Frank Vann "Willy Messerschmitt" pp. 158–165. *Milch concedes authority for aircraft production to Speer:* David Irving "The Rise and Fall of the Luftwaffe" pp. 288–289. *P-38 strengths and weaknesses:* Martin Caidin "Forktailed Devil."

CHAPTER 53

Development of P-51 Mustang: William Newby Grant "P-51 Mustang." Also Graham Smith "North American P-51 Mustang." Also Larry Davis "P-51 In Action."

CHAPTER 54

US 8th Air Force bombing attack of 11 January 1944: "Combat Chronology of the US Army Air Forces January 1944." *Biographical sketch and combat exploits of Major James H. Howard:* "One Man Air Force," True Magazine June 1944. *P-51s transported to Europe on tankers of US Merchant Marine:* Author's experience WWII. *Allied bombing attacks during Big Week:* "United States Air Forces in World War II." Also "RAF Bomber Command Campaign Diary February 1944." *Göring goes on three-week leave:* Milch diary 24 February 1944. *Milch steps up defenses, establishes Fighter Staff:* David Irving "The Rise and Fall of the Luftwaffe" pp. 267–276.

CHAPTER 55

Fatal crash of Me-262V6 at Lager Lechfeld 9 March 1944: Willy Radinger and

Walter Schick "Messerschmitt Me-262" p. 44. *Me-262V8 damaged by collapse of nose gear:* Ibid p. 46. *RAF loses 95 bombers in attack on Nurem-berg 30 March:* David Irving "The Rise and Fall of the Luftwaffe" pp. 275–276.

CHAPTER 56
Erwin Rommel strengthens defenses of the Atlantic Wall: David Irving "The Trail of the Fox" pp. 315–355. *Hitler turns over responsibility for construction of Me-262 factories to Xaver Drosch:* David Irving "The Rise and Fall of the Luftwaffe" pp. 278–281. *Milch defends Speer to Hitler, who says Milch can tell Speer he's very fond of him:* Ibid p. 281. *General Korten fears death of the bomber force:* Ibid p. 282. *Conference in which Göring says long-range bombers are needed:* Ibid p. 283. *Meeting with Hitler at the Berghof:* Ibid p. 284. *Hitler berates Milch, who responds unwisely:* pp. 284–285.

CHAPTER 57
Gradual loss of power by Milch: Ibid p. 286–287. *Messerschmitt blames Milch for errors in building the Me-262:* Ibid p. 287. *D-day, Allied invasion of France:* William L. Shirer "The Rise and Fall of the Third Reich" pp. 1036–1042. Also Randy Holderfield and Michael J. Varhola "D-Day: The Invasion of Normandy June 6, 1944."

CHAPTER 58
Launch of V-1 flying bombs against England: Winston Churchill "Triumph and Tragedy" pp. 38–56. Also David Irving "The Rise and Fall of the Luftwaffe" pp. 162–163. Also David Johnson "V-1, V-2: Hitler's Vengeance on London." *P-47 in action:* Hub Zemke and Roger A. Freeman "Zemke's Wolf Pack" pp. 46–70. *New name, Sturmvogel, for the Me-262:* Joseph Goebbels' propaganda magazine "Spiral" Summer 1944. *Formation of Erprobungskommando 262:* John Foreman and S.E. Harvey "Me-262 Combat Diary" p. 29. *Ekdo 262 commander killed in crash:* Ibid p. 33. *Formation of Kommando Schenk:* Ibid pp. 34–35. *Erwin Rommel wounded:* William L. Shirer "The Rise and Fall of the Third Reich" pp. 1041–1042. Also David Irving "The Trail of the Fox" pp. 418–420.

CHAPTER 59
Conspiracy to assassinate Hitler: William L. Shirer "The Rise and Fall of the Third Reich" pp. 1014–1076. Also James Forman "Code Name Valkyrie: Count Von Stauffenberg and the Plot to Kill Hitler."

CHAPTER 60
Encounter between Mosquito and Me-262 26 July 1944: RAF combat report no. 2256 by pilot A.E. Wall. Also Luftwaffe combat records.

CHAPTER 61
3rd Staffel of KG(J)51 under command of Hauptmann Wolfgang Schenk sent to Chateaudun: John Foreman and S.E. Harvey "Me-262 Combat Diary" pp. 34–35.

Allied advances in France following invasion: William L. Shirer "The Rise and Fall of the Third Reich" p. 1076. *Operation Cobra:* David Mason "Breakout: Drive to the Seine." *Leutnant Schreiber attacks Spitfire:* John Foreman and S.E. Harvey "Me-262 Combat Diary" p. 35. *Leutnant Joachim Weber attacks Mosquito:* Ibid. *Feldwebel Wolfgang Martin rams B-17:* Anthony Pritchard "Messerschmitt" p. 115. *Disputes with Fritz Seiler:* Frank Vann "Willy Messerschmitt" p. 219. *Messerschmitt again hospitalized:* Ibid. pp. 215–216.

CHAPTER 62

Battle between Mosquito and Me-262 on 15 August 1944: Records of RAF and 60th Squadron of the Royal South African Air Force.

CHAPTER 63

Allies capture of Paris: Larry Collins and Dominique Lapierre "Is Paris Burning? How Paris Miraculously Escaped Adolf Hitler's Sentence of Death in August 1944." *Operation Dragoon, the invasion of southern France:* Winston Churchill "Triumph and Tragedy" pp. 95–100. *Operation Market-Garden:* Cornelius Ryan "A Bridge Too Far." *Participation of Me-262s in Operation Market-Garden:* John Foreman and S.E. Harvey "Me-262 Combat Diary" p. 39. *Allies advance into Germany:* William L. Shirer "The Rise and Fall of the Third Reich" pp. 1085–1089. *V-2 flying bomb:* David Johnson "V-1, V-2: Hitler's Vengeance on London." *Heinkel He-162 Volksjaeger:* Aeronautical Staff of Aero Publishers Inc. "Heinkel He-162." *Feldwebel Helmut Lennartz destroys B-17:* John Foreman and S.E. Harvey "Me-262 Combat Diary" p. 38. *Oberfeldwebel Lauer attacked by P-47:* Ibid p. 39.

CHAPTER 64

RAF area bombing continued: Norman Longmate "The Bombers: The RAF Offensive Against Germany 1939–1945." *Shortened training period for Luftwaffe pilots:* Author interview with former Luftwaffe instructor Heinz Suhrbeer. *Typical raiding of training schools for instructors to fly in combat:* Ibid. *General Doolittle requests more fighters:* USAAF archives. *General Galland urges Hitler to increase volume of Me-262 production:* Adolf Galland "The First and the Last."

CHAPTER 65

Components of Me-262 produced in dispersed facilities: Willy Radinger and Walter Schick "Messerschmitt Me-262" p. 97. *Various small assembly operations:* Ibid. *Death of Rommel:* David Irving "The Trail of the Fox" pp. 440–445. *Messerschmitt writes to Hitler, asking that Dr. Langbehn be spared:* Frank Vann "Willy Messerschmitt" pp. 223–225. *Death of Theo Croneiss:* Ibid pp. 217–219. *Jet victories in September 1944:* John Foreman and S.E. Harvey "Me-262 Combat Diary" pp. 41–46.

CHAPTER 66

Atmosphere at Lager Lechfeld: Author interview with former Me-262 pilot Heinz Suhrbeer. *Oberfeldwebel Helmut Baudach of Ekdo 262 attacks American raiders:*

John Foreman and S.E. Harvey "Me-262 Combat Diary" pp. 42–43. *Mustang shot down by Baudach:* 8th Air Force records of air battle 11 September 1944.

CHAPTER 67
Problems of disguising jet airfields: Author interview with former Me-262 pilot Heinz Suhrbeer. *Me-262 combat tactics:* Edward H. Sims "Fighter Tactics and Strategy 1914–1970" pp. 173–175. *General Galland orders Nowotny to take charge of Me-262 unit with Hitler's approval:* Adolf Galland "The First and the Last" pp. 266–267. *Record of Major Walter Nowotny:* "Aces of the Luftwaffe."

CHAPTER 68
Lt. Urban Drew in combat against Me-262s: Urban Drew "Fighter Ace: Exploits of a P-51 Mustang Fighter Ace." *Friendship between Drew and Luftwaffe pilot Georg-Peter Eder:* John Foreman and S.E. Harvey "Me-262 Combat Diary" p. 128. *Me-262s in action October 1944:* Ibid pp. 47–59. *Two-seat bomber Me-262 A-2a/U2:* Willy Radinger and Walter Schick "Messerschmitt Me-262" p.70.

CHAPTER 69
Career of Chuck Yeager: Chuck Yeager, Leo Janos "Yeager: An Autobiography."

CHAPTER 70
General Galland inspects Kommando Nowotny: John Foreman and S.E. Harvey "Me-262 Combat Diary" p. 64. *Air battles, Nowotny killed in combat:* Ibid p. 66. Also Adolf Galland "The First and the Last" pp. 266–267.

CHAPTER 71
Record of Major Georg-Peter Eder: "Aces of the Luftwaffe." *Original Luftwaffe plan for the Great Blow:* Adolf Galland "The First and the Last" p. 240. *Göring's loss of power:* Ibid p. 244. *Orders for Great Blow cancelled, Galland ordered to send forces to the western front:* Ibid p. 241.

CHAPTER 72
Use of takeoff-assistance rockets in the Me-262: Willy Radinger and Walter Schick "Messerschmitt Me-262" p. 51. *Interceptor II powered by BMW turbojets with integrated rocket fuel engine:* Ibid p. 67. *Eberhard Stromeyer de Raulino, aeronautical engineer and test pilot with Messerschmitt AG:* Author interview with Eberhard Stromeyer. *General Galland's summation of the Luftwaffe's need for more Me-262s:* Adolf Galland "The First and the Last" pp. 260–261. *Messerschmitt's experiments with various alternative armament combinations for the Me-262:* Willy Radinger and Walter Schick "Messerschmitt Me-262" p. 61. *Engineers test rockets, favor R4M:* Ibid p. 62. *Development of Me-262 night fighter:* Ibid pp. 71–72. *Oberleutnant Kurt Welter achieves victory over Lancaster in night combat:* "Aces of the Luftwaffe." Also Hugh Morgan and John Weal "German Jet Aces of World War II."

CHAPTER 73
Meeting of German generals at Hitler's secret command center at Zeigenberg:
William L. Shirer "The Rise and Fall of the Third Reich" pp. 1089–1092.

CHAPTER 74
RAF Flight Lt. Jack Boyle in battle 25 December 1944: John Foreman and S.E.
Harvey "Me-262 Combat Diary" pp. 78–79. *RCAF Squadron Leader J.E. Collier
in battle same day:* Ibid p. 79. *Battles 29 December:* Ibid p. 80. *Feldwebel Baudach
in battle 31 December:* pp. 80–81. *Operation Bodenplatte:* Ibid pp. 82–83. *Battle
of the Bulge:* Francis Trevelyan Miller "History of World War II" pp. 788–797.
General Galland relieved as General of the Fighter Arm: Adolf Galland "The First
and the Last" p. 244.

CHAPTER 75
Joseph Goebbels' condemnation of Allied Bomber crews as Terrorfliegers: Spiral
Magazine January 1945. *Norden bombsight:* Top-secret Norden Bombsight "War
Monthly Issue 23." *Bombing reduces German fuel supply:* Johannes Steinhoff "The
Final Hours" p. 47. *Natter Viper:* Luftwaffe Resource Center. Also Johannes
Steinhoff "The Final Hours" p. 75. *General Galland discusses losses of Luftwaffe
pilots:* Adolf Galland "The First and the Last" pp. 260–261. *Göring insists on Me-
262 as bomber, rejects use as fighter:* Ibid pp. 263–264.

CHAPTER 76
*Five Luftwaffe pilots meet with Göring to protest his orders and his treatment of
the Jagdstaffe:* Johannes Steinhoff "The Final Hours" pp. 101–109. Also Adolf
Galland "The First and the Last" pp. 245–247.

CHAPTER 77
Göring takes revenge on pilots: Johannes Steinhoff "The Final Hours" pp. 109–111.
Galland exiled from Berlin: Adolf Galland "The First and the Last" pp. 245–247.
Reduction in coal production: William L. Shirer "The Rise and Fall of the Third
Reich" p. 1098. *Fuel shortages curtail Luftwaffe operations; attacks on Leuna syn-
thetic chemical center:* Air Force Magazine "Twenty Missions In Hell" April 2007.
Battles 9 February: John Foreman and S.E. Harvey "Me-262 Combat Diary" pp.
95–96. *Action over Berlin same day:* Ibid pp. 96–07.

CHAPTER 78
Allied forces closing in on Rhine: William L. Shirer "The Rise and Fall of the Third
Reich" pp. 1099–1100. *Bombing of Dresden:* Alexander McKee "Dresden 1945,
The Devil's Tinderbox." Also Paul Addison "Firestorm: The Bombing of Dresden,
1945." *Me-163 Komet in action:* Anthony Pritchard "Messerschmitt" pp. 33–147.
Hitler countermands Göring's orders re Galland: Adolf Galland "The First and the
Last" p. 247.

CHAPTER 79

General Galland visits Karinhalle, is told by Göring to form a jet unit with a select group of pilots: Adolf Galland "The First and the Last" pp. 247–248. Also Jonannes Steinhoff "The Final Hours" pp. 119–120.

CHAPTER 80

Galland and Steinhoff begin organizing and equipping the new Me-262 fighter unit, JG44, at Brandenburg: Johannes Steinhoff "The Final Hours" pp. 122–124. *Pilots wear new outfits:* Ibid p. 125. *Steinhoff and Leutnant Blomert fly Me-262s over Berlin, engage Russian fighters:* Ibid pp. 124–129.

CHAPTER 81

Me-262s in action 22 February 1945: John Foreman and S.E. Harvey "Me-262 Combat Diary" pp. 102–105. *Air battles 23–24 February:* Ibid pp. 105–106. *Further action 25 February with grim results for Me-262s:* Ibid pp. 106–108.

CHAPTER 82

Greater numbers of Me-262s allocated to bomber units: Adolf Galland "The First and the Last" p. 264. *US Army forces take the bridge at Remagen:* Ken Hechler "The Bridge At Remagen." *Hitler's reaction to loss of the bridge:* William L. Shirer "The Rise and Fall of the Third Reich" p. 1101. *Arado 234B bombers and Me-262s attack the bridge:* John Foreman and S.E. Harvey "Me-262 Combat Diary" p. 115.

CHAPTER 83

Me-262 accidents, including crash of aircraft flown by Leutnant Hans Busch: Author interviews with former Luftwaffe pilot Busch. *Me-262 testing procedures:* Author interviews with former Luftwaffe pilot Heinz Suhrbeer. *Eberhard Schmidt defection:* Frank Vann "Willy Messerschmitt" p. 226. *Messerschmitt complains about mismanagement of the company by Seiler and Kokothaki:* Ibid pp. 219–221.

CHAPTER 84

R4M air-to-air rockets: Deutsche Waffen Und Munitions Fabrik archives. Also Anthony Pritchard "Messerschmitt" pp. 161–162. Also Pierre Clostermann "The Big Show." *Air battles 18 March 1945, in which R4M rockets made first appearance:* John Foreman and S.E. Harvey "Me-262 Combat Diary" pp. 119–122.

CHAPTER 85

Air battles 19–24 March: Ibid pp. 122–123. Also archives of US 8th and 15th Air Forces. *Me-262 pilot Heinz Suhrbeer bails out near Schwerin:* Author interview with Suhrbeer. *Factory test pilot Hans Fay flies Me-262 fighter-bomber Rhein-Main, surrenders to Americans:* John Foreman and S.E. Harvey "Me-262 Combat Diary" p. 136. RCAF bombers attacked by Me-262s: Ibid pp. 138–141.

CHAPTER 86

Leutnant Hans-Dieter Weiss shot after bailing out: Ibid p. 121. *Reaction of Luft-*

waffe pilots to USAAF order to strafe Germans in parachutes: Author interview with former Luftwaffe pilot Hans Busch. *Hitler orders to shoot captured Allied airmen:* William L. Shirer "The Rise and Fall of the Third Reich" p. 1100. *Hitler takes drugs ordered by Dr. Morell:* Ibid p. 1102. *Albert Speer resists Hitler's scorched-earth policy:* Ibid p. 1104. *Professor Messerschmitt argues with Gauleiter Wachtler against defense of Bamberg:* Frank Vann "Willy Messerschmitt" p. 228–229. *Staff car destroyed by strafing Thunderbolts:* John Foreman and S.E. Harvey "Me-262 Combat Diary" p. 128. *Air battles 4 April:* Ibid p. 144. *Oberfeldwebel Hermann Buchner leads jets after Major Sinner shot down:* Hermann Buchner "Stormbird" p. 135.

CHAPTER 87

Hajo Hermann plans Operation Werewulf: Angelos Thalassinos "Rammkommando Elbe." Also David Irving "Göring, A Biography." Also John Foreman and S.E. Harvey "Me-262 Combat Diary" p. 149.

CHAPTER 88

Air battles 8 April: Ibid p. 150. *Galland and Steinhoff visit pilots' rest home at Lake Tegernsee:* Johannes Steinhoff "The Final Hours" pp. 133–136. *Other pilots join JV-44:* Ibid p. 137. *Steinhoff and Fahrmann attack Lightnings, then B-24s:* Ibid pp. 137–144.

CHAPTER 89

Air battles 10 April: John Foreman and S.E. Harvey "Me-262 Combat Diary" pp. 155–157. *Losses so severe JG7 will never recover:* Ibid pp. 158–159.

CHAPTER 90

Goebbels learns of the death of Roosevelt, informs Hitler: William L. Shirer "The Rise and Fall of the Third Reich" pp. 1109–1110. *Hitler jubilant, but refuses to acknowledge dire straits of German forces:* Ibid p. 1110. *Hitler has mistress Eva Braun brought to bunker in Berlin, prepares to marry her:* Ibid p. 1111. *Air battles involving Me-262s 14 April:* Also John Foreman and S.E. Harvey "Me-262 Combat Diary" pp. 159–160. *General Galland leads pilots of JV44 into combat:* Adolf Galland "The First and the Last" pp. 275–276. *Airfield under attack:* Ibid p. 275. *Galland leads nine Me-262s into action 17 April:* John Foreman and S.E. Harvey "Me-262 Combat Diary" pp. 162–163.

CHAPTER 91

Oberst Steinhoff attempts takeoff in Me-262, crashes: Johannes Steinhoff "The Final Hours" pp. 156–181. *General Galland leads five jets against 400 American fighters:* John Foreman and S.E. Harvey "Me-262 Combat Diary" pp. 166–167. *Heinz Bar shoots down two Thunderbirds:* Ibid p. 167. *On 24 April jets attack B-26 Marauders, Franzl Lützow is killed:* Ibid pp. 171–172. *Galland vows to fight on, JV44 pilots will follow him to the end:* Adolf Galland "The First and the Last" p. 277.

CHAPTER 92

Willy Messerschmitt presses work on next generation jet fighter: Anthony Pritchard "Messerschmitt" p. 168. Also Frank Vann "Willy Messerschmitt" p. 230. *Kreisleiter Shiede directs Messerschmitt to turn over 81 members of his design staff for military training:* Ibid pp. 229–230. *Heinrich Himmler plots to take over German government:* William L. Shirer "The Rise and Fall of the Third Reich" pp. 1114–1115. *Hitler calls General Ritter von Greim to Berlin, puts him in command of Luftwaffe:* Ibid pp. 1118–1119. *General Galland leads flight of Me-262s in attack on B-26 Marauders, crashes and is badly wounded:* Adolf Galland "The First and the Last" pp. 277–279.

CHAPTER 93

Kreisleiter Shiede again directs Messerschmitt to turn over 81 members of design staff; Messerschmitt again refuses: Frank Vann "Willy Messerschmitt" pp. 230–232. *American forces enter Oberammergau:* Ibid p. 232. *Agents seize plans for P-1101, send them to France:* Ibid P. 232. *Messerschmitt arrested, flown to London for interrogation:* Ibid p. 233. *Mussolini and mistress captured and shot:* William L. Shirer "The Rise and Fall of the Third Reich" p. 1131. *Death of Hitler:* Ibid pp. 1131–1134. *Admiral Doenitz attempts to negotiate a surrender; Eisenhower refuses:* Ibid p. 1138.

CHAPTER 94

Me-262s burned: Adolf Galland "The First And The Last" p. 280. *Oberleutnant Fritz Stehle's last flight:* John Foreman and S.E. Harvey "Me-262 Combat Diary" p. 180. Also author interview with former JG7 pilot Heinz Suhrbeer.

BIBLIOGRAPHY

Addison, Paul. *Firestorm: The Bombing of Dresden, 1945* (Chicago 2005).

Beaulieu, Gerard. *The Republic in Danger: General Maurice Gamelin and the Politics of French Defense 1933–1940* (New York 1993).

Bendiner, Elmer. *The Fall of Fortresses* (New York 1980).

Berg, A. Scott. *Lindbergh* (New York 1998).

Bewlay, Charles. *Hermann Göring* (Gottengen 1956).

Blond, Georg. *Born to Fly* (London 1964).

Boyne, Walter J. *Arrow to the Future, The Me-262* (Atglen, PA 1994).

Brockdorff, W. *Der Landser Ritterkreuztrager NR 153 Oberst Günther Lützow* (Munich 1970).

Buchner, Hermann. *Stormbird* (London 2000).

Davis, Burke. *The Billy Mitchell Affair* (New York 1967).

Caidin, Martin. *Me-109* (New York 1968).

Caidin, Martin. *Forktailed Devil—The P-38* (New York 1973).

Cain Charles W. and Gerram Mike. *Fighters of World War II* (New York 1979).

Cajus, Bekker. *The Luftwaffe War Diaries* (New York 1967).

Churchill, Winston. *The Gathering Storm* (London 1949).

Churchill, Winston. *Their Finest Hour* (London 1949).

Churchill, Winston. *The Grand Allliance* (London 1950).

Churchill, Winston. *Triumph and Tragedy* (London 19).

Clostermann, Pierre. *The Big Show* (New York 1958).

Collier, Richard. *Eagle Day* (London 1966).

Combat Chronology of the US Army Air Forces January 1944.

Copp Dewitt S.. *A Few Great Captains: The Men and Events that Shaped the Development of US Air Power* (New York 1980).

Craig, James. *The Messerschmitt Bf-109* (New York 1968).

Davis, Burke. *The Billy Mitchell Affair* (New York 1967).

Davis, Larry. *P-51 in Action* (New York 1991).

Diedrich, Georg-Peter. *German Rocket Fighters of World War II* (Atglen, PA 2005).

Douhet, Guilio. *Command of the Air* (Washington DC 1983).

Drew, Urban. *Fighter Ace: Exploits of a P-51 Mustang Fighter Ace* (New York 1975).

Dugan, James and Stewart, Carroll. *Ploesti, the Great Ground Air Battle of 1st August 1943* (New York 1973).

Elstob, Peter. *Condor Legion* (New York 1973).

Ellis, Major L.F. *The War in France and Flanders 1939–1940* (Nashville 1996).

Emerson, William R. *Operation Pointblank: A Tale of Bombers and Fighters* (Colorado Springs 1962).

Esposito, Vincent J. Ed. *The West Point Atlas of Wars Vol. II* (New York 1997).

Estes, Lt. Col. Richard H. *General Douhet: More on Target Than He Knew* (Air Power Journal 1990).

Foreman, John, and Harvey, S.E. *Me-262 Combat Diary* (New Malden, Surrey 1990).

Forman, James. Code Name Valkyrie: *Count Von Stauffenberg and the Plot to Kill Hitler* (New York 1973).

Freeman, Roger A. *The Mighty Eighth* (London 1996).

Frisbee, John L. *Into the Mouth of Hell* (Air Force Magazine, September 1988).

Galland, Adolf. *The First and the Last* (New York 1957).

Gobbels, Joseph. *Speeches and Essays 1940.*

Grant, William Newby. *P-51 Mustang* (London 1980).

Green, William. *Rocket Fighter* (London 1969).

Green, William. *Famous Fighters of the Second World War* (London 1976).

Haberlen, Klaus. *A Luftwaffe Bomber Pilot Remembers* (Atglen, Pa 2001).

Hansell, Heywood S. Jr.. *The Air Plan That Defeated Hitler* (Atlanta 1972).

Hechler, Ken. *The Bridge at Remagen* (New York 1969).

Herlin, Hans. *Der Teufels Flieger* (Munich 1974).

Hitler, Adolf. *Speech on 8 December 1941* (Munich 1941).

Holderfield, Randy and Varhola, Michael J. *D-Day: The Invasion of Normandy June 6, 1944* (Cambridge, MA 2000).

Horn, Alistair. *How to Lose a Battle; France 1940* (New York 2006).

Hutton, Joseph. *Hess, The Man and His Mission* (New York 1971).

Imperial War Museum Archives. *BBC broadcasts 7–8 December 1941*.

Irving, David. *The Rise and Fall of the Luftwaffe* (New York 1974).

Irving, David. *The Trail of the Fox* (New York 1977).

Ishoven, Armand van. *Messerschmitt, Aircraft Designer* (London 1975).

Jackson, Robert. *Combat Legend De Havilland Mosquito* (New York 2003).

Jackson, Robert. *Bomber! Famous Bomber Missions of World War II* (New York 1980).

Johnson, David. *V-1, V-2: Hitler's Vengeance on London* (New York 1982).

Kennedy, R.M. *The German Campaign in Poland 1939* (Washington, DC 1956).

Koniarek, Jan; Greer, Don; Tullis, Tom. *Polish Air Force 1939–1945* (Carollton, TX 1994).

Lewis, Jon E., editor. *The Mammoth Book of Fighter Pilots* (Berkeley, CA 2002).

Longmate, Norman. *The Bombers: The RAF Offensive Against Germany 1939–1945* (London 1988).

Lucas James S. *War on The Eastern Front: The German Soldier in Russia 1941–45* (New York 1985).

MacDonald, Callum. *The Killing of SS Obergruppenfuhrer Reinhard Heydrich* (New York 1989).

Makana, Philip. *Himmelssturmer* (Munich 1995).

Manstein, Feldmarschal Erich von. *Verlorene Siege* (Bonn 1955).

Mason, David. *Breakout: Drive to the Seine* (New York 1968).

Messerschmitt, Willy. *Front und Heimat Feb. 1940*.

McKee, Alexander. *Dresden 1945, The Devil's Tinderbox* (New York 2000).

Miller, Francis Trevelyan. *History of World War II* (Philadelphia 1945).

Morgan, Hugh and Weal, John. *German Jet Aces of World War II* (London 1998).

Moriarty, David. *Rudolf Hess, Deputy Fuhrer* (New York 1988).

Musgrove, Gordon. *Operation Gomorrah—Hamburg Firestorm Raids* (New York 1981).

Nossack, Hans Erich. *The End: Hamburg 1943* (Chicago 2007).

"One Man Air Force," True Magazine June 1944.

Pack, S.W.C. *Operation Husky, The Allied Invasion of Sicily* (London 1977).

Parton, James. *Air Force Spoken Here: General Ira Eaker and the Command of the Air* (New York 1986).

Pokryshkin, Alexander. *Sky of War* (Moscow 1959).

Price, Alfred. *Instruments of Darkness* (London 1970).

Pritchard, Anthony. *Messerschmitt* (New York 1975).

Proctor, Raymond. *Hitler's Luftwaffe in the Spanish Civil War* (London 1983).

Radinger, Willy and Schick, Walter. *Messerschmitt Me-262* (Munich 1992).

RAF Bomber Command Campaign Diary February 1944.

Rudel, Hans Ulrich. *Stuka Pilot* (New York 1958).

Ryan, Cornelius. *A Bridge Too Far* (New York 1974).

Schror, Werner. *Fighters Over the Desert.*

Sharp, C., Martin, D.H. *History of De Havilland* (London 1982).

Shirer, William L. *The Rise and Fall of the Third Reich* (New York 1960).

Sims, Edward. *Fighter Tactics and Strategy* (New York 1970).

Skorzeny, Otto. *Skorzeny's Special Missions* (London 1997).

Smith, Graham. *North American P-51 Mustang* (New York 1991).

Speer, Albert. *Inside the Third Reich* (New York 1970).

Spiral Magazine Summer 1944.

Steinhoff, Johannes. *The Final Hours* (Munich 1974).

Thalassinos, Angelos. *Rammkommando Elbe.*

Udet, Ernst. *Ace of the Iron Cross* (New York 1970)

US Air Force Historical Study No. 253.

Vann, Frank. *Willy Messerschmitt* (London 1993).

Volkischer Beobachter. *Articles 7–8 December 1941.*

Wallace, Graham. *RAF Biggin Hill* (London 1969).

Weber, Eberhard and Uwe Feist. *Focke-Wulf 190, Wurger* (New York 1968).

Webster, Sir Charles and Frankland, Noble. *Strategic Air Offensive Against Germany 1939–1945* (London 1961).

Wernick, Robert. *World War II: Blitzkrieg* (New York 1976).

Werstein, Irving. *The Cruel Years* (New York 1971).

Yarnell, Harry E. *Papers of Harry E. Yarnell* (Washington, DC 1955).

Yeager, Chuck; Janos, Leo. *Yeager: An Autobiography* (New York 1985).

Zemke, Hub and Freeman, Roger A. *Zemke's Wolf Pack* (New York 1994).

INDEX

Freyer, Margaret, 307
Friedeburg, Admiral Hans von, 360
Friedrichshafen, Germany, 8
Froelich, Leutnant Gottfried, 361
Fromm, General Friedrich, 225, 226, 227
FuG 25A radio, 124

Gable, Clark, 32
Gabreski, Francis ("Gabby"), 221
Galland, Oberleutnant Adolf, 37–38, 67,
    76–78, 82, 103, 118, 143–144,
    167–169, 194, 198, 206, 214, 218, 232,
    245, 251, 261–262, 267, 272–275, 277,
    279–283, 285, 287, 290–295, 298,
    300–302, 310–313, 318, 321, 326, 335,
    337, 339, 346–350, 352–356
Gamelin, General Maurice, 65–66
Gaulle, General Charles de, 66, 241
General Electric Company (GEC), 85
Gehlker, Obergefreiter Fritz, 329
Geisthövel, Feldwebel Heiner, 339
George, King, 96
Gerb, Lieutenant W.T., 268
Gerlach, Captain Heinrich, 185, 186
German A-4 (V-2) rocket, 211
German aircraft:
    Albatros D.V., 21
    Amerika Bomber. See Me-264
    Arado Ar-234, 32–33, 72, 123, 141,
        195, 213, 319
    Arado Ar-234B bomber, 319–320
    Bertha. See Bf-109B
    Betti. See S-16b
    Bf-108, 31, 45, 70
    Bf-108B, 31–32
    Bf-109, 1, 33, 34, 37–39, 43–47, 51, 53,
        55–58, 60, 62, 67, 67–68, 70, 75,
        77–79, 83, 88–92, 101, 103, 105,
        116, 124–125, 129, 134, 139,
        141–143, 149, 152–153, 163, 167,
        178, 181, 187–188, 193, 202, 205,
        207, 209, 235, 241, 248, 251, 259,
        261, 263–264, 270, 272, 275,
        279–280, 283–284, 297, 305, 207,
        315, 322, 327, 335–337, 342, 346,
        362, 365
    Bf-109B, 38
    Bf-109C, 44
    Bf-109E, 52, 78
    Bf-109F, 117
    Bf-109G, 116, 126, 141, 153, 169,
        170–171
    Bf-110, 34, 52, 58, 75, 76, 79, 82–83,
        93–94, 150–151, 162, 169, 178,
        188, 205, 208–209, 222, 229, 235,
    249, 255, 284, 298, 328
    Bf-110F4, 169, 171
    Bücker-131, 247
    Butcherbird. See Fw-190
    Clara. See Bf-109
    Dackelbauch. See Bf-110
    Dornier Do-11, 30
    Dornier Do-17, 58, 75, 78, 81
    Focke-Wulf, 4, 32–33, 52, 63, 72, 82,
        90–91, 103, 136, 149, 152, 258,
        262
    Focke-Wulf Fw-190, 1, 53, 89–2, 92,
        105, 116, 134–135, 142, 149, 153,
        169, 188, 192, 205, 209, 221, 243,
        251, 258–259, 262–263, 265, 272,
        274–275, 284–285, 297, 315, 322,
        327, 336–338, 342
    Focke-Wulf Fw-190A, 153
    Fokker D-VII, 2
    Friderich fighter, 62, 103, 116–117
    Gigant, 105. See also Me-321
    Heinkel He-45, 30
    Heinkel He-51, 33, 35–36, 39, 41
    Heinkel He-70, 36
    Heinkel He-111, 38, 58, 66, 75, 78, 108,
        152, 183, 225
    Heinkel He-111B, 36
    Hienkel He-112, 33, 34
    Heinkel He-162, 245
    Heinkel He-177, 51, 103, 213
    Heinkel He-178, 55
    Heinkel He-219, 195, 284, 298
    Heinkel He-219s, 209, 285
    Heinkel He-280, 88, 139, 141
    Heinkel He-343, 141
    Jagdbomber (Jabo), 140
    Junkers Ju-52, 35, 36, 60, 105, 116,
        128, 184, 195, 328
    Junkers Ju-87, 32, 42, 57, 78, 154
    Junkers Ju-88, 78, 80–81, 99, 100,
        151–153, 156, 162, 209, 213, 241,
        284, 298, 299, 303, 313
    Junkers Ju-287, 141
    M-17, 18–20
    M-18, 20, 22
    M-18b, 20
    M-19, 20
    M-20, 23, 25
    M-20b, 25–27
    M-21, 27
    M-22, 27
    M-23, 26
    M-27, 30
    M-29, 29–30
    M-35, 31